Tatiana Zhurzhenko

BORDERLANDS INTO BORDERED LANDS

Geopolitics of Identity in Post-Soviet Ukraine

With a foreword by Dieter Segert

ibidem-Verlag
Stuttgart

Bibliografische Information der Deutschen Nationalbibliothek
Die Deutsche Nationalbibliothek verzeichnet diese Publikation in der
Deutschen Nationalbibliografie; detaillierte bibliografische Daten sind im
Internet über http://dnb.d-nb.de abrufbar.

Bibliographic information published by the Deutsche Nationalbibliothek
Die Deutsche Nationalbibliothek lists this publication in the Deutsche Nationalbibliografie;
detailed bibliographic data are available in the Internet at http://dnb.d-nb.de.

Cover Picture: The International Festival of Slavic Peoples "Slavic Unity 2007" that took place in the Homel region not far from the spot where the state borders of Ukraine, Russia and Belarus meet. © RIA Novosti, 2007.

Editorial assistance: Olena Sivuda

© Maps design: Dmytro Vortman, 2009.
© Photographs in the texts: Tatiana Zhurzhenko.

Gedruckt auf alterungsbeständigem, säurefreien Papier
Printed on acid-free paper

ISSN: 1614-3515

ISBN-10: 3-8382-0042-X
ISBN-13: 978-3-8382-0042-2

© *ibidem*-Verlag
Stuttgart 2010

Alle Rechte vorbehalten

Das Werk einschließlich aller seiner Teile ist urheberrechtlich geschützt. Jede Verwertung außerhalb der engen Grenzen des Urheberrechtsgesetzes ist ohne Zustimmung des Verlages unzulässig und strafbar. Dies gilt insbesondere für Vervielfältigungen, Übersetzungen, Mikroverfilmungen und elektronische Speicherformen sowie die Einspeicherung und Verarbeitung in elektronischen Systemen.

All rights reserved. No part of this publication may be reproduced, stored in or introduced into a retrieval system, or transmitted, in any form, or by any means (electronical, mechanical, photocopying, recording or otherwise) without the prior written permission of the publisher. Any person who does any unauthorized act in relation to this publication may be liable to criminal prosecution and civil claims for damages.

Printed in Germany

Soviet and Post-Soviet Politics and Society (SPPS) Vol. 98
ISSN 1614-3515

General Editor: Andreas Umland, *The Catholic University of Eichstaett-Ingolstadt,* umland@stanfordalumni.org

Editorial Assistant: Olena Sivuda, *Drahomanov Pedagogical University of Kyiv,* SLS6255@ku-eichstaett.de

EDITORIAL COMMITTEE*

DOMESTIC & COMPARATIVE POLITICS
Prof. **Ellen Bos**, *Andrássy University of Budapest*
Dr. **Ingmar Bredies**, *University of Regensburg*
Dr. **Andrey Kazantsev**, *MGIMO (U) MID RF, Moscow*
Dr. **Heiko Pleines**, *University of Bremen*
Prof. **Richard Sakwa**, *University of Kent at Canterbury*
Dr. **Sarah Whitmore**, *Oxford Brookes University*
Dr. **Harald Wydra**, *University of Cambridge*
SOCIETY, CLASS & ETHNICITY
Col. **David Glantz**, *"Journal of Slavic Military Studies"*
Dr. **Rashid Kaplanov**, *Russian Academy of Sciences*
Dr. **Marlène Laruelle**, *ISDP, Stockholm*
Dr. **Stephen Shulman**, *Southern Illinois University*
Prof. **Stefan Troebst**, *University of Leipzig*
POLITICAL ECONOMY & PUBLIC POLICY
Prof. em. **Marshall Goldman**, *Wellesley College, Mass.*
Dr. **Andreas Goldthau**, *Central European University*
Dr. **Robert Kravchuk**, *University of North Carolina*
Dr. **David Lane**, *University of Cambridge*
Dr. **Carol Leonard**, *University of Oxford*

Dr. **Maria Popova**, *McGill University, Montreal*
FOREIGN POLICY & INTERNATIONAL AFFAIRS
Dr. **Peter Duncan**, *University College London*
Dr. **Taras Kuzio**, *University of Toronto*
Prof. **Gerhard Mangott**, *University of Innsbruck*
Dr. **Diana Schmidt-Pfister**, *University of Konstanz*
Dr. **Lisbeth Tarlow**, *Harvard University, Cambridge*
Dr. **Christian Wipperfürth**, *N-Ost Network, Berlin*
Dr. **William Zimmerman**, *University of Michigan*
HISTORY, CULTURE & THOUGHT
Dr. **Catherine Andreyev**, *University of Oxford*
Prof. **Mark Bassin**, *University of Birmingham*
Dr. **Alexander Etkind**, *University of Cambridge*
Dr. **Gasan Gusejnov**, *Moscow State University*
Prof. em. **Walter Laqueur**, *Georgetown University*
Prof. **Leonid Luks**, *Catholic University of Eichstaett*
Dr. **Olga Malinova**, *Russian Academy of Sciences*
Dr. **Andrei Rogatchevski**, *University of Glasgow*
Dr. **Mark Tauger**, *West Virginia University*
Dr. **Stefan Wiederkehr**, *BBAW, Berlin*

ADVISORY BOARD*

Prof. **Dominique Arel**, *University of Ottawa*
Prof. **Jörg Baberowski**, *Humboldt University of Berlin*
Prof. **Margarita Balmaceda**, *Seton Hall University*
Dr. **John Barber**, *University of Cambridge*
Prof. **Timm Beichelt**, *European University Viadrina*
Prof. em. **Archie Brown**, *University of Oxford*
Dr. **Vyacheslav Bryukhovetsky**, *Kyiv-Mohyla Academy*
Prof. **Timothy Colton**, *Harvard University, Cambridge*
Prof. **Paul D'Anieri**, *University of Florida*
Dr. **Heike Dörrenbächer**, *Naumann Foundation Kyiv*
Dr. **John Dunlop**, *Hoover Institution, Stanford, California*
Dr. **Sabine Fischer**, *EU Institute for Security Studies*
Dr. **Geir Flikke**, *NUPI, Oslo*
Dr. **David Galbreath**, *University of Aberdeen*
Prof. **Alexander Galkin**, *Russian Academy of Sciences*
Prof. **Frank Golczewski**, *University of Hamburg*
Dr. **Nikolas Gvosdev**, *Naval War College, Newport, RI*
Prof. **Mark von Hagen**, *Arizona State University*
Dr. **Guido Hausmann**, *University of Freiburg i.Br.*
Prof. **Dale Herspring**, *Kansas State University*
Dr. **Stefani Hoffman**, *Hebrew University of Jerusalem*
Prof. **Mikhail Ilyin**, *MGIMO (U) MID RF, Moscow*
Prof. **Vladimir Kantor**, *Higher School of Economics*
Dr. **Ivan Katchanovski**, *Harvard University, Cambridge*
Prof. em. **Andrzej Korbonski**, *University of California*
Dr. **Iris Kempe**, *Heinrich Boell Foundation Tbilisi*
Prof. **Herbert Küpper**, *Institut für Ostrecht Regensburg*
Dr. **Rainer Lindner**, *CEEER, Berlin*
Dr. **Vladimir Malakhov**, *Russian Academy of Sciences*
Dr. **Luke March**, *University of Edinburgh*

Prof. **Michael McFaul**, *US National Security Council*
Prof. **Birgit Menzel**, *University of Mainz-Germersheim*
Prof. **Valery Mikhailenko**, *The Urals State University*
Prof. **Emil Pain**, *Higher School of Economics, Moscow*
Dr. **Oleg Podvintsev**, *Russian Academy of Sciences*
Prof. **Olga Popova**, *St. Petersburg State University*
Dr. **Alex Pravda**, *University of Oxford*
Dr. **Erik van Ree**, *University of Amsterdam*
Dr. **Joachim Rogall**, *Robert Bosch Foundation Stuttgart*
Prof. **Peter Rutland**, *Wesleyan University, Middletown*
Dr. **Sergei Ryabov**, *Kyiv-Mohyla Academy*
Prof. **Marat Salikov**, *The Urals State Law Academy*
Dr. **Gwendolyn Sasse**, *University of Oxford*
Prof. **Jutta Scherrer**, *EHESS, Paris*
Prof. **Robert Service**, *University of Oxford*
Mr. **James Sherr**, *RIIA Chatham House London*
Dr. **Oxana Shevel**, *Tufts University, Medford*
Prof. **Eberhard Schneider**, *University of Siegen*
Prof. **Olexander Shnyrkov**, *Shevchenko University, Kyiv*
Prof. **Hans-Henning Schröder**, *University of Bremen*
Prof. **Yuri Shapoval**, *Ukrainian Academy of Sciences*
Prof. **Viktor Shnirelman**, *Russian Academy of Sciences*
Dr. **Lisa Sundstrom**, *University of British Columbia*
Dr. **Philip Walters**, *"Religion, State and Society," Oxford*
Prof. **Zenon Wasyliw**, *Ithaca College, New York State*
Dr. **Lucan Way**, *University of Toronto*
Dr. **Markus Wehner**, *"Frankfurter Allgemeine Zeitung"*
Dr. **Andrew Wilson**, *ECFR, London*
Prof. **Jan Zielonka**, *University of Oxford*
Prof. **Andrei Zorin**, *University of Oxford*

* While the Editorial Committee and Advisory Board support the General Editor in the choice and improvement of manuscripts for publication, responsibility for remaining errors and misinterpretations in the series' volumes lies with the books' authors.

Soviet and Post-Soviet Politics and Society (SPPS)
ISSN 1614-3515

Founded in 2004 and refereed since 2007, SPPS makes available affordable English-, German- and Russian-language studies on the history of the countries of the former Soviet bloc from the late Tsarist period to today. It publishes approximately 15-20 volumes per year, and focuses on issues in transitions to and from democracy such as economic crisis, identity formation, civil society development, and constitutional reform in CEE and the NIS. SPPS also aims to highlight so far understudied themes in East European studies such as right-wing radicalism, religious life, higher education, or human rights protection. The authors and titles of all previously published manuscripts are listed at the end of this book. For a full description of the series and reviews of its books, see www.ibidem-verlag.de/red/spps.

Note for authors (as of 2009): After successful review, fully formatted and carefully edited electronic master copies of up to 250 pages will be published as b/w A5 paperbacks and marketed in Germany (e.g. vlb.de, buchkatalog.de, amazon.de) and internationally (e.g. amazon. com). For longer books, formatting/editorial assistance, different binding, oversize maps, coloured illustrations and other special arrangements, authors' fees between €100 and €1500 apply. Publication of German doctoral dissertations follows a separate procedure. Authors are asked to provide a high-quality electronic picture on the object of their study for the book's front-cover. Younger authors may add a foreword from an established scholar. Monograph authors and collected volume editors receive two free as well as further copies for a reduced authors' price, and will be asked to contribute to marketing their book as well as finding reviewers and review journals for them. These conditions are subject to yearly review, and to be modified, in the future. Further details at www.ibidem-verlag.de/red/spps-authors.

Editorial correspondence & manuscripts should, until 2011, be sent to: Dr. Andreas Umland, ZIMOS, Ostenstr. 27, 85072 Eichstätt, Germany; e-mail: umland@stanfordalumni.org

Business correspondence & review copy requests should be sent to: *ibidem*-Verlag, Julius-Leber-Weg 11, D-30457 Hannover, Germany; tel.: +49(0)511-2622200; fax: +49(0)511-2622201; spps@ibidem-verlag.de.

Book orders & payments should be made via the publisher's electronic book shop at: www.ibidem-verlag.de/red/SPPS_EN/

Authors, reviewers, referees, and editors for (as well as all other persons sympathetic to) SPPS are invited to join its networks at www.facebook.com/group.php?gid=52638198614
www.linkedin.com/groups?about=&gid=103012
www.xing.com/net/spps-ibidem-verlag/

Recent Volumes

89 *Aygul Ashirova*
Stalinismus und Stalin-Kult in Zentralasien
Turkmenistan 1924-1953
Mit einem Vorwort von Leonid Luks
ISBN 978-3-89821-987-7

90 *Leonid Luks*
Freiheit oder imperiale Größe?
Essays zu einem russischen Dilemma
ISBN 978-3-8382-0011-8

91 *Christopher Gilley*
The 'Change of Signposts' in the Ukrainian Emigration
A Contribution to the History of Sovietophilism in the 1920s
With a foreword by Frank Golczewski
ISBN 978-3-89821-965-5

92 *Philipp Casula, Jeronim Perovic (Eds.)*
Identities and Politics During the Putin Presidency
The Discursive Foundations of Russia's Stability
With a foreword by Heiko Haumann
ISBN 978-3-8382-0015-6

93 *Marcel Viëtor*
Europa und die Frage nach seinen Grenzen im Osten
Zur Konstruktion ‚europäischer Identität' in Geschichte und Gegenwart
Mit einem Vorwort von Albrecht Lehmann
ISBN 978-3-8382-0045-3

94 *Ben Hellman, Andrei Rogachevskii*
Filming the Unfilmable
Casper Wrede's 'One Day in the Life of Ivan Denisovich'
ISBN 978-3-8382-0044-6

95 *Eva Fuchslocher*
Vaterland, Sprache, Glaube
Orthodoxie und Nationenbildung am Beispiel Georgiens
Mit einem Vorwort von Christina von Braun
ISBN 978-3-89821-884-9

96 *Vladimir Kantor*
Das Westlertum und der Weg Russlands
Zur Entwicklung der russischen Literatur und Philosophie
Ediert von Dagmar Herrmann
Mit einem Beitrag von Nikolaus Lobkowicz
ISBN 978-3-8382-0102-3

97 *Kamran Musayev*
Die postsowjetische Transformation im Baltikum und Südkaukasus
Eine vergleichende Untersuchung der politischen Entwicklung Lettlands und Aserbaidschans 1985-2009
Mit einem Vorwort von Leonid Luks
Ediert von Sandro Henschel
ISBN 978-3-8382-0103-0

Contents

List of Abbreviations 7

List of Images 9

Foreword: Ukraine en route to where? (Dieter Segert) 11

Acknowledgements 15

Introduction 19

I   Remapping the Post-Soviet Space

1. "Eurasia" and its Uses in the Ukrainian Geopolitical Imagination 43

2. Slavic Sisters into European Neighbours: Ukrainian-Belarusian relations after 1991 75

II   Bordering Nations, Transcending Boundaries

3. Under Construction: the Ukrainian-Russian Border from the Soviet Collapse to EU Enlargement 125

4. Boundary in Mind: Discourses and Narratives of the Ukrainian-Russian Border 155

5. "Slobozhanshchyna": Re-inventing a Region in the Ukrainian-Russian Borderlands 191

III   Living (with the) Border

6. Making Sense of a New Border: Social Transformations and Shifting Identities in Five Near-Border Villages 237

7. Becoming Ukrainians in a "Russian" Village: Local Identity, Language and National Belonging 281

List of Abbreviations

AEBR	Association of European Border Regions
BUMAD	"Belarus, Ukraine, Moldova Against Drugs" UNDP Project
CDC	Community of Democratic Choice
CFE	Treaty on Conventional Armed Forces in Europe
CIS	Commonwealth of Independent States
CSTO	Collective Security Treaty Organization
ENPI	European Neighbourhood and Partnership Instrument
EU	European Union
EUBAM	European Border Assistance Mission to Moldova and Ukraine
EurAsEC	Eurasian Economic Commonwealth
IOM	International Organization for Migration
JHA	Justice and Home Affairs
KGB	Komitet Gosudarsvennoi Bezopasnosti (Committee for State Security)
MFA	Ministry of Foreign Affairs
NATO	North Atlantic Treaty Organization
NIS	New Independent States
ODED-GUAM	Organization for Democracy and Economic Development (Georgia, Ukraine, Azerbaijan and Moldova)
OSCE	Organization for Security and Co-operation in Europe
OUN	Orhanizatsiia Ukrainskykh Natsionalistiv (Organization of Ukrainian Nationalists)
PACE	Parliamentary Assembly of the Council of Europe

SEA	Single Economic Area
TACIS	Technical Assistance to the Commonwealth of Independent States
UNDP	United Nations Development Program
UPA	Ukrainska Povstanska Armiia (Ukrainian Resurgent Army)
USSR	Union of Soviet Socialist Republics
UWCC	Ukrainian World Coordination Council
WMD	Weapons of Mass Destruction

List of Images

Map of Ukraine (2009)	41
Map of Belgorod and Kharkiv Oblasts	42
Prokhorovka Memorial (Bell Tower)	86
Peter and Paul Cathedral in Prokhorovka	88
Names of Soviet soldiers engraved on the inner walls of the cathedral	89
The Bell of Unity	91
Derzhprom / Gosprom building in Kharkiv	202
Lenin Monument in Kharkiv	203
V.Karazin Kharkiv National University	204
Belgorod oblast administration with Lenin monument	207
Belgorod State University	208
Hoptivka-Nekhotkeevka, on the highway Moscow-Crimea, is the main crossing point at the Kharkiv-Belgorod part of the border	213
Street in Udy	240
Post office in Shchetinovka	245
National and regional symbols in Shchetinovka school	246
Public library in Zhuravlevka	248
Kozacha Lopan, a railway station at the Ukrainian-Russian border, halfway between Kharkiv and Belgorod. The border guards patrol is on its way to check the local train	252

People waiting for border and customs controls to enter the local train Kharkiv-Belgorod	254
The monument for the liberation of Udy from German fascist occupation dominates the central square of the village. 506 inhabitants of the village died in the Second World War	287
The remnants of the trade centre in Udy, built in the 1970s	289
Memorial cross erected after 1991 at the place of the old Orthodox church destroyed in the 1930s	291
New Orthodox church recently opened in the former Udy cafeteria	292
Pavel Kusnetzov, the former Udy school director and local history enthusiast, with one of the teachers	294
Udy's school (built in 1910) is the only one in the Zolochiv rayon to teach in Russian	306
The class room for Ukrainian studies in Udy's school. Objects of Ukrainian folklore are presented to promote Ukrainian national identity among pupils	311
Vasyl, private farmer and Yushchenko supporter	319

Foreword

Ukraine *en route* to where?

Among the features of the post-socialist transformation of Eastern Europe over the past two decades have been the conflicts over collective identities. Sometimes these have led to military confrontations between new nations, at great human cost. In the case of Ukraine, the identities of the various regions, and the related conflicts over the country's geopolitical orientation towards either "Eurasia" or Europe, clash peacefully, yet constantly.

The re-interpretation of national history plays an important role in all post-socialist conflicts over political identity. Not only in the Balkans is there too much history per square metre. In Ukraine, too, the interpretation of national history has been used as a political weapon, particularly by Viktor Yushchenko, who became president after the Orange Revolution of 2004. Yet it is not only politicians that are involved in these conflicts, but also historians, journalists, writers – in short, intellectuals. In a constructivist understanding of international politics, such as that offered by Tatiana Zhurzhenko in the present book, these symbolic struggles are themselves part of the debate over possible futures.

The following study offers a perspective on an important conceptual (discursive and political) context of post-Soviet relations between Russia, Ukraine, and other post-Soviet states. Although foreign policy at core revolves around economic and power interests, the verve, the emotional effort, and the obstacles facing real-politics cannot be understood without studying the conflicts over cultural identities. The book begins by sketching the discourse on Eurasia, which first emerged among intellectuals in Russian émigré circles during the interwar period, and which in the post-Soviet ideological vacuum after 1991 influenced the debate among Ukrainian and Russian elites with renewed strength. The Soviet and post-Soviet discourse on "Eastern

Slavic Unity" and the "Great Patriotic War" is retraced in a similar way. Particularly interesting are Zhurzhenko's references to the shifting interpretations and instrumentalizations of these myths in the present day.

The first part of the book, having discussed this intellectual discourse, goes on to chart the geopolitical options for Ukraine, especially in relation to Russia. This is followed by an analysis of the relations between Ukraine and Belarus, a subject that until now has received little attention in the scholarly literature. Here, too, there is a discussion of the images of the other and their role in the debate over the future of the nation. The author shows how the relation to the neighbouring country and its path of development becomes an argument for or against particular domestic alternatives.

In the second part of the book, the main axis of the study becomes visible: an analysis of the borders between the new nation-states, with the emphasis on the new border between Russia and Ukraine. Drawing on the distinction used in border studies between "hard" and "soft" borders (the latter being "narrative constructs"), the author discusses the real production and symbolic construction (legitimation) of this border, along with its significance for both states' re-orientation towards each another. "Narratives of security" and "narratives of integration" both play a role in this symbolic production of the border.

The first chapter in this part also focuses on EU security interests in the Ukrainian border regime, analysing the development of a concomitant policy, particularly following the EU enlargement in 2004. The result, as we learn from the study, is that Schengen standards are shaping the entire Ukrainian border regime, including in the east.

Large stretches of the Ukrainian-Russian border run through heavily populated areas that traditionally have close economic ties. The study describes how the installation and modernization of the border regime and of a regime of trans-border cooperation is closely connected to the construction of new identities, thus becoming the object of conflict between political camps in Ukraine. Ukrainian discourses about borders are variously identified as pro-Russian, Ukrainian nationalist and pro-European, Russian discourses as nationalist, imperialist and liberal. In the third chapter, the author analyses a particular cross-border region (that between Kharkiv and Belgorod,) and the central role of regional economic elites in the shaping of the Euroregion "Slobozhanshchyna".

In the third part, the author summarizes the results of a field study in five villages (three in the Kharkiv region, two in the Belgorod region) in 2003 and 2004. She describes the empirical methods used in order to obtain her results. Among the list of questions used in this research are those asking into the history and the identity of the villagers, their trans-border economic interests and their perception of the Ukrainian-Russian border. Zhurzhenko selects a sample of research objects that differ in their historical and ethnic characteristics. Her own contradictory identity as Ukrainian citizen whose mother tongue is Russian is also discussed in this context.

The observations and the interpretations of the conversations and interviews visualize the evolution of new borders (and, connected with this, the formation of the different national identities of the populations on both sides the border). For me, a particularly significant discovery of the field study was how much the sustainability of the various processes of symbolic construction depends on the economic success of the village or the region. "The new border represents the irreversibility of the post-1991 political and social changes, thus separating not only Ukraine from Russia, but also the present, real Ukraine from an imagined Soviet Union." On the basis of the results of the field study described, the book concludes by analysing how in one of the villages (Udy), "Russians" become "Ukrainians" – in other words how the process of nation-building takes place at the local level.

The book can be highly recommended to students of East European Studies, especially post-Soviet Politics. Its approach is informed by an intimate familiarity with the scholarly literature on border studies across the humanities and social sciences, combined with a politological analysis of the relations between Ukraine and its two northerly and easterly neighbours, Belarus and Russia. The book provides an insight into the intellectual and political discourse that frames the dispute over new, post-Soviet identities in this region. It also presents the results of an interesting field study on life on the Ukraine-Russia border. Where is the Ukraine heading today? Is it en route to Europe, or to a Russia-dominated Eurasia? Might it act as an important bridge if in the future Russia draws closer to Europe? Which of these political alternatives to opt for will not only be decided at the level of rational politics; symbolic constructions and their public reception will also play an influential role. This book reveals in detail this interplay of politics and collective identities.

Dieter Segert
Vienna, February 2010

Acknowledgments

This book is based on the results of my research project *The Ukrainian-Russian Border in National Imagination, State Building and Social Experience* (2002-2004). My host institution in Austria, the Institute for East European History at the University of Vienna provided me with valuable scholarly expertise, access to library resources and a vibrant academic environment. I am grateful to Andreas Kappeler, a leading specialist in Russian and Ukrainian history, for his institutional and personal support and intellectual inspiration. He introduced me to his research team working on the research project *Multikulturelle Grenzstädte in der Westukraine 1772-1914* (Multicultural Border Towns in Western Ukraine 1772-1914; 2004-2006), an experience which helped me to better understand the specificities of historical research on borders and borderlands. I also profited from participating in the lectures and seminars of the Doktoratskolleg *Das österreichische Galizien und sein multikulturelles Erbe* (2007-2010). My research project was generously funded by the FWF (Austrian Science Fund), which granted me a Lise Meitner Fellowship providing the crucial time for research and writing and made possible not only field trips to the border regions of Kharkiv and Belgorod but also presentations of my work at various international conferences. Among them were the Annual Convention of the Association for Study of Nationalities at Columbia University (2003); *Border Regions in Transition* – Sixth International Conference on Regionalisation: *EU Enlargement, Shifting Borders of Inclusion and Exclusion* in Pécs (Hungary, 2003); the Association for Borderlands Studies European Conference in Graz (2004); the Seventh World Congress of the ICCEES in Berlin (2005).

I also owe a lot to my Moscow colleagues Vladimir Kolossov and Olga Vendina from the Institute of Geography of the Russian Academy of Sciences, who shared their personal insights and scholarly expertise with me. Together with them and their French colleague Wanda Dressler we travelled to Belgorod, Kharkiv, Lviv and Lutsk in 2005-2006 in the framework of an international research project on post-Soviet borders. The inspiring meetings we had in these regions, the valuable firsthand information we collected and the intensive intellectual exchange made these journeys unforgettable. The results of our joint common project were presented at the Eighth BRIT International Conference in Lublin (2006) and at the workshop *Dynamiques transfrontalières et politiques de voisinage aux confins de l'Europe* at the University Paris X Nanterre (2006).

I am particularly obliged to Kerstin Zimmer, whose knowledge of Ukrainian regional politics and expertise on the Donetsk region was highly stimulating for my research. She introduced me to the project on region making in Eastern Europe led by Melanie Tatur at the Institute for Comparative Politics and International Relations at Johann Wolfgang Goethe University in Frankfurt (Main), and in May 2003 invited me to a workshop where I had the opportunity to discuss my project with her colleagues. Another inspiring event was the international seminar on *Borders, Frontiers and Border Regions in History* at Viadrina University in Frankfurt (Oder) in 2004 where I was invited to present my project. I am grateful to Helga Schultz, Andrea Komlosy, Katharina Stoklosa and other participants of this seminar for their useful comments on my project. The *First Danyliw Annual Research Seminar in Contemporary Ukrainian Studies* at the University of Ottawa (2005) offered a valuable opportunity to discuss my work with colleagues from North America. I am particularly grateful to Dominique Arel, Catherine Wanner, Tania Richardson and Jessica Allina-Pisano, who read my paper and commented on it. Finally I would like to thank the Center for Advanced Studies and Education at the European Humanities University in Minsk-Vilnius for the opportunity to participate in its long term project *East-Central Borderlands in the Context of European Studies*. My debates with Pavel Tereshkovich, Svetlana Naumova, Igor Bobkov and many other colleagues inspired me to apply the concept and methodology of Border Studies to the lands in between the EU and Russia.

Several friends and colleagues read earlier versions of chapters or contributed in other ways to this book. I would like to especially express my thanks to the late Peter Gowan as well as to Marco Bojcun, Sabine Dullin, Madeleine Hurd, János M. Kovács, Eva Kovács, Hiroaki Kuromiya, Sergey Oushakine and Dieter Segert.

Special thanks go also to my colleagues from Kharkiv University: Olexander Fisun, Olga Filipova, Volodymyr Kravchenko and Alexei Kiriukhin. Together with them and in cooperation with the Kennan Institute (Kyiv) we organized the international seminar *The Ukrainian-Russian Borderlands: Geopolitics, History, Identity* (2003) which was one of the first attempts to attract academic interest for this issue. The last two chapters draw on results of focus group and individual interviews conducted in near border villages of Kharkiv and Belgorod oblasts in summer 2003, 2004 and 2005. I thank my friend and colleague Liudmyla Kulik for her assistance. I am also grateful to the heads of my department, Olexander Mamalui and Ivan Karpenko, and to the rector of Kharkiv University, Vil Bakirov, for their organizational and personal support over many years.

Parts of this book have appeared elsewhere in a different form and sometimes in other languages. I am obliged to the publishers for granting permission to incorporate them in this book. An earlier version of chapter 1.1 was published in French in: *Eurasie: Espace mythique ou réalité en construction?*, edited by Wanda Dressler (Brussels: Bruylant, 2009); a shortened Russian version appeared in *Politicheskaya Nauka*, no. 2, 2006. An earlier version of chapter 1.2 was published in: *Belarus: External Pressure, Internal Change*, edited by Hans-Georg Heinrich and Ludmilla Lobova (Bern and Berlin: Peter Lang Verlag, 2009). Chapters 2.1, 2.2, and 2.3 are based on two articles also published before: "Cross-border Cooperation and Transformation of Regional Identities in the Ukrainian-Russian Borderlands: Towards a Euroregion 'Slobozhanshchyna'?", in: *Nationalities Papers*, vol. 32, no. 1 (March 2004) and vol. 32, no. 2 (June 2004); "Europeanising the Ukrainian-Russian Border: from EU Enlargement to the Orange Revolution", in: *Debatte: Review of Eastern and Central European Studies*, no. 13 (2005); "Ukraine's Border with Russia before and after the Orange Revolution", in: *Die Ukraine: Zerrissen zwischen Ost und West?*, edited by Martin Malek, *Schriftenreihe der Landesverteidigungsakademie*, no. 2 (2007). Chapter 3.1 is based on a conference paper presented on a panel on "Proximity and Asymmetry in Border Encounters" at the *EASA* Conference in Vienna (2004); a part of this paper was published under the title "The New Post-Soviet Borderlands: Nostalgia, Resistance to Changes, Adaptation: A Case Study of Three Near-Border Villages in Kharkiv Oblast, Ukraine", in: Borderland Identities, edited by Madeleine Hurd (Eslöv: Förlags ab Gondolin 2006). The last chapter, 3.2, draws on a paper presented at the First Danyliw Annual Research Seminar in Contemporary Ukrainian Studies in the University of Ottawa (2005). For the purpose of this publication I have significantly rewritten, re-edited and updated all chapters in 2009. Most of this work was done at the Institute for Political Science of the University of Vienna, where I am currently an Elise Richter Research Fellow.

I have used an adapted Library of Congress system for transliteration, ignoring diacritical marks and soft signs. Certain Anglicisms have been retained (Crimea, Dnieper, etc.). The names of persons who publically use a Romanized version of their names are usually rendered in the orthography used by these persons.

Last but not least I am very grateful to Andeas Umland, the editor of the *Post-Soviet Politics and Societies* series of *ibidem* Verlag for supporting the idea of this book. Many thanks also to Jason Heilman (Duke University) for his editorial work. This book would not have been possible without the support of my husband and colleague Klaus Nellen, who encouraged me to start a new life in Vienna, shared my fascination with the post-Soviet borders and accompanied me in my journeys. He was the first reader and professional editor of my texts and gave me the confidence to publish this book.

Tatiana Zhurzhenko
Vienna, January 2010

Introduction

1   Remapping Eastern Europe: the geopolitical context

This book was prepared for publication during 2009 – the year when a united Europe commemorated the fall of the communist regimes in Eastern Europe. While Berlin became the epicentre of political and cultural events celebrating the regained German unity, similar festivities also took place in many other sites along the former Iron Curtain which used to divide the European continent into "East" and "West". Political speeches, academic conferences, art and photo exhibitions reminded the Europeans of a border that has disappeared but remains in the collective memory as a symbol of political oppression, ideological blindness and mutual hostility. With the process of integration, the national borders within the European Union change their political status, their functions and their attached symbolic meanings – they become places of encounter, communication and exchange; they are seams where Europe, in words of Karl Schlögel, "grows together".

The success of a new Europe "without borders" is only one side of the story, however. At the margins of the European continent the collapse of communism brought about the disintegration of the Soviet Union and the break-up of Yugoslavia. For the new independent states, national borders not only represent an important attribute of state sovereignty and a symbolic link between the nation and its territory; here borders are crucial elements of national security and, to use Friedrich Ratzel's term, "power barometers" in relations with neighbouring countries. Border disputes, territorial conflicts and separatist movements make it difficult to imagine the political map of the post-Soviet space as finally settled. But even if the new borders are legitimized by international treaties, territorial and border issues often reflect the renegotiation of the power balance between neighbours, a changing geopolitical status or national identity problems. Post-Soviet borders have a pre-history as administrative boundaries of the former Soviet republics; but as international borders they are "young" and often lack symbolic power or, in the words of Claus Eder, "narrative plausibility". Competing geopolitical ambitions of the

EU and NATO, on the one hand, and of Russia as a re-emerging great power, on the other, add to the political tensions that surround border issues. In fact, in the last two decades, borders in the post-Soviet space – in particular in its European part – served as unique laboratories where processes of nation and state building overlap globalization and European enlargement.

The texts collected under this cover mainly deal with the Ukrainian-Russian border after 1991, but are not restricted to this subject. It is rather the processes of re-mapping, re-narrating and re-bordering the Western post-Soviet borderlands that are of interest for me. Covering Ukrainian-Russian and, to a lesser extent, Ukrainian-Belarusian relations, the book addresses the emergence of new borders and the transformation of collective identities in the processes of post-Soviet disintegration and nation building. Since 1991, national identities in Ukraine, Russia and Belarus have been re-narrated and new national borders established and legitimized; former Soviet republics search for their place on the geopolitical map of the European continent and re-discover each other as neighbours, competitors and partners facing similar challenges. At the same time, the new borders are often politically contested by controversial attempts to re-establish an albeit imagined former unity, like a common "East Slavic" or "Eurasian" geopolitical and geo-cultural space. The Ukrainian-Russian border in particular became a site (and an indicator) of conflict between two integration projects – the European and the post-Soviet one. Although the EU's enlargement ambitions are quite limited when it comes to Ukraine, the prospect of EU accession plays an enormous symbolic role in Ukrainian foreign and domestic politics. Without advancing further east geographically, the European Union influences the geopolitical status and regime of Ukraine's eastern border. Most Ukrainian experts and politicians consider the still porous and non-demarcated border with Russia to be a sign of unfinished nation building, an indicator of power imbalance in bilateral relations and an obstacle for European integration. Meanwhile, certain functions of the EU's external borders (such as the monitoring and prevention of illegal migration) have been delegated to the Ukrainian-Russian border. The same is true for the Ukrainian-Moldavian border, where in 2005 the EUBAM Project (European Border Assistance Mission to Moldova and Ukraine, 2005-09) was implemented with the aim of enhancing the capacities of the border guard and custom services of both countries. In the framework of the new European Partnership initiative launched May 2009 in Prague Ukraine and Belarus agreed on the delimitation and demarcation of their common border. The EU will provide technical and financial assistance for this project.

However, the role of these "new" borders appears quite different in the context of the post-Soviet integration projects initiated and led by Russia. Cross-border cooperation between the Ukrainian and Russian border regions is seen as a "small-scale integration", which is supposed to complement more ambitious integration projects such as EurAsEC or the Single Economic Area (SEA). In the discourse of post-Soviet integration the new borders appear artificial, dividing the "natural" unity of the "East Slavic civilization" and undermining the historically proven "brotherhood". From the Russian point of view, Ukraine's integration into NATO and EU institutions would inevitably turn the border between the two countries into a new dividing line cutting Russia off from the rest of Europe.

It is the "new" Eastern Europe, the borderlands between Russia and the enlarged EU – Belarus, Moldova, and to some extent the Caucasus region, but first of all Ukraine – which are at stake in this conflict between two centres of power on the European continent. And while the attraction of the EU as a "soft power" lies in the European model of democracy, respect for human rights and appeal to civil society, Russia still uses traditional instruments of "hard power" for persuading its neighbours to the advantages of post-Soviet integration. The 2004 Orange Revolution in Ukraine became a revealing illustration of this persisting geopolitical competition projected into the domestic politics of post-Soviet states as a conflict between pro-Russian and pro-European orientations. In 2009 the Eastern Partnership program was initiated by the EU in order to facilitate cooperation and provide the foundation for new association agreements with six post-Soviet countries – Ukraine, Belarus, Moldova, Georgia, Armenia and Azerbaijan. While the promotion of human rights and the rule of law are the priorities of this new initiative, it is obviously aimed at countering Russia's influences in its "backyard". Strengthening democratic institutions and capacities of the new independent states (including border management) serves as an instrument of European "post-modern" geopolitics. Meanwhile, recovered from the shock of the "Colour Revolutions", Moscow is also learning to use "soft power" instruments such as NGOs and youth movements. The Russian-speaking population of Ukraine's eastern borderlands, where hybrid identities and double loyalties are widespread, is a target of this new Russian politics. As long as the architecture of security in Europe remains incomplete, EU-Russian relations will not be settled and their zones of influence are disputed; the symbolic status of the Ukrainian-Russian border in the national and international politics will have to be contested and re-negotiated.

While writing this book, however, I was not driven by the national security considerations central to most analysts writing about post-Soviet borders. In the case of the Ukrainian-Russian border, this "security discourse" usually focuses on its strategic role, on the threats and disadvantages for Ukrainian foreign policy resulting from its "unaccomplished" status. Nor was I inspired by nostalgia for the lost Soviet unity or by the pan-Slavic visions shaping the discourse of post-Soviet integration. Rather, the idea of this book was to approach the post-Soviet borders as a construct produced by different political actors through various narratives; to go beyond the dominant discourses of security and integration and demonstrate their role in the processes of border construction. In doing so, I address not only the elitist discourses produced by politicians and intellectuals, but also the narratives of ordinary people living near the new border and experiencing it in their everyday lives. In addition, I use a regional scale of analysis to understand the role of the border in the political strategies of the regional elites, the uses of border issues and cross-border cooperation in region making, in power negotiations with the centre and in re-shaping relations with the neighbouring states. Here once again I try to take some distance from the affirmative discourse and move beyond the positivist analysis of the advantages of and obstacles to cross-border cooperation.

Although "border studies" are flourishing, the Ukrainian-Russian border has rarely been addressed in academic literature. The classical historical work of Hiroaki Kuromiya on the Soviet Donbas,[1] recent studies by the political scientists Jessica Allina-Pisano[2] on the post-Soviet land reform in the

---

1 Hiroaki Kuromiya, *Freedom and Terror in the Donbas: A Ukrainian-Russian Borderland, 1870s-1990s*, New York: Cambridge University Press 1998.
2 Jessica Allina-Pisano, *The Post-Soviet Potemkin Village: Politics and Property Rights in the Black Earth*, New York: Cambridge University Press 2008.

Black Earth region, Kerstin Zimmer[3] on power elites in Donbas and Peter Rodgers on school education and identity in Sumy, Luhansk and Kharkiv[4] have analyzed the political and social transformations in the Ukrainian-Russian borderlands. However, they do not focus on the border or on the processes of border construction.[5] My intention was to fill in this research gap and apply new approaches and concepts developed in the relatively young field of border studies to the Ukrainian-Russian case. The lack of academic interest in the Ukrainian-Russian border is particularly visible in comparison to the western border of Ukraine, which has attracted the attention of Ukrainian and international scholars from economists and political scientists to historians and anthropologists.

The lack of interest in the eastern border can be itself an object of analysis; it seems to be a symptom of a deeper problem, having to do with the symbolic hierarchy and the hegemony of discourses. Western Ukrainian border regions actively re-brand themselves as a "bridge" or a "gate to Europe", and the border with Poland, Slovakia and Hungary – the new EU members – today embodies Ukraine's strategic choice. In contrast, the Ukrainian-Russian borderlands appear as part of a non-differentiated, stagnating, ambiguous "post-Soviet space"; they are either ignored or bear rather negative connotations. Ukraine's border with Russia seems not fascinating enough for researchers: in their eyes it offers neither cultural contrasts and historical conflicts nor interesting projects and civic initiatives. And the way the border is presented in public discourse reduces it to a "security problem". In contrast, this book makes the very ambiguity of the Ukrainian-Russian border a subject of inquiry.

---

3   Kerstin Zimmer, *Machteliten im ukrainischen Donbass – Bedingungen und Konsequenzen der Transformation einer alten Industrieregion*, Münster: LIT 2006.
4   Peter Rodgers, *Nation, region and history in post-communist transitions. Identity Politics in Ukraine, 1991-2006*, Stuttgart: Ibidem 2008.
5   Vladimir Kolossov and Olga Vendina, "Social gradients, identity and migration flows (by the example of Belgorod and Kharkiv oblasts)", *Migration and Border Regime: Belarus, Moldova, Russia and Ukraine*, Kyiv: National Institute for International Security Problems 2002, pp. 21-46 (in Russian); Olga Vendina and Vladimir Kolossov, "Partnership that Bypasses Barriers", *Russia in Global Politics*, no. 1 (2007).

2 Frontiers, boundaries and borderlands: the conceptual framework

Borders, borderlands and the construction of borders are the key concepts of this book. Widely used in various academic disciplines (international law, political geography, history, anthropology, political science), the notion of "border" is far from being well defined and unequivocal. Therefore a brief theoretical introduction is needed here to outline my approach. In other words, after having situated this book (geo)politically, I will now try to position it conceptually. While particular theories and methodological issues are discussed in the respective chapters, here I would like to discuss the key concepts and their applicability to the post-Soviet borders, in particular to the Ukrainian-Russian border.

If we start with the question of terminology, such notions as "border", "boundary" and "frontier" are often used as interchangeable in academic literature. However, historically they have considerable nuances. *Frontier* implies etymologically "in front", an area which is "ahead of the hinterland"; it is often called the foreland, or borderland, or march.[6] In his classic work of border research, Ladis Kristof noted that "in its historical origin the frontier was (1) not a legal concept, and (2) not, or at least not essentially, a political or intellectual concept. It was rather a phenomenon of 'the facts of life' – a manifestation of the spontaneous tendency for growth of the ecumene."[7] It was in a similar sense that the concept of frontier was introduced by Frederic Jackson Turner in relation to American history: a transition zone with a dynamic character.[8] The American frontier had analogues in world history.[9] According to Andreas Kappeler, this notion can be applied to the early modern Russian state and its south and east margins: as a geographic frontier (between forest and steppe), as a social frontier (between settled and nomadic cultures), as a military frontier (between different military formations) and finally as a reli-

---

6   Ladis K.D. Kristof, "The Nature of Frontiers and Boundaries", *Annals of the Association of American Geographers*, vol. 49, no. 3 (1959), pp. 269-282.
7   Kristof, "The Nature of Frontiers and Boundaries", p. 270.
8   Frederick Jackson Turner, *The Frontier in American History*, New York: Henry Holt and Co. 1935 (1893).
9   Hans-Heinrich Nolte, "Deutsche Ostgrenze, russische Südgrenze, amerikanische Westgrenze. Zur Radikalisierung der Grenzen in der Neuzeit", in: Joachim Becker and Andrea Komlosy (eds.), *Grenzen Weltweit. Zonen, Linien, Mauern im historischen Vergleich*, Vienna: Promedia 2004, pp. 55-74.

gious and cultural frontier (between "civilization" and "barbarism").[10] In the pre-modern state, "frontier was quite literary 'the front': the *frons* of the *imperium mundi* which expands to the only limits it can acknowledge, namely, the limits of the world. Thus, the frontier was not the end ('tail') but rather the beginning ('forehead') of the state."[11] Similarly, the French term for state border, *frontière*, was borrowed from the military vocabulary and in the 16th and 17th centuries still "referred to the idea of movement, advance, clash, repulse".[12] Later, with the formation of the modern French state, the notion of *frontière* absorbed the meaning of *limite* (border in the juridical sense).[13]

The term *boundary* "indicates certain established limits (the bounds) of a given political unit, and all that which is within the boundary is bound together, that is, it is fasten by an internal bound."[14] To put it roughly, a boundary is a frontier which has become a demarcated line; it implies stabilization and peace instead of expansion.[15] To use Kristof's helpful metaphor, the frontier is a manifestation of centrifugal forces, while the boundary indicates centripetal forces; the latter marks "the outer line of effective control exercised by the central government".[16] If the frontier is a historical phenomenon, the boundary is more of legal and political development, and if the frontier is about integration and communication, the term "boundary" implies quite the opposite meaning: delimitation and separation. In medieval Europe an exact territorial delimitation was scarcely possible, because different legal claims by secular and clerical powers often overlapped the same territory. The feudal land properties were full of enclaves and exclaves and therefore did not represent homogeneous territorial entities. In this sense, the idea of the bound-

---

10 Andreas Kappeler, "Rußlands Frontier in der Frühen Neuzeit", in: Ronald G. Asch, Wulf Eckart Voß and Martin Wrede (eds.), *Frieden und Krieg in der Frühen Neuzeit. Die europäische Staatenordnung und die außereuropäische Welt*, Munich: Wilhelm Fink 2001, pp. 599-613; here p. 600.
11 Kristof, "The Nature of Frontiers and Boundaries", p. 270.
12 Lucien Febvre: "Frontière. Le mot et la notion", *Revue de synthèse historique*, no. 45 (1928), pp. 31-44, cited in: "Einleitung", in: Eva Horn, Stefan Kaufmann and Ulrich Bröckling (eds.), *Grenzverletzer. Von Schmugglern, Spionen und anderen subversiven Gestalten*, Berlin: Kulturverlag Kadmos 2002, pp. 7-22; here p. 13.
13 Febvre in: Horn et al., *Grenzverletzer*, p. 14.
14 Kristof, "The Nature of Frontiers and Boundaries", p. 270.
15 Cf. Stephen B. Jones, "Boundary Concepts in the Setting of Place and Time", *Annals of the Association of American Geographers*, vol. 49, no. 3 (1959), pp. 241-255; here p. 250.
16 Kristof, "The Nature of Frontiers and Boundaries", p. 272.

ary as a clear continuous line defining the limits of state authority is quite new. This is an attribute of a modern state exercising authority over a given territory and conducting a policy aimed at homogenizing the population living on this territory. In international relations the idea of the boundary as a line delimitating exclusive territorial/political communities goes back to the Peace of Westphalia (1648), which initiated a new political order based on the concept of a sovereign state.

In this book I prefer the term "border" to both "boundary" and "frontier" for various reasons. In fact "border" is the most popular term, often used as a synonym for the latter two. Its meaning cannot be reduced to legal and technical aspects and it has no specific historical or ideological connotations; the term also refers to the political, social and cultural aspects of territoriality. "Border" usually combines both meanings discussed above: as a dividing line it assumes delimitation, demarcation and separation, while at the same time, as a zone of interaction, it signifies communication and integration. The new post-Soviet borders, which used to be largely irrelevant administrative boundaries two decades ago, are now subject to demarcation on the territory. As an attribute of the newly acquired state sovereignty they have to be strictly controlled and technically modernized to fulfil their function of separation, both in terms of security and national identity formation. At the same time, post-Soviet borders remain zones of intensive traffic and communication and, in many cases, zones of ongoing assimilation and integration; they continue to produce hybrid and overlapping identities.

The opposition between frontier and boundary is of course only analytical. The nature of borders is ambivalent and historically changing; their interpretations reflect the spirit of a particular epoch and the constellation of certain political forces. The idea of territorial sovereignty combined with the principle of national self-determination adopted in 1918 was built into the fundament of the new international order established in Europe after World War I. The idealist political principles promoted by Woodrow Wilson sought to create a stable system of international relations based on the rule of law and on fair and legitimate borders. However, this ambitious attempt to redraw the borders on the European continent according to principles of national self-determination and sovereignty failed to secure stable peace. Revisionist forces in the interwar Europe used, among others, the organicist and evolutionist ideas of the German geographer Friedrich Ratzel. He argued that a strong state follows the imperative of territorial expansion, the natural tendency of the state organism seeking to enlarge its *Lebensraum*. According to Ratzel, "the frontier is, as the peripheric organ of the state, the bearer of its growth and its security, conforming to all changes of the state organism".[17] This expansionist concept of the border was instrumentalized by Nazi politics in Europe and thus politically compromised. The system of post-WWII international boundaries was more stable and hardly changed until 1989 as the threat of a global nuclear conflict between the two superpowers had made territorial revisionism a taboo. The system of post-war boundaries was stabilized through the enemy-friend logic.[18] The Iron Curtain, a clear-cut boundary between East and West, can serve as an example for an almost perfect separation and isolation unique in human history. At the same time both systems could hardly hide their expansionist ambitions which sometimes provoked local military conflicts in other parts of the world. Not by accident, in the Cold War era the concept of frontier was used again to reflect the opposition between the two ideological systems and hostile political blocks. Ladis Kristof suggested in 1959 that the very principle of territorial sovereignty is undermined by the opposition of political blocks, because class and ideological loyalties override the loyalty to the nation state.

With the fall of the Iron Curtain, barbed-wire fences and concrete walls were removed, but the "border of prosperity" between Western and Eastern European states still persists.[19] The process of European integration has been changing the nature of state boundaries once again. Supranational institutions limit the national sovereignty of the EU member states and the processes of regionalization and globalization render EU internal borders less relevant. New traffic routes, transport corridors and networks determine the

---

17 Friedrich Ratzel, "Die Gesetze des räumlichen Wachstums der Staaten", cited in: Stephen B. Jones, *Boundary Concepts*. Ratzel uses the German term *Grenze*.
18 Mathias Bös and Kerstin Zimmer, "Wenn Grenzen wandern. Zur Dynamik von Grenzverschiebungen in Osten Europas", in: Monika Eigmüller and Georg Vobruba (eds.), *Grenzsoziologie: Die politische Strukturierung des Raumes*, Wiesbaden: VS Verlag 2006, pp. 157-184; here p. 172.
19 Andrea Komlosy and Joachim Becker, "Grenzen und Räume – Formen und Wandel", in: idem (eds.), *Grenzen Weltweit*, pp. 21-54; here p. 33.

geography of Europe more than state boundaries.[20] To Karl Schlögel this post-modern European territoriality in some aspects reminds of a pre-modern one: "Powerful forces are working to overcome the old borders... The map that is emerging does not bear much similarity to the one on the classroom wall I grew up with: with the variously coloured nation states, with the provisional borders of post-war Europe marked either in thick or hatched lines. The new map is more reminiscent of early modernity, of the trade and pilgrimage routes, of the links between holy cities and routes of world communication."[21]

The Soviet bloc collapsed, but the border between the two political blocs did not disappear completely. With EU and NATO enlargement it was shifted to the east; it now separates the new EU members and their Eastern neighbours.[22] The new external EU border is technically superior to the former Iron Curtain, but its permeability varies significantly for various nationals and different social groups. Visa regimes and a strictly regulated access to EU labour markets are meant to keep the citizens of the new independent states "out". At the same time new political incentives such as association agreements and regional cooperation programs seek to turn the new Eastern European states into a "ring of friends" – EU satellite states sharing democratic principles and providing security along the Schengen borders. In this way the former Soviet republics along the eastern border of the EU represent a "frontier" in the almost classical sense: a transitional area to be "civilized" and assimilated to Western political values. At the same time, Russia also sees these territories through the frontier lens: as its former Western borderlands which it had to give up, but over which it still hopes to regain political and economic influence.

3 Nation-building, nomadic borders and shifting identities

It seems that in the modern era, the stability of political boundaries on the European continent has been an exception rather than a rule. While some borders have remained unchanged for centuries, many others – particularly in

---

20 Cf. Karl Schlögel, "Europe tests its boundaries", *Eurozine*, www.eurozine.com/articles/article_2004-11-24-schloegel-en.html (last accessed February 7, 2010).
21 Karl Schlögel, "Places and strata of memory. Approaches to Eastern Europe", *Eurozine*, www.eurozine.com/articles/2008-12-19-schlogel-en.html (last accessed February 7, 2010).
22 Komlosy and Becker, "Grenzen und Räume – Formen und Wandel", p. 34.

Eastern and Central Europe – have changed their location, geopolitical status, economic and social functions and symbolic meanings many times. The rise of modern nationalism, the collapse of three continental empires (the Austro-Hungarian, the Russian and the Ottoman), two World Wars, the Cold War, the end of the bi-polar world order and, most recently, EU enlargement have been constantly changing the political map of Europe. German sociologists Mathias Bös and Kerstin Zimmer argue that we usually associate borders with the migration of people, but in fact it is often borders that "migrate" and move over the populations.[23] "Nomadic borders" is another metaphor that has been suggested by the Russian sociologists Viktor Voronkov and Olga Brednikova.[24] The "migration of borders" destroys old communities and shapes new ones; it causes resettlements, deportations, and even ethnic cleansing, while creating new minorities or homogenizing the population inside the new borders. With these border changes, not only do the political and legal systems become subjects of reform; school education, official national symbols, dominant historical narratives, and even the official language can change as well.[25] Border shifts reshape the collective memories and identities of populations, and challenge their loyalties and emotional attachments.[26] A new nation state usually requires a new national history; it needs symbols and myths for the majority of its population to identify with.

The institutionalization of the new borders in the post-Soviet space cannot be understood without taking into account the nation building processes following the disintegration of the Soviet Union. The literature on (post-)Soviet nation building is vast, but according to Ukrainian historian Serhy Yekelchyk, the debate is dominated by two main approaches. The first one, represented by Richard Pipes and Robert Conquest, supports "the traditional view of the oppressive Soviet empire, which had imposed its ideology on pre-existing nationalities and was finally undone by its peoples' long-suppressed national stirrings". The second, "revisionist" view, represented by Grigor Suny, Robert

---

23 Mathias Bös and Kerstin Zimmer, "Wenn Grenzen wandern", p. 156-157.
24 Olga Brednikova and Viktor Voronkov (eds.), *Nomadic Borders*. Proceedings of the Seminar held in Narva, 12-16 November 1998, St. Petersburg: CISR, Working Paper no 7 (1999).
25 Bös and Zimmer, "Wenn Grenzen wandern", p. 161.
26 Tatiana Zhurzhenko, "Borders and Memory", in: Doris Wastl-Walter (ed.), *Ashgate Research Companion to Border Studies*, Farnham: Ashgate 2010 (forthcoming).

Kaiser and Yuri Slezkine, sees the Soviet Union "as a creator of territorial nations with their own modern high cultures, political elites and state symbols".²⁷ Indeed, the Soviet politics of national territorialization was rather ambivalent. The Soviet Union was formally a federation of fifteen Soviet republics, each representing their titular "socialist nations". Together with the other ethnic groups whose territorial rights were recognized in the form of "autonomous republics" and "autonomous districts", they formed the Soviet hierarchy of nationalities. This institutional territorialization of ethnicity in a complex system of administrative divisions sought to establish a link between an ethnic group and the territory it "possessed". However, the administrative boundaries between the Soviet republics were neither demarcated nor controlled and had no particular symbolic meaning. The (supra-)national identity and political loyalty of Soviet citizens were bound to the whole territory of the Union, while ethnicity was de-politicized and mainly reduced to folklore and exotic tradition. In particular, Russians "were encouraged to identify their national interests with Soviet interests".²⁸ After 1991 the bonds between nation and territory have been (re-)created in the new independent states in the process of "homeland making".

Political geographer Robert Kaiser sees the "construction of homelands" as a process in which the nationalist elites mobilize "the myths and images of a primordial homeland to reinforce the depiction of the nation as an ancient community of belonging, an organic singularity 'rooted' to a particular place."²⁹ Indeed, political elites and intellectuals have been playing a leading role in the processes of reterritorialization of the post-Soviet nations. This is done through the creation of maps and other cartographic representations, producing motherland images and designing symbolic landscapes and commemorative sites. School education, in particular the teaching of national history and geography, is essential in the process of "territorial socialization" of the citizens, while national media and cultural industry aim to re-shape the territorial

---

27   Serhy Yekelchyk, *Stalin's Empire of Memory. Russian-Ukrainian Relations in the Soviet Historical Imagination,* Toronto: University of Toronto Press 2004, p. 3.
28   Terry Martin, *The Affirmative Action Empire: Nations and Nationalism in the Soviet Union, 1923-1939,* Ithaca: Cornell University Press 2001, p. 461.
29   Robert J. Kaiser, "Homeland making and the territorialization of national identity", in: Daniele Conversi (ed.), *Ethnonationalism in the Contemporary World. Walker Connor and the study of nationalism,* London and New York: Routledge 2002, pp. 229-247; here p. 230.

consciousness of the older generations. However, these political strategies of the elites are not entirely manipulative; they appeal to the cultural memory of the nation, to powerful historical symbols and narratives. For Anthony Smith the "territorialization of memory" is not induced by the elites but starts with an ethnic community which endows its territory with a particular collective emotion. Smith introduces the notion of "ethnoscapes" which "cover a wider extent of land, present a tradition of continuity and are held to constitute an ethnic unity, because the terrain invested with collective significance is felt to be integral to a particular historical culture, community or ethnie, and the ethnic community is seen as an intrinsic part of that poetic landscape".[30] Some ethnoscapes are endowed with an extraordinary meaning and generate powerful feelings of reverence and belonging – according to Smith they become "sacred territories" central for ethnic identity. Smith's approach can be particularly applied to border conflicts, where "two communities compete for possession of the selfsame homeland territories"[31] (as in case of Ulster, Kosovo or Nagorno-Karabakh).

Regardless what comes first – an ethnic group that endows a specific terrain with a deep symbolic meaning, or the elites that draw national borders and educate masses to give them the idea of "our land" – nationalism can be seen as a "territorial ideology" (David Harvey). The intrinsic ambition of nationalism is to bring state and ethnic (national) boundaries together, to make them congruent. This is a project which usually requires a certain degree of symbolic if not physical violence. The population of border regions, which is often suspected of being "de-nationalized" and lacking loyalty to the new state, experience this symbolic violence more often. The nationalization of borderlands becomes one of the strategic tasks of nation and state building. John Augelli described these processes at the border between the Dominican Republic and Haiti, and his analysis is also relevant for the post-Soviet countries: "The borderlands between two emerging states tend historically to be zones of cultural overlap and political instability where the national identity and loyalties of the people often become blurred. In the absence of a sharply defined international boundary and an effective political control by the central

---

30 Anthony Smith, *Myths and Memories of the Nation*, New York: Oxford University Press 2000, p. 150.
31 Smith, *Myths and Memories of the Nation*, p. 154.

governments, the frontier provides an excellent opportunity for interpenetration and sway. Border populations are little concerned with jurisdictional limits; residents work out intimate economic and social reciprocity with their neighbours in the adjoining country; and the ties that bind them to compatriots in their national core areas are often tenuous. These conditions are tolerated only when a state is immature and the power of the central authority is weak. Ultimately governments tend to pursue strong nationalization policies along their territorial borders. The vague frontier zone is replaced by a sharp boundary line; border people are infused with a marked sense of national purpose or are supplemented by settlers from the core area of the country. Efforts are made to integrate the borderlands with the rest of the national territory".[32]

The Ukrainian-Russian borderlands provide some examples of such nationalization politics and the difficulties it faces in the post-Soviet states. In the eastern regions of Ukraine, near the Russian border, mixed and overlapping identities pose a challenge to the politics of the central government aimed at the assimilation of the post-Soviet population to Ukrainian culture. The significant percentage of ethnic Russians and Russian speakers makes it difficult to pursue a strategy of Ukrainization to create a new national identity and loyalty; the language issue – and more recently, the memory of the Soviet past – have been used by some regional elites to mobilize mass opposition against the national-democratic government. Donetsk in particular has become the most prominent example of such political opportunism since 2004. The oblast[33] and city councils in Kharkiv and Luhansk use similar strategies threatening the centre with "linguistic separatism". In turn, Russia encourages active opposition to and passive sabotage of the Ukrainization policy in Ukraine's border regions, using this issue as political leverage in bilateral relations. The Russian media and cultural industry, which still dominate the Ukrainian market, reproduce this affiliation with the former "common homeland". In general, Russia's politics for the territorialization of national identity in the Ukrainian-Russian borderlands is twofold. In the Russian Federation

---

32 John P. Augelli, "Nationalization of Dominican Borderlands", *The Geographical Review*, no. 70 (1980), pp. 19-35; here p. 19.
33 In Ukraine and Belarus *oblast* is an administrative division one step below the national level; in Russia *oblasts* are not only administrative units, but also subjects of the Federation. Oblasts are further subdivided into *raions* (districts).

"elites affiliated with the state are seeking to reterritorialize Russian national identity towards the boundaries of the Russian state, and Russians outside the borders of the Russian federation are officially treated as members of the nation living in diaspora".[34] At the same time, Russians, as the group that was formally dominant in the USSR, still perceive the whole territory of the now defunct country as their "imagined homeland" – and for historical and cultural reasons, Ukraine constitutes an integral part of it. Russian political elites appeal to these nostalgic feelings and instrumentalize them for the legitimation of their re-integration projects.

4 "Borderlands into bordered lands"

The title of the book – "Borderlands into Bordered Lands" – refers to the politics of territorial delimitation and nationalization in the post-Soviet borderlands addressed above. I borrowed it from Jeremy Adelman and Steven Aron, historians working on the evolution of the US-Mexico borderlands. They demonstrate that with the implosion of the Old World empires in the late 18th and early 19th centuries, contested colonial zones of influence in North America turned into modern states with borders recognized by international treaties. "This shift from inter-imperial struggle to international coexistence turned borderlands into *bordered* lands".[35] Significantly, this transition was not for the benefit of the indigenous populations of the borderlands. "With states claiming exclusive dominion over all territories within their borders, Indians lost the ability to play off rivalries; they could no longer take advantage of occupying the lands 'in between'. Thus, as colonial borderlands gave way to national borders, fluid and 'inclusive' intercultural frontiers yielded to hardened and more 'excusive' hierarchies".[36]

It is clear that this scheme of bordering the (post-)colonial space cannot be directly applied to the post-Soviet realities as an analytical model; at the same time, it is certainly much more than a useful metaphor. It helps us to understand post-Soviet processes of disintegration of the common political and symbolic space, of nationalization of the "shared past" and imposition of

---

34 Kaiser, "Homeland making", p. 237.
35 Jeremy Adelman and Stephen Aron, "From Borderlands to Borders: Empires, Nation-States, and the Peoples in Between in North American History", *The American Historical Review*, vol. 104, no. 3 (1999), pp. 814-841; here p. 815.
36 Adelman and Aron, "From Borderlands to Borders", pp. 815-816.

clear cut national identities and explicit state loyalties. Diffuse and ambiguous zones "in between" turn into delimited and demarcated territories, where contingent cultures, hybrid identities and fuzzy ethnic definitions have to be clarified and disciplined. One could probably suggest that in certain geopolitical areas that are often associated with "cleavages" or transition zones between civilizations such processes can have a cyclic character and often remain unfinished. The history of Ukraine, a country historically situated on the European steppe frontier and whose name etymologically refers to "margins" or "borderlands", provides multiple examples of such ambiguity and various attempts to cope with it. Most efforts to colonize "borderlands" and tame cultural ambiguity were made from the outside – by the Russian empire, Poland, the Soviet regime and the Nazis. Since 1991, Ukrainian national elites have more or less consequently pursued a policy of cultural homogenization and national consolidation intended to pull the country out of this ambiguous "borderlands" zone and bring it into Europe. The ideal of the "European", "civilized" border – clearly marked, controlled and well-protected – has become part of this project.

In her "Biography of No Place", Kate Brown[37] demonstrates how throughout the 20th century the *kresy*, the former Polish territory lost to Tsarist Russia and later to the Soviet state, was transformed from multiethnic borderlands into a largely homogeneous Ukrainian heartland. Eastern Ukraine also experienced multiple transitions from borderlands to heartland and then to "bordered lands" throughout history. Most of the territories along the Ukrainian-Russian border used to be borderlands between the Polish-Lithuanian Commonwealth, the Muscovite state and the Tatar Khanate in early modern era. Once they were incorporated into the core of the Russian empire during the 18th century, they lost the characteristics of a military frontier. The modern history of the Ukrainian-Russian border started in 1917 with the collapse of the Russian empire. In early 1918 the delegation of the Ukrainian People's Republic participated in the Brest-Litovsk negotiations, where Ukrainian territorial claims were recognized by the Central Powers. In 1919 this demarcation line became Soviet Ukraine's border with the Russian Federation, legitimised by an official agreement. However, during the 1920s, with the politics

---

37 Kate Brown, *A Biography of No Place. From Ethnic Borderlands to Soviet Heartlands*, Cambridge, MA: Harvard University Press 2004.

of *korenizatsiia*[38] and the administrative-territorial reforms, the border was renegotiated by the communist governments of Soviet Ukraine and the Russian Federation.[39] While Ukrainian leaders had to concede the majority of the Russian Shakhty region and a part of Taganrog area, their claims for a much larger portion of the RSFSR territory – namely parts of the Briansk, Kursk and Voronezh guberniias[40] – were satisfied only partly, leaving millions of ethnic Ukrainians within the Russian Federation. They became an object of Ukrainization policy in 1928-32, which resulted in a major political crisis that culminated with Stalin's repressions against "national Communists". In this respect, Terry Martin argued that the RSFSR-Ukrainian border dispute became a turning point in Soviet nationalities policy. The Great Famine, repressions and the return to Russification policy contributed to the transformation of the Ukrainian-Russian borderlands into Soviet heartland. But in the long-term perspective the border settled at the end of 1920s created a legitimate basis for the peaceful disintegration of the Soviet Union and for Ukraine's state independence some decades later. During the Soviet era the boundary between the two republics was not an obstacle to economic integration or to close social and cultural cross-border ties between populations. It was in 1991 that the territories which used to be de facto Soviet heartland – core industrial regions, the productive Black Earth zone with its ethnically mixed population largely assimilated to Russian language and sharing Soviet identity – became a new border area. However, demographically, economically and politically these regions have too much weight to be easily assimilated and incorporated into the new national core. Having no articulated political project of their own, the eastern border regions of Ukraine constantly challenge the nation building efforts of the centre (which is itself captured by the regional interest groups).

At the same time, these territories today are becoming part of the new "borderlands", which have emerged with the end of the East-West divide and the collapse of the Iron Curtain. This so-called "new Eastern Europe" is often understood as a "grey zone" between Russia and the EU, as a waiting room

---

38   *Korenizatsiia* was the policy of supporting the use of non-Russian languages and the creation of non-Russian elites in the non-Russian territories of the USSR, 1923-1932. Cf. Terry Martin, *The Affirmative Action Empire*, p. 463.
39   Martin, *The Affirmative Action Empire*, pp. 273-282.
40   *Guberniias* were an administrative subdivision of the Russian Empire and were retained for a few years under the Soviet Union.

for countries like Ukraine, Belarus or Moldova, which have yet to make their "return to Europe". This geopolitically amorphous zone "in between" bears the classical characteristics of borderlands: it generates hybrid models and creates political, economic and cultural practices which combine mutually excluding values and principles, while the political space has been torn between Western and Eastern vectors.[41] The persisting situation of a "final choice" to be made between West and East, between the EU and Russia – a "mission impossible" – produces a whole gamut of "multivector politics" on the national as well on the regional level. External pressure reproduces and strengthens this political ambivalence. Led by its own interests, the EU wants to see its Eastern neighbours as "bordered lands", encouraging the delimitation and demarcation of the borders between the post-Soviet countries as well as the improvement of border management and control of illegal migration. Russia, which is rather interested in preserving the status quo in its Western borderlands, views these EU "bordering politics" with suspicion. Moreover, the prospect of NATO expansion to the east invests the Eastern European borderlands with some characteristics of a political and military frontier which is seen from Moscow as a new *cordon sanitaire*.

Can transition from "borderlands into bordered lands" in the "new" Eastern Europe be accomplished? Modern – or as Ukrainian politicians prefer to say, "civilized" – borders are an important attribute of a sovereign state, and in this sense "border making" is one of the central tasks of nation and state building in the new independent states. The legal and technical aspects can be settled relatively easy, while symbolic delimitation might take more than one generation. However, everywhere in the contemporary world, the sovereignty of the nation state has been eroded by processes of both regional integration and globalization, and the functions of state borders have been adapting to new challenges: increased mobility of capital, re-structuring of labour markets, brain drain, formation of new diasporas, growing and often illegal migration and, as a consequence, problems of social integration. "As the political order in general, also the border regimes in the era of globalization are *per se* neither 'softer' nor 'harder' in comparison to the national institutional states – they are just more flexible. The filters of exclusion and inclu-

---

41 Igor Bobkov and Pavel Tereshkovich, "Instead of an Introduction", *Perekrestki*, no. 1-2 (2004), pp. 5-9; here p. 6.

sion are per se neither finer no rougher – they have been constantly readjusted".[42] The post-Soviet borders are also subject to these new challenges and will not stay unchanged. In the geopolitical sense, the "borderland" situation will persist as long as the competition between "the elephant and the bear" – the reluctant empire of the European Union and the reluctant ex-empire of Russia[43] – determines the map of the European continent. From the political perspective the accomplishment of the border is dependent on the success of nation and state building in Ukraine and Russia, on the dynamics of their bilateral relations and on new forms of cross-border and regional cooperation emerging in the former Soviet space. And from an anthropological perspective every border regime always finds its "violators" – be they smugglers, political refugees, or illegal labour migrants. Border violations legitimize the border regime; the violator is "indispensible as an imagined enemy in a war that keeps the order visible and welds loyal citizens together into a single, no less imagined 'We'".[44] Residents of the border areas, who have to deal with the border in their everyday lives and often abuse the border regime for pragmatic reasons, also challenge the ideal of a "civilized" border and at the same time are subject to the disciplining practices of state power.

5 Structure of the book

This book is not a monograph in the strict sense, but rather a collection of texts united by a common subject. Most of them are based on the results of my research on the Ukrainian-Russian border and have been published before in academic journals and collected volumes. The chapters were updated and re-written for the purpose of this publication in order to take new developments into account, to avoid redundancies and to fill some thematic gaps. The advantage of this collection is that it can be read selectively, allowing every chapter to find its own readers. The book combines several disciplines and methodological approaches: from the history of ideas and theories of in-

---

42 Horn, Kaufmann and Bröckling, "Einleitung", p. 21.
43 Both metaphors belong to Michael Emerson, *The Elephant and the Bear: The European Union, Russia and their Near Abroads*, Brussels: CEPS 2001.
44 Horn, Kaufmann and Bröckling, "Einleitung", p. 9.

ternational relations to discourse analysis, political science and social anthropology.

This book is structured according to three major levels of analysis: (1) the symbolic geography and geopolitics of the post-Soviet space/"new" Eastern Europe; (2) the Ukrainian-Russian border in bilateral relations, in the nation and state building processes and in regional politics, and (3) the micropolitics of border construction and the role of the border in everyday life. Thus, the seven chapters are organized in three parts.

The first part deals with the symbolic aspects of border making: the disintegration of the grand narrative of "East Slavic unity", the re-invention of "Eurasia" and the symbolic re-mapping of the "new" Eastern Europe. Chapter 1.1 examines "Eurasia" as a political and cultural construct, which has been re-narrated and used in multiple political and cultural discourses after the disintegration of the Soviet Union. It offers a view on "Eurasia" from a Ukrainian perspective, addressing the role of Ukrainians in the Eurasianist movement(s) and the place of Ukraine in imagined Eurasia(s). This chapter juxtaposes two dimensions: the evolution and conflict of ideologies on the one hand, and the actual dilemmas of regional integration in the "Eurasian" space on the other. Chapter 1.2 examines Ukrainian-Belarusian relations in the context of European enlargement to the East and Russia's reactions to this challenge. The modified Soviet concept of "East Slavic unity" as constitutive for Ukrainian-Belarusian relations is supplemented today by new discourses on (Eastern) Europe. This chapter demonstrates how the former "sister republics" and now independent states Ukraine and Belarus re-invent each other in the process of their respective post-Soviet transformations as new neighbours, allies and competitors. The ruling elites, the political opposition and the intellectuals in both countries not only appeal to the similarities and close historical roots of both peoples, but also use them as political symbols embodying particular values and models of transition. The chapter analyses Ukraine's policies towards Belarus after the Orange Revolution and the reasons for its ambivalence.

In the second part of the book the reader finds three chapters dealing with the construction of new post-Soviet borders in the context of nation and state building, EU enlargement and regional cooperation. Chapter 2.1 addresses the recent history of the Ukrainian-Russian border, its role in the bilateral relations of the two countries and cross-border cooperation initiatives between the Ukrainian and Russian regions. It shows that the unfinished delimitation and demarcation of the border, as well as the issue of Ukraine's territorial integrity as it is regularly evoked in official Russian rhetoric, is a symptom of deeper problems in bilateral relations. Moreover, the contested geopolitical status of the Ukrainian-Russian border reflects the power struggle over the "new Eastern Europe", torn between Russia and the enlarged EU. As a result of the Orange Revolution and EU enlargement to the East, Ukrainian-Russian relations have been "Europeanized" and internationalized. And despite Ukraine's weak prospects for EU accession, the Ukrainian-Russian border has been integrated into the European security system. In Chapter 2.2 the Ukrainian-Russian border is analysed as a discursive construct and a symbolic reality. Not only its geographic location, but also its geopolitical status and regime of crossing are justified by historical, linguistic and political arguments; they are constantly subject to discussion and negotiation. Two competing meta-discourses – the discourse of security and the discourse of integration – shape the perceptions and images of the common border both in Ukraine and Russia. A more detailed account allows for differentiating between pro-Russian, Ukrainian nationalist and pro-European discourses in Ukraine as well as the nationalist/imperialist and liberal discourses in Russia. Their analysis demonstrates how the border as a symbolic reality reflects geopolitical fears and historical traumas in both countries. Moving one step lower, Chapter 2.3 addresses the regional level of border making, focusing on the cross-border cooperation between Kharkiv and Belgorod oblasts. Discussing region making and cross-border cooperation in the post-Soviet context, this chapter focuses on the Euroregion "Slobozhanshchyna" initiated by Kharkiv and Belgorod regional elites. This Ukrainian-Russian cross-border project shows the dilemmas of a Euroregion "in absence of Europe". Can it contribute to the political and economic modernization of Ukraine and its eventual accession to the EU; or rather does it represent the geopolitical alternative to the "European choice"? This chapter also explores mechanisms for constructing the regional identity, the ambiguity of the historical "Slobozhanshchyna" myth and the multiplicity of its political uses.

Finally, the third part of this book is based on interviews and focus group conversations conducted in several near border villages in both the

Kharkiv and the Belgorod oblasts. Chapter 3.1 reflects the experiences of the new border in the everyday life of the local population – from visiting friends and relatives, to shopping and work in the neighbouring country, to education and career strategies. My research demonstrates how local and national identities are performed at (and transformed by) the border. This chapter seeks to show how the particular experience of "becoming a borderland" has been connected to another experience – that of becoming Ukrainians or Russians. It also shows how the border re-shapes political loyalties and local patriotism, induces nostalgia and strengthens or weakens the feeling of national belonging. Neither by Russian nor by Ukrainian citizens is the new border perceived as a cultural boundary. Instead, different social provisions related to citizenship as well as economic asymmetry make the border "real" for the local populations. Chapter 3.2 deals with one particular village, which I found the most interesting among the cases I studied: Udy, a near-border village in the Kharkiv oblast, on the Ukrainian side of the border, used to be ethnic Russian by its origins and still preserves a sense of "otherness" within its Ukrainian ethnic environment. Poor economic performance in contrast to its Russian neighbours has made many locals feel isolated and abandoned since the emergence of the new border. Most people in Udy speak Russian, but their "Russianness" is based rather on collective memory, and the dominant language of communication is subject to constant contestation and re-negotiation. The village school, with Russian as its official language of instruction, is a good example of the ambivalence and flexibility characteristic of the borderlands: attracting Russian-speaking families and teachers to the village serves to reproduce its "Russianness"; at the same time, the school administration gives in to the indirect pressure of Ukrainization and promotes a new national identity not only among children, but also their parents. The experience of the Orange Revolution, which at the first glance seemed to even more alienate Udy residents from the nation building project, in fact raised their awareness about Ukrainian political life and strengthened their emotional engagement in Ukrainian politics, thus accelerating the break with the Soviet past.

UKRAINE, 2009

KEY

1 - Russia
2 - Slovakia
3 - Transnistria (self-proclaimed Transnistrian Moldovan Republic)
4 - Autonomous Republic of Crimea, within Ukraine
5 - Montenegro
6 - Kosovo*
7 - Macedonia
8 - Abkhazia (self-proclaimed Republic of Abhkazia)

* As of July 11, 2009, 62 out of 192 United Nations members (including 22 out of 27 European Union members and 24 out of 28 NATO members) recognized the Republic of Kosovo. Serbia, Russia, China, India, Ukraine, Greece, Spain, Romania, Slovakia are among those that have not recognized independent Kosovo.

Map of Ukraine (2009)

Map of Belgorod and Kharkiv Oblasts

I   Remapping the Post-Soviet Space

1   "Eurasia" and Its Uses in the Ukrainian Geopolitical Imagination

In the post-Soviet space the ideas of Eurasianism, a product of a narrow intellectual circle of Russian émigré intellectuals, have begun a second life as an influential and even state-sponsored ideology. Not only in Russia, where it occupies a prominent place in the new imperial thinking, but also in other post-Soviet republics, Eurasianism offers a solution for the painful problem of finding a new geopolitical identity in a globalizing world. In this sense "Eurasia" is a substitute for the disappearing Atlantis of the Soviet civilization. To claim the intermediate position between "Europe" and "Asia" is one of the few possible options for those countries which do not belong to the "West", but do not want to be stigmatized as a part of the "Third World". In its various versions "Eurasianism" reflects a compromise between modernization and tradition, between the need to integrate into the global economy and to assume the newly acquired state sovereignty, between authoritarian rule and democratic institutions, between the actual multiethnicity and the pressure of the "nationalizing state". At the same time, for the Western-oriented national elites, "Eurasianism" often represents a betrayal of the true European values, and "Eurasian" became a denomination for all negative features of post-Soviet reality: disrespect for human rights, corruption and authoritarian rule.

The present chapter illustrates these tendencies using the case of post-Soviet Ukraine. It seeks to combine two dimensions: the evolution and clash of ideologies, on the one hand, and the actual dilemmas of post-Soviet regional cooperation, on the other. The first part addresses classical Eurasianism in relation to the issue of Ukrainian geopolitical identity, the place designed for Ukraine in the "Eurasia House",[1] but also the original tradition of "Ukrainian Eurasianism". The second part explores the role Eurasianism plays in the contemporary debate about Ukrainian geopolitical identity. The third and last part deals with the geopolitics of the post-Soviet space and the position of Ukraine in the regional integration projects, where it confronts the painful dilemma of European or "Eurasian" integration.

In this chapter, I deal with Eurasia not as a geographical notion, but as a political and cultural construct. What has to be stressed here is the plurality of Eurasianist discourses. Classical Eurasianism placed Ukraine inside the borders of "Russia-Eurasia", whereas Ukrainian Eurasianists were rather anti-Russian and considered Ukraine an integral part of Europe. Today many in Ukraine (and in Russia) would agree that the border between "Europe" and "Eurasia" runs through Ukraine and separates its west from the rest of the country. Nowadays "Eurasia" has been re-invented not only in Moscow, Kyiv or Astana; some Western politicians and journalists are also eager to use this geographic label to mark the new divide on the post-EU-enlargement map of the European continent. In their eyes, the winners of the post-communist transition have deservedly received their entry tickets to Europe, while the losers (like Belarus, Ukraine or Moldova) still belong to "Western Eurasia", the latter used as a synonym of authoritarianism, corruption and poverty.

1.1 Imagining Eurasia, re-inventing Ukraine

The Ukrainians in the "Eurasia House"

Eurasianism as a geopolitical doctrine and a political movement emerged in the Russian émigré community of the 1920s as a reaction to the disaster of the Bolshevik Revolution and as a strategic vision of Russia's future.[2] The protagonists of the Eurasianist movement, among them geographers, historians and philosophers, denied Russia's European identity and at

---

[1] I refer here to the title of Roman Szporluk's article: "The Eurasia House. Problems of Identity in Russia and Eastern Europe", *Cross Currents: A Yearbook of Central European Culture*, no. 9 (1990), pp. 3-15.

[2] For more information on the conceptual premises of Eurasianism see: Dmitry Shlapentokh (ed.), *Russia Between East and West: Scholarly Debates on Eurasianism*, Leiden: Brill 2006; Marlene Laruelle, *Russian Eurasianism: An Ideology of Empire*, Baltimore: Johns Hopkins University Press 2008.

the same time disagreed with the Slavophiles who saw Russia as part of a greater Slavic civilization. Instead, Eurasianists considered it a civilization in its own right – "Russia-Eurasia" – a unique blend of Slavic and non-Slavic, mostly Turkic, people. Eurasianists radically reassessed the roles of Western and Eastern influences in Russian history. They saw the Bolshevik Revolution as an outcome of a mistaken policy of Westernization, unsuited to Russia's nature, and hoped that the Soviet regime would embrace their ideas.

It was the beneficial influences of Turkic-Mongol civilization on Russia and the "Asian" dimension of Russian identity that were the focus of the Eurasianists of the 1920s and 1930s. But as for Ukraine and the other western territories of the former Russian Empire, they were not very innovative.[3] Interestingly, although quite a few representatives of Eurasianism had Ukrainian family origins, they did not reflect much on the role of Ukraine in their doctrine. The geographer Petr Savitskii (1895-1968), one of the fathers of Eurasianism, had Ukrainian roots. His father, who belonged to the Ukrainian gentry from Chernihiv (Central Ukraine), actively worked for the local self-administration (*zemstvo*). Under his influence Petr Savitskii developed some academic interest in Ukraine and even a kind of Ukrainophilia. But like many of his compatriots of that time, he made his choice in favour of Russian culture and identity, which he considered more universal, and his Ukrainophilia remained a personal matter. Savitskii stressed his Ukrainian ("Little Russian") origins in his polemics with the Ukrainian autonomists, who accused the Eurasianists of being simply narrow-minded Russian nationalists. Moreover, the historian and active Eurasianist Georgii Vernadskii (1887-1973), a son of the famous scientist Vladimir Vernadskii (1863-1945), also had Ukrainian roots. Both Vernadskiis have been rediscovered now in Ukraine as a part of the national academic tradition. Another representative of Eurasianism who was Ukrainian by origins was Petr Suvchinskii (1892-1985).

Even more interestingly, "Ukrainian traces" can be found in some early sources, which may have inspired the Eurasianists. Already in the 1850s the historian Franciszek Duchinski (1816-1893), who was a Polonized Ukrainian,

---

3   One of the rare exceptions is the article of Nikolai Trubetskoi "On the Ukrainian Problem", *Evraziiskii vremennik*, no. 5 (1927). Trubetskoi argued that the Muscovite culture in the 17th and the beginning of th 18th centuries was exposed to strong Ukrainian influences.

developed, in a negative form, some ideas which later became fundamental for Eurasianism.[4] Duchinski summarized them in his main work "Peuples Aryas et Tourans, agriculteurs et nomades" published in 1864 in Paris. According to the author, the Dnieper River marks the boundary between Christian humanist Europe and the despotic "Turanian World", which ends in the Far East. This "political geography" reflected of course the historical conditions and the political mood of the Polish elite in the 19th century Russian Empire. Similar to Savitskii later, Franciszek Duchinski had some kind of double identity, stressing his Ukrainian ("Ruthenian") roots and at the same time, his commitment to a more "universal" Polish identity and pro-Polish political orientation. Duchinski supported the idea of a geopolitical and cultural unity of Ukraine and Poland in opposition to the "Turanian" Russia.

These examples are not given here in order to claim Polish or Russian historical figures as a part of the Ukrainian national tradition. Rather they show that long before Ukraine emerged on the political map as a nation state, its "borderland" situation between Europe and Russia was reflected in those personal "geopolitical" choices which the representatives of the (proto-) Ukrainian intellectual elite had to make. It is therefore legitimate to ask how by imagining "Eurasia" Ukraine was re-invented and defined in the various "Eurasianist" discourses. Do Ukraine and the Ukrainians belong to the "Eurasia House"? How do the borders of Ukraine correlate with the western boundary of Eurasia?

Although the Eurasianists had witnessed the Bolshevik revolution, the birth of an independent Ukrainian state, a brutal civil war in Ukraine and the incorporation of the country into the formally federal union of Soviet republics, this experience did not much alter the traditional view of Ukraine that was typical for the Russian intelligentsia. Ukrainian independence was not seen as a historical normality, but rather as one of those short episodes in the sequence of separatist movements associated with the chaos of revolution. The Eurasianists shared this attitude in principle; moreover, as Eurasianism propagated the territorial reintegration of Russia it offered itself as an ideology against the threat of separatism.

---

4   Vadym Skurativskyi, "The Eurasian Syndrome", *Politychna Dumka*, no. 2-3 (1995), pp. 81-87, here p. 82 (in Ukrainian).

Eurasianists, looking rather East than West, did not reflect much on why Ukraine should belong to the new "Russia-Eurasia"; their arguments in this sense were rather intuitive than rational. They did not regret the losses of Finland, the Baltic provinces and Poland; in their eyes these territorial changes made Russia even more "Eurasian" and therefore more coherent and stable. But they did not accept the loss of orthodox Bessarabia to Romania and claimed the former Austrian Galicia: "in their view Ukrainians, indeed, formed a subunit within a broader Russian nation along with the Great Russians and Byelorussians, and together with them belonged to the Eurasian nation".[5]

With regards to the role of Ukraine in Eurasia, Eurasianists showed some ambivalence. On the one hand, their arguments were inherited from the Slavophiles and quite traditional for Russian nationalism. They defined the western border of Eurasia according to cultural and religious criteria and drew it between Greek Christianity (Orthodox and Uniate) and Latin Christianity. Ukraine was a part of the Orthodox world, but influenced and claimed by Latin Europe. The Greek Catholic (Uniate) Church in Galicia was seen as a marginal form of cultural and political alienation from Orthodoxy.[6] Opposition to the Latin cultural tradition, and anti-Europeanism was one of the ways to define "Eurasia". On the other hand, Eurasians, unlike Slavophiles, were looking for a modern scientific justification to legitimize the borders of Eurasia. A geographic case, which presented the western border of Eurasia as a "natural", was made by Petr Savitskii. He drew parallels between the climate differences, zones of particular types of vegetation, local dialects and forms of economy (pig-breeding and sheep-breeding) that determine the cultural as well as the natural border between Europe and Eurasia.[7] Moreover, one of his central postulates was the congruence of the natural borders of Eurasia with its cultural ones. According to Savitskii, the western border of Eurasia runs from the Baltic Sea to the Black Sea. In one of their collective works, the

---

5   Szporluk, p. 10. Note that after 1991 the name "Byelorussia" was changed into "Belarus".
6   The Uniate Church in Galicia emerged in 1596 with the Union of Brest. Some of the Orthodox clerics accepted the Union with Rome while keeping Church autonomy and Eastern rite.
7   Petr Savitskii, "Geographical and Geopolitical Basics of Eurasianism", in: idem, *Kontinent Evraziia*, Moscow: Agraf 1997, p. 295-303, here p. 299 (in Russian).

Eurasianists drew this border along the Neman, western Bug and San Rivers to the Danube Delta.[8] Geographic arguments were additionally used to legitimize the border that followed religious and cultural divisions and reflected the geopolitical realities in Europe after the Second World War. Eurasianists stressed that it was the very geo-morphological structure of the Eurasian territory (the East European Plain) that caused the failure of separatist movements. (Interestingly, Ukrainian geographer Stepan Rudnytskyi, whose ideas will be discussed below, saw the absence of a "natural" border at the east of Ukraine as one of the main geopolitical challenges for the nation).

At the same time, by shifting the focus from language and culture to territory, the Eurasianists changed the accents in the traditional Slavophile argumentation for Russian-Ukrainian unity. Sceptical of Pan-Slavism, they believed that the Western Slavs belonged to Europe, not to Eurasia, and that only language connected the Russians with the other Slavic peoples in Europe. According to Eurasianism, the so called "Turanian" cultural influences are more important for Russian identity than Slavic origins, and Russians have more in common with the peoples of Eastern Asia than with Western Slavs. In their attempts to construct a Eurasian nation, the Eurasianists believed that it is not so much linguistic and ethnic closeness, but rather a shared territory that creates the foundation of a national community. "Territory creates a common destiny",[9] which then realizes itself in a common state. However, Eurasianists implicitly assumed that it is not only territory that keeps Russians and Ukrainians together. Re-positioning Russia in relation to Europe, to the Western Slavic nations and to the East Asian peoples, the Eurasianists seemed to leave intact the old Slavophile myth about Ukrainians as a branch of the Russian nation.

According to them, Ukraine belongs to the Eurasian space but keeps its ambiguity as the western borderland of Eurasia. This ambiguity becomes evident in light of the historical arguments of the Eurasianists. They re-evaluated Russian historiography, which they considered Europe-centred, from their own perspective. According to Savitskii, Kievan Rus was a European and not

---

8   Cf. the chapter "Eurasianism" in: Savitskii, *Kontinent Evraziia*, pp. 13-78, here p. 41.
9   Marlene Laruelle, *L'ideologie eurasiste Russe ou comment penser l'empire*, Paris: L'Harmattan 1999. Cited from the Russian translation, Moscow: Natalis 2004, p. 116.

a Eurasian state formation, and therefore marginal in the history of Russia-Eurasia. Its main positive heritage was Orthodox Christianity, which defined the Eurasian identity as different from both Latin Europe and Islamic Asia. Kievan Rus had no ambitions to integrate the nomadic steppe, and only with the Mongol invasion were the Rus drawn back into Eurasian history.[10] It is the period of the Mongol domination over the Rus which was positively re-evaluated from an anti-European position, first of all by Georgii Vernadskii, Nikolai Trubetskoi (1890-1938) and Petr Savitskii. They argued that the civilization and culture of the nomadic steppe had profoundly shaped the Russian mentality and tradition of statehood. Therefore Rus territories that became part of the Grand Duchy of Lithuania, and did not experience Mongol dominance, became alienated from Eurasian history. This "other Rus" was dominated by Latin influences and became instead part of the European history.[11] But rejecting the Eurasian, "truly Russian" character of the western Rus territories, the Eurasianists at the same time denied the right of Ukraine and Belarus for state independence and even for autonomy. They continued to argue that the split between Eastern Slavs is a cultural fiction and that they have a common political destiny. The French historian Marlene Laruelle noted that "by representing the Kievan Rus as a European country, Eurasianists could unintentionally legitimize the historical process of dividing Eastern Slavs into two, or rather three nations". Paradoxically, it was the Ukrainian "Eurasianists" who, using the same arguments in a negative way, contributed to this task.

A "Ukrainian Eurasia"?

Slavophilia and later Eurasianism were reactions to the dilemmas resulting from the delayed modernization of the Russian Empire. The ideological response to the analogous situation in Ukraine, an imperial periphery, was different. Ukrainian nationalism, according to Mykola Riabchuk, "could not afford a direct anti-Western attitude. Just the opposite, because the discourse of Russian domination was to a large extent nativist and anti-Western, a discourse of Ukrainian emancipation had to be pro-Western... A centrifugal movement away from Russia necessarily meant a centripetal movement to-

---

10 Laruelle, *L'idéologie eurasiste Russe*, p. 199.
11 Laruelle, *L'idéologie eurasiste Russe*, p. 202.

wards Europe".[12] The leaders of modern Ukrainian nationalism followed the patterns of the Polish and Czech national liberation movements and strived for the international recognition of Ukraine as a European nation. Their pro-Western orientation was not always consistent, but "Europe" as a symbolic alternative to "Moscow" was constitutive for political as well as cultural discourses in Ukraine. For example, Mykola Khvylovyi, a devoted communist and a highly regarded Ukrainian writer, believed that Ukraine's mission was to initiate an "Asian Renaissance" that would synthesize elements of both East and West. However, the only path he could see to a cultural breakthrough in Ukraine necessitated emancipation from Russian influences and openness to Europe. The "imagined Ukraine" was certainly a European country, and this Europeanism had an "anti-colonial", defensive character. Ukrainian Eurasianism was not as developed and coherent as the Russian version, and contrary to the latter, it combined a distinctive European national identity with some Eurasian geopolitical ambitions.

From Mykhailo Hrushevskyi on, Ukrainian historiography stressed Ukraine's participation in European history, the close political and cultural ties of "Ukraine-Rus" with Western Europe and the important role Ukrainian lands played in protecting Europe from the Mongol invasion. In the ethnocentric paradigm of Ukrainian history the neighbourhood of the Asiatic steppe was usually seen negatively: for example, the Mongol invasion caused the devastation and decay of the Kievan Rus and isolated most of its territories from Europe; in the 16th and 17th centuries, Crimean Tatars and Turks terrorized the Ukrainian population, turning huge numbers of captured men and women into slaves and profiting economically from human trafficking. Only after the Crimean Khanate was finally defeated by Catharine II (with the crucial help of Cossack military formations) could the colonization of the southern steppe become possible.

At the same time, the long term historical contacts of Ukrainians with Crimean Tatars were difficult to ignore, and already Hrushevskyi stressed the role of the Tatars in the Cossack uprising. In the 1920s and early 1930s, oriental studies developed intensively in Soviet Ukraine; historians, anthropologists and linguists studied Ukrainian contacts with the Middle East and

---

12   Mykola Riabchuk, "Westernizers Despite Themselves: Paradoxes of Ukrainian Nativism", *Perekrestki*, no. 1-2 (2004), pp. 33-60, here p. 50 (in Russian).

Byzantium, with the nomadic peoples of the southern steppe and Crimea. The academic journal "Eastern World" appeared from 1927-1931 in Kharkiv, and Agatangel Krymskyi, a famous Ukrainian orientalist, published his "History of Turkey".[13] As a parallel to Eurasianism in Russian émigré circles, some Ukrainian historians in exile (e.g. Viacheslav Lypynskyi, Ivan Lysiak Rudnytskyi) suggested a new paradigm of Ukrainian history – "Ukraine as a synthesis between East and West". However, they associated "the East" mainly with Byzantium, and never blurred the ethnic boundary between Ukrainians and nomadic Tatars. If this can be considered as some kind of embryo of Ukrainian Eurasianism, it never had the messianic character of Russian Eurasianism.

The Ukrainian political geographer Stepan Rudnytskyi (1877-1937) was the first to make an attempt to define the borders of Ukraine and to formulate the geopolitical challenges and tasks of the country. It was Rudnytskyi who developed some basic ideas of Ukrainian Eurasianism as a geopolitical doctrine.[14] Defining the territory of Ukraine according to ethnographic criteria, he believed that the Don basin, the North Caucasus and the Caspian steppe belonged to Ukraine in the ethnographic sense. According to Rudnytskyi, Ukrainians made use of their marginal position in Europe and expanded their territory enormously by peaceful peasant colonization to the east and south. As these new lands are thinly populated they provide ample space for the Ukrainian ethnos in the future.[15] Moreover, "in the direct neighbourhood of Ukraine there are huge territories with thin population (Caucasus, Central Asia, Southern Siberia)", which are crying for Ukrainian colonization. The prospects for future colonization were connected for Rudnytskyi with the population growth, so it was no wonder that his other main academic interest was in demography. He saw the relation between territory and population in Darwinist terms and was rather optimistic when it came to the demographic perspectives of the Ukrainian ethnos.

---

13   For more details see: Oleksandr Halenko, "In Search for Crimea in the Past and Present of Ukraine", *Krytyka*, no. 12 (2004) (in Ukrainian).

14   See the analysis of Ukrainian Eurasianist geopolitical tradition in: Andrew Wilson, *The Ukrainians: Unexpected Nation*, New Haven and London: Yale University Press 2004.

15   Stepan Rudnytskyi, "The Ukrainian Question from the Point of View of Political Geography", in: *Chomu my hochemo samostiinoi Ukrainy?* Lviv: Svit 1994, pp. 93-208, here p. 105 (in Ukrainian).

Rudnytskyi emphasized the mediating position of Ukraine between Europe and Middle Asia, and predicted that Ukraine can profit a lot from its transit location. It is the Black Sea that plays the most important role in his geopolitical and geo-economic doctrine. The Black Sea unites the Ukrainian river network into one system and provides communication with neighbours, while at the same time protecting Ukraine's southern border. According to Rudnytskyi the decline of Kievan Rus was caused by the Mongol expansion and the isolation of the Rus from the Black Sea. Later the Russian Empire was more interested in developing trade contacts via the Baltic region, at the cost of Ukraine's economic interests related to the Black Sea. Rudnytskyi believed that the economic revival of Ukraine depends on the effective use of the Black Sea and the country's river network, and proposed a system of channels connecting the Black, the Baltic and the Caspian Seas. Consequently the main geopolitical task of Ukraine was to secure an access to the Black Sea and to protect the territory from the east and south-east, where Ukraine has no "natural" borders.

Although Rudnytskyi definitely considered Eurasia an important sphere of Ukrainian geopolitical interests, he did not attribute any symbolic significance to it, nor did he believe in a common identity and geopolitical mission of the Eurasian peoples. Just the opposite: in his research he showed little interest in the indigenous peoples inhabiting territories he saw as an object of Ukrainian colonization. According to Rudnytskyi, these territories offer a good chance for the Ukrainian ethnos to preserve its language and culture (which is more difficult for the Ukrainians in Northern America, for example). Influenced by the powerful ideological tendencies of his time, in his demographic works, Rudnytskyi warned against the danger of mixed marriages, especially with close neighbours and "racially inferior peoples". This also applied to his estimations of the historical encounter between Ukrainians and nomadic peoples of the steppe: since Ukrainian culture was superior, it was practically immune to the influences of these nomadic civilizations.

Rudnytskyi's ideas were developed by Yurii Lypa (1900-1944), who presented his geopolitical doctrine in three books: "Destination of Ukraine" (1953), "The Black Sea Doctrine" (1947), and "The Partition of Russia" (1941). During the Second World War, Lypa fought in the Ukrainian Resurgent Army and fell in 1944. His geopolitical vision was radically nationalist and anti-Russian. He developed Rudnytskyi's ideas into the "Black Sea doctrine" and saw Russia as Ukraine's main rival in the region. According to Lypa, after the unavoidable collapse of Russia, Transcaucasia will become Ukraine's natural source of energy and raw materials, and its bridge to the east.[16] Through this Caucasian gateway, Ukraine could expand its connections with Turkey, Iran, India and China. Lypa's book "The Partition of Russia" presents historical, economic and anthropological arguments for the thesis that Russia, in its contemporary borders, was an artificial creation. After its imminent territorial disintegration, he argued, four new formations will emerge: Ukraine with Transcaucasia and the Caspian steppe, Kazakhstan and Middle Asia, Siberia, and "Russia proper", which will be reduced to the borders of the Muscovite state of the 16th century. It is interesting that Lypa borrowed some arguments from the Russian Eurasianists and insisted on the cultural closeness between Russians and the indigenous peoples of the Russian North and Siberia, which due to intermarriages with Russians already formed some kind of supra-ethnos. Unlike the Russian Eurasianists, who avoided that era's anthropological discourse on "race" and "blood", Lypa used this type of argumentation.[17] He cited "medical research" to claim that Ukrainians and peoples of Transcaucasia are anthropologically very different from Russians and cannot be assimilated by them.

Ukrainian Eurasianism of the first part of 20th century was openly nationalist and, unlike its Russian counterpart, did not make universalist claims to represent "Eurasia" as a whole. It articulated the transitional position of Ukraine between Europe and Asia and the emerging geopolitical interests of Ukraine in the east and south. Russia was seen by both Rudnytskyi and Lypa as a rival and an enemy; both of them used geographic and demographic arguments to demarcate Ukraine's territory and the Ukrainian sphere of influence from the Russian one. Rudnytskyi and Lypa used "Eurasianist" arguments about the natural character of the border between Christian Europe and "Turanian" Russia-Eurasia, but these arguments are reflected in the mir-

---

16   Wilson, *The Ukrainians*, p. 294-295.
17   Yurii Lypa, *Rozpodil Rosii*, L'viv: Academy of Sciences 1995. I refer here to the American edition: Youriy Lypa, *Partition of Russia*, New York: Nobles Offset & Printing Co. 1954, p. 32-36 (in Ukrainian); Youriy Lypa, *Pryznachennia Ukrainy (Destination of Ukraine)*, 2nd edn, New York: "Howerla" Ukrainian Book Store 1953, pp. 121-174 (in Ukrainian).

ror of Ukrainian nationalism. As Franciszek Duchinski had in the 19th century, they constructed Ukrainian identity in opposition to "Turanian" Russia.

In contemporary Ukrainian geopolitics, Russian and Ukrainian visions of "Eurasia" paradoxically intertwine, complementing in various ways the dominant pro-Russian and pro-European discourses.

1.2 (Anti-)Eurasianism after communism

Neo-Eurasianism in post-communist Russia: Ukraine as a threat

The renaissance of Eurasianist ideas is one of the most striking phenomena of Russia's contemporary ideological landscape. Neo-Eurasianism has many faces: some of its aspects were developed in the aggressive, revanchist doctrine of Aleksandr Dugin[18] and in the anti-Atlanticism of Sergei Panarin;[19] others in Lev Gumilev's esoteric theory of ethnogenesis or, more recently, in the "post-Eurasianist" geopolitical essays of Vadim Tsymburskii (in particular, his concept of an "island Russia").[20] To some extent Eurasianism has been built into the official ideological doctrine of the Kremlin (most clearly articulated in the version of the president's adviser Gleb Pavlovskii) – as a legitimization of Russia's special interests in the post-Soviet space. According to the Russian geographer Vladimir Kaganskiiy, the popularity of Eurasianism can be explained by nostalgia for a big and strong country that was respected in the world, by fears of separatism which have been stoked by the Chechen war, and by the difficulties to define the new Russian identity.[21] Responding to post-Soviet nostalgia and frustration, neo-Eurasianism restores the continuity of Russian statehood and rehabilitates the Soviet Un-

---

18 Aleksandr Dugin, *Osnovy geopolitiki: Geopoliticheskoe budushchee Rossii*, Moscow: Arktogeia-Center 1999.
19 Sergei Panarin, *Rossia i tsivilizatsionnyi protsess: mezhdy atlantizmom i evrazianizmom*, Moscow: Nauka 2004 (in Russian).
20 Vadim Tsimburskii, "Island Russia", *Polis*, no. 5 (1993), pp. 11-17; "Geopolitics for the 'Eurasian Atlantis'", *Pro et Contra*, vol. 4 (1999), no. 4, pp. 141-175; "Peoples between Civilizations", *Pro et contra*, vol. 2 (1997), no. 3, pp. 154.184 (all in Russian).
21 Vladimir Kaganskii, *Kultyrnyi landshaft i sovetskoe obitaemoe prostranstvo*, Moscow: NLO 2001, p. 412.

ion as a historical form of the Eurasian empire. In fact, neo-Eurasianists argue that Russia is conceivable only as an empire.

In the mid-1990s, observers associated Eurasianism with the "realistic", moderate line in Russian foreign policy debates, as an approach that could balance the extremes of the pro-Western liberal and radical nationalist discourses.[22] It seemed reasonable that Russia cannot simply integrate within the West, that it has interests in Asia as well as in Europe, that its identity is multiethnic and cannot be easily transformed into a European one.[23] In this context, Russia could be seen as a natural mediator between the West and the East. In his essay published in 1990, Roman Szporluk saw in Eurasianism a positive potential for solving the problem of post-Soviet Russian identity.[24] Referring to Nikolai Trubetskoi's article "All-Eurasian Nationalism" (1927) Szporluk suggested that Eurasianism could provide a common identity for the peoples of the Russian Federation. Such a civic identity, which would be based on territory and would not privilege Russians above non-Russian peoples, would help to create a single Eurasian nation that is multiethnic but non-imperial.

Indeed, Eurasianism had a chance to develop into a Russian version of multiculturalism, but unfortunately this positive anti-imperial potential was never realized. Under Vladimir Putin's presidency the historical continuity of Russian statehood was restored, presenting post-Soviet Russia as a successor of the Russian Empire. New Russian nationalism was combined with old imperial symbols. As a result, Eurasianism was left instead for external use: it became more and more associated with anti-Western isolationism and increasingly instrumentalized as an ideology of re-integration in the former post-Soviet space. With respect to Ukraine and Belarus, neo-Eurasianism was combined with the ideology of East Slavic unity.[25]

---

22 See for example Neil Macfarlane, "Russian Conceptions of Europe", *Post-Soviet Affairs*, vol. 10 (1994), no. 3, pp. 234-269.
23 In historiography, according to Mark von Hagen, the anti-paradigm of Eurasia emerged as a sign of "normalization" of Russian / East European history, which in the era of the Cold War was seen only through the lens of "orientalism" or "modernization". Cf. Mark von Hagen, "Empires, Borderlands, and Diasporas: Eurasia as Anti-Paradigm for the Post-Soviet Era", *The American Historical Review*, vol. 109 (2004), no. 2, pp. 445-468.
24 Szporluk, "The Eurasia House".
25 See the following chapter in this book.

The classical Eurasianism of the 1920s and early 1930s reflected the new geopolitical reality resulting from the collapse of the Russian Empire. But in the 1920s, the Soviet Union reintegrated most of the former territories of the empire into a new state. Neo-Eurasianists today have to answer to more dramatic geopolitical changes. The new Russia in its present borders has never existed before. Not only have the peripheral republics of Central Asia gained state sovereignty, but also Ukraine and Belarus, which are much more important for Russian identity. Former Soviet satellites and even the Baltic states have joined the European Union, while some other former Soviet republics do not hide their own Euro-Atlantic aspirations. Today Moscow has to compete with the European Union and the US even in the "near abroad". Russia's sphere of direct influence has dramatically shrunk, and a majority of its political elite sees democratic alternatives in the former Soviet republics as a threat to Russia's security and geopolitical status. This became especially evident during the 2004 presidential elections in Ukraine, when the Kremlin actively supported its preferred candidate Viktor Yanukovych. The extremely hostile reaction to the Orange Revolution in Ukraine as well as to the new pro-Western government in Georgia – both of which are perceived by the Kremlin as part of a Western plot against Russia – have revealed irreconcilable visions for the geopolitics of the post-Soviet space.

In this new situation, Russian neo-Eurasianism in its most aggressive form (à la Aleksandr Dugin) opposes itself to "Atlanticism", which is perceived as the main geopolitical threat coming from the West. Accordingly Dugin considers independent Ukraine to be a Trojan horse: "Russia and Ukraine found themselves on the opposite sides of the geopolitical barricades. But their functions are different. While Russia by definition even in reduced form remains the centre of Eurasia, Ukraine plays the role of a *cordon sanitaire* and becomes the outpost of NATO".[26] According to Dugin, Russia lost its control over the Black Sea's northern coast with the independence of Ukraine, a fact that threatens the very existence of "Russia-Eurasia". The only acceptable solution for him is a new protectorate of Moscow over Ukraine.

The only alternative scenario would be to partition the country. Here Samuel Huntington's map of Ukraine as divided between two different civiliza-

---

26   Dugin, *Osnovy geopolitiki*, p. 798.

tions comes to mind. Russian Eurasianists and nationalists believe that the people of eastern and southern Ukraine feel culturally closer to the Russians than to their Galician compatriots, and together with Belarusians constitute some kind of "natural" East Slavic community. Characteristically, Aleksandr Dugin also supports the idea that the west of Ukraine belongs to Central Europe, and its autonomy and closer integration with Europe would be "very useful". In this way, the rest of Ukraine would become more "Eurasian" and digestible for Moscow's integration projects. In contrast to their predecessors, the neo-Eurasianists gave up their claims to Ukrainian Galicia; they typically see the Greek Catholic Church as an enemy of the Russian Orthodoxy, and as an agent of Catholicism and Western cultural aggression.

The other pole of the Eurasianist discourse in relation to Ukraine is represented by the young Russian political scientist Andrei Okara. He is convinced that it is not nation states but civilizations that compete today in the international arena, and both Ukraine and Russia can survive this competition only as parts of one single civilization. Okara admits that the old paradigm of a Moscow-centred imperialism has lost its influence today and cannot be attractive for the new Ukrainian elite. Instead, he suggests that Kyiv should be a new imperial centre.[27] This "third way" for Ukraine (not a European nation state, but not a province of Russia either) means that Kyiv would become the centre of a "Big Eurasian Space", of the hinterland of the Eurasian civilization. There would be a division of roles: Kyiv as a "spiritual centre" would share its leadership with Moscow as a centre of political and military power ("Moscow as a Third Rome and Kyiv as a Second Jerusalem"). There are two preconditions for this geopolitical project: first, Ukraine must give up its pro-European ambitions, and second, Kyiv must not monopolize its imperial role or offer itself as a "European" alternative to "Asiatic" Moscow. This new role for Kyiv also presupposes changes in the cultural identity of the Ukrainians: Byzantine influences should be seen as central and decisive, and Polish-Latin influences as an attempt to change the cultural paradigm. This variant of Eurasianism (Ukraine as a potential partner in empire-building) seems to be just

---

27 Andrei Okara, "In Search for an Imperial Perspective", *Russkii Arkhipelag* (2001), www.archipelag.ru/geopolitics/nasledie/cosmopolis/36/ (in Russian) (last accessed February 7, 2010).

the opposite of Dugin's neo-Eurasianism (Ukraine as an agent of Atlanticism in Eurasia), but in fact they are two sides of the same coin.

The Russian elites are interested in the integration of their country into the global economy, and therefore some old-fashioned ideas of classical Eurasianism (for example, economic autarky) seem to be obsolete today. In contrary, the idea of messianism and the imperial destiny of Russia have become indispensable today as a means to legitimize Russian ambitions in the post-Soviet space. Even Anatolii Chubais, the author of the privatization campaign, suggested "liberal imperialism" as the new Russian ideology. "Ukraine is a critical mass for any project in the Eurasian space" (Okara), and therefore it is very important for neo-Eurasianist geopolitical conceptions. Russian-led integration projects in the post-Soviet space and Ukraine's reaction to these initiatives will be discussed below. The next section will summarize Ukrainian intellectual debates around Eurasianism.

Ukraine between "Europe" and "Eurasia"

The meaning of "Eurasia" has also been re-negotiated in the Ukrainian political debate on national identity and geopolitical choice, which started at the end of 1980s. In this debate the concepts of "Europe" and "Eurasia" mutually presuppose one another, with "Eurasia" being most often associated with neo-imperial Russia, and "Europe" identified with the EU and seen as the final destination of post-communist transition.

The idea that Ukraine is an integral part of Europe became central for national self-identification after the collapse of Soviet Union. At the level of political rhetoric, it was appropriated by virtually all political forces, with the notable exception of the Communists. What does "Europe" mean for Ukraine, and what are the political implications of a "European identity" for a post-Soviet nation? The national democrats, who are the ideological successors of the *Narodnyi Ruch* movement, believe that "European identity" means full integration of Ukraine into the EU and NATO as a guarantee for the final break from the Soviet Empire. For many of them, Ukraine (or at least its western part) has a Central European identity and should follow the path of Poland, Hungary, the Czech Republic and Slovakia. Central European identity (in the sense of Milan Kundera) also assumes that as an original part of Europe, Ukraine was kidnapped by the Soviet (Russian) empire and now has to return to its European roots. The journalist and political essayist Mykola Riabchuk and the writer Yurii Andrukhovych, among others, represent this position in the Ukrainian cultural debate. Their vision of "Europe" presupposes that Ukraine constitutes an integral part of Europe, while Russia represents a culturally and politically different civilization. This approach is rooted in the long tradition of an orientalization of Russia and Soviet communism, characteristic of right-wing and conservative political forces in the West.

In this context "Eurasian" becomes a substitute for "post-Soviet" and signifies a lack of "Europeanness": an authoritarian state, a deficit of democratic culture and disrespect for human rights. It is in this sense that the concept of "Eurasia" is used by the Ukrainian political scientist Olexandr Derhachov. According to him, deeply rooted but suppressed "European" characteristics of Ukrainian society coexist with "Eurasian" features which are partly immanent, partly imposed by the communist regime. This internal ambiguity corresponds to the ambiguity of Ukrainian geopolitical identity and its "multi-vector policy". While "Europe" is still important for Ukrainian national self-identification, the post-Soviet or Eurasian space seems to be more "comfortable" for the Ukrainian political elites: it is less competitive and does not demand any particular level of democracy. "The post-Soviet space is united by the Soviet heritage, first of all by the genetic closeness and the interdependency of the ruling elites, and, what is very important, by their isolation from ... the democratic world".[28] "Eurasian" political culture associated with Kuchma's regime was seen by his critics as the main source of misunderstandings between Ukraine and the EU.[29]

For the national democrats "Eurasia" signifies the post-colonial status of Ukraine, the heritage of Russian and Soviet imperial rule and the continuing political and cultural dominance of Russia in the post-Soviet space. "Eurasia" symbolizes political tendencies in the countries east of the new EU border: the rise of authoritarian regimes in former post-Soviet republics, the suppression of civil society and independent media, and widespread corruption. Eurasianism is associated with the ideology of Russian-led projects aimed at

---

28   Oleksandr Derhachov, "Ukraine in the European and Eurasian Interior", *Politychna Dumka*, no. 3-4 (2000), p. 91 (in Russian).
29   Taras Kuzio, "EU-Ukrainian Relations Hampered by Clash of Civilizations", *Eurasia Daily Monitor*, July 12, 2004.

the re-integration of the post-Soviet space – projects that are seen as an option excluding Ukraine from European integration. In particular, the presidential elections of 2004 were presented by the national democratic camp as a decisive choice between "Europe" and "Eurasia" (= Asia). For them (and for most Western observers) the victory of Viktor Yushchenko has proved the "European identity" of the country. The anti-Eurasian oppositional discourse aimed against Kuchma's regime, lost most of its critical pathos after 2004. However it still serves to shift the primary responsibility for the country's numerous problems outside Ukraine, and ascribes them to Russian interference or to the Communist past.

Other positions in this debate are not so consolidated. The Russian-oriented intelligentsia in Ukraine has been trying to combine both pro-Russian and pro-European orientations. This position (usually condemned by the national democrats as "Little Russian" and "colonial") has a long historical tradition going back to the status of Ukrainian elites in the Russian Empire and their active participation in its westernization. From this point of view "Europe" has blurred boundaries: it also includes Russia and assumes that Ukrainian and Russian identities overlap to some extent. This also means that the geopolitical orientations of both countries do not contradict each other, that "Eurasia" does not radically oppose "Europe". However, even Russophiles associate political and economic modernization with "Europe" and do not suggest a special "Eurasian way" as an alternative. This approach can have various political implications. In 2002, left-wing and even some centrist political forces took up the motto "To Europe with Russia": they argued that cooperation with Moscow would be beneficial for Ukrainian economy and therefore work for and not against the "European dream". The official strategy of Kuchma's administration was formulated as "integration into Europe and cooperation with the CIS". This so called "multi-vector policy" was heavily criticized by the national democratic opposition as a political syndrome of post-Soviet schizophrenia.[30] After the Orange Revolution the Party of Regions has represented the updated version of this position, claiming that EU membership is a long-term outlook in the best case and therefore should not prevent pragmatic cooperation with Russia. Representatives of the Party of Regions criticize

---

30   Mykola Riabchuk, "The End of Ukrainian Multi-Vector Policy?", *Suchasnist*, no. 12 (2002), pp. 58-83 (in Ukrainian).

President Yushchenko for his political and cultural policy (first of all his urging of NATO accession plans as well as the instrumentalization of the Holodomor for national identity politics), which provokes Russia and undermines any partnership between the two countries.

Neo-Eurasianism in Ukraine is openly exploited only by a few relatively marginal pan-Slavists and left populists, who support the idea of a re-union between Russia and Ukraine and oppose the "East Slavic" civilization to the West, preferring "Eurasia" to the "Euro-Atlantic civilization". The Progressive Socialist Party of Ukraine led by Natalia Vitrenko and, to some extent, the Communist Party of Ukraine often instrumentalize these kinds of ideas, as in 2007 during anti-NATO protests in Crimea. However, this brand of "neo-Eurasianism" is merely an ideological and political import from Russia, basically identical to the ideas of Aleksandr Dugin.

There are of course other contexts within Ukrainian political debate where the concept of "Eurasia" and "Eurasian space" can be found. In the discussions on energy politics, "Eurasia" is increasingly associated with the region of the Caspian Sea and with the oil and gas exporting countries (Iran, Iraq, Kazakhstan, Turkmenistan and Azerbaijan). In this sense "Eurasia" is associated with the perspectives of dynamic economic development and foreign investments. This region represents a potential interest for Ukraine as an alternative source for its energy supply. With its pipeline system, Ukraine would profit from the transit of oil and gas from this region to Europe and in this sense could become the "gateway to Eurasia". In this context Eurasia has no negative connotation and can be associated with such projects of regional cooperation as GUAM (which will be discussed later in this chapter) and, in a broader context, with the search for new partners for cooperation in a globalized multi-polar world.

The official political discourse in Ukraine since the middle of the 1990s has paradoxically combined elements of both Eurasianism and Europeanism and fluctuated between them. President Kuchma, elected in 1994 on a pro-Russian political platform, promoted a specific version of "Ukrainian Eurasianism" at the beginning of his presidency. In his inaugural address, Leonid Kuchma claimed that "Ukraine is historically a part of the same Eurasian economic and cultural space" as Russia and Belarus and rejected any depiction of Ukrainian-Russian relations in Manichean terms.[31] Dmytro Tabachnyk and Dmytro Vydrin, advisors to president Kuchma in his first term, developed a Ukrainian version of Eurasianism in opposition to "Eurocentrism", "isolationism and artificial hostility towards Russia".[32] This Eurasianism reflected the interests of the East-Ukrainian industrial elites in re-establishing economic contacts with Russia and the former Soviet republics and in preserving traditional markets for Ukrainian industry. At the same time, it assumed that Ukraine could have its own interests in the region and that the Ukrainian concept of "Eurasia" would not necessary coincide with the Russian version. (GUAM, an alliance of several post-Soviet republics excluding Russia, was initiated by Kuchma's Ukraine). Despite this flirtation with Eurasianism, the Kuchma government made significant steps in establishing relations with the EU. It was in his second term that Kuchma's rhetoric became pro-European, which paradoxically coincided with a political rapprochement between Ukraine and Russia. As a consequence, the deepening political and economic dependence from Russia compromised Kuchma's initial "Eurasianism". Additionally, anti-democratic tendencies in Russia, the strengthening of authoritarian regimes in the post-Soviet space and the new division of Eastern Europe into accession states and "neighbours" of the EU also contributed to a devaluation of the Ukrainian version of Eurasianism. The official discourse shifted from Eurasianism to Europeanism and appropriated some of the national democratic, "anti-Eurasian" rhetoric. Anatolii Halchynskyi, the executive director of the National Institute for Strategic Studies and adviser to Kuchma in the last years of his presidency, also joined the position that Ukraine and Russia belong to two different civilizations. The integration of Ukraine into Europe goes along with the revival of the country's national identity. But for Eurasian Russia, he argued, "the integration into Europe would mean a change of its civilization code".[33]

After the Orange Revolution the conceptions of Eurasianism that were associated with a pro-Russian cultural and political orientation were significantly marginalized. The new Ukrainian leadership developed an ambition to

---

31   Wilson, *The Ukrainians*, p. 295.
32   Wilson, *The Ukrainians*, p. 295.
33   Anatolii Halchynskyi, *Chas natsionalnogo probudzhennia*, Kyiv: National Institute for Strategic Studies 2004, p. 92 (in Ukrainian).

become a pro-European leader of democratization in the post-Soviet space, in this way challenging Russia politically, if not economically. For the advocates of cooperation with Russia it has become more and more difficult to combine pro-European and pro-Russian views, as Moscow had strengthened its domination within the post-Soviet space, positioning itself as an alternative to the West and as a competitor rather than a partner of the EU. The gas wars between Moscow and Kyiv meant the eventual transition to a language of pragmatism and national interests and demonstrated the end of a certain type of Eurasianism built on the model "geopolitical loyalty in exchange for cheap gas". Yushchenko's politics of accelerated NATO accession and his attempts to get international recognition for the Holodomor as a genocide of the Ukrainian nation not only met a harsh political response from Moscow, but also provoked some extremist actions organized by radical nationalist organizations, most notably the so-called "Eurasian Youth Union". This group, ideologically subscribed to Aleksandr Dugin's doctrine, took active part in the 2006 anti-NATO protests in Ukraine. In October 2007 activists from this organization demolished Ukrainian national symbols which had been erected on Ukraine's highest mountain, the Hoverla. They claimed that these actions were prompted by Yushchenko's decision to commemorate Roman Shukhevych, the legendary commander of the UPA (Ukrainian Resurgent Army). This episode, which was widely discussed in the Ukrainian media, has contributed further to the negative image of the Russian Eurasianist movement. Particularly after the Russian-Georgian military conflict in August 2008 the idea of Eurasianism as based on Russia's "natural" leadership in the post-Soviet space has been heavily compromised.

1.3 Integrating Post-Soviet Eurasia

Ukraine in the Russian-led integration initiatives

Soon after the *perestroika* dreams of a "Common European House" had faded away, it became clear that the geopolitical ambitions of the Ukrainian and Russian political elites were quite different. Unlike Ukraine, Russia has no ambitions to join the European Union; it considers Europe a "strategic partner" and wants to be treated by the EU as an "equal". Instead, Russia has initiated several integration projects attempting to re-establish its leading role in the post-Soviet space. First of all, the Commonwealth of Independent States (CIS) was established in 1991 by Belarus, Russia and Ukraine with the aim to fill the geopolitical vacuum that had emerged after the dissolution of the USSR. Other former Soviet republics, with the exception of the Baltic states, joined it shortly after. The CIS was initially supposed to ensure the new independent states a "civilized divorce" and to provide a platform for discussing problems of security, economic relations and humanitarian issues. Since the early 1990s Moscow has attempted to turn the CIS into an economically and politically integrated union, but without much success. The Eurasian Economic Commonwealth (EurAsEC) was initiated in 2000 with aim of creating a customs union and coordinating common policies on trade, migration, currency exchange and infrastructure development. It included Russia, Belarus, Kazakhstan, Kyrgyzstan and Tajikistan (Uzbekistan joined in 2006 and withdrew in 2008), while Ukraine, Moldova and Armenia limited their participation to an observer status. Finally, in 2003 the presidents of Russia, Ukraine, Belarus and Kazakhstan announced their plans to create another international association, the Single Economic Area (SEA). This was supposed to facilitate, in several stages, a customs union and a free trade zone in the region, ensure harmonization of foreign trade policy, of tax regulations, and to some extent, of monetary and credit policy. If fully implemented, the SEA agreement would have created a new regional bloc similar to the EU. This initiative was impeded from the beginning, however, by Ukraine's ambivalent position (see below). Additionally, the CIS Collective Security Treaty (1992) was transformed in 2003 into the Collective Security Treaty Organization (CSTO), with the aims of ensuring military cooperation and providing regional security. The main goal of all these integration initiatives was to consolidate the "pro-Russian" camp within the CIS, combining geopolitical loyalty with trade preferences, cheap energy resources and credit.

Under Yeltsin's rule, integration projects in the CIS benefited first of all from the psychological inertia of the post-Soviet elites and populations, and usually were not seen as an alternative to Russia's rapprochement with the West. Putin realized that the CIS is too diffuse and ineffective to be an instrument of integration and therefore emphasized pragmatic bilateral relations with its members. However, this did not at all mean that Putin had given up the project of a Eurasian integration; rather, he turned it into a vehicle for regaining Russia's influence in the post-Soviet space and for reasserting Russia's geopolitical identity. According to this logic, if Russia is going to reemerge as an influential player on the world stage, it should start in the "near abroad". Dmitri Trenin, the executive director of the Moscow Carnegie Center, predicted in 2004 that in the next years, Moscow is going to concentrate mainly on the "near abroad" because it cannot compete with the US in the global arena or claim a more important role on the European continent.[34] The recent EU and NATO enlargements to the East and the apparent Euro-Atlantic ambitions of the former Soviet republics of Georgia and Ukraine in particular have stimulated Moscow's efforts to protect and consolidate its traditional sphere of influence. In response to these developments, the concept of Eurasian integration was updated by the Kremlin's political adviser Gleb Pavlovskii, who in the mid-2000s suggested the project of *EvroVostok* (European East) as a second centre of European integration under Russian geopolitical responsibility: "Russia acts on the European East as an initiator of new forms of European unity, not as an obstacle to it and not at all as an anti-European force".[35] This new ideology of Eurasian integration as a component of European integration processes reflected the fears of the Russian political elite: exclusion and isolation from the enlarged Europe and growing US influences in European political affairs – particularly in the post-Soviet space. No wonder the Orange Revolution in Ukraine was perceived as an expansion of

---

34 Dmitri Trenin, "Moscow's *Realpolitik* ", *Nezavisimaia Gazeta*, February 9, 2004 (in Russian).
35 Gleb Pavlovskii, "The Presumption of Stability. Has Russia lost all Soviet positions?", *Centrasia*, May 3, 2004, www.centrasia.ru/newsA.php?st=1085981520 (in Russian) (last accessed February 7, 2010).

the EU backed by Washington and thus a direct challenge to Russia in its traditional "zone of responsibility".

Due to its territory, population, economic potential and geopolitical location, Ukraine is an indispensible partner for any integration project in the Eurasian space. For those who believe that Russia can only be an empire, Ukraine is the key to its very existence. Although Moscow officially recognized the national sovereignty of Ukraine, it has always expected Ukraine to remain its loyal ally and to take part in common integration projects. According to Dmitri Trenin, Russia's "agreement on the borders was implicitly tied to Ukraine's full integration in the CIS and its 'friendly attitude to Russia'".[36] The Russian political elite, with minor exceptions, imagined relations with Ukraine as a special partnership based on Kiev's geopolitical loyalty to Moscow, "common history" and a shared cultural identity.

Contrary to Russia, Ukraine proclaimed its integration into the Euro-Atlantic structures as its strategic choice. However, at least until 2004 post-Soviet Ukraine remained a part of the "Eurasian space", particularly in the geopolitical and economic sense. Moscow received semi-official guarantees of loyalty from Kyiv and did not take its pro-European declarations seriously. In the early 2000s Moscow succeeded in binding Ukraine economically, using low gas prices and trade preferences to get strategic dividends, such as in the case of the reverse use of the Odessa-Brody pipeline. Despite attempts to diversify the energy supply, the Ukrainian economy remained dependent on Russian oil and gas. In the process of the privatization of the Ukrainian economy, Russian business gained control over key economic positions. This allowed the critics of Kuchma's political course to say that Ukraine's *de facto* involvement in the Eurasian integration had increased during his presidential term despite his declared "European choice".

At the same time Ukraine has managed to keep at least a symbolic distance from the Eurasian integration initiatives. Whatever declarative the "European choice" of the Kuchma administration was, Ukraine tried to avoid formal membership in Russian-led integration projects and bound itself only with a minimum of obligations. Being one of the founders of the CIS in 1991, Ukraine in fact never signed the CIS Charter and joined only a small part of

---

36 Dmitri Trenin, *The End of Eurasia: Russia on the Border between Geopolitics and Globalization*, Moscow: Carnegie Moscow Center 2001, p. 165.

the collective agreements in the framework of CIS. It has systematically resisted Moscow's attempts to create supranational institutions in the CIS and did not join the Tashkent Treaty on Collective Security. Ukraine's position was that CIS should stay a consultative body: "a mechanism of civilized divorce", according to the first president of Ukraine Leonid Kravchuk. Kyiv refused to join the Union State of Russia and Belarus, it also rejected the full membership in EurAsEC and limited itself to an observer status. If there was something constant in the multi-vector policy of Kyiv, it was the reluctance to join any integration project led by Russia.

Against this background Kuchma's decision to join the Single Economic Area Agreement (SEA) created by Russia, Belarus and Kazakhstan looked rather inconsistent. The agreement, which was signed in September 2003 and ratified by the Ukrainian Parliament in April 2004, included ambitious plans for regional economic integration. The SEA was a reaction to the expected EU enlargement, but even more importantly, it represented the last attempt to pull Ukraine into the Eurasian integration processes. The Ukrainian government was interested in some aspects of the agreement, like a free trade zone, but was very suspicious of the idea of a customs union and a central executive body controlled by Moscow. The agreement was heavily criticized by the political opposition in Ukraine as a "betrayal of the European choice", as being both unconstitutional and economically unacceptable. Three leading ministers of the Ukrainian government openly opposed signing this treaty, and these reservations were reflected in the final text of the document, which states that Ukraine will fulfil its obligations only if they do not infringe on the Ukrainian constitution.

The principles and forms of cooperation with Russia and their compatibility with the "European choice" were the subject of heated political debate in the last years of Kuchma's presidency. How to distinguish between Ukraine's national interests and the interests of some business groups? How to decide between Ukraine's short-term and long-term interests? As the Ukrainian government tried to secure a cheap gas supply from Russia, the critics of Kuchma's regime suspected that the main profiteers of this deal might be the big private companies beyond public control. Moreover, by deepening economic cooperation with Russia, the critics argued, Ukraine would preserve its technological backwardness instead of profiting from Western know-how. Critics of the "Eurasian integration" stressed that "all integration projects in the region have required minimizing reforms and maximizing the efforts to preserve isolation".[37] Both the Ukrainian and the Russian economies suffer from low productivity, unfair competition, and monopolist and protectionist tendencies; therefore their integration would merely maintain these negative features.[38] The same applies to the standards of democracy in the post-Soviet space: political integration in the region and isolation from the rest of the world will only strengthen authoritarian tendencies.

During the 2004 presidential election campaign the opposition promised to reconsider Ukraine's participation in the integration projects with Russia, especially in the notorious SEA agreement. After his appointment, the new foreign minister Boris Tarasiuk promised that it would be re-evaluated by experts. In February 2005 Russia's new initiatives – creating a CIS Security Council and a Humanities Cooperation Council – were rejected by the Ukrainian government. Ukraine confirmed its position towards the CIS: no supranational political institutions should be created, and the CIS should eventually transform into a free trade zone. The perspectives for the SEA agreement were also addressed by Putin at his first short meeting with Yushchenko in Moscow immediately after the inauguration of the Ukrainian president. Putin expressed his hope that Ukraine would adhere to it. Disappointed by the results of the 2004 presidential elections in Ukraine, Moscow did not give up its projects but rather adopted a "wait and see" attitude. In winter 2005-06 the dramatic gas conflict between Gazprom and Kyiv preoccupied the Ukrainian leadership and caused an internal political crisis. This conflict was followed by trade restrictions on Ukrainian exports, and the diplomatic confrontations on the issue of Ukraine's NATO membership, on the status of the Russian Black Sea Fleet and on Yushchenko's politics of history changed the tenor of Ukrainian-Russian relations. As a consequence the issue of regional integration has been put on ice.

Almost two decades after the collapse of Soviet Union it has become clear that the post-Soviet integration projects have failed to consolidate the

---

37 Oleksandr Derhachov, "Russian-Ukrainian Relations: The Autumn of the Decade", *Dzerkalo tyzhnia*, August 21-27, 2004 (in Ukrainian).
38 Oleksandr Vlasiuk, "Ukraine and Russia after EU Enlargement: Models of Relationship", *Ekonomist*, no. 5 (2003), www.niss.gov.ua/book/eko052003.htm (in Ukrainian) (last accessed February 7, 2010).

new independent states into the regional political and economic bloc, as most of them preferred to integrate into the global economy on their own. The younger generation of the political elites in post-Soviet countries does not share a common Soviet mentality and political culture and does not see integration with Russia as a "natural" option. The Orange Revolution in Ukraine and, more recently, the Russian-Georgian military confrontation in August 2008 showed the actual crisis of the CIS, which in both cases was not able to articulate its collective position. The fact that these events further consolidated the division of the CIS into two camps – pro-Russian and pro-Western – can be seen as a failure of Eurasian integration. During the second term of Putin's presidency Moscow also started to feel some kind of "tiredness" with regards to integration projects and preferred to focus on bilateral relations using the "carrot and stick" of gas price politics. According to Bertil Nygren, the "CIS structures in more than one sense seem to be too old-fashioned for the 'liberal empire' that Putin is trying to create".[39] Under these new conditions, when the US and the EU actively compete with Russia for geopolitical influence in the post-Soviet space, the instruments and concepts of "Eurasian integration" no longer seem effective for the purposes of the Russian political elites.

GUAM – Eurasia without Russia?

Ukraine's reservations against "Eurasian integration" dominated by Russia do not mean that Ukraine has no political and economic interests in the Eurasian space. In the 1990s Ukraine helped to launch a regional initiative that brought together Georgia, Ukraine, Azerbaijan and Moldova (GUAM).[40] This initiative emerged in 1997, when the leaders of the four countries started political consultations during the negotiations on the Treaty on Conventional Forces in Europe.[41] Facing the same challenge of Russian domination, they decided to coordinate their positions and speak collectively

---

39 Bertil Nygren, *The Rebuilding of Greater Russia. Putin's foreign policy towards the CIS countries*, London: Routledge 2007, p. 45.
40 Uzbekistan joined the group in 1999 and left in 2005; during this period the name of the organization was GUUAM. I use the acronym GUAM regardless of the year.
41 Oleksandr Pavliuk, "GUUAM: The Maturing of a Political Grouping into Economic Cooperation", in: Renata Dwan and Oleksandr Pavliuk (eds.), *Building Security in the New States of Eurasia: Subregional Cooperation in the Former Soviet Space*, Armonk, NY: M. E. Sharpe 2000, pp. 33-56; here p. 34.

in various issues. The primary goal of GUAM was therefore a political one: cooperation in solving common problems (e.g., military conflicts, regional separatism), counterbalancing Russian influence in the post-Soviet space and enhancing regional security. The GUAM leaders also declared their interest in Euro-Atlantic integration. The economic dimension of the GUAM initiative is secondary, since the level of bilateral trade between its members is rather low. It is the issue of energy security that has high priority. The problems of dependency on Russian energy supply and access to the Russian energy transport system are common for all GUAM members. Ukraine and Moldova, in particular, are interested in diversifying their oil supplies by cooperating with Azerbaijan and developing alternative pipelines transporting Azeri oil to Europe, bypassing Russia. In 1997 the leaders of Georgia, Ukraine, Azerbaijan and Moldova declared their intention to cooperate in the construction of a "Eurasian Trans-Caucasian Transport Corridor", an alternative transport route from Europe to Asia, which would be shorter and cheaper than the traditional route via Russia.

The emergence of GUAM signified a potential alternative to the Russian-led integration projects. As Taras Kuzio put it, "GUAM has merely institutionalized what always existed in the CIS from the moment it was created in December 1991 – a division between the supporters of the Russian idea of integration around itself (after the Soviet centre was removed) and the Ukrainian idea of 'divorce'".[42] No wonder that Russia reacted rather negatively to the new regional initiative. Official Moscow expressed its concern of a possible turn of GUAM into a military bloc and criticized the exclusion of Russia as a sign of political hostility. Russian media interpreted GUAM as a product of US policy and NATO's plans to encircle Russia with a *cordon sanitaire*.

However, GUAM did not become a viable alternative to the CIS; the economic interests of its members were too closely bound to Russia and the other post-Soviet states from the "pro-Russian" camp. According to Olexandr Pavliuk, "in most cases, the policies of individual GUAM countries toward Russia are still reactive rather than proactive. To this extent, the Russia-GUAM relationship is influenced more by Russia than by its GUAM part-

---

42 Taras Kuzio, "Geopolitical Pluralism in the CIS: The Emergence of GUUAM", *European Security*, vol. 9 (2000), no. 2, pp. 81-114; here p. 84.

ners".[43] Russia's policy towards the post-Soviet space was more successful. Under Putin's presidency, Russia developed bilateral relations and offered its partners beneficial deals, binding them with long-term agreements. GUAM had little to offer against this strategy. In the early 2000s some experts argued that GUAM had fulfilled its initial tasks: strengthening the national sovereignty of the new states, removing Russian military forces from their territories and reducing their dependence on Russia.[44] According to Pavliuk, long-term integration projects are much more difficult to realize: "Almost insurmountable challenges for a substantive economic cooperation within GUAM are presented by the poor economic situation, the absence of an institutional mechanism for multilateral economic cooperation , the slow progress of economic and structural reforms in each and every GUAM state, the underdevelopment of the private sector and the almost complete lack of a middle class, the geographic remoteness, the inconsistent and varying external trade tariffs, and the inadequacies of national legislations. It remains an open question how much GUAM countries are willing and able to make concrete steps to harmonize their foreign trade regulations, adjust national legal systems, and become more closely integrated by giving up portions of their sovereignty".[45] It is also not clear to what extent European partners are likely to cooperate in such ambitious projects as the Eurasian Transport Corridor, and if they would accept the exclusion of Russia.

It was the Orange Revolution in Ukraine that gave the GUAM its second wind. Yushchenko's leadership, optimistic about its prospects for EU membership, declared Ukraine a "locomotive of democratization processes" in the post-Soviet space. Ukraine was supposed to play this ambitious role in tandem with the pro-Western reformist government of Georgia. In 2005 Ukraine and Georgia launched the Community of Democratic Choice (CDC) initiative with the aim of making the region of the "three seas" – Baltic, Black, and Caspian – an "area of democracy, stability, and security". Profiting from personal sympathies between Yushchenko and Saakashvili, Ukrainian-Georgian relations became the motor for renewing GUAM. At the 2005 Chisinau sum-

---

43   Oleksandr Pavliuk, "GUUAM", p. 47.
44   "Problems and Perspectives of Ukraine's Relations with the countries of GUUAM and EVRAZES. Materials of an academic seminar", *Politychna Dumka*, no. 1-2 (2001), pp. 99-121 (in Ukrainian).
45   Pavliuk, "GUUAM", p. 52.

mit, which was devoted to regional disputes, the GUAM members expressed their concern over Russia's dominance in the peacekeeping processes in the post-Soviet space. In regard to the Transnistrian problem, president Yushchenko suggested a peace plan that was supported by the EU. It featured free elections in Transnistria under international supervision and an increase in the number of Ukrainian peacekeepers in the conflict zone. Additionally, Ukraine changed its customs regulations so that goods coming to Ukraine from Transnistria could be cleared only if their clearance is certified by the Moldovan Customs Service. This decision, also supported by the EU, was supposed to put economic pressure on the separatist government of Tiraspol. Yushchenko's peace plan failed, however, not least due to the ambivalent position of Chisinau and the collapse of the "Orange coalition" in Ukraine. Throughout this episode, Moscow was rather sceptical about the Ukrainian efforts in Transnistria and saw Kyiv as an agent of Western influence.

Nevertheless, the GUAM members managed to bring the issue of post-Soviet regional conflicts on the world stage: in September 2006 the "frozen conflicts" in Nagorno-Karabakh, Abkhazia, South Ossetia, and Transnistria were discussed at the UN General Assembly. However, since Russia was interested in the separatist movements as an instrument of political control in the "near abroad", it opposed the efforts of the GUAM members. In particular, the idea of creating GUAM joint peacekeeping forces was met with a negative response from Moscow and was eventually blocked by Chisinau.

At the Kyiv summit in May 2006, GUAM was restyled as the Organization for Democracy and Economic Development (ODED-GUAM). Among its primary aims the renewed GUAM sought the promotion of democracy and deepening European integration, as well as energy security across the Caspian-Caucasus-Black Sea axis and a free trade area among the member states. The ODED-GUAM calls for a higher degree of regional integration, based on shared political principles, but it still lacks effective institutions and working mechanisms. The geopolitical orientations and the level of commitment to democracy and human rights among GUAM members also vary significantly. While Moldova sticks to its "neutral" status and distances itself from military cooperation projects, Azerbaijan has developed into a semi-authoritarian political regime. During the Russian-Georgian conflict in summer 2008 the GUAM members failed to respond to this challenge with a single voice. Baku and Chisinau did not join the demonstration of solidarity with the Saakashvili government, which on August 13 brought together in Tbilisi the leaders of Latvia, Estonia, Lithuania, Poland and Ukraine.

In conclusion, Ukraine was an initiator and a catalyst of the GUAM. The support from Ukraine was vital for Azerbaijan, Georgia and Moldova during the early stages of their sovereignty. Contrary to its role on the level of European or Russian relations, in its relations with its GUAM partners Ukraine was not just an object but could shape geopolitics as a subject. "For Ukraine, GUAM has become an important political means of asserting itself as a regional leader".[46] In this sense some visions of Stepan Rudnytskyi and Yurii Lypa on Ukrainian Eurasia turned out to be not that far off the mark. However, its internal weakness has prevented the new Ukrainian leadership from living up to its initial ambition to become a democratic leader in the post-Soviet space.

Conclusion

As we have seen, there is a plurality of discourses and political options underlying the popular opposition between "Europe / the West" and "Eurasia / Russia". Ukraine has its own tradition of geopolitical thinking where Eurasianism plays an important role. However, in contemporary Ukrainian political discourse "Eurasia" is usually associated with Russian authoritarianism and neo-imperial politics in the post-Soviet space, and is opposed to "democratic and free" Europe. As a strategy of re-asserting the new national identity and of claiming Ukraine's place in Europe, this "anti-Eurasianist" discourse tends to deny Russia's Europeanness and serves to externalize the problems of Ukrainian nation and state building.

The Colour revolutions showed that "Eurasia" as a Russian-made construct can be challenged in Kyiv, Tbilisi or anywhere else in the post-Soviet space. With the Orange Revolution, Ukraine became a challenge and a chance for "Eurasia", raising hopes for the democratization of the political regimes in the post-Soviet space. Democratic Ukraine got a chance to become an alternative leader in the region and opened opportunities to shape its own

---

46   Pavliuk, "GUUAM", p. 40.

"Eurasian" politics. However, the weakness of the democratic institutions and the split among the political elites blocked political and economic reforms in Ukraine and limited the country's potential of regional leadership. Democratic consolidation and a decisive progress towards integration into the EU remain crucial preconditions for Ukraine to become a strong and independent player in the post-Soviet space. Unfortunately, a confrontation with Moscow in this matter is difficult to avoid, and Ukraine's position in the EU-Russia-Ukraine triangle is still the weakest one. This means that the dichotomy of "Europe / the West" vs. "Eurasia / Russia" will remain an important symbolic axis of Ukrainian politics for years to come.

2 Slavic Sisters into European Neighbours: Ukrainian-Belarusian relations after 1991

Ukraine and Belarus are the two countries that today constitute the main part of the strategically important "new" Eastern Europe. Since 2004 they have shared a common border with the EU and have become potential candidates for EU membership. In the 1990s Ukraine and Belarus were commonly perceived as part of the "grey" zone between Russia and the EU and attributed to the sphere of Moscow's legitimate geopolitical interests. But the EU enlargement to the East and the relative political stabilisation of the Balkans have made these countries more visible for Brussels. Western disappointment with Russia's democratic reforms and Putin's politics in the "near abroad" – especially his use of "gas blackmail", which is seen as a potential threat to European security in general – are additional factors explaining the EU's increasing interest in Ukrainian and Belarusian affairs. The engagement of Brussels and of some European governments in Ukraine during the Orange Revolution, the growing political pressure on Lukashenka's regime and the introduction of sanctions against its officials in 2006 indicated a serious commitment of the EU for this region.

Although political transformations in Ukraine and Belarus are often discussed and compared, the problems of Ukrainian-Belarusian relations and their role in Eastern Europe are rarely addressed. This is not surprising given that for more than sixty years, relations between the Soviet republics were mediated by Moscow. For more than a decade after the collapse of the USSR, Ukraine and Belarus remained corners of the "East Slavic triangle" dominated by Russia. During the 1990s the new bilateral relations between Kyiv and Minsk developed mainly in the framework of the Commonwealth of Independent States (CIS) as the successor of the disintegrated "Soviet empire". With the Orange Revolution in 2004 and the pro-Western orientation taken by the new Ukrainian leadership, the geopolitical context of Ukrainian-Belarusian relations has changed. Ukraine, which after the Revolution claimed democratic leadership in the post-Soviet space, has joined the chorus of critics of Lukashenka's regime, though only half-hearted. At the same `time, the recent gas conflict between Minsk and Moscow opened new possibilities in Ukrainian-Belarusian relations.

This chapter uses a constructivist approach in International Relations in order to analyse how the new independent nations and former Slavic "sisters" Ukraine and Belarus have been reinventing each other since 1991 as new neighbours / allies / competitors in the process of post-Soviet transformations. The ruling elites, the political opposition and the intellectuals in both countries refer to "Belarus" or "Ukraine" as symbols of a(n) (un)desirable alternative, use them as examples to demonstrate their own successes or failures or seek mutual support and solidarity with them. Although Russia and Europe remain the dominant constitutive "Others" for the national identities of both Belarus and Ukraine, the processes of mutual re-discovering and re-mapping of the two East European countries have been intensifying, especially after the Orange Revolution. With the EU enlargement to the East and the changing role of Russia in the post-Soviet space, Ukrainian-Belarusian relations have become important for the political stability and security of Europe.

2.1 Chronology and basic facts of Ukrainian-Belarusian relations

Ukraine and Belarus established diplomatic relations on December 27, 1991, only a few weeks after the *Belovezhskaia Pushcha* Accords – the act that dissolved the USSR – had been signed by the leaders of Russia, Ukraine and Belarus. In June 1992 the embassy of Ukraine was opened in Minsk and in October 1993 the embassy of Belarus started to operate in Ukraine. During the official visit of President Leonid Kuchma in Minsk in July 1995 the basic *Treaty on Friendship, good neighbourhood and cooperation* was signed (effective from August 1997).[1]

In May 1997 Leonid Kuchma and Alyaksandr Lukashenka signed the *Treaty on State Borders* between Ukraine and Belarus. This treaty has not yet been ratified by the parliament of Belarus, a fact that for years has been seen in Kyiv as the main obstacle in Ukrainian-Belarusian relations. The Ukrainian

---

1 Official information from the web site of the Embassy of Ukraine in Belarus: www.belarus.mfa.gov.ua/belarus/ua/publication/content/5394.htm (last accessed February 7, 2010).

Ministry of Foreign Affairs considers the delimitation and demarcation of the national border an important issue of national security and a necessary condition for the accession to NATO and EU. But official Minsk uses the ratification of the Border Treaty as a bargaining chip in the negotiations over the so called "Ukrainian debt". This debt emerged in 1992 with the interruption of economic relations between Ukrainian and Belarusian enterprises and their asynchronous departure from the "rouble zone". Ukraine, being afraid of creating a precedent, refused to recognize a "state debt" and prefers to call it a corporate debt. While avoiding recognition of the fact of a state debt officially, Kyiv offered a partial compensation scheme in order to de-block the ratification of the Border Treaty. Compromise was nearly reached in 2002, but then the Belarusian government refused. In 2003 Leonid Kuchma officially recognized the problem of debt, and later Viktor Yanukovych, at that time a prime minister, signed a protocol, where the sum of the debt (134 million dollars) was indicated. However, the new Ukrainian president Viktor Yushchenko did not recognize the debt; neither did the "Orange" prime-minister Yurii Yekhanurov, who visited Minsk in 2005.[2]

During Kuchma's presidency (1994-2004) the leaders of Ukraine and Belarus met 19 times; half of these meetings took part during official visits, the other half on the CIS summits and other multilateral meetings of the leaders of the former Soviet republics. Since 2004, president Yushchenko and Lukashenka have met three times, always on the occasion of CIS summits. During the twentieth anniversary commemoration of the Chernobyl disaster in April 2006, an official visit of Lukashenka to Ukraine was planned and widely announced, but did not take place. As this visit had been scheduled for just one month after the highly ambiguous Belarusian presidential elections and the wave of repressions against the political opposition, it would certainly have helped Lukashenka to overcome his international isolation and legitimise his regime. In exchange, the Ukrainian side had hoped for the ratification of the long-awaited Border Treaty. Moreover, both sides were supposed to sign an agreement on simplified border crossing at the Slavutych-Komarin crossing point, which the Ukrainians urgently need for the maintenance of the

---

2 Volodymyr Kravchenko, "Sweets from Batka", *Dzerkalo tyzhnia*, April 15-21, 2006; Volodymyr Kravchenko, "Ukraine-Belarus: A treaty in exchange for money", *Dzerkalo tyzhnia*, November 1-7, 2003 (both in Ukrainian)

Chernobyl nuclear station.[3] Nevertheless, Lukashenka did not arrive in Slavutych. The meeting of the two presidents was then rescheduled for spring 2007, already after the dramatic gas conflict between Minsk and Moscow. The new issue of energy cooperation was therefore added to the agenda. But the visit was again postponed, now due to the political crisis in Kyiv that led to the dissolution of the Ukrainian parliament and new elections in September 2007.

In 1998 both countries signed the *Agreement on economic cooperation for the period of 1998-2008* and adopted the *Program for long-term economic cooperation*. Despite the obvious stagnation of political contacts, economic cooperation continues to develop quite well. From 2003 to 2007 the trade turnover between the two countries more than quadrupled – a fact that correlates with the sustainable economic growth in both Belarus and Ukraine at the same period. Trade relations between the two countries are relatively balanced and mutually profitable, but concentrated on raw materials and semi-finished products (oil products, fertilizers, ferrous metal, mixed fodder, etc.). At the same time, trade relations are seriously undermined by antidumping measures practiced by both sides. In 2007 the *Agreement on Free Trade* between Ukraine and Belarus has come into effect, which however does not exclude antidumping measures completely. Despite the hidden political tensions, in May 2007 the first national exhibition entitled "Products of Ukraine" took place in Minsk. Industrial cooperation, especially in machine construction (motors and other devices for tractors, harvest combines, locomotives etc.), is developing well due to the long Soviet tradition of cooperation and compatibility of the technical standards. However, mutual investments are rather low, especially from the Ukrainian side, reflecting Lukashenka's economic protectionism and the uncertain political prospects.

Ukraine sells electric power to Belarus and plans to increase its supply in the near future. For this purpose, a new line from Rivno Nuclear Station in Ukraine to the Belarusian town Mikashevichi will be built. Following the gas conflict with Moscow the Belarusian government has taken measures to diversify the energy supply. Among them are projects to increase the purchase of Ukrainian coal (two new coal power stations are planned in Belarus – in the

---

3   Kravchenko, "Sweets from Batka".

Brest and Hrodno oblasts). Minsk also indicated its interest in other common energy projects in the region (for example, the reverse use of the Odesa-Brody pipeline) that would decrease its energy dependence from Moscow.

Further promising prospects for Ukrainian-Belarusian cooperation include such projects as the common use of the transport infrastructure (especially of the Ukrainian sea ports and the Dnieper River) and the development of transit routes. In 2006, an agreement on military-technical cooperation was signed between Belarus and Ukraine.

Although Belarus is not so prevalent in Ukrainian public debates on national identity and geopolitical orientation, mutual contacts on the levels of populations, civil organizations and cultural institutions have always been very important. Ukrainians compose 2.4% of the Belarusian population and form the third largest national minority group. Ukrainian settlements are traditionally concentrated in the near-border oblasts Homel and Brest. But the main part of the Ukrainian minority in Belarus is of Soviet origin: most Ukrainians are former labour migrants and live in urban areas. Thirty percent of Belarusian academics are ethnic Ukrainians.[4] The Ukrainian embassy in Minsk actively promotes Ukrainian culture and language in Belarus and tries to consolidate the Ukrainian Diaspora.[5] There are several cultural associations of Ukrainians in Belarus. Ukrainian studies are taught at the Belarusian State University, but there have been very few Ukrainian classes in the Belarusian schools.

In Ukraine, Belarusians compose 0.6% of the entire population. A compact zone of Belarusian settlements can be found at the border with Belarus (Rivno oblast), although many of them now are assimilated to the Ukrainian language.[6] From the 17th to the 19th centuries, several Belarusian settlements emerged in the east and south of Ukraine encouraged by the tsarist migration policy. Most of them now are ethnically mixed, and the population assimilated to the Russian language. As is the case with the Ukrainians in Belarus, the

---

4   Yurii Voloshyn, "Ukrainians in Belarus", *Dzerkalo tyzhnia*, January 21-27, 2006 (in Ukrainian).
5   This is the general policy of the Ukrainian MFA. For example, the law on the status of the overseas Ukrainians, adopted in 2004, grants special privileges to foreign citizens of Ukrainian origin.
6   Historically "Polissia" (Russ. Poles'e), which today is a borderland between Ukraine and Belarus, was part of the Polish Kresy where the national identity of the local peasants remained undefined at least until the end of World War II.

number of Belarusians in Ukraine particularly increased in the Soviet period. At the end of the 1980s almost half of the Belarusians in Ukraine were urban citizens, and according to the census of 1989, the percentage of specialists with higher and special technical education among Belarusians was higher than among the Ukrainians.[7] The relatively high social status of both national minorities in the neighbouring countries, combined with the cultural closeness, the low level of national mobilization and the absence of any ambitions of territorial autonomy create no ground for interstate conflicts at least in this respect. Ukraine and Belarus have signed several humanitarian agreements: on the rights of migrants and their families (2003), on the rights of national minorities (1999), on a simplified procedure of changing citizenship of Ukrainians living in Belarus and vice versa (1999).

2.2 (Re)constructing East Slavic "Sisterhood"

After the disintegration of the Soviet Union Ukraine and Belarus have been looking for their new place on the European continent, between the reluctantly enlarging European Union and the ambitious post-imperial Russia. Taking rather different paths of post-Soviet transition, both countries struggle for a new national identity, make geopolitical choices and look for new partners in the region. Struggling with the heritage of "East Slavic unity" and a common "post-Soviet destiny", Belarus and Ukraine have been reinventing themselves as European nations (even if this is only a "minority faith",[8] as it is the case with Belarus). These processes open a new space for solidarity, competition and learning from each other. The Orange Revolution in Ukraine and the turbulent presidential elections of 2006 in Belarus have accelerated this process (which will be discussed extensively in the next section). The old paradigm of East Slavic unity has not died with the collapse of Soviet Union in 1991 but has been reinvented, a metamorphosis which deserves our attention.

---

7 Valerii Vorona et al., "Belarusians in Ukraine", *Viche*, no. 8 (1995), pp. 104-112 (in Ukrainian).
8 I refer here to the title of the well-known book by Andrew Wilson, *Ukrainian nationalism in the 1990:. A Minority Faith*, New York: Cambridge University Press 1996.

"East Slavic unity" as a Soviet construct

In the formally multinational federal structure of the Soviet Union the East Slavic core played, of course, a central role.[9] This can be seen in the concept of "Sisterhood" which was a well-known metaphor for the relations between the Soviet republics.[10] Naturally, not only Russia, Ukraine and Belarus were referred to as "sister republics". The metaphor of "sisterhood" was meant to stress equal, non-exploitive relations between the subjects of the Soviet federation. At the same time, Russia, Ukraine and Belarus had a special position in the Soviet family of the fifteen republics. Indeed, in their case "sisterhood" was not just a thin metaphor for a community in principle open to any nation and based on the shared communist ideology, but a thick metaphor for the "blood ties" of the three East Slavic nations.

The official paradigm of Soviet historiography, established in the 1930s and fully developed after World War II, considered the Kievan Rus a common cradle of the three East Slavic peoples – Russians, Ukrainians, and Belarusians.[11] Separated due to unfortunate historical circumstances, they were predestined to reunite, and this mission was finally fulfilled in the form of the Soviet federation. This narrative of common ancestry was partly borrowed from 19th century Russian imperial historiography which "saw Ukrainians and Belarusians as prodigal sons of the single Russian nation and estimated historical events and persons from such a perspective. Differences between Russians, on the one hand, and Ukrainians and Belarusians on the other, were considered the result of damaging Polish influences."[12] An anti-Polish pathos was also characteristic for many Ukrainian historians of the "populist" school (the so called *narodnyky*), which associated Polish national oppression with the economic and social exploitation of the Ukrainian and Belaru-

---

9   This was confirmed in 1991 by the *Belovezhskaia Pushcha Accords* signed by the three leaders of Russia, Ukraine and Belarus: Boris Yeltsin, Leonid Kravchuk and Stanislau Shushkevich. Other former Soviet Republics ratified this agreement later in Alma-Aty.

10   The concept of "Sisterhood" was famously represented by the "Friendship of Peoples" fountain at the All-Union Exhibition of People's Economic Achievements in Moscow.

11   For a detailed account of this issue see Serhy Yekelchyk, *Stalin's Empire of Memory: Russian-Ukrainian Relations in the Soviet Historical Imagination*, Toronto: University of Toronto Press 2004.

12   Zenon Kohut, *Korinnia identychnosi. Studii z rann'omodernoi ta modernoi istorii Ukrainy*, Kyiv: Krytyka 2004, p. 11.

sian peasantry. This narrative was later merged with the Marxist concept of "class struggle". Soviet historiography, while admitting the existence of Ukrainian and Belarusian national cultures and languages, stressed their direct "kin" relations with Russian culture. The paradigm of East Slavic unity was based on the (constructed) cultural and linguistic closeness of the three peoples and carefully selected historical myths. Thus, the Pereiaslav agreement was celebrated as an act of unification of Ukraine with Russia, Hetman Mazepa's alliance with Sweden was considered a betrayal of Russia, and the conquest and destruction of Belarusian Smolensk by the Russian army in 1654 was downplayed.

In the Soviet period, a new important myth was added to the construct of East Slavic unity – the myth of the Great Patriotic War. As the Ukrainian historian Vladyslav Hrynevych put it: "The myth of the War, creating common heroes and common enemies, aimed at the integration of the whole population of the USSR into a single 'Soviet people'. However, every national republic and every Soviet ethnos created its own small myth, adding to this colossal ideological construction."[13] Thus, Belarus, the "partisan republic", was glorified for its mass resistance and became at the same time a symbol of suffering under Nazi repressions (famously, every fourth Belarusian died in the war). And in Ukraine traditions of national liberation and historical memory of Cossackdom were mobilized by the Soviet propaganda and integrated into the Ukrainian myth of the Great Patriotic War. It was the territories of Ukraine and Belarus that were completely occupied by the Nazis and became sites of the cruellest battles, with most of the cities destroyed and with huge losses of the civil population. Being under Nazi occupation for more than two years, it was Ukrainians and Belarusians who survived hunger and repressions and had to choose between resistance and collaboration in their everyday life, being torn between occupational authorities, partisans, the communist underground and nationalists. Finally, it was Ukraine and Belarus that became the main site of the Holocaust east of the Polish border. No wonder the memory of World War II in Ukraine and Belarus differed from the dominant Russian

---

13 Vladislav Hrynevych, "Split memory. The Second World War in the historical consciousness of Ukrainian society", in: Mikhail Gabovitch (ed.), *Pamiat o voine 60 let spustia: Rossiia, Germaniia, Evropa*, Moscow: NLO 2005, p. 420 (in Russian). German version: "Gespaltene Erinnerung. Der Zweite Weltkrieg im historischen Bewusstsein der Ukraine", *Osteuropa*, no. 4-5-6 (2005), pp. 88-104.

official narrative of the Great Victory; but these differences could be openly articulated only after the disintegration of the USSR. In the late Soviet era the common victory over fascism became a new myth cementing the "friendship of peoples" and their East Slavic core. The myth of the "Great Patriotic War", officially constructed in the Brezhnev era,[14] thus stressed the solidarity of the East Slavic peoples in their common fight with an external threat (once again coming from the West!).

Of course this coherent narrative of "sisterhood", grounded in common struggling and suffering, became possible only due to the exclusion and suppression of certain "unwanted" episodes and aspects. Among them were the upsurge of national self-consciousness in Ukraine and Belarus at the beginning of World War II and the hopes for national revival nationalists naively connected with the new Nazi administration. Thus, members of the OUN (Organization of Ukrainian Nationalists) as well as the UPA (Ukrainian Resurgent Army) were unambiguously condemned by the Soviet regime as fascist collaborationists (the same can be said about the structurally similar but less representative phenomenon of the Belarusian nationalist anti-Soviet resistance).

Another less known but very telling example is the story of Khatyn, an ordinary Belarusian village that became a symbol of fascist crimes against civilians in Belarus.[15] The inhabitants of Khatyn, accused of collaboration with Soviet partisans, were burned alive, including children. Only a few people survived this extermination by chance, and the village was completely destroyed. After the war Khatyn was made the main memorial site of World War II in Belarus, with its world famous symbolic cemetery of the 628 Belarusian villages, destroyed by the Nazis. But the fact that the Khatyn inhabitants were actually executed not by Germans but by a special police unit consisting mainly of Ukrainians is not well known. The chief of this unit, Hryhorii Vasiura, was coincidentally found by the KGB at the end of the 1980s (he was a Communist party member and kept a rather high position in the Kyiv oblast). He was arrested and sentenced to death as a war criminal by a military tribu-

---

14   Boris Dubin, "Goldene Zeiten des Krieges. Erinnerung als Sehnsucht nach der Breznev-Aera" (Golden times of war. Memory as nostalgia for the Brezhnev era), *Osteuropa*, no. 4-5-6 (2005), pp. 219-234.
15   Not to be confused with Katyn (Smolensk oblast), the place where thousands of Polish officers and civilians were massacred in 1940 by the NKVD.

nal. Interestingly, Soviet media did not mention this case at all; the first information appeared only much later in a Latvian newspaper. As it became known later, the First Secretary of the KPU Central Committee, Volodymyr Sherbytskyi, put this case under his personal control. Only selected journalists were allowed to the tribunal, and no materials about it were ever published.[16] It is easy to understand what was at stake here for the Soviet authorities: the myths of East Slavic unity, of the common anti-Nazi struggle and of the common victory.

Despite certain similarities between the two republics, the status of Belarus and Ukraine in the Soviet federation differed substantially. Ukraine was more important economically and geopolitically (as Zbigniew Brzezinski formulated it, without Ukraine Russia ceases to be an empire). Ukrainian nationalism was therefore seen as a dangerous challenge, as was the Ukrainian dissident movement since the beginning of 1960s. Respectively, the Ukrainian party elite was more retrograde and the Ukrainian political regime even more repressive than the Kremlin itself. Belarus was less of a headache for Moscow in this sense. Virtually rebuilt from scratch after World War II, it had the reputation of a shop window of socialism. The Belarusian party *nomenklatura* had the reputation of being the least corrupted in the USSR, and its communist leader Petr Masherov, a former partisan, was widely respected in the republic, contrary to his Ukrainian counterpart Volodymyr Shcherbytskyi. Masherov's sudden death in a car accident caused numerous speculations about the "hand of the KGB". One can probably say that at the beginning of *perestroika*, the Soviet regime was less compromised in Belarus than in Ukraine, which partly explains the different paths taken by the two republics.

---

16 Bogdan Gordasevich, "The truth about Khatyn. What do we know about the tragedy of the exterminated Belarusian village?", *Kievskii Telegraf*, April 8-14, 2005, http://telegrafua.com/256/history/3964/ (in Russian) (last accessed February 7, 2010); see also Natalia Petrouchkevitch, *Victims and Criminals: Schutzmannschaft Bataillon 118*, Thesis, University of Western Ontario 1999, pp. 102-104, www.collectionscanada.ca/obj/s4/f2/dsk1/tape9/PQDD_0001/MQ44823.pdf (last accessed February 7, 2010).

East Slavic unity reloaded?

How could the idea of East Slavic unity survive the disintegration of the Soviet Union? What kind of evolution did it go through? This concept, which in Soviet times helped legitimise the coexistence of the three Slavic nations in one state, has been reinvented after 1991 by the post-communist political elites as an ideology of reintegration in the post-Soviet space. Explicitly or tacitly, the idea of East Slavic unity has been present in such geopolitical projects as the Commonwealth of Independent States (CIS), the Eurasian Economic Community (EurAsEC), the Common Economic Area (CEA) and the Union of Russia and Belarus. Initiated and dominated by Russia, these projects were unimaginable without the reintegration first of all of the former East Slavic republics. In case of success, the East Slavic core would once again become a gravitation centre for the fragments of the Soviet empire. In this way, the East Slavic unity fitted into the more vague concept of a "Eurasian" integration after the model of a "Russian nested doll". It was especially at the end of the 1990s, with the growing international isolation of Lukashenka's as well as Kuchma's regimes, that the political rapprochement between Kyiv and Moscow and the institutionalisation of the Union of Belarus and Russia revitalized the ideas of a common historical destiny and geopolitical identity of the East Slavic peoples.

How does this reinvented East Slavic unity differ from the old Soviet construct? First, its cultural and religious component is much more present, especially if one looks at the important political and symbolic role of the Orthodox Church in the reconstruction of the "East Slavic civilisation".

Second, one can observe a relative devaluation of Soviet symbolism and historical myths (although Lukashenka's regime manages to combine both). The meaning of the Communist past has been reduced to a "common historical experience" and thus has become just one element of the East Slavic unity. The myth of the Great Patriotic War is still important as a common point of reference, although in all three countries one can observe a tendency to a nationalization of the World War II historical memory.[17]

---

17 It is probably Lukashenka's version of the "Great Patriotic War" narrative, still very much Soviet, which is the most inclusive.

Prokhorovka Memorial (Bell Tower)

The reinvented post-Soviet version of East Slavic unity is represented, for example, by significant changes in the memorial landscape of the Kursk battle. In 1943 the Prokhorovka village in the Belgorod oblast (Russia), not far from the Ukrainian border, was the site of the biggest tank battle of the Second World War, where the Soviet Army defeated the Germans troops at a heavy cost of lives. During Soviet times several important memorial sites were constructed in Belgorod and its surroundings, which became a locus of organized pilgrimage and official commemorative events.

In 1995 a new war memorial complex was created in Prokhorovka on the occasion of the 50th anniversary of the Victory. The project of an impressive memorial site was supported by president Yeltsin and reflects the attempts of Moscow to reinvent post-Soviet Russian identity. Communist and Soviet symbols are virtually absent here. Instead, orthodox symbolism is extensively used. The most important symbolic element of this memorial site is the Bell Tower crowned with a statue of Mary, Mother of God, erected in the fields behind the village.

The four sides of the tower are covered with images of saints and Russian military heroes of the past canonized by the Orthodox church. They also carry some of the most worshipped Orthodox icons. These images surround the heroic figure of Marshal Zhukov. The Bell Tower is supplemented by a new cathedral in Prokhorovka named after Peter and Paul. The names of the Soviet soldiers fallen in the battle are engraved on the inner walls of the church, thus including them in the imagined community of the "Orthodox".

The replacement of the old Soviet symbolism with the Orthodox one manifests the essence of the new state-sponsored Russian identity. At the same time, the myth of the "Great Patriotic War" is transformed into an important element of "common history" and Orthodox culture shared by Russians, Ukrainians and Belarusians.

Peter and Paul Cathedral in Prokhorovka

BORDERLANDS INTO BORDERED LANDS 89

Names of Soviet soldiers engraved on the inner walls of the cathedral

This interpretation of the new memorial site was explicit in the official speeches of presidents Putin, Kuchma and Lukashenka, who met in Prokhorovka on May 4, 2000, to celebrate the 55th anniversary of victory in the Great Patriotic War. Patriarch Alexii II, who initiated the invitation of the Ukrainian and Belarusian presidents, noted at this occasion that the new millennium opens an opportunity for coexistence in love and peace for the Slavic peoples of Ukraine, Russia and Belarus.[18] The Patriarch stressed that the dead cannot be divided and that it is a common duty to cherish the unity of Slavic peoples in the future. As a part of the official ceremonies, Patriarch Alexii II consecrated the "Bell of Unity", which is decorated with the icons of three orthodox saints – the protectors of Russia, Ukraine and Belarus.

The "Bell of Unity" represents another element of the memorial site, connecting the shared cultural and religious symbols with the "common future" of the Eastern Slavic peoples embodied in the post-Soviet integration projects. Three young trees planted by the presidents during their meeting add to this symbolic landscape. Visits to the Prokhorovka memorial site have become an obligatory part of various official events and meetings of politicians and officials from Ukraine, Russia and Belarus, which were especially frequent in Kharkiv and Belgorod from 2000 to 2004.

Thus, in the reinvented paradigm of East Slavic unity, the old dominant ideological opposition of capitalism and communism has been replaced by the new cultural opposition of "the West" and the "East Slavic world". The geopolitical choice for Belarus and Ukraine is now represented as a cultural choice à la Samuel Huntington: between the European civilisation and the East Slavic, or Orthodox civilisation.

The new post-Soviet concept of East Slavic unity is of course not a coherent, centrally produced ideology. Rather it is represented by a range of narratives and symbols instrumentalized in different ways by various political forces in all three countries.

---

18   "His Holiness Alexii II, Patriarch of Moscow and All Russia, and the presidents of Russia, Ukraine and Belarus visited Belgorod and Prokhorovka on May 17, 2000", www.mospat.ru/archive/nr005172.htm (in Russian) (last accessed February 7, 2010).

The Bell of Unity

In Ukraine under Kuchma the official political discourse combined this concept with the rhetoric of a "European choice"; and even the pro-presidential political forces preferred to formulate their relations with Russia in the context of the European integration ("To Europe with Russia!"). In fact the idea of East Slavic reunification was fully supported only by forces of the political margins (Communists, pro-Russian parties and left populists such as Nataliia Vitrenko). At the same time, in the election campaign of 2004, the Party of Regions successfully used some elements of the East Slavic unity myth to mobilize votes in the east and south of Ukraine.

In the Russian version, East Slavic unity was transformed into a neo-imperialist ideology aimed at consolidating Russia's sphere of influence in the near abroad and keeping the satellites Ukraine and Belarus under control. Popular among the left and the right margins of the political spectrum and feeding popular nostalgia for the lost status of a "great power", this ideology got into competition with the new Russian nationalism, which is hostile and suspicious to Russia's new neighbours. For Putin, particularly in his second term, the language of East Slavic unity was too archaic; he preferred the aggressive language of national interests.

Only Lukashenka seems to have succeeded in keeping the Soviet version of East Slavic unity somehow intact. It still forms a part of his usual rhetoric: "our relations are proved by centuries old ties of Slavic brotherhood", Russians – or Ukrainians, depending on the circumstances – "are not aliens in Belarus, they feel at home here"; "we defend the western border of Russia"; "Russian is also our language, it is not a foreign language in Belarus"; "Belarusians understand Ukrainian without translation".[19] For him the unity of the Eastern Slavs reaches back into history as far as the Battle of Kulikovo against the Tataro-Mongols (1380) and the Battle of Poltava (1709). But the most important shared value is the Soviet past: "together we created a mighty state". In Lukashenka's highly populist version it was the short-sighted politicians and the egoistic elites who betrayed the Slavic unity and destroyed the Soviet state – damage he feels called upon to repair. This rhetoric, which had earlier been addressed mainly to the Russian audience, is now adapted to the Ukrainian one. During a meeting with Ukrainian journalists in November

---

19 Citations taken from the official web site of Lukashenka: www.president.gov.by (last accessed February 7, 2010).

2006 Lukashenka discussed the possibilities of an integration "in the interest of the Ukrainian and Belarusian peoples", speculating even on the possibility of a union state with Ukraine instead of Russia.[20]

In short, the longevity of the East Slavic unity paradigm helped the populations of the three countries to adapt to the disintegration of the USSR and to survive the trauma of imperial collapse through the firm believe in some kind of union between Russia, Ukraine and Belarus. From the mid-90s, the instrumentalization of the idea of an East Slavic unity between Russia, Ukraine and Belarus indeed secured a broad support for the leaders of these countries: for Yeltsin not less than for Kuchma and Lukashenka. They used the East Slavic unity paradigm at various points of their political careers: in 1994 Lukashenka was elected president while promising a reunification with Russia; in the same year Leonid Kuchma defeated Kravchuk by responding to the pro-Russian sympathies of the eastern Ukrainians; and in 1996 Yeltsin was re-elected by instrumentalizing the project of a Russian-Belarusian Union State in his fight against the communist candidate Gennadii Ziuganov. For both Kuchma and Lukashenka, East Slavic unity was basically reduced to a special partnership with Russia, a fact that reveals a lot about the hierarchy and asymmetry in this triangle construction. Russia still remains the constituting "Other" for the national identities of both Ukraine and Belarus.

While marking the contours of the disappearing Soviet civilization in geopolitical terms, East Slavic unity is a phantom – as the ongoing polarisation in the post-Soviet space demonstrates: while Belarus still remains in the "pro-Russian" camp (it is a member of the Tashkent Collective Security Treaty, of EurAsEC, and supports the Single Economic Area project with Russia and Kazakhstan), Ukraine claims its ambitions to lead a "pro-Western" camp. It did not join the Tashkent Treaty, limited itself to an observer status in EurAsEC and is rather reluctant when it comes to a participation in the SEA. Instead, Ukraine created the GUAM group (together with Georgia, Azerbaijan and Moldova) as a counterbalance to Russian geopolitical and economic dominance; and in 2005, together with Georgia, it initiated the Community of

---

20 "Press-conference of President Lukashenka for Ukrainian journalists", November 23, 2006, www.president.gov.by/press38014.html#doc (in Russian) (last accessed February 7, 2010).

Democratic Choice (which includes also Moldova, Estonia, Latvia and Lithuania, Slovenia, Romania and the Republic of Macedonia).

The Ukrainian-Russian gas conflict in winter 2005-06 and the similar conflict between Belarus and Russia one year later have revealed the true geo-economic fundament of post-Soviet East Slavic unity. Besides their similar mentalities and political cultures, the post-Soviet elites of the three countries thrived on the compatibility of their political and economic interests: cheap oil and gas for Ukraine and Belarus in exchange for cheap transit and geopolitical loyalty to Moscow. This kind of deal helped to secure relative social stability, contributed to strengthening the power of the oligarchs in Ukraine and consolidated the authoritarianism in Belarus. However, the "reorganisation" of the Russian business elites during Putin's second presidential term and the changing political role of Gazprom made this deal obsolete. The nostalgic language of East Slavic unity on the Russian side was replaced by the pragmatic language of "market prices" and "national interests". Thus, the Belarusian official news agency BELTA in its commentary on Russia's conflict with Georgia accused Moscow of a policy of "turning the former sister republics into whores of the Gazprom harem".[21] At the same time, the rise of Russian nationalism[22] and Putin's power politics in the near abroad indicates the political death of the East Slavic unity paradigm even more than the Orange Revolution. Although the idea of a close cooperation between Russia, Ukraine and Belarus is still popular in all three countries,[23] the option of an interstate integration is supported only by marginal parts of the national elites.

---

21 Viktor Gavrysh, "The Georgian-Russian conflict will split the CIS", *Belta* - Belarusian news agency, November 2, 2006, www.belta.by/ru/actual/comments/?id=119193 (in Russian) (last accessed February 7, 2010).
22 See Aleksandr Tsypko, "A Slavic farewell: Is the Russian national revolution under way?" *Literaturnaia Gazeta*, February 26 - March 4, 2003 (in Russian).
23 According to the NISS sociological survey conducted in Ukraine in 2006, 31,7% of the respondents supported the idea of East Slavic integration, 13,7% supported a cooperation with the CIS countries, 9,9% a cooperation mainly with Russia, 15,2% a cooperation with Western countries, 20,3% were for an independent development of Ukraine. See: "Citizens attitudes to the foreign policy orientations of Ukraine (2005-2006)", www.niss.gov.ua/Monitor/Monitor30_n/01.htm (in Ukrainian) (last accessed February 7, 2010).

2.3 Claiming European identity, reinventing the neighbour

Perestroika and the disintegration of the Soviet Union opened the way to alternative historical narratives both in Ukraine and in Belarus, presenting them as European nations rather than parts of Russia-dominated East Slavic civilization. While during the Soviet period these alternative narratives were marginal and even officially banned, they became very popular with the rise of the national-democratic movements. In the early 1990s they were partly institutionalised through the education system and official memory politics.[24] Pro-European narratives corresponding to the political emancipation of the former Soviet republics from Moscow became important in the process of a symbolic re-mapping of Eastern Europe. This process has been marked by compromises, however, since the Soviet historical identity and the above-mentioned concept of East Slavic unity remained instrumental for the post-Soviet elites. Moreover, since 1994 Belarus has been experiencing a come-back of the Soviet historical narrative as the result of Lukashenka's politics of national identity.

The reconstruction of the history of Ukraine as a European nation brings some new aspects to the fore.[25] Among them are the long-term historical ties that Ukrainian lands had with Europe while part of the Grand Duchy of Lithuania and later of the Polish-Lithuanian Commonwealth, the openness of the Ukrainian elite to European cultural influences, Ukraine's role as a cultural bridge to Europe and as a supplier of intellectual resources for Russia in the 17th century, and the role of the Greek Catholic church in Ukrainian nation revival. While before 1991 these aspects of Ukrainian history could be developed only in Western and Diaspora literature, today they are included in school textbooks. Another important element of Ukraine's European historical identity is owed to Western Ukraine, in particular to Halychyna, which was part of the Polish Kingdom since the 14th century and during the 19th century was a province of the Habsburg Empire. Not only the architecture, but also

---

24 Catherine Wanner, *Burden of Dreams: History and Identity in Post-Soviet Ukraine*, University Park, PA: Pennsylvania State University Press 1998.
25 Among other publications, see Roman Szporluk, "Die Entstehung der modernen Ukraine – die westliche Dimension, *Transit* 29 (2005); Yaroslav Hrytsak, "Are we also in Europe?", in: idem, *Strasti za natsionalizmom*, Kyiv: Krytyka, pp. 309-324 (in Ukrainian).

the mentality and political culture of this region are seen as "European" in contrast to the more Sovietised east and south. Thus, western Ukraine claims the role of a locomotive pulling the "Ukrainian train" to Europe.

In the case of Ukraine, however, the emergence of a pro-European national historical narrative did not mean a radical break with the Soviet one. Volodymyr Kravchenko, among other authors, pointed to the ambivalence of the post-Soviet politics of history in Ukraine:[26] while initiating a pompous celebration of the 350th anniversary of the Pereiaslav Agreement in 2004, which was criticized by many Ukrainian intellectuals; President Kuchma just one week later issued a decree on the official commemoration of the Holodomor. And the jubilee of Volodymyr Shcherbytskyi, the First Secretary of the Communist Party of Ukraine from 1972-1989 was celebrated in parallel with another jubilee – that of the famous Ukrainian dissident and leader of the national democratic movement, Viacheslav Chornovil, a victim of the political repressions under Shcherbytskyi. This ambivalence of the new post-Soviet historical narrative in Ukraine reflected the historical compromise between the former communist elite, which in the early 1990s faced the challenge of building a nation-state, with the national democrats, who endowed this project with their ideology and symbolic resources. From my point of view, the relatively smooth transition to a new national historical narrative was supported by the reinterpretation of some historical topics and figures that had been fundamental already for the Soviet Ukrainian identity (Kievan Rus, Cossackdom, Bohdan Khmelnytsky's uprising, Taras Shevchenko, Ivan Franko, etc.). Mykhaylo Hrushevskyi, the famous Ukrainian historian and first president of the short-lived Ukrainian People's Republic, was soon added to this new pantheon, based on a shaky compromise between anti-Soviet and post-Soviet political forces. In particular, the popular myth of Cossackdom, already accepted by Soviet historiography, has become a cornerstone of the new Ukrainian historical narrative. The new nationalized version represents the Cossacks as a European phenomenon. Khmelnytskyi's uprising is often compared with the English Revolution and seen as one of the key events in European history of the 17th century. The democratic tradition of the Cossacks (as opposed to

---

26 Vladimir Kravchenko, "Fighting the shadow: The Soviet past in the historical memory of contemporary Ukrainian society", *Ab Imperio*, no. 2 (2004), pp. 329-368 (in Russian).

Muscovy despotism) and the numerous contacts Hetmanate leaders had in the Europe of that time are often underlined in this context, as well as the fact that one of the first constitutions in Europe was written by Hetman Pylyp Orlyk.

Belarus does not have such a "Piedmont" and "inner Europe" as Ukrainian Halychyna, nor does it have something comparable to the Cossack mythology. The heritage of the Kievan Rus also turned out to be rather marginal for the new national historical narrative, which, in radical opposition to the Soviet one, puts Belarus in the context of the Polish and Lithuanian history. It was the national democrats who interpreted the Grand Duchy of Lithuania as a proto-Belarusian state and made it the new founding national myth. However, represented by only a rather narrow segment of the Belarusian intelligentsia, this narrative remained marginal. Unlike in Ukraine, no compromise between national democrats and post-communist elite was reached in Belarus in the early 1990s. Instead, Lukashenka's restoration of the Soviet narrative only increased the polarisation between the two versions of history. The absence (or weakness) of symbols and historical figures that could bridge the old Soviet and the new European narrative of Belarusian history partly explains the revival of Soviet ideology and symbolism under Lukashenka. While Lukashenka's official historiography is still anti-Polish,[27] focusing on the negative consequences of Polonization and Catholicism for the Belarusian lands,[28] some young historians try to re-assess the Polish factor in Belarusian history and claim the heritage of the Polish-Lithuanian Commonwealth, with its tradition of civil society, its parliamentary system, its self-administration and religious tolerance.[29] In the national democratic movement and later among the opposition various versions of "Litvinism" have become popular.[30] Litvinism as a supranational regional patriotism was an ideology widespread among the Polish and Polonized regional elites in the end of 19th and the beginning

---

27 A fact which corresponds to the latent tensions between official Minsk and Warsaw as well as with Lukashenka's conflicts with the Polish minority in Belarus.
28 Aleksandr Smolenchuk, "'Polish presence' in Belarusian history", *Perekrestki*, no. 1-2 (2006), pp. 55-72 (in Russian).
29 Gennadii Saganovich, *Narys gistoryi Belarusi ad starazhytnastsi da kantsa 18 stagodzia*, Minsk 2001 (in Belarusian).
30 Aliaksei Iankovich, "Anthology of Litvinism: origins, idea, realization", *Palitychna Sfera*, no. 6 (2006), pp. 11-18 (in Belarusian).

of the 20th century, and died only after the World War II.[31] The Belarusian version reinvented at the end of the 1980s considers the Grand Duchy of Lithuania a de facto Belarusian state, which was destroyed by Russian imperial aggression. Cultural Litvinism sees Belarus as a site of ongoing conflicts between Western (Latin) and Eastern (Byzantine, or Muscovite) civilizations, and as an outpost of the Latin world. Political Litvinism (represented by the Belarusian Popular Front "Renaissance" and by the former leader of Belarusian nationalism Zenon Pazniak) promotes the idea of a Baltic-Black Sea Association that would unite Belarus, Lithuania and Ukraine as nations sharing not only a common history, but also common interests in the West and similar problems with Russia.[32]

As one can see from this short glance into the politics of history and identity formation in Ukraine and Belarus, both nations are in a process of re-inventing themselves as European nations. Of course, what in Ukraine has become a state-sponsored policy (especially after the Orange Revolution), in Belarus is still an oppositional discourse. (However, this can change quickly, and even before Lukashenka's fall, as his conflict with Moscow and the recent attempts to win European sympathy show.) Still, there are many similarities in the strategies of reinventing a "European" identity and distancing themselves from the "East Slavic triangle" dominated by Russia, as both national elites share similar cultural resources and face similar challenges. In this way they also re-discover each other not only as new/old neighbours, but also as potential partners on their way to Europe. The new geopolitical identity of both countries is increasingly defined as "East-Central European" or even "Central European" by their intellectuals and politicians. Ukrainians and Belarusians claim common historical roots in the Grand Duchy of Lithuania, which is often interpreted as a common state of Lithuanians, Belarusians and Ukrainians (the latter two called at that time Ruthenians), with Ruthenian language, traditions and public institutions dominating. The ancestor of the Lithuanian kingdom, the Polish-Lithuanian Commonwealth whose policy was less inclusive towards the Ukrainians and Belarusians, is still considered to be culturally closer to them than the "Asiatic" and despotic Muscovite state.

---

31 Timothy Snyder, *The Reconstruction of Nations: Poland, Ukraine, Lithuania, Belarus, 1669-1999*, New Haven: Yale University Press 2003.
32 See Iankovich, "Anthology of Litvinism".

According to theses new narratives Ukraine and Belarus, being for centuries objects of geopolitics rather than active subjects, have common European roots, a long history of mutual contacts, but practically no burden of conflicts and mutual violence in the past. However, until recently, there was no political need for such a narrative of political and cultural closeness between the two nations. Both have been preoccupied with Russia and Europe, and the pro-western and democratic forces in Ukraine and Belarus are too weak to profit from the newly discovered Europeanness of their respective neighbour.

However, the new "European" narratives in Ukraine and Belarus get some support from outside, especially with the EU enlargement to the East. Particularly some new EU members like Poland, Slovakia and Lithuania have shown solidarity with the pro-Western Ukrainian and Belarusian national elites and have developed some sensibility for their European aspirations. Poland especially sees its historical mission in encouraging democratisation in Ukraine and Belarus and in pleading for their eventual accession to the European Union. The strategic vision of Polish politics is easy to understand: strengthening democracy in Ukraine and encouraging a regime change in Belarus would contribute considerably to the security of Eastern Europe and of Poland in particular. The ambition of Poland to expand European values and norms to the East can be seen as a sublimated, post-nationalist form of traditional Polish nationalism. And the success of such an *Ostpolitik* would also strengthen Poland's position in the EU. Given the difficult past – a long history of tensions and conflicts between Ukrainians and Poles which culminated in the mutual ethnic cleansings of 1943-44 – the ability of the Polish political elites to differentiate "between state interests and national memories"[33] is rather exceptional for this part of Europe. Poland's politics of reconciliation has been welcomed and embraced by Ukraine, for whom Poland is an influential neighbour, an advocate of Ukrainian interests in the EU and a counterweight to Russian influence. During the Orange Revolution it was due to the initiatives of the Polish and Lithuanian leaders that the EU played an important mediating role in solving the political crisis.

---

33   Snyder, *The Reconstruction of Nations*, p. 274.

Although Polish-Belarusian relations are less burdened with past mutual violence than Polish-Ukrainian relations, they are not harmonious at all. Lukashenka considers Poland's politics towards Belarus to be a threat to his power (and accordingly the pro-Lukashenka media characterize it as "Cold War"). Poland and Lithuania are both determined to support democratic changes in Belarus, but their political means are limited. While in the Ukrainian case one of the most promising long-term programs proved to be cross-border cooperation (institutionally supported within the European Neighbourhood Program since 2007), such regional initiatives are not welcomed in Minsk and are limited by administrative barriers. Another strategy, which does not require cooperation with the regime, is the support of cultural and educational projects such as fellowships for Belarusian students, the project of a Polish-Ukrainian-Belarusian university in Lublin, etc. One should not forget that Lithuania gave asylum to the European Humanities University, the first independent higher educational institution in the country closed by Lukashenka in 2005 for being too pro-Western. The existence of a Belarusian university in the Lithuanian capital Vilnius, a city which has been claimed by Polish, Lithuanian and Belarusian nationalists for almost a century, would be unimaginable without the EU enlargement. It symbolizes the re-establishment of old historical ties in the new Europe in spite of the hostilities of the recent era of nationalism. All this represents a new geopolitical context which is conducive for the narrative of a "European Belarus".

2.4 The uses of the Other

The title of this paragraph is borrowed from Iver Neumann, whose influential book on the role of the Other in European identity formation and European geopolitics contributed significantly to the constructivist approach in International Relations as an academic discipline. Of course Russia and Europe are the most important constituting "Others" preoccupying the national imagination of both Belarus and Ukraine, as it was already demonstrated in the previous paragraphs. At the same time, the two former Soviet republics have been reinventing each other as neighbours / allies / competitors in the new Eastern Europe. The ruling elites, the political opposition and the intellectuals in both countries refer to "Belarus" or "Ukraine" as symbols of a(n) (un)desirable alternative, use them as examples to demonstrate their own successes or failures or seek for mutual support and solidarity.

Since the end of the 1990s the image of Ukraine in the West has been profiting from the comparison with its northern neighbour. Against the background of authoritarian Belarus, even the problematic democracy of Ukraine looks like a partial success. This contrast, by the way, was skilfully used by President Leonid Kuchma for promoting his European and democratic image and strengthening the legitimacy of his rule. Although critical of the lack of affirmative national identity politics, the national democrats and the Ukrainian Diaspora in the West had to admit that the situation in Ukraine was still much better than in neighbouring Belarus, where Lukashenka reintroduced Soviet ideology and made Russian the second state language. At the same time, Lukashenka's Belarus represented a "worst-case scenario" for the pro-Western Ukrainian political and intellectual elites: the danger of falling into authoritarianism and giving up the nation-building project. The threat of a "Belarusian scenario" seemed to be growing especially in the second term of Kuchma's presidency (1999-2004). The attempts of the presidential administration to control media and harass independent journalists, to put pressure on the political opposition and on pro-Western NGOs looked like a "Belarusization" of Ukrainian politics. The political isolation of Kuchma's regime from the West, caused by the Gongadze case[34] and some corruption scandals (for example, the "Kolchuga story"[35]), as well as the growing political rapprochement with Putin's Russia suggested that Ukraine was sliding into Lukashenka's path. Therefore the pro-Western Ukrainian intellectuals' discourse

---

34 Georgii Gongadze was a Ukrainian journalist kidnapped and murdered in 2000. Secret tape recordings made by Mykola Melnychenko, a former presidential bodyguard, revealed a possible involvement of president Kuchma in this affair. The circumstances of Gongadze's death caused a national scandal and a wave of mass protests against Kuchma's regime.
35 Kolchuga is a Ukrainian early warning radar device. In 2002 the US State Department accused president Kuchma of personally approving the sale of the Kolchuga system to Iraq, a clear violation of UN Security Council Resolution 661.

on Belarus was actually more about the fate of Ukraine and could be summarized as "Today's Belarus is tomorrow's Ukraine".[36]

By the end of Kuchma's second presidential term the historical alternative posed for the Ukrainian nation was often formulated as a choice between "good and evil": "Either Ukraine will continue to build bridges to Western Europe, or it will become an isolated island like its northern neighbour – Belarus".[37] The feeling of reaching a dramatic turning point where the fate of both nations would be decided was reflected in the democratic Ukrainian media in October 2004: while the highly politicised Ukrainian society was approaching its first truly competitive presidential election, the Belarusians once again supported their *"Batska"*, approving in a referendum changes to the constitution that allowed Lukashenka to run as a candidate for a third presidential term.[38] Observers noticed that Yanukovych's election program had astonishing similarities with Lukashenka's in 1994 (giving up multi-vector policy and Euro-Atlantic integration, the promise to give Russian the status of a state language and to grant dual citizenship) and warned about the serious danger of a Belarusian scenario for Ukraine.[39] Representatives from both "Our Ukraine" and Yulia Tymoshenko's Block criticized the results of the Belarusian referendum of October 17, 2004, and denounced it as a falsification. Anatolii Hrytsenko, later a minister of defence in the Orange government, expressed his concern with the situation in Belarus, particularly "with the conditions journalists and opposition work under". He noted that "Belarus is a problem because it conserves 'Asiatic values'. At the same time, the country has an opportunity to break through and widen the post-Soviet space".[40] Oleksandr Turchynov, Tymoshenko's right hand man, stressed that Ukraine can-

---

36   Maksym Strikha, "Belarus today – Ukraine tomorrow?", *Ukrainska pravda*, October 6, 2004, http://pravda.com.ua/news/2004/10/6/12431.htm (last accessed February 7, 2010).
37   "If the elections are recognized unfair, it will lead to Kuchma's isolation – Financial Times", *Ukrainska Pravda*, April 2, 2002, http://pravda.com.ua/news/2002/4/2/22230.htm (in Ukrainian) (last accessed February 7, 2010).
38   Kyrylo Orovetskyi, "Lukashenka's victory and the Ukrainian choice of October 31", *Ukrainska Pravda*, October 20, 2004, http://pravda.com.ua/news/2004/10/20/12824.htm (in Ukrainian) (last accessed February 7, 2010).
39   Strikha, "Belarus today – Ukraine tomorrow?".
40   "The headquarter of Yanukovych does not criticize Lukashenka's falsification", *Ukrainska Pravda*, October 19, 2004, http://pravda.com.ua/news/2004/10/19/12815.htm (in Ukrainian) (last accessed February 7, 2010).

not cooperate with the Belarusian regime, if it wants to be recognized as a civilised country."[41]

The prevailing pro-Western discourse on the Belarusian transition as a total failure is in obvious contradiction to the image of a relatively stable and prosperous country which Belarus enjoys in a part of Ukrainian society, especially in the east. The Ukrainian Communists and Nataliia Vitrenko's Party of Progressive Socialists – political forces which traditionally are sympathetic to Lukashenka – see the "Belarusian model" as a preferable option for Ukraine. In October 2004 both parties welcomed the results of Lukashenka's referendum and condemned the Orange coalition for interfering in the internal affairs of the neighbouring country. In the Ukrainian communist and left populist discourses Belarus is the only example of a post-Soviet state that managed to avoid criminal privatisation and to preserve the social achievements of Soviet socialism. Especially praised are the absence of unemployment, the relatively high pensions and social benefits as well as Stalinist methods used by Lukashenka against corruption. Ukrainian Communists solidarize with the Belarusian regime in its confrontation with the West and promote the idea of East Slavic reintegration. Nataliia Vitrenko, a populist politician fighting against NATO and EU membership and advocating the Russian language has been his most enthusiastic supporter up to the present day.

The Party of Regions and its candidate for the presidential elections 2004, Victor Yanukovych, also took advantage of pro-Belarusian sentiment in Ukraine. In October 2004, Serhii Tigipko, at that time head of Yanukovych's election team, refused to criticize the controversial Belarusian referendum, referring to the economic success of Lukashenka's policy. "Today the average wage in Belarus is higher than in Ukraine. Belarusians will decide themselves",[42] he commented, on the option for a third term for Lukashenka.

The other way round, Ukraine also serves as the Other for Lukashenka, who eagerly makes use of it in his populist propaganda of the "Belarusian model", which according to his definition is a social welfare state based on direct plebiscitary democracy and taking care of people's needs. Lukashenka used Kuchma's Ukraine, which had become notorious for its wide-spread corruption, growing social inequality and the rule of oligarchic clans, as a con-

---

41 "The headquarter of Yanukovych".
42 "The headquarter of Yanukovych".

trast case, showing his own policy in a positive light. He presented himself to the Belarusians as a true people's president, who is able to prevent such catastrophic developments in his own country. For example, in August 2003 the official newspaper of the presidential administration *Sovetskaia Byelorussia* published an editorial under the title "Who is rich in Ukraine?" The article was devoted to clan politics in the neighbouring country and discussed the new administrative appointments made by the Ukrainian president: "Achmetov's men" Victor Yanukovych and Vitalii Haiduk had become prime minister and vice-prime minister on energy issues. Referring to the Polish magazine *Wpost,* which published a list of Russian and Ukrainian billionaires, *Sovetskaia Byelorussia* pointed to the close relations that Ukrainian oligarchs had to president Kuchma. The Ukrainian case as a negative example is opposed to Belarus: "There are no ministers in Minsk, who own 'enterprises and ships'[43], no almighty media barons and 'members of the family', who operate in the world of capital and open the door to the presidential office by foot".[44]

At first glance it seems strange that Kuchma and Lukashenka, who at the beginning of 2000s were both marginalized by the West (for example, at the end of 2003 they both were ignored by the NATO summit in Prague), showed so little solidarity for each other. In fact, until his last days in office, Kuchma cared much about his democratic and European image (one of the reasons why he refused to use repression against demonstrators) and did not want to be put into the same category as Lukashenka. He probably saw the developments in Belarus – its sliding into the hands of Moscow – as a warning that strengthened his policy of keeping both doors open as long as possible. Contrary to Kuchma, Lukashenka consciously chose integration with Russia and isolation from the West. He repeatedly showed his frustration with Putin's cool response to his integration plans, and was evidently jealous of his more independent Ukrainian colleague, who was still respected by Moscow. Behind Lukashenka's ritualised rhetoric of East Slavic brotherhood one could notice that he was irritated by Kuchma's flirting with the EU and the United States, by Kuchma's lack of enthusiasm for the CIS, EurAsEC and other pro-

---

43 A reference to Maiakovskii's poem "Mister Twister".
44 Cited from: "Lukashenka attacks Kuchma because of Akhmetov", *Ukrainska Pravda,* August 21, 2003, http://pravda.com.ua/news/2003/8/21/29798.htm (in Ukrainian) (last accessed February 7, 2010).

jects, and by his moderate nationalism and ambivalent attitude towards Moscow.

For the Belarusian opposition – especially for its liberal and national democratic wing – Kuchma's Ukraine, despite its rather moderate democratic achievements, served as an inspiring example. The democratic accounts of Poland and Lithuania, two other neighbours, were definitely more substantial, but they were on their way to the EU and already members of NATO, moving into a completely different geopolitical context. Ukraine was a more comparable case, and it was more advanced in terms of press freedom, civil society and consolidation of the political opposition. This made Ukraine an object of special interest for Belarusian democrats. Since the end of the 1980s there have been not only regular contacts and mutual learning between the national democratic movements in both countries, but also a common vision of a democratic Ukraine and Belarus as allies and geopolitical partners (for example, the idea of a Baltic-Black Sea Association). However, the democratic forces were too weak and fragmented to act beyond the borders of their own countries. The few acts of solidarity with the Belarusian opposition organized by Ukrainian civil society were purely symbolic. Of course, professional contacts between civil society activists, journalists and intellectuals[45] and youth organizations had existed long before the turning point of 2004, but the frame for them was in most cases provided by Western NGO's and sponsors. The Orange Revolution inspired the pro-Western part of the Belarusian society, especially young people, as an example how a peaceful democratic change is possible also in this part of Europe. Hundreds of Belarusian democratic activists and ordinary students took part in mass demonstrations in Kyiv, and Belarusian journalists followed the Ukrainian events closely. The Orange Revolution was probably the first moment since 1991 when Ukraine attracted so much attention in both Belarusian society and the regime that it almost replaced Russia as the constituting Other.

---

45   The best example is shown by two European-oriented journals, the Belarusian *Arkhe* and the Ukrainian *Krytyka*, which regularly exchange materials and publish articles on the situation in the neighbouring country.

2.5 After the Orange Revolution: a new policy towards Belarus?

Considered by Lukashenka as a direct threat to his rule, the Orange Revolution became a symbol of hope and a model for action for the Belarusian opposition. Not only was it a proof that a peaceful transition from authoritarianism is possible, but it also offered a technology of regime change, a template for the opposition which in Belarus could be applied to the coming elections: parallel vote counting, exit polls, and in case of fraud, mass street protests organized by the leaders of the opposition. In one of his interviews, the candidate from the united opposition, Aleksandr Milinkevich, held that the Belarusian situation is rather similar to the Ukrainian one. In case the regime fails to guarantee free and fair elections, he "would not exclude calling people to take to the streets, as it happened in 2004 in Kyiv."[46] The Orange Revolution also demonstrated the need for consolidation of the opposition and for a charismatic leader, and proved the efficiency of the "round table" model as a mechanism for a peaceful shift of power. The Belarusian youth organization *Zubr* was created according to the Ukrainian *Pora* model. Ukrainian events taught Belarusian activists a lot of practical skills: how to mobilize masses and keep their enthusiasm, how to organize peoples' needs, block police actions, and so on.[47] Especially for those who spent the decisive weeks on the Kyiv Maidan, this experience was a real school of revolutionary action (in this case, the geographic proximity between Minsk and Kyiv and the absence of a visa regime was a considerable advantage).

But even more important than the "technology" of the Orange Revolution was the moral and organizational support that the opposition in Belarus expected from the new Orange leadership in Ukraine. The very fact of having a democratic and pro-European neighbour who closely and critically follows Belarusian political life would increase, one hoped, the pressure on Lukashenka's regime. In his article "The new role of Ukraine" published in the Ukrainian weekly *Dzerkalo tyzhnia* in May 2005, Andrey Sannikov, the inter-

---

46 Aleksandr Milinkevich, "The Ukrainian experience is very important for us", *Tribuna*, October 27, 2005, http://tribuna.com.ua/articles/politics/110852.htm (in Russian) (last accessed February 7, 2010).
47 A discussion of the problem why the Belarusian Maidan failed would exceed the scope of this article. For this question see: Vitali Silitski, "Belarus: Learning From Defeat", *Journal of Democracy*, vol. 17, no. 4 (October 2006), pp. 138-152.

national coordinator of the civil initiative "Charta '97", stressed the importance of the Orange Revolution for his own country, Belarus.[48] He argued that Ukraine has a chance to become a new leader in the post-Soviet space and to initiate and support the democratic tendencies in the region. Sannikov warned Ukrainian politicians against a "pragmatic" approach to Lukashenka's regime, and argued that the support of democratic forces in Belarus would serve the national interests of Ukraine and its new mission in Eastern Europe. Aleksandr Milinkevich, in the above cited interview, also pointed to the special role of Ukraine as show case for Belarus: "Your political and economic achievements are especially important for us now. They calm the fear of reforms people have."[49]

No wonder that Alyaksandr Lukashenka considered the Ukrainian Orange Revolution as a serious challenge to his regime. The new Ukraine represented a double threat for authoritarian Belarus: an external one, as Ukraine had joined the geopolitical interests of the EU and the USA in the region; and an internal one, as the Belarusian opposition could follow the Ukrainian example and draw on the Ukrainian experience. Although the official presidential rhetoric pretended to be neutral during the election campaign of 2004, it became rather aggressive with the victory of Yushchenko and with the approaching presidential elections in Belarus. In his annual address to the parliament in April 2005, Lukashenka called the revolutions in Georgia and Ukraine "open banditry in democratic guise"[50]. A counter propaganda film, prepared by the First National TV channel and entitled "Conspiracy Theory: Controlled Chaos", once again presented the opposition in Belarus as the puppets of obscure international forces interested in the destabilization of the post-Soviet countries and in weakening Russia's geopolitical position.[51] Until autumn 2006, when Gazprom announced its plans to raise the gas price for Belarus, Lukashenka defined the colour revolutions as a Western conspiracy aimed first of all at Russia and its interests in the near abroad.

---

48 Andrei Sannikov, "The new role of Ukraine", *Dzerkalo tyzhnia*, no. 17, May 7-13, 2005 (in Ukrainian).
49 Milinkevich, "Ukrainian experience".
50 "The President of Belarus addresses the Belarusian people and the parliament", April 19, 2005, www.president.gov.by/press10257.html (in Russian) (last accessed February 7, 2010).
51 Igor Slavinskii, "Manageable Chaos", *Sovetskaia Belarussiia*, no. 50, March 17, 2006 (in Russian).

In 2004 some Belarusian experts (for example Valerii Karbalevich) believed that Minsk could in fact be interested in a victory of pro-Western Yushchenko, creating a scenario which would push Russia and Belarus closer to each other.[52] A victory for Yanukovych, Karbalevich argued, would not be in the interest of Lukashenka, because in this case Ukraine would replace Belarus as a key partner of Russia in the post Soviet space – a view that certainly underestimated the pragmatic economic nationalism of the Donetsk clan and the Party of Regions. On the contrary, other experts considered the possible victory of Yushchenko a clear threat for the Belarusian-Russian integration: "It would discredit the ability of the Russian leadership to defend their geopolitical interests, stimulate the activities of the national and pro-Western political forces in Belarus and their anti-Russian rhetoric, thus weakening the public support for the integration projects."[53] Whatever the complex and unpredictable geopolitical consequences of the Ukrainian elections of 2004 for Belarus, the immediate threat to Lukashenka's regime of personal power was certainly coming from the victory of the democratic forces in Ukraine.

As some observers had predicted, Lukashenka took preventive measures against a possible "Orange scenario" in Belarus.[54] Imposing administrative and financial limitations for NGO activities, harassing activists and independent journalists, threatening students with administrative sanctions, and a counter-propaganda campaign in the pro-presidential media – all this was used to keep the opposition isolated and fragmented. Police forces were strengthened and trained to act properly in case of street actions. At the same time, the conflicts and corruption scandals in the Ukrainian Orange team were instrumentalized by Lukashenka's administration in order to demonstrate the failure of the revolution and to warn Belarusian voters of a "false choice". Publications in the pro-presidential media, with characteristic titles such as "Self-Liquidation of the Orange Virus", "Love has Gone, Oranges have Shriv-

---

52 Aleksandr Zaitsev, "Minsk has not decided yet which colour suits Ukraine", www.rol.ru/news/misc/newssng/04/12/19_004.htm (in Russian) (last accessed February 7, 2010).
53 "Analysis of the chances to export the Orange Revolution to Belarus", Informatsionnyi i analiticheskii sait Soiuznogo gosudarstva, 11 Dec 2004, http://soyuz.by /ru/?guid=11198 (in Russian) (last accessed February 7, 2010).
54 Cf. Silitski, "Has the Age of Revolutions Ended?", *Transitions online*, January 13, 2005, www.tol.cz/look/TOL/article.tpl?IdLanguage=1&IdPublication=4&NrIssue=98 &NrSection=4&NrArticle=13298(last accessed February 7, 2010).

elled" or "*Maidan* has Become a Cemetery", systematically made the pro-European, democratic political forces in Ukraine look ridiculous.

Were the Belarusian expectations and fears with respect to the Ukrainian Orange Revolution really grounded? Did Yushchenko and his team have a principal position on Belarus, a clear political course? The initial intention of the victorious Orange team was to support democratisation in the post-Soviet space unambiguously. The new Ukrainian leadership, which imagined itself already with one foot in the EU, had a strong ambition to play the same role of democratic patron in relation to Belarus, as Poland had for Ukraine before.

Yulia Tymoshenko, the first prime-minister in the Orange government, was especially optimistic about the prospects of a Belarusian "Orange Revolution". In an interview she gave in Paris in June 2005, Tymoshenko advocated "to study and apply" the Ukrainian experience in other countries, first of all in Belarus.[55] At the end of August 2005, some days before she was ousted from office, Tymoshenko argued that Ukraine, Poland and the Baltic lands will develop a common position and coordinate their policies towards Lukashenka's regime.[56] No wonder that Tymoshenko's dismissal was enthusiastically welcomed and commented by official Minsk. But Anatolii Lebedko, the leader of the United Civic Party, optimistically believed that Yulia Tymoshenko, now out of office and not bound by diplomatic obligations, could give even more support to the Belarusian opposition.[57]

In the beginning of his presidency, Victor Yushchenko also took a rather resolute attitude towards Lukashenka's regime. In January 2005 a joint statement from the presidents George W. Bush and Victor Yushchenko condemned the non-democratic regimes of Cuba and Belarus.[58] A clear commitment to democracy in Belarus was expressed also in a special declaration of the Forum of the Community of Democratic Choice, held in December 2005

Yulia Tymoshenko, "Belarus can learn from the Ukrainian experience", *Khartyia97*, June 15, 2005, www.charter97.org/bel/news/2005/06/15/timoshenko (in Russian) (last accessed February 7, 2010).

56   "Lukashenka heckled", *Dzerkalo tyzhnia*, August 27 - September 2, 2005 (in Ukrainian).

57   Viktor Martinovich, "Orange is ripe", *Belgazeta*, no. 36, September 12, 2005 (in Russian).

58   "A New Century Agenda for the Ukrainian-American Strategic Partnership", Joint Statement by President George W. Bush and President Viktor Yushchenko, www.whitehouse.gov/news/releases/2005/04/20050404-1.html (last accessed Nov 3, 2008).

in Kyiv under the patronage of Yushchenko.[59] The Ukrainian Ministry of Foreign Affairs, led by the pro-Western Boris Tarasiuk, actively supported this political course. In a session of the UN Commission on Human Rights held in May 2005, Ukraine, despite the pressure of the Russian and Belarusian delegations, voted for a resolution condemning human rights abuse in Belarus. Ukraine also joined several EU declarations expressing concern over the state of democracy in Belarus.

In spring 2005, the Ukrainian MFA took a firm position in the diplomatic conflict with Minsk caused by the detention of five Ukrainian citizens during the annual April 26 commemoration of the Chernobyl disaster. Ukrainian students, activists for the NGO "National Alliance", were detained among 33 other young people (including eight Russians) near the presidential residence, where they assembled to submit a petition to the head of the state. They received sentences of 9-15 days in prison. The arrested Russians were released after a few days at the request of the Russian Foreign Ministry. In case of the arrested Ukrainians, however, Minsk did not make any concessions despite the angry protests from the Ukrainian MFA. Ukrainian Foreign Minister Tarasiuk accused Minsk of applying double standards and called these arrests politically motivated.[60] The MFA not only deployed all diplomatic means to help its citizens, but actually solidarized with the students' political position, an unprecedented case for Ukraine. A similar situation happened one year later, some days before the presidential elections in Belarus. On March 12, 2006, several Ukrainian citizens were detained during the meeting in support of the oppositional candidate Milinkevich, among them TV journalists from the Ukrainian "5th Channel". They were arrested during the live reportage from the meeting. The Ukrainian supporters of Milinkevich, most of them members of *Studentske Bratstvo* (Students' Brotherhood) organisation, were sentenced to 10 days of arrest. In its note, the Ukrainian MFA called

---

59 "Forum of the Community of Democratic Choice took place in Kyiv on December 2", Mission of Ukraine to European Communities, http://ukraine-eu.mfa.gov.ua/eu/en/news/detail/1377.htm (last accessed February 7, 2010).
60 David Marples, "Belarus triggers dispute with Ukraine", The Jamestown Foundation. Eurasia Daily Monitor, vol. 2, issue 90 (May 9, 2005). http://www.jamestown.org/publications_details.php?volume_id=407&issue_id=3325&article_id=2369721, last accessed Nov 3, 2008.

upon the Belarusian authorities to immediately release the Ukrainian citizens, to respect democratic norms and to guarantee free and fair elections.[61]

However, despite all the official declarations and diplomatic demarches, Ukraine's position in relation to Belarus has been rather ambiguous. Ukraine has not officially recognized the results of the presidential elections of 2006, but also did not join EU sanctions against Belarusian top officials accused in the West of kidnapping journalists and oppositional politicians in Belarus. The Ukrainian president, although having little personal sympathy for the "last dictator of Europe", did not boycott Alyaksandr Lukashenka and repeatedly stressed that "a total isolation of Belarus would be a mistake". Moreover, Victor Yushchenko invited Milinkevich, as a candidate from the united opposition, to the Forum of Democratic Choice in Kyiv, but did not find the time to meet him personally.[62] Already the official visit of Prime Minister Yurii Yekhanurov to Minsk in October 2005 signalled that Ukraine's relations with Belarus were slowly returning to the old Kuchma model: "pure business, no politics".[63] Yekhanurov did not touch the painful questions; he admired the economic development in Belarus and praised the social achievements in the countryside, which, he said, Ukraine should copy. Both sides focused on trade and economic cooperation (however with no breakthrough in the border delimitation issue). Lukashenka profited from this visit symbolically by using it to strengthen the legitimacy of his regime. In conclusion, one can say that the Orange coalition, not able to find a common position even in burning issues of Ukrainian politics, actually delegated the "Belarusian question" to the NGO sector.

And indeed the pro-European part of Ukrainian civil society has been more active and determined in this respect than official Kyiv. Ukrainian youth organizations (such as *Pora*, "National Alliance", *Studentske Bratstvo* etc.) not only sent their people to Minsk to support the opposition during the elections of 2006, but also put moral pressure on the Ukrainian authorities, forcing

---

61   "Statement of the Ministry of Foreign Affairs of Ukraine relating to the arrest of Ukrainian citizens in Belarus", Ministry of Foreign Affairs of Ukraine, http://www.mfa.gov.ua/mfa/en/publication/content/5333.htm (last accessed February 7, 2010).
62   Volodymyr Kravchenko, "The Belarusian question", *Dzerkalo tyzhnia*, March 25-31, 2006 (in Ukrainian).
63   This visit was planned during the meeting of the two presidents in Kazan. If Tymoshenko had not left office she would have been the head of the official Ukrainian delegation to Minsk.

them to take a more resolute position. Thus, in April 2005, in the midst of the diplomatic crisis between the two countries, *Pora* called to ban entry of Lukashenka and his top officials into Ukraine, to strengthen the role of the NGO sector in Ukrainian-Belarusian relations and to base them on democratic standards and on the respect of human rights.[64] An open letter signed by prominent Ukrainian intellectuals in May 2006 blamed the government for replacing democratic standards in Ukrainian-Belarusian relations with pragmatism and for neglecting the "ideals of Maidan", the rule of law and European integration. The letter called president Yushchenko to openly solidarize with the victims of political repressions by joining EU sanctions against the Belarusian regime and to refuse its officials entry into Ukraine.[65] (A similar letter, appealing to the solidarity of the Ukrainian leadership, was signed later by Belarusian intellectuals, human rights activists and oppositional politicians.) However, no official reactions followed these initiatives.

With Victor Yanukovych's return to power in August 2006, Ukraine's policy towards Belarus was switched from pragmatism to Byzantinism. There were several events that signalled a clear relapse into anti-democratic politics and the cooperation of the executive forces in both countries against "disturbing elements"; the following case is just one demonstrating how efforts to establish the rule of law were obstructed in the end. In the night of November 24-25, 2004, Ukrainian policemen had illegally arrested four Belarusian activists – representatives of "Charta 97", the "European Coalition" and *Zubr* – at the Ukrainian-Belarusian border. They were on their way from Kyiv, where they had been taking part in protest rallies in support of Viktor Yushchenko. In the process of detention, Ukrainian policemen, border guards and "people in camouflage" used brutal force against them. Released by the court after only a few days, the Belarusians called this incident the revenge of the old regime and a joint operation by the Belarusian and Ukrainian security forces. The fact that in February 2005 a criminal case was opened against the Ukrainian po-

---

64 "*Pora* calls for a ban on Lukashenka to enter Ukraine", *Korrespondent.net*, April 22, 2005, http://ua.korrespondent.net/ukraine/256697/ (in Ukrainian) (last accessed February 7, 2010).
65 "Open letter of the Ukrainian intelligentsia to the President of Ukraine on violation of Human Rights in Belarus and the need of democratic solidarity", *Lvivska gazeta*, May 17, 2006, http://www.gazeta.lviv.ua/articles/2006/05/17/15280/ (in Ukrainian) (last accessed February 7, 2010).

licemen involved in the incident was considered an important step towards democracy and the rule of law in Ukraine.[66] Dmitrii Bondarenko, one of the Belarusian activists, expressed hope that the investigation would become a model case, particularly for his country, where the police often uses brutal force on street protesters. However, the case was dismissed in August 2006, a couple of weeks after Yanukovych's return to power. Belarusian activists perceived this news to be a sign of an authoritarian backlash in Ukraine.[67]

Another example signalling the retreat from democratic standards in Ukraine was revealed in September 2006 by the Belarusian newspaper *Nasha niva*. It reported on recent cases in which Ukrainian security forces harassed and threatened Belarusian activists. Serzhuk Vysotski, the director of the Belarusian National Democratic Centre in Kyiv, who was the victim of such harassment, suspected a possible collaboration between the Belarusian KGB and the Ukrainian Security Service.[68]

Why did Ukraine's "new" Belarusian policy become half-hearted and return so quickly to the old pattern of "pragmatism"? Why did Ukraine after the Orange Revolution fail to support democratic changes in Belarus? There are several reasons for this failure:

First of all, obvious pragmatic considerations did play a role, such as the hope for a resolution of the border delimitation issue and more generally, the unwillingness of Kyiv to turn a neutral neighbour into a hostile one (given the already problematic relations with Moscow and the still rather marginal geopolitical status of Ukraine). Second, the fragile balance of political forces behind the Orange coalition as well as the permanent political crisis made it difficult for Yushchenko to develop a consistent Belarusian policy. With the return of Victor Yanukovych to power this project became even more difficult. Ukraine turned out to be too weak for its newly claimed role of a democratic leader in Eastern Europe. Third, the Belarusian political opposition was not

---

66 "Ukraine probes into arrests of Belarusians a year ago", *Khartyia 97*, 30 Nov 2005, http://www.charter97.org/rus/news/2005/11/30/delo (in Russian) (last accessed February 7, 2010).
67 "The file on arrests of Belarusians in Ukraine has been closed", Ukrainska khelsynska pravozakhystna grupa, October 11, 2006, http://www.helsinki.org.ua/index.php?id=1160580861 (in Ukrainian) (last accessed February 7, 2010).
68 "Belarusian oppositionists are harassed in Kyiv", *Nasha Niva*, October 17, 2006, http://www.nn.by/index.php?c=ar&i=4371 (in Belarusian) (last accessed February 7, 2010).

successful during the presidential elections in March 2006, despite mass street protests. Although Lukashenka's victory was rather ambivalent, the election results, even if partly falsified, demonstrated a relatively high support for his rule. Despite the fact that they were not recognized by the West, the results helped to legitimise Lukashenka's regime and consolidate his power. This has made an export of the Orange Revolution to Belarus rather improbable, at least for another four years. Fourth, the EU has not shown sufficient clarity and resoluteness in the Belarusian case. It does not dare to go much further than soft political isolation of the regime. Although the Belarusian opposition continues to call on the EU to use economic sanctions against Lukashenka, it is rather unlikely that such hard measures will be taken against Minsk. Effective isolation and international pressure would require the support of Russia, which at the moment is not inclined to cooperate with the EU. And as the Ukrainian leadership's initial optimism about the prospects for EU membership has faded, it does not see a reason to identify too much with the political line coming from Brussels. The fifth and last factor, the new gas conflict between Belarus and Gazprom in 2006 and its impact on Ukrainian-Belarusian relations, will be analysed in the next section.

2.6 Gas wars: partners despite themselves?

The first open conflict for the gas prize between Minsk and Moscow emerged in February 2004.[69] In the midst of winter, Gazprom switched off the gas supply for Belarus, which impaired the gas transit to Europe for some days. Already at that time Lukashenka demonstrated his political will, his ability to act quickly and pragmatically and to change his political rhetoric radically in one day. And the Belarusian leader won this war of nerves: after a few days, Gazprom restored the gas supply and both sides started negotiations.

---

69 Already in the 1990s Gazprom was pressing Belarus to pay its debts and offered to rent the assets of Beltransgaz in exchange for a supply guarantee, but due to the political priorities of Moscow at that time could not pursue its economic interests. With its new head Alexei Miller, Gazprom has intensified its pressure on Belarus since 2002. (Cf. Roland Goetz, "Ukraine and Belarus: Their Energy Dependence on Russia and their Roles as Transit Countries", in: Daniel Hamilton, Gerhard Mangott (eds.), *The New Eastern Europe: Ukraine, Belarus, Moldova*, Vienna: Austrian Institute for International Affairs 2007, p. 165).

As a result, in 2004 the gas price for Belarus was raised by 50%, from $30 to $47 per 1,000 m³ — still less than the other former Soviet republics had to pay. However, it seems that Lukashenka did not really learn from this conflict. At least his pro-Russian political orientation did not change, and nothing was done to overcome Belarus's almost total economic and energy dependency on Moscow. In an interview to the *Rossiiskaia gazeta* in December 2005, Lukashenka explained why Belarus should be treated preferentially in terms of gas price and will never get into a precarious situation like Ukraine: first, because Belarusian tariffs for gas transit are much lower than in Ukraine; second, because Belarus allows the free deployment of Russian troops on its territory and does not charge money for military infrastructure; and third, because Belarus does not strive for NATO membership and remains Russia's strategic ally.[70] The harshest critics of Russian "energy imperialism", who called the Gazprom ultimatum for Ukraine in 2005 "the price for democracy", in fact followed Lukashenka's logic. Similar arguments were used by Yushchenko's political opponents, who blamed his pro-NATO course for the raised gas price.

However, the events of the subsequent winter would prove correct those analysts who were inclined to see in Gazprom a capitalist enterprise led by the normal logic of profit maximization, rather than an instrument of political control in the "near abroad". In 2006 Gazprom announced its intention to raise the gas price for Belarus to $200 per m³ and demanded a 50% participation of Gazprom in Beltransgaz, which would mean that Belarus nearly loses control over its pipeline system. Long negotiations brought no results, and at the end of 2006, Gazprom threatened again to stop the gas supply to Belarus. Lukashenka, internationally isolated more than ever after the controversial March 2006 presidential elections, nevertheless did not give in to pressure. He rejected Gazprom's conditions appealing to the union agreements with Russia, which allegedly allowed Belarus to buy gas at the Russian internal price. Finally both sides gave in, and on December 31, 2006, Gazprom and Belarus signed a new contract for 2007-2011. According to this contract, Belarus pays $100 per 1,000 m³ in 2007, and the price will gradually

---

70   Aleksandr Lukashenko, "Russians are our brothers in blood", *Rossiiskaia gazeta*, December 29, 2005, http://www.rg.ru/2005/12/29/lukashenko.html (in Russian) (last accessed February 7, 2010).

increase in the following years up to the "European level" in 2011. Gazprom also buys 50% of Beltransgaz assets for $2.5 billion – a price much higher than what was initially offered.

It is difficult to determine if Minsk made a better deal with Gazprom than Kyiv had one year earlier (the official price for Ukraine in 2006 was $130, although it paid only $90 to RosUkrEnergo, a mediating company; besides, Ukraine kept control over its transportation system). More interesting for us was the perception of both gas wars in the public opinion at home and in the neighbouring country. While Kyiv's conflict with Gazprom, which ended in the obscure RosUkrEnergo deal, was seen as a professional and political failure of the Ukrainian government, cast a shadow on "Our Ukraine" and on president Yushchenko, raised the issue of corruption, and considerably contributed to the public frustration with the Orange Revolution, Lukashenka's regime rather profited from his dispute with Gazprom. Once again he got a chance to demonstrate to the Belarusian public his strong hand and his personal control over key issues, his ability to defend national interests and to resist external pressure. Lukashenka managed to use this conflict to consolidate his power, and even some representatives of the political opposition supported him against the Moscow dictate. The Ukrainian media also compared Lukashenka's firm position vis à vis Gazprom with the failure of Kyiv in a similar situation one year earlier. As it was noticed in the media, Ukraine's bargaining conditions were better than those of Belarus: The Belarusian energy sector uses mainly gas fuel, while Ukraine has also nuclear power stations and a coal industry; Belarus is dependent on Russia, while Ukraine formally buys Turkmenian gas; and finally the volume of the Ukrainian transit is more significant than the Belarusian one.[71] In the eyes of the democratic press, the fact that Ukraine failed to use these advantages in its negotiations with Gazprom can be explained only by corruption and by the pro-Moscow mentality of the Ukrainian government. "Even if there is corruption in Belarus, its scale does not pose a threat to national security and state interests, as it is

---

[71] "Gazprom and Belarus: Not a distant gas war", *Ekonomichna pravda*, December 29, 2006, http://epravda.com.ua/news_print/2006/12/29/51765.htm (in Ukrainian) (last accessed November 3, 2008).

the case in Ukraine,"[72] wrote *Dzerkalo tyzhnia*, a pro-Western Ukrainian weekly which is usually rather critical of Lukashenka. In the eyes of the pro-Western Ukrainian public, the conflict with Gazprom did not make Lukashenka a democrat, but turned him into a potential ally in the gas wars with Russia – into a "nationalist despite himself". Some Ukrainian observers regretted that the two countries were not able to defend their interests jointly against the pressure of the "energy empire".

With the gas crisis tapering, Lukashenka easily gave up his traditional pro-Russian rhetoric and started to look for new allies. The Belarusian government approached its neighbours in the West with cooperation initiatives, but the new EU members did not hurry to shake hands with the "last dictator of Europe". In the second half of 2006 some business propositions were made to Kyiv, which had already before demonstrated its pragmatic approach to the Belarusian issue. Pushed by the urgent need to diversify its energy supply, Belarus showed interest in renting reactors in Ukrainian nuclear stations, in increasing the electricity import from Ukraine, and in purchasing Ukrainian coal for its thermal power stations. According to media sources, the Belarusian side asked for the re-export of the 10 billion m^3 of gas from the Ukrainian quota of RosUkrEnergo, but Naftogaz Ukrainy showed little enthusiasm.[73] Minsk indicated its wish to join the Odesa-Brody project[74]; and the Belarusian media speculated on the possibility of cooperation between Ukraine and Belarus in transporting Azerbaijani oil to Europe. In October 2006 the heads of Beltransgaz and Ukrtransgaz met to discuss the possibili-

---

72   Mykhaylo Honchar, "Drained 'Druzhba' stinks like hell", *Dzerkalo tyzhnia*, January 13-19, 2007 (in Ukrainian).
73   "Yushchenko will not help Lukashenka with gas", *Khartyia 97*, October 25, 2006, http://www.charter97.org/rus/news/2006/10/25/gaz (in Ukrainian), (last accessed February 7, 2010).
74   The Odesa-Brody pipeline (in operation since 2002) is a 674 km long crude oil pipeline between the Ukrainian city of Odesa at the Black Sea and Brody in Western Ukraine. The pipeline was originally intended to transfer oil from the Caspian Sea (Kazakhstan) to the Polish Black Sea port Gdansk and from there to the rest of Europe. The pipeline should have helped Ukraine diversify its energy supply and thus make the country less dependent on Russia. Under Russian pressure, however, the Kuchma government in 2004 accepted reverse flow allowing Russia to transfer oil southwards to the Black Sea. After the Orange Revolution the new Ukrainian government returned to the Odesa-Brody project. The pipeline is planned to be extended to Plock in Poland in order to use it in the direction originally intended.

ties of coordinating the transit tariffs for Russian gas.[75] Moreover, as Minsk was afraid of Russian trade sanctions, it showed some interest in exporting Belarusian products to Ukrainian markets.

In November 2006 Lukashenka met a large group of Ukrainian journalists and spoke about the possibilities of Belarusian-Ukrainian cooperation for the first time. He avoided criticising the pro-Western course of Ukraine, praised Yushchenko as a good banker and even speculated on the possibility of a Union state for Ukraine and Belarus. The last idea sounded sensational, but nobody in Ukraine took it seriously and considered it instead to be a message addressed to Moscow.

However, Lukashenka's new initiatives did have some response in Ukraine. Contacts intensified not only on the governmental level; the head of the Ukrainian presidential administration, Viktor Baloha, visited Minsk in December 2006 in order to prepare Lukashenka's visit to Kyiv planned for the first months of 2007. The energy security of Belarus and Ukraine and their possible cooperation in this sphere was supposed to become a central subject to be discussed by the two presidents. Both sides were supposed to sign a memorandum on cooperation in energy issues,[76] including the increase of electric energy export from Ukraine to Belarus (with the construction of a new power line between Rivne, Ukraine, and Mikashevichi, Belarus) and the shared use of the gas transit infrastructure (pipelines and gas storages). The idea of a Ukrainian-Belarusian-Azerbaijani consortium for the export of Caspian oil to the West was also mentioned. On February 15, 2006, Viktor Yushchenko told journalists that he supports Lithuanian president Valdas Adamkus's idea to develop a common energy policy for Lithuania, Belarus and Ukraine as transit countries. Lithuania has been in conflict with Russia since summer 2006 because it sold its refinery "Mazeikiu nafta", in which Russia was interested, to a Polish company. In response, the Russian oil company Rosneft closed the Druzhba pipeline "for technical reasons", leaving Lithuania without oil and transit profit. As the shutting down of Druzhba caused also

---

75 "Does the gas price unite?", *Dzerkalo tyzhnia*, October 14-20, 2006 (in Ukrainian).
76 "Lukashenka proposes Kyiv to make friends against Moscow", *Khartyia 97*, March 12, 2007, http://www.charter97.org/rus/news/2007/03/12/kiev (in Russian); "Ukraine confirms meeting of Yushchenko and Lukashenka", *Khartyia 97*, February 21, 2007, http://www.charter97.org/rus/news/2007/02/21/storona (in Russian) (both last accessed February 7, 2010).

significant losses for the Belarusian budget, Adamkus's proposition was timely and reasonable. It was not completely new, since the idea of a common EU energy strategy had been put forward by Poland already in 2006, and a possible cooperation between Poland and Ukraine in energy security had been already discussed. But the proposition to include Belarus in this "anti-Russian" coalition was somewhat unexpected and caused an outrage in the Russian media. It was even speculated (also mainly in Russia) that Belarus might join GUAM.

However, no geopolitical sensations happened and the Krakow energy summit in May 2007[77] took place without Belarus. Probably Lukashenka hesitated to show too much disloyalty to Moscow as he was hoping to get a credit from Russia to stabilize the state budget. And the European partners might not have been eager to have him sit at the same table. The EU did not change its position and, in June 2007, deprived Belarus of its trade preferences. Also the planned visit of Lukashenka to Kyiv did not take place in 2007; it was postponed for an indefinite time due to the outbreak of the political crisis in Ukraine. None of the key political players in Ukraine were interested in addressing the Belarusian issue in the wake of the new parliamentary elections. A political rapprochement with Lukashenka's Belarus could compromise Ukraine's Euro-Atlantic aspirations and, at the same time, irritate Moscow, which was suspicious of any effort to pull Belarus into the pro-Western camp.

In 2006-07 the Ukrainian political elite once again proved to be split on the Belarusian question. The Party of Regions, because of its "anti-Russian" orientation, did not support the idea of an "energy union" between Ukraine and Belarus.[78] Unlike Yushchenko, Prime Minister Yanukovych and Yurii Boiko, the minister of energy, did not make any comment on the Adamkus proposition of cooperation between Ukraine, Belarus and Lithuania. The Ukrainian government did also not have a clear position to the conflict between Minsk and Gazprom and even tried to profit from it. The energy minis-

---

[77] The Krakow Energy Summit brought together the presidents of Azerbaijan, Poland, Ukraine, Lithuania and Georgia; the president of Kazakhstan changed his plans and preferred to meet Vladimir Putin, who made his Central Asian tour at the same time.
[78] "Nezavisimaia gazeta: Lukashenka creates alliance against Russia", *Khartyia 97*, January 31, 2007, http://www.charter97.org/rus/news/2007/01/31/ng (in Russian) (last accessed February 7, 2010).

ter proposed to increase gas transit through Ukraine in order to "fully satisfy the needs of the Ukrainian neighbours".[79] When the *Druzhba* pipeline was closed by Russia in January 2007, Ukraine, according to some media, profited from the additional transit of oil, earning $25 million extra (although according to other sources, Ukraine instead lost money due to the same measure).

The "gas war" between Minsk and Gazprom in 2006 created the precondition for at least a temporary alliance between Ukraine and Belarus and a possible coordination of their energy politics. It caused some confusion across the spectrum of Ukrainian political forces, shifting their traditional attitudes to Lukashenka's regime. While "Our Ukraine" and the Tymoshenko Block applauded Lukashenka's move away from Moscow and his firm defence of national sovereignty and state interests, and hoped that distancing from Moscow could push his regime to democratisation, the traditionally Lukashenka-friendly Communists and Vitrenko's Progressive Socialists avoided commenting on the gas conflict. Moreover, the criticism of the state of democracy in Belarus made by Prime Minister Victor Yanukovych during his visit to Brussels on March 27, 2007, became a small sensation.

However, the "gas war" with Moscow did not make Minsk change its geopolitical orientation in favour of the West, but rather let it return to the well-tried "multivector" policy of balancing between Russia and the EU. Not at all convinced by Lukashenka's democratic rhetoric and his cosmetic reforms, but rather having realized that further isolation would push Belarus even more towards Russia, Brussels has softened its attitude to the authoritarian regime in Minsk. Although the OSCE criticised the parliamentary elections in September 2008 for falling short of democratic norms, it noticed some improvements.[80] In October 2008 the European Union took the decision to resume contacts with Minsk at the highest level and to suspend the visa ban against a number of high-ranking Belarusian officials, including the president. The EU High Representative for Common Foreign and Security Policy, Javier Solana,

---

79   "Ukraine is ready to raise transit of Russian gas to Europe", *Podrobnosti*, December 26 , 2006, http://www.podrobnosti.ua/economy/energetical/2006/12/28/382325.html (in Russian) (last accessed February 7, 2010).

80   "The parliamentary elections in Belarus fell short of OSCE commitments in spite of minor improvements, observers say" (press-release), http://www.osce.org/item/33272.html (last accessed February 7, 2010).

visited Minsk and met President Lukashenka on February 19, 2009. In 2009 Belarus together with five other post-Soviet countries (Ukraine, Moldova, Armenia, Azerbaijan, and Georgia) was invited to participate in the Eastern Partnership, a new program designed to strengthen political and economic cooperation between the EU and its Eastern and Caucasian neighbours. An official Belarusian delegation attended the Eastern Partnership summit in Prague on May 7, 2009. In June 2009 PACE (Parliamentary Assembly of the Council of Europe) voted in favour of restoring the Special Guest status of the Belarusian Parliament (which had been suspended since 1997) making a moratorium on death penalty the only condition.[81] Lukashenka's office celebrated these new tendencies as a "breakthrough of the political blockade" and used them to counterbalance the one-side dependency from Moscow, still highly interested in a military-strategic cooperation with Belarus and in its geopolitical loyalty. In particular, Moscow expects official recognition of Abkhazia's and South Ossetia's independence by Minsk, a promise that Lukashenka successfully traded for concessions in economic and energy issues.

Brussels' softening of its political line affected also the atmosphere in Ukrainian-Belarusian relations. In the first half of 2009 the presidents of Ukraine and Belarus met twice, finally resuming official contacts after the Orange Revolution. On January 20 in Chernyhiv they focused on current issues of trade and economic cooperation. The second meeting took place in Homel on June 6, in the wake of the Prague EU summit, and was devoted to the perspectives of the Eastern Neighbourhood program. While the first meeting was commented in the media and met the criticism of the Belarusian democratic opposition,[82] the second one went almost unnoticed. Perceived as a sign of "normalisation" of bilateral relations, the talks between the two presidents nevertheless brought no breakthrough in the key issues of Ukrainian-Belarusian relations. The Ukrainian president invited Belarus to cooperate in energy issues and common transit projects, and Lukashenka confirmed his

---

81 "Belarus: PACE committee calls for the restoration of Special Guest status", Council of Europe, http://assembly.coe.int/ASP/Press/StopPressView.asp?ID=2175 (last accessed February 7, 2010).
82 "Yushchenko's meeting with Lukashenka is betrayal of Orange Revolution", *Khartyia 97*, January 20, 2009, http://charter97.org/ru/news/2009/1/20/14173/ (in Russian) (last accessed February 7, 2010).

interest in a common use of the Odesa-Brody-Plotsk oil pipeline. However, Ukraine and Belarus are not only too weak economically and politically for such projects, they are also competitors as transit countries and far from being able to coordinate their efforts. Thus, in January 2009 the Belarusian Prime Minister Sidorskii put forward the idea of the new gas pipeline Yamal-Europe-2, which is bypassing Ukraine.[83] Although permanent trade wars with Russia and the prospect of rising gas prices force Minsk to seek new cooperation partners, Ukraine cannot replace Russia for the Belarusian economy. The rapprochement with Ukraine first of all allows Lukashenka to demonstrate to Moscow his independence. As for President Yushchenko, he can get some geopolitical dividends presenting Ukraine as an advocate of Belarus in the EU, at least in the framework of the Eastern Neighbourhood program.

Conclusion

With the collapse of the Soviet Union in 1991, Ukraine and Belarus rediscovered each other as new neighbours, partners and competitors facing similar challenges in the process of post-Soviet transformations. As the national elites seek to redefine the collective identities and the place of their countries in Europe, the Russia-led reintegration projects based on the "Slavic triangle" lose their attraction. Although the old paradigm of East Slavic unity is still popular in mass consciousness and is often instrumentalized by various political forces, democratic politicians, NGOs and pro-Western intellectuals increasingly appeal to the normative force of "European" democratic principles and justify the European identity of their countries using cultural and historical arguments. In the course of their post-Soviet transitions, both Ukraine and Belarus faced similar authoritarian tendencies, but developed into different types of political regimes. The project of "Europeanization" put forward by the leaders of the Orange Revolution was enthusiastically received by the democratic opposition in Belarus. At the same time the more conservative post-Soviet political elites in both countries denounced this project as a Western plot. After the Orange Revolution, the new Ukrainian gov-

---

83 "Sidorskii: second line of Yamal-Europe would allow to increase gas transit to Europe considerably", *Belarusskie novosti*, http://naviny.by/rubrics/economic/2009/01/18/ic_news_113_304824/ (in Russian) (last accessed February 7, 2010).

ernment claimed its ambition to initiate and support democratic tendencies in the post-Soviet space. In relation to Lukashenka's regime, Ukraine initially solidarized with Western critics, but due to internal political conflicts soon shifted back to a more pragmatic attitude.

The pragmatic turn in Russia's politics towards the CIS countries and the common challenges of energy security push Kyiv and Minsk to coordinate their interests vis à vis Moscow. Moreover, the general enlargement fatigue in the EU and the stabilization of its eastern border also urge both countries towards cooperation and lobbying common interests in Brussels. But the political and economic weakness of both countries, the differences between their political systems and ideologies, and the growing competition for Russian oil and gas transit render the perspectives of a sustainable alliance rather bleak. While Russia and the European Union intensify their geopolitical contest for the post-Soviet borderlands, energy security and the stability of EU-Russian relations seem to be the priority for Brussels. This constellation deepens the political polarisation in Ukraine, torn between the West and Russia, but at the same time creates a "grey zone" which secures a certain leeway and immunity for the Belarusian authoritarian ruler.

II Bordering Nations, Transcending Boundaries

3 Under Construction: the Ukrainian-Russian Border from the Soviet Collapse to EU Enlargement

In 1991, with the collapse of the Soviet Union, the administrative boundary between two former Soviet republics, Ukraine and the Russian Federation, became an international border. The Ukrainian-Russian border measures 2,295.6 km (with 1,974 km of land border), which is almost one-third of the overall length of the Ukrainian state borders. It crosses densely populated territories and industrial zones that are of crucial importance for the economies of both countries, and despite the introduction of custom and passport controls remains one of the "busiest" borders in the region. The Ukrainian-Russian border is not a site of ethnic tensions or military conflict, as is the case with other post-Soviet borders, but it is not unproblematic in other respects. The scale of illegal crossing, contraband and human trafficking (especially illegal transit migration) is a serious challenge for Ukraine, but also for Russia and the EU. Although the legal status of the border is basically settled between Ukraine and Russia, some issues such as the land border demarcation and the delimitation of the Azov Sea still remain open and have often been instrumentalized by politicians in both countries. The symbolic status of the border with Russia, a former "imperial power", is a highly sensitive subject in Ukrainian political discourse. The 2004 Orange Revolution in Ukraine marked an escalation of the political confrontation between the two countries and also changed the geopolitical and even military-strategic context of this border, in particular with regards to a possible NATO accession of Ukraine.

The enlargement of the European Union to the East in May 2004 endowed the Ukrainian-Russian border with increased international relevance. However, the main interest of the EU and other international actors with regards to this border is determined rather by security agenda and does not necessarily include economic and humanitarian cooperation, as is the case with the internal and even external EU borders. The cross-border cooperation between Ukrainian and Russian regions that was launched in the 1990s with the aim of restoring broken economic ties and compensating for the shock of the Soviet collapse now serves mainly the narrow group interests of local business.

The changing visions of "national interests" and "national security" in both countries, their search for national identity and geopolitical choice, the competing influences of Russia and the EU in the post-Soviet space, the EU enlargement and the institutionalization of its Eastern policy, and the ongoing power negotiations between regional elites and national centres – all this is reflected in the politics of border making on both sides. This chapter addresses the complex process of constructing a new border and analyzes its political and symbolic role in the Ukrainian-Russian relations and its place in the European security system.

3.1 Ukraine's border with Russia: the heritage of the Soviet past and the new challenges

In 1991, Ukraine as a newly independent state inherited the territory and the boundaries of the former Ukrainian Soviet Socialist Republic. The system of Ukraine's national borders is therefore twofold: it includes "old" and "new" borders, which differ not only in age, but also by the border regime and the level of infrastructure development. Ukraine's western border coincides with the former external frontier of the Soviet Union, which was well protected and hardly permeable before 1991, thus contributing to the Soviet policy of isolation from the West. Having a common border with the countries of the "socialist camp" (Poland, Hungary, Slovakia, Romania), Ukrainians could not really profit from their western neighbourhood: border management and cross-border contacts were strictly controlled by Moscow. On the contrary, Ukraine's borders with its neighbouring Soviet Republics (Russia, Belarus, Moldova) were purely administrative lines, which were not controlled and not demarcated; they did not matter in terms of labour market, social provisions or education system.

Therefore, with state independence Ukraine faced very different challenges at its "old" and "new" borders. The infrastructure of the western border had to be modernized to answer the needs of the growing cross-border traffic, to facilitate contacts between the populations of the near-border regions and to attract western tourists. New crossing points have been opened and the old ones have been modernized in order to reduce waiting time for freight and passenger traffic. Modern technical equipment is supposed to simplify border control and custom procedures. These changes correspond to the Ukrainian policy of integration into Europe, openness to the West and the new status of Ukraine as an EU neighbour.[1]

At the "new" borders of Ukraine with the former Soviet republics the challenges are of a rather different kind. Both the delimitation and the demarcation of the new borders have yet to be finished, which is not only a technical but also a political issue. The infrastructure of border and custom controls has to be built here from zero, which is an additional financial burden on the limited state budget.[2] Populations in the near border areas usually speak the same language, share a common historical memory and culture, and have family and friendship contacts across the border. Illegal crossing is often seen by these people as legitimate and the simplest way to keep contact with the other side.[3] For the border control service this means an additional challenge of educating people and keeping them in check while at the same time winning their loyalty. In case of the Ukrainian-Moldovan border, which is in fact a

---

[1] From the beginning of the 1990s, Ukrainian citizens had enjoyed a visa-free border regime with Poland, Hungary and Slovakia. Due to their accession to the EU in 2004, these countries were forced to introduce visas for Ukrainian citizens, a measure which was criticized in Ukraine (and in Poland) for impeding cross-border trade and local business. With the accession of these countries to the Schengen Agreement in 2007 their visa regimes with Ukraine were even tightened. In order to cushion the consequences for near border residents Ukraine and Hungary signed an agreement on small cross-border movement in the end of 2007. According to this agreement, residents of the 50-km border zone – some 700 towns and villages – are issued special certificates allowing them to cross the Ukrainian-Hungarian border by without Schengen visa. A similar agreement between Ukraine and Poland was enacted on July 1, 2009.

[2] The basis for state borders construction and management policy in Ukraine was laid by the Law "On the State Border of Ukraine" (1991) and by the "Comprehensive Program on the Development of State Borders of Ukraine" enacted by Presidential decree in 1993.

[3] On the attitudes of the population in near-border areas to the new border see chapter 3.1.

border with the unrecognized separatist Transnistria region,[4] the frozen conflict has become a source of instability and cross-border criminality. Ukraine's border with Belarus is not very busy in terms of traffic as this zone is only thinly populated , but it runs through territories heavily polluted as a result of the Chernobyl nuclear accident in 1986.

However, the biggest challenge for Kyiv seems to be the border with Russia. It crosses urbanized and densely populated territories, which have a crucial importance for the economies of both countries and which until recently were deeply integrated. The main transport routes from Moscow to the South go through the territory of Ukraine. The Ukrainian-Russian border is also one of the busiest among post-Soviet borders: around 20 million persons cross it per year. Presently Russian and Ukrainian citizens can cross it with internal passports; a visa is not required, but a migration card has to be filled in. In 2006, international passports were to be introduced as obligatory for crossing the border, but this measure was postponed as both sides were not prepared for it technically. The biggest problem for travellers is the long waiting time at the border, especially during summer holidays. Until autumn 2004 an official registration of Ukrainian visitors (entering the country for more than three days) with the local police offices was required by Russia. This unpopular measure was abolished in the wake of the presidential election campaign in Ukraine, as Vladimir Putin's present to the electorate of the pro-Russian candidate Viktor Yanukovych. Official registration for Ukrainians was reintroduced in 2008, according to the new migration rules for the citizens of NIS countries adopted by the Russian government in 2007.

The scale of contraband, illegal crossing and human trafficking (especially illegal transit migration to the EU countries) at the border with Russia is a serious challenge for the Ukrainian state. The open flat landscape of the southern steppe makes the task of fighting contraband rather difficult, especially in summer, when the smugglers' trucks can easily take small roads or just go through the fields. Part of the population in the near border area makes their living from smuggling vodka, cigarettes, sugar and petrol (this assortment changes according to the price dynamics). But an even more se-

---

4   A separatist region within the former Moldavian SSR that declared independence from Moldova in 1990, followed by a military conflict in 1992. Also known as Trans-Dniester, Transdniestria or Pridnestrovie.

rious problem is the large scale contraband and corruption of the border and customs control services.

Due to its geographic position Ukraine faces the challenge of transit migration (first of all from China, Afghanistan, and countries of East-South Asia) to the EU. Given the relatively open border with Russia, these illegal migrants often are stopped only at the Polish or Slovak border. Some of them stay in Ukraine, having no opportunity to get into the EU, but others make it. Therefore, from the end of the 1990s the Ukrainian-Russian border has been in the focus of EU interest. Also the OSCE, the International Organization for Migration (IOM) and UN Development Program launched some related projects here. Ukrainian experts warn that with the tightening of EU's external border, Ukraine will have to deal with a growing number of refugees and asylum-seekers. The agreement between Ukraine and Russia on re-admission was signed in 2006; it is supposed to facilitate chain deportation of illegal migrants from Ukraine to Russia and possibly further to the countries of origin. However the readmission agreement has not been ratified yet by the Russian parliament.

Although the legal status of the Ukrainian-Russian border has been basically settled by international treaties, some problems such as the demarcation of the land border and the delimitation of the Azov Sea and the Kerch Strait still remain open. For a long time, Russia had objected to the demarcation of the land border and continues to block it despite the formal agreement.[5] Negotiations on the Azov Sea are continuing but no progress has been made during the last years. Even more worrying is the fact that with the "ice age" in the Ukrainian-Russian relations after the Orange Revolution issues settled long ago were reanimated for political purposes. It is particularly Kyiv's plans for NATO accession and declaring the 1932-33 Great Famine in Ukraine a genocide of the Ukrainian people that irritates Moscow. In response to the new gas price, Ukraine threatened to raise the rent for the Russian naval base in Sevastopol and to reconsider the agreement on the Black Sea Fleet. In May 2006, the lower House of the Russian Parliament, or State Duma, sent the government an official inquiry "On the possibility of returning

---

5   "Ukraine threatens Russia with unilateral land border demarcation", *Johnson's Russia list*, no. 58 (2008), http://www.cdi.org/russia/johnson/2008-197-58.cfm (last accessed February 7, 2010).

Crimea to Russia". These developments confirm what Russian political analyst Dmitri Trenin wrote about the Ukrainian-Russian border in 2001: "The border issue as such is not a major problem, but it could become a symptom of the bilateral and even regional political dynamics."[6]

In Ukrainian politics and society the status of the border with Russia is a highly sensitive subject. The still not demarcated and relatively open eastern frontier is often associated in domestic public debates with Ukraine's vulnerable position vis à vis Russia as a former imperial centre, with the postcolonial status of the Ukrainian culture, with the dominance of Russian media and Ukraine's economic dependency. The supporters of the European integration have been pointing to the necessity of arranging Ukraine's eastern border according to Schengen standards in order to liberalize the border regime with EU countries. In 2008 the issue of the border with Russia emerged again in public debates after negotiations between Ukraine and the EU on a visa-free regime for Ukrainian citizens had been announced. The unresolved demarcation of the border and the readmission agreement between Russia and Ukraine, which has yet to be ratified by Moscow, are seen as main obstacles to a visa-free regime with the EU. Moreover, in order to reach this long-term goal Ukraine will have to introduce visas for Russian citizens (and face a symmetric policy from the Russian side). However, this would be difficult to implement given the intense cross-border traffic between two countries.[7]

The alarmist discourses of experts and politicians on the openness of the eastern border often contradict the nostalgic mood, the "common sense" and the pragmatic attitudes of the population. According to a survey conducted by the Centre for Peace, Conversion and Foreign Policy of Ukraine (CPCFPU) in 2001,[8] the overwhelming majority of Ukrainian experts (87.5%) assessed the transparent and not demarcated border with Russia negatively, as "a proof of Ukraine's exposure to potential risks." Of the experts 56.2%

---

6   Dmitri Trenin, *The End of Eurasia: Russia on the Border between Geopolitics and Globalization*, Moscow: Carnegie Moscow Centre 2001, p. 169.
7   Vitalii Martyniuk, "Are Schengen visas to be expected by Ukrainians?", *Ukrainska Pravda*, January 25, 2008, http://www.pravda.com.ua/news/2008/1/25/70432.htm (in Ukrainian) (last accessed February 7, 2010).
8   *Borders of Ukraine. Effective Policy Implementation*, Center for Peace, Conversion and Foreign Policy of Ukraine, http://cpcfpu.org.ua/en/projects/borders/papers/polls/document_1 (last accessed November 3, 2008).

voted for a "Ukrainian border equally protected along its entire perimeter", another 25.0% were for "the western border being more open than the eastern one." In contrast, the results of a general opinion poll demonstrated that the majority of Ukrainians (59.75%) see the transparent status of the eastern border "positively, as a proof of a special relationship between Ukraine and Russia," and almost half of the respondents (46.7%) would like to see the eastern border "more open than the western one." The rather successful political instrumentalization of this issue by Viktor Yanukovych in the 2004 presidential election campaign has shown that this attitude still persists, especially in the eastern Ukraine. By promising dual (Ukrainian and Russian) citizenship as well as to give the Russian language an official status and to simplify border crossing for inhabitants of the near border regions, Yanukovych could win the sympathies of the pro-Russian part of the eastern Ukrainian electorate.

The idea of federalisation and the threat of territorial separatism in the eastern regions was instrumentalized by the Party of Regions to challenge their political opponents in the 2004 presidential election campaign. This strategy, originally aimed against the Orange coalition, continued after the 2006 parliamentary elections: referring to the European Charter for Regional or Minority Languages ratified by the Ukrainian parliament, oblast and city councils in the east and south of Ukraine have declared Russian the "second official language" in their regions. This "parade of language separatism" as it was called in the Ukrainian media, coincided with the anti-NATO campaign in Crimea. Mass protests organized by pro-Russian political parties forced U.S. troops, which had been sent there to prepare for joint manoeuvres, to withdraw from Ukraine.

The instrumentalization of border issues in the internal political fight can be illustrated by the following example. In May 2006, the State Border Service of Ukraine announced its plans to dig a 400-km ditch throughout the length of the Russian-Ukrainian border in the Luhansk oblast in order to reduce the criminal activities of smugglers. The ditch was planned to be 1 meter wide and 1.5 meters deep. Being first of all an anti-contraband measure, this action had also a symbolic dimension. It was seen by many as a *de facto* demarcation of the Ukrainian territory. Not only was the reaction of the Russian media to this measure hostile and ironic; it also found little support in the Luhansk oblast, controlled by the Party of Regions. The engineering work has already started, but was interrupted due to the opposition of the Luhansk oblast council, which accused the Border Service of ignoring the law and the interests of the local farmers.[9] Like the "language separatism" and the anti-NATO campaign, the protests against the technical modernization of the border with Russia were aimed at undermining the Orange political forces and challenging President Viktor Yushchenko's political course.

The persisting political speculations on the problems of Crimea and the Black Sea Fleet by some political forces in Russia as well as the ongoing politicization of border-related issues in Ukraine demonstrate that the status of the Ukrainian-Russian border has still not been completely settled. Unlike any other part of Ukraine's border, it is connected with the legitimacy of the new Ukrainian state and as such still remains a "symbol of unfinished nation building".[10]

3.2 Border issues in the Ukrainian-Russian relations

Nation and state-building processes in both countries, problems of "divorce" and of building new relations based on principles of national sovereignty have shaped the context of the Ukrainian-Russian border issue since 1991. Particularly during Kuchma's era, it reflected the ambivalence in Ukrainian-Russian relations: a declared "strategic partnership" and persisting economic interdependency on the one hand and growing divergence in geopolitical orientations, accumulated tensions, mutual claims and negative stereotypes on the other.

According to Roman Szporluk, "it was of critical importance that Russia defined itself within the borders of the Russian Federation as it existed in Soviet times".[11] Indeed, the Kremlin never directly put forward territorial claims to

---

9 "Luhansk does not want to be separated from Russia by a ditch", 16.05.2006, http://www.portal.lg.ua/content/view/1518/282/ (in Ukrainian) (last accessed February 7, 2010).
10 Nataliia Parkhomenko and Oleksandr Sushko, "Borders of Ukraine: a symbol of unfinished nation building", *Dzerkalo tyzhnia*, July 14-20, 2001 (in Ukrainian).
11 Roman Szporluk, "Reflections on Ukraine after 1994. The Dilemmas of Nationhood", in: idem, *Russia, Ukraine, and the Breakup of the Soviet Union,* Stanford: Hoover Institution Press 2000, p. 332.

Ukraine, although unsettled and disputed issues were often used for putting pressure on Kyiv. At the same time, various parties and politicians (from the nationalists to the communists) did not hesitate to claim Crimea and parts of eastern Ukraine on historical and language-related grounds.[12] The Russian State Duma has often indulged in anti-Ukrainian rhetoric, and some politicians (nationalist hardliner Vladimir Zhirinovskii, Moscow Mayor Yurii Luzhkov, Communist Party leader Gennadii Ziuganov, Duma deputy and director of the Moscow-based Institute for the CIS States Konstantin Zatulin and others) built their careers on playing with anti-Ukrainian sentiments. In Ukraine, similar territorial claims to Russia (most often for Kuban as a former Ukrainian ethnic territory) have been only marginal and limited to radical nationalist milieu.

---

12   The modern history of the Ukrainian-Russian border goes back to 1917. After the February Revolution and the collapse of the Russian empire, the first Ukrainian government *(Tsentralna Rada)* claimed the autonomy of Ukraine; the related territory consisted of nine *guberniias* (administrative units of Tsarist Russia). The Provisional Government in Saint-Petersburg was ready to accept the autonomy of Ukraine, but reduced it to only five *guberniias*. An agreement could not be reached, and later the October events and the civil war in Ukraine changed the situation considerably. In the beginning of 1918, a delegation of the Ukrainian government participated in the Brest-Litovsk negotiations, where the Ukrainian National Republic and its territorial claims were recognized by the Central Powers. As a result, in 1918 the Ukrainian-Russian border, which corresponded in fact to the demarcation line negotiated between the German and the Russian sides, was defined according to the old administrative division of the Russian empire: the Ukrainian territory now consisted of the nine *guberniias,* as it had been claimed earlier by the *Tsentralna Rada*. But the Ukrainian claims for Taganrog, Kuban, and some parts of the Voronezh and the Kursk *guberniias* with predominant Ukrainian speaking populations were rejected. This demarcation line became the border of Soviet Ukraine with the Russian Federation in 1919 and was legitimized by the border agreement signed by Ukraine with the other Soviet Republics. In 1920 the Donbas industrial region under the jurisdiction of Ukraine was formed by adding some Russian territories (including Taranrog). After the USSR came into being in 1922 and with the beginning of the administrative-territorial reforms the border issue emerged again. The Ukrainian government claimed mainly some parts of the Kursk and Voronezh *guberniias,* inhabited by a Ukrainian-speaking population. As a result of the border dispute of the 1920s, Ukraine was granted approximately one third of the claimed territories, while the Taganrog and Shakhty districts went back to the Russian Federation. By 1927, the administrative border between the Russian Federation and the Ukrainian Republic was finally established; further small changes were made according to Soviet law. The only exception was the transfer of Crimea from Russian to Ukrainian jurisdiction in 1954. This transfer was initiated by Nikita Khrushchev to celebrate the 300th anniversary of the "unification of Ukraine with Russia" and was regarded as a symbolic act in the framework of the USSR as a united state. At the time, no provision was taken for the case of an possible dissolution of the USSR.

It took years for the Russian political elites to accommodate to the fact of Ukrainian independence, and the Ukrainian-Russian border issue remained open until the mid 1990s. Tensions on the territorial status of Sevastopol, a Russian military base in Crimea for more than two centuries, and on the future of the Black Sea Fleet were among the main obstacles for compromise, but they were basically settled in the second half of the 1990s. One of the reasons why Moscow was slow in dealing with the Ukrainian border issue was that "keeping the issue suspended, Moscow though it could use its eventual concession as a bargaining chip".[13] According to Trenin, it was the first Chechen war in 1994 that forced Moscow to cooperate with the central governments of the former Soviet republics, rather than with the separatist regions. The 1994 election of Leonid Kuchma as Ukrainian president on a pro-Russian platform made it easier for Moscow and Kyiv to reach a final agreement on borders. In 1996 the Ukrainian-Russian Subcommittee on State Borders was created. In 1997 the *Treaty on Cooperation, Friendship and Partnership* was signed by both presidents (Boris Yeltsin and Leonid Kuchma) and, despite the resistance of the nationalist opposition in the Russian Duma, ratified by both parliaments. This so-called Big Treaty recognized for the first time the territorial integrity of Ukraine *as an independent state* within the boundaries of the Ukrainian Soviet Republic. Also the Crimean knot seemed to be unravelled: Sevastopol remained Ukrainian territory with the military facilities leased to Russia, and the Black Sea Fleet was granted the right to stay there for twenty years.

In a sense, Ukraine was lucky with Yeltsin as the first president of Russia: elected on a democratic platform, Yeltsin stood for a peaceful dissolution of the "Soviet empire". The Big Treaty with Ukraine was a natural continuation of his foreign policy course and an important argument against the communist opposition. The opponents of the Big Treaty considered it a concession to Ukraine and a big political mistake. Thus, one of its main political opponents, Konstantin Zatulin, called it "the betrayal of the century".

While accepting Ukrainian territorial integrity in its present borders, Russia expected Ukraine to remain its ally and integrate fully into the CIS, which was seen in the 1990s as the main instrument for the re-integration of

---

13   Trenin, *The End of Eurasia*, p. 166.

the post-Soviet space. But in Ukraine, the Treaty was seen only as a point of departure. The CIS was considered by most Ukrainian politicians not as an integration project with prospects for the future, but rather as a transitional mechanism, an instrument for a "civilized divorce", according to the first Ukrainian President Leonid Kravchuk. For Ukraine, to have its borders legitimized by international treaties and equipped according to international standards was a necessary precondition for building an independent statehood. In this respect, the Ukrainian political elites always demonstrated a firm consensus, and Kuchma, despite his electoral pro-Russian declarations, continued his predecessor's policy aiming at strengthening the formal attributes of national sovereignty. Ukrainian diplomats lobbied for the full delimitation and demarcation of the border, but the Russians remained rather reluctant in this respect. For Russia in the 1990s, the border with Ukraine was not the issue of first priority: Russia had to cope with new borders of around 13,000 km in total length, some of them going through zones of military and ethnic conflicts. But the deeper reason was political rather than technical: Russia considered the borders inside the CIS "internal" and declined any discussions on demarcation as not compatible with "partnership relations". The transparency of the Ukrainian-Russian border (as well as a common jurisdiction over the issues of defence policy and national security) was seen during Yeltsin's presidency as a substantial part of this "partnership", also based on a common history and on close cultural identities.[14]

At the same time, official Russia's position on demarcation did not prevent the institutions in charge from strengthening the border regime against contraband, illegal migration and trans-border criminality; border guard services of both countries developed a successful cooperation in this respect.
Putin's presidency marked a pragmatic turn in Russian policy towards Ukraine. During his first term in office he favoured the development of bilateral relations and common projects led by economic interest. At the same time, since the end of the 1990s, Kuchma's government, isolated from the West due to a lack of democratic reforms and to scandalous corruption, be-

---

14   "The Legal Status of the Russian-Ukrainian Border: Problems and Prospects", *Borders of Ukraine. Effective Policy Implementation*, Center for Peace, Conversion and Foreign Policy of Ukraine, http://cpcfpu.org.ua/en/projects/borders/papers/security/document_2 (last accessed November 3, 2008).

came rather vulnerable to political pressure from Moscow. Under these conditions some progress has been achieved concerning the status of the Ukrainian-Russian border, but at the cost of concessions in another strategic issue – Ukraine's participation in the Russia-led project of regional integration, the *Single Economic Area Agreement*. In January 2003, the *Agreement on the State Border between Ukraine and Russia* was signed by Putin and Kuchma and ratified by both parliaments in April 2004. This agreement finalized the negotiations on the delimitation of the Ukrainian-Russian border (concerning its land part), a process which took around four years. However, the controversial issues of the delimitation of the Azov Sea and the Kerch Strait, which unexpectedly caused the Tuzla crisis in Ukrainian-Russian relations in October 2003, have not been settled by this agreement. Ukraine insisted on the delimitation of the Azov Sea by the water surface along the administrative border existing between Russia and Ukraine in Soviet times, while Russia opted for defining only responsibility zones on the coast and for the joint use of the Kerch Strait and Azov Sea by both countries. The same is true for the demarcation of the land part of the border, which was not even mentioned in the text of the document. Russia refused to discuss the problem of demarcation of the land part of the border, referring to its high costs and low priority. In Ukraine, the long-awaited agreement was not perceived as a sensation but merely as a symbolic gesture, connected to the opening of the "Year of Russia" in Ukraine.[15]

The Tuzla conflict, which broke out in October 2003 and turned into a serious crisis between the two countries, has shown how fragile the show case of "strategic partnership" is. In September 2003, Russia started some construction work with the aim of connecting the Taman peninsula with the Ukrainian island of Tuzla. From the Russian side, the project was justified by an ecological argument: it was supposed to protect the Taman sea coast from storms. Russians also claimed that until the 1920s Tuzla was not an island, but a spit connected with the Taman peninsula, and therefore originally Russian. The Ukrainian side referred to some documents confirming that the island was officially attached to Crimea some years before it became part of the Ukrainian territory in 1954. The conflict culminated in an exchange of hos-

---

15 See the comments in Ukrainian media, for example: Ivan Sahaidachnyi, "Sammit of neformaly", *Dzerkalo tyzhnia*, February 1-7, 2003 (in Ukrainain).

tile statements between Ukrainian and Russian officials and in an open demonstration of military force by both sides. It was the first time that Ukrainian border guards appeared on Tuzla Island, and a virtual border became real. After intensive consultations between the Ukrainian and Russian Ministries of Foreign Affairs the crisis was solved, and negotiations on the delimitation of the Azov Sea started.

The unexpected Tuzla conflict seemed to have done only little damage to the official Ukrainian-Russian "strategic partnership", but for the Ukrainian elites it was a shock revealing the lack of transparency in Ukrainian-Russian relations. It became evident that Russia remained an unpredictable partner and that Ukraine's international isolation, especially from the West, poses a serious problem.[16] While the immediate effect of the Tuzla crisis on Ukrainian society was not significant – according to opinion polls, only a quarter of the Ukrainian population felt provoked by Russia's behaviour – its political implications became visible one year later, during the Orange Revolution. When Moscow repeated the same pattern by supporting its candidate for the Ukrainian presidency at any cost, the opposition managed to mobilize public opinion in the country and abroad against the Kremlin's political intervention. And unlike in the Tuzla conflict, the West, and in particular the EU, did not remain indifferent observers in this critical moment.

In December 2004 the presidents of both countries signed an agreement for cooperation in the exploitation of the Azov Sea and the Kerch Strait (known as "Kerch Agreement"). This agreement confirmed the status of the Azov Sea as "inland waters" of both countries (defined already in the Border Agreement of 2003). This remains Russia's main achievement in the Azov Sea negotiations. The status of "inland waters" prevents third-country military vessels from entering the Azov Sea, something Russia wants to avoid in case Ukraine joins NATO. According to the Kerch Agreement the rights for exploiting the Kerch channel were assigned to a joint Ukrainian-Russian corporation. Russia agreed in principle to delimit the surface of the Azov Sea.

---

16 See the analysis of the Tuzla crisis consequences in the CPCFPU analytical paper no. 14, 2004, *Present challenges for Ukraine-Russia bilateral relations*, http://foreign policy.org.ua/eng/papers/archive.shtml (last accessed November 3, 2008). See also Taras Kuzio, "Behind the Tuzla Island controversy", *Kyiv Post*, October 30, 2003.

However, a final agreement on the delimitation of the Azov Sea and the Kerch Strait has not been achieved yet. The Ukrainian side defers to international practice and proposes to draw the border along the old Soviet administrative boundary. This solution would allow Ukraine to control the traffic to and from the Azov Sea and to profit from the main sturgeon fisheries. Probably even more importantly, there are also potential oil and gas fields at the continental shelf that are at stake in this dispute. The Russian diplomats, who understandably try to support their country's geopolitical and economic interests in this region, insist on a "combined" approach to delimitation. According to Ukrainian experts, the uncertain status quo is beneficial for Russia, which dominates in the Azov Sea due to its economic power.[17]

From the Ukrainian point of view, it is the status of "inland waters" that is the main obstacle for delimitation according to international law. Ukrainian diplomats thus suggest changing the status of the Azov Sea from inland waters to international waters and inviting international observers to the negotiations on delimitation. Changing the status of the Azov Sea would mean an amendment of the Kerch Treaty, and not surprisingly, the Russian attitude to this proposal was negative. In response to this dead end situation, the Ukrainian Ministry of Foreign Affairs is considering the option to appeal to the international court in The Hague. While Moscow accuses the Ukrainian diplomats of politicizing the issue, Kyiv suspects that Russia's reluctance and lack of interest in solving the problem is a means to prevent Ukraine's accession to NATO.[18] Meanwhile, the unsolved dispute damages not only bilateral relations but also regional economic development. The project of a bridge across the Kerch Strait, which was about to be launched in 2008, was suspended by the Ukrainian MFA until the delimitation issue is settled.[19]

As mentioned above, Russia has for a long time resisted the demarcation of the land part of the Ukrainian-Russian border. The Border Agreement of 2003 between Ukraine and Russia did not even mention the issue of de-

---

17 Volodymyr Kravchenko, "Rewriting the Bible", *Dzerkalo tyzhnia*, June 10-16, 2006 (in Ukrainian).
18 "Russia blames Ukraine for inactivity in establishing the border", *Ukrainska Pravda*, January 29, 2009, http://www2.pravda.com.ua/news/2009/1/29/88764.htm (in Ukrainian) (last accessed February 7, 2010).
19 "Ukrainian MFA suspended construction of a bridge to Russia", Novosti@mail.ru, October 21, 2008, http://news.mail.ru/politics/21.12098 (in Russian) (last accessed November 22, 2008).

marcation; otherwise, according to Russian Foreign Ministry officials, the agreement would have had no chance of being ratified by the Russian parliament.[20] From 2005 the Russian position seemed to soften in this respect. According to information from the Ukrainian TV Channel 5 from May 2006, the joint Ukrainian-Russian commission on demarcation was about to start its work.[21] The softening of Russia's position on demarcation can be explained by its new accent on "sovereignty" as the centre of its national doctrine. It assumes not only the ability to conduct its own political course, independent from the West, but also full control over economic resources and national territory. State borders that are demarcated, equipped according to the international technical standards and well controlled correspond to this doctrine of "national sovereignty". The crisis of the CIS and the bleak perspectives of other Russia-led integration projects have certainly contributed to Moscow's changing attitude in the demarcation issue. With the continuing disintegration of the post-Soviet space, "transparent borders" have become expensive and non-effective. The fact that the demarcation still has not started yet could be explained by Russia's intention to use it as a bargaining chip in the Azov Sea negotiations.[22] Meanwhile the Ukrainian MFA has declared that it might start the demarcation process unilaterally.[23]

Paradoxically, it was the Orange Revolution that forced the Russian political class to realize these irreversible changes in the CIS, and opened the way for demarcation of the Ukrainian-Russian border. At the same time, Moscow prefers to wait and does not rush to make concessions. It still hopes for political changes in Kyiv, which would remove the main proponents of Euro-Atlantic integration from the Ukrainian political scene and bring to power more compliant partners.

---

20 Volodymyr Kravchenko, "Stumbling block at the Ukrainian-Russian border", *Dzerkalo tyzhnia*, January 25-31, 2003 (in Ukrainian).
21 "Ukrainian-Russian border will get clear contours", http://5tv.com.ua/print/101/56/25994/ (in Ukrainian) (last accessed November 22, 2008).
22 Personal conversation with Oleksandr Sushko on June 8, 2006.
23 "Ukraine can draw the border with Russia on its own", *Rosbalt*, October 24, 2008, http://www.rosbalt.ru/2008/10/24/535676.html (in Russian) (last accessed February 7, 2010).

3.3 Cross-border cooperation

The ambivalent status of the border, which is symptomatic of the whole complex of Ukrainian-Russian relations, also affects the prospects for cross-border cooperation between the two countries.[24] The border between Ukraine and Russia crosses urbanized and densely populated territories. Moreover, it divides a socio-economic system, which only recently was still integrated, in particular concerning settlement and transportation. Cross-border cooperation has developed in post-war Europe as a solution for the specific problems of border regions with the aim to soften the dividing effect of international borders. Similarly, in the 1990s cross-border cooperation between the CIS countries was seen as a means of restoring broken economic ties and compensating for the psychological shock afflicted to the local populations by the breakup of Soviet Union. Particularly for the Ukrainian-Russian borderlands, with their developed economic ties and common cultural background, cross-border cooperation looked like an important prospect for regional development. However, during the 1990s, cross-border cooperation between Ukraine and Russia reflected contradictory political tendencies. On the one hand, both new independent states, afraid of economic and territorial disintegration, concentrated their efforts on gaining control over their borderlands and on enhancing the capacity of state institutions such as customs and state border services.[25] Cross-border initiatives and direct contacts of the border regions were sometimes viewed with suspicion by the centre. On the other hand, cross-border cooperation was considered by post-Soviet elites as an important pillar of the re-integration processes in the framework of the Eurasian Economic Community (EurAsEC) and later the Single Economic Area (SEA). "Cross-border cooperation" copied from the European model and adapted to the "Eurasian" space assumed important elements of supranational integration, such as harmonization of legislation, free trade, cooperation in security

---

[24] For more on cross-border cooperation between Ukraine and Russia see Tatiana Zhurzhenko, "Regional Cooperation in the Ukrainian-Russian Borderlands: 'Wider Europe' or/and Post-Soviet Integration?", in: I. Nagy and J. Scott (eds.), *EU Enlargement, Region-Building and Shifting Borders of Inclusion and Exclusion*, Aldershot: Ashgate 2006.

[25] Vladimir Kolossov and Alexei Kiriukhin, "Cross-border cooperation in the Russian-Ukrainian relations", *Politia*, no. 1 (2001), pp. 141-165 (in Russian).

and defence issues.

Efforts to develop cross-border cooperation had already been made in the early 1990s. In 1994, the *Council of the Border Regions of Russia and Ukraine* (which has also come to include Belarus) was created. It became the main organization lobbying in Moscow and in Kyiv for the interests of the border regions. In 1995 the *Agreement on the Cooperation of the Border Regions* was signed by the two governments. Since 2000, with the political rapprochement between Ukraine and Russia, prospects for cross-border cooperation projects seemed to be even more optimistic. Economic forums, bringing together businessmen and politicians from both countries became a regular practice, most often in Kharkiv and Belgorod. In February 2002, the Russian and Ukrainian presidents signed the *Program of interregional and cross-border cooperation* (2001-2007) in Dnipropetrovsk (in October 2006 it was modified and prolonged until 2010). For the first time, this document officially mentioned the possibility of establishing the Euroregions in the Ukrainian-Russian borderlands. In 2004 the Law on Cross-Border Cooperation was adopted in Ukraine. With the support of the *Council of Border Regions*, various projects were initiated in the border regions: the development of the near border infrastructure (transport routes, border crossing points), the common usage of water resources and the protection of the Siversky Donets River, an experiment on encouraging cross-border trade. In order to facilitate cooperation in education and research and to provide broader opportunities for students in both countries, the *Consortium of Near-Border Ukrainian and Russian Universities* was created in 2004. In 2003, heads of the Kharkiv and the Belgorod oblasts' administrations signed an agreement on the creation of the *Euroregion "Slobozhanshchyna"* – the first project of this kind on the Ukrainian-Russian border.[26] In April 2006, an agreement on the rules of border crossing for the residents of near-border territories was signed between the Ukrainian and Russian governments.

At the same time, with EU enlargement stimulating Ukraine's Euro-Atlantic aspirations and with the continuing disintegration of the post-Soviet space, the geopolitical context of the Ukrainian-Russian border has changed. Ukraine preferred to see cross-border cooperation with Russia rather prag-

---

26   For more on the Euroregion "Slobozhanshchyna" see next chapter.

matically – as complementary and subordinated to EU integration. Contradictory economic interests and divergent geopolitical orientations of both countries made the tasks of harmonization of tax and customs legislation, of prospective cooperation in high-tech industrial projects, and of coordination of security and defence policy very difficult. Euroregions as well as other regional bureaucratic initiatives remain on paper and serve mainly as a representative façade for the regional elites. Besides, the pervasive corruption is to be blamed for the systematic abuse of cross-border cooperation initiatives by organized criminal groups. Special privileges in the border regions (e.g. "free zone" and "special regime of investments") were used in Kuchma's Ukraine for massive contraband, money laundering and tax evasion. In 2005 Tymoshenko's government announced a large-scale campaign against corruption and contraband cancelling "free zones" and other regional privileges. The Customs Service was purged and special police units were formed in order to fight contraband. These measures of the new leadership were also symbolic and stressed its break with Kuchma's Ukraine, associated with corruption and "porous borders". However, the issue of corruption, contraband and cross-border criminal business remains unsolved.[27]

Some cross-border cooperation projects have been existing on paper for years, such as the plans for an international Ukrainian-Russian airport at the border halfway between Kharkiv and Belgorod, near the crossing point Hoptivka.[28] It is supposed to be used by both countries according to the model of EuroAirport Basel-Mulhouse-Freiburg. Supplemented by an exhibition hall, a business centre and entertainment facilities, the airport is expected to stimulate business and economic development in the region. However, this ambitious project lacks serious investors as well as political support from Moscow and Kyiv. A common project modernizing the transit highway Moscow-Crimea, which has already started, seems more realistic. It will improve the border crossing infrastructure and reduce waiting time at the border, particularly during summer holidays.

---

27 "Tarasiuk failed to see the border with Russia", *Ukrainska Pravda*, June 24, 2007, www.pravda.com.ua/news/2007/6/24/60724.htm (in Ukrainian) (last accessed February 7, 2010).
28 "Airport for two: international airport is going to be built at the Ukrainian-Russian border," *Korrespondent*, no. 17 (2005) (in Russian).

Not surprisingly, the political shock of the Orange Revolution also affected cross-border cooperation with Russia. The "cold war" between Moscow and Kyiv, the defeat of the "pro-Russian" Party of Regions and the priority of Euro-Atlantic integration for the new Ukrainian leadership did not contribute to its development. For example, Yevhen Kushnar'ov, the former governor of the Kharkiv oblast, who was the initiator of the "Slobozhanshchyna" Euroregion from the Ukrainian side, became notoriously famous by his attempt to play the separatist card in order to support Yanukovych and was eventually dismissed from his position.[29] With the symbolic defeat of "Eastern Ukraine" in the Orange Revolution the idea of cross-border cooperation with Russia also seemed to be compromised. The new governors of the east Ukrainian regions appointed by President Yushchenko were concerned with the consolidation of their power and did not give priority to relations with their Russian neighbours. The other way round, the Russian partners, who anyway had prejudices against the Orange Revolution, saw this lack of interest as an expression of the new political line.[30] Indeed, Kharkiv governor Arsen Avakov, who officially supports the Euroregion "Slobozhanshchyna", unlike his predecessor Kushnar'ov, has never yet officially visited Belgorod. In March 2006, the Party of Regions won the local elections in eastern Ukraine, thus partly restoring the "pre-revolutionary" status-quo. However, the political elites of eastern Ukraine are still divided and too much involved in the current political crisis to be able to develop strategic plans for cross-border cooperation with Russia.

Nevertheless, despite the turbulent relations between Moscow and Kyiv, some progress has been made in establishing an institutional framework for cross-border cooperation. When visiting Kyiv in December 2006, Vladimir Putin called for the development of cooperation between the border regions of Russia and Ukraine and the creation of favourable conditions for common business projects. In April 2006, the foreign ministers of Ukraine and Russia signed an agreement on simplifying border crossing procedures for border residents. People living close to the border and crossing it frequently are now able to do so at special checkpoints without fulfilling all formalities.

---

29 In January 2007 Kushnar'ov tragically died after a hunting accident.
30 Interviews with regional and state officials made by the author in Kharkiv and Belgorod in October 2005.

As it was mentioned before, Ukraine signed the agreement on re-admission with Russia, which is still has to be ratified by the Russian parliament.

On the other hand, Russia's economic sanctions and trade wars against Ukraine (such as limitations on the export of Ukrainian milk and milk products) certainly have affected cross-border economic relations. In June 2006, Russia tightened the border crossing rules for Ukrainian border residents who carry agricultural products to Russia for sale. Before, up to 500 kg was allowed according to the simplified rules; according to the new rules, an official registration and licence for export is required for such commercial activities.[31] The introduction of such measures (especially in June) threatened the survival of the small Ukrainian farmers and businessmen specialized in supply of agricultural products to the neighbouring Russian territory – and surely stimulated contraband.

Cross-border cooperation today is not about the "restoration of broken economic ties" and the preservation of the "common cultural space" as it used to be in the 1990s. Cross-border projects are usually shaped by the interests of the new economic actors and are entirely pragmatic. Still, even such pragmatic business projects remain suspended because of the political instability of Ukrainian-Russian relations, which makes private investors long for more security. Meanwhile, the institutions of cross-border cooperation (Council of Border Regions, Euroregions, etc.) serve as a representative façade for the regional authorities and hardly influence regional development. Ukrainian and Russian public and civil societies hardly participate in these institutions and are not included in decision-making.

3.4   Interests and activities of the EU and other international actors

In the first half of the 1990s the new post-Soviet borders were in the focus of the EU's concern mainly as sites of possible military and ethnic conflicts in the aftermath of the collapse of the Soviet empire. Both the US and the EU tacitly accepted the responsibility of Russia for the stability of the post-

---

31   "Russia made border crossing more difficult for Ukrainian citizens", *Ukrainska Pravda*, June 13, 2006, http://www2.pravda.com.ua/news_print/2006/6/13/42861.htm (in Ukrainian) (last accessed February 7, 2010).

Soviet space and its legitimate geopolitical interests in the "near abroad". Ukraine's borders (with the exception of the potentially conflict-prone Crimea) seemed to be unproblematic compared to the Caucasus and the Republics of Central Asia. Although the attitudes of the EU and the US to Ukraine as a newly independent state were rather different (Washington quickly realized the key geopolitical importance of this country in the region, while Brussels only saw it as a satellite of Russia), Ukraine's state borders were not a subject of special international attention.

But with the beginning of the following decade, several factors changed this situation and raised interest in the borders of Ukraine and the Ukrainian-Russian border in particular:

- First, the EU enlargement to the East – the accession of Poland, Hungary, and Slovakia in 2004 and Romania in 2007 turned Ukraine into a direct neighbour of the European Union. Ukraine's western border became an external EU frontier and, since 2007, a Schengen border. Thus, the security of Ukraine's state borders now directly concerns the EU.
- Second, the attitude of both the European Union and the USA to Russia has changed. Of course, Russia is still seen by Brussels as a strategic partner and regional power, and Washington considers it an ally in the issues of global security. However, the monopoly of Russian influence in the post-Soviet space is now challenged. The West was disappointed by Russia's ambivalent democratic reforms, and the war in Chechnya already undermined the geopolitical claims of Russia to be the only guarantor of security in the post-Soviet space. In the last years the gas conflicts with Ukraine, which threatened the energy supply of EU countries, and the war with Georgia in the summer of 2008 demonstrated that Moscow is ready to use all means from economic pressure to military intervention to preserve its domination of the post-Soviet space. It has become clear to the Western partners that Russia alone is not able to provide regional stability and that its power monopoly can be dangerous. Both the US and the EU now act more actively in the post-Soviet space and openly challenge Russia's positions. Support for the Orange Revolution in Ukraine, international isolation of Alexander Lukashenka's regime in Belarus and attempts to solve the Transnistrian conflict are

examples of active EU intervention in post-Soviet affairs. In this context the new post-Soviet borders are getting more international attention. For example, in 2005 the European Commission sent its monitoring mission to the Ukrainian-Moldovan border. Ukraine deliberately uses this to internationalize its border disputes with Russia (for example, during the Tuzla conflict in 2003, and in 2006 by suggesting the invitation of international experts to the Azov Sea negotiations).

- Third, new global threats related to international terrorism gave state borders new significance. Not only the US and the EU try to secure their external frontiers against potential terrorists and arms smuggling. State borders in other regions have become important sites for preventing the proliferation of technologies and materials that can be used for developing nuclear, chemical or biological weapons of mass destruction. In the eyes of Western security experts, the partly abandoned Soviet military facilities, unemployed specialists, political corruption and insufficient border controls in the post-Soviet countries create a potentially dangerous situation.
- Fourth, NATO enlargement into the post-Soviet space is another important factor. A NATO accession of Ukraine would certainly change the geopolitical status of its border with Russia. Already today Ukraine cooperates with NATO on issues of border management.

The above-mentioned factors have all contributed to the "Europeanization" and internationalization of the Ukrainian-Russian border.

The European Union

Political and economic stability in Ukraine is very important for European security. Given Ukraine's large migration potential, the impoverishment of the population, its position of a transit country and its ecological situation, the EU is interested in developing a selective cooperation with this country without committing itself too much to Ukraine's internal problems – a cooperation following the principle of "exporting stability without importing instability". The EU's "Country Strategy Paper 2002-2006" on Ukraine stressed that enlargement increases "EU awareness of 'soft' security threats from Ukraine, in the field of environment, nuclear safety, justice and home affairs (illegal migration, organised crime, money laundering, etc.) and public health".[32] Among the various risks connected to Ukraine as a neighbour the issue of illegal migration is one of the most urgent problems. Ukraine is the biggest transit country on the way of many migrant flows from the Middle East and China to Europe. No wonder that the issue of Ukraine's borders is of primary interest to the EU.

Since the beginning of their official relations (Partnership and Co-operation Agreement 1994) the EU and Ukraine have cooperated in Justice and Home Affairs (JHA); border management has become one of the focal points in this matter. Already the *Common EU Strategy on Ukraine* (1999) included concrete proposals about security policy, justice and internal affairs, and cooperation in border security issues in particular. The next document, the *Country Strategy Paper 2002-2006*, included the *National Indicative Programme 2002-2003* (total budget 115 million Euros) and set the support for institutional, legal and administrative reforms as the number one priority with a budget of 59 million Euros, including 22 million for border management. The Program for the next two years (2004-2006), with a total budget of 212 million Euros, allocated 60 million for JHA (including border management).[33] The aim of this part of the program was to improve the overall border management system in Ukraine, with a view towards facilitating movement of goods and people, while combating illegal activities. Not surprisingly, the main attention was given to the western border of Ukraine with the purpose of supporting the construction or refurbishment of key border crossing points, training programs for border guards, customs and other related agencies, assistance in the form of equipment and facilities, legislation development and implementation. These measures do not contradict the European aspirations of Ukraine because they are aimed at the modernization of a former Soviet frontier which was designed not for communication but for effective isolation. According to the EU-Ukraine Action Plan from 2005 additional financial assistance became available for Ukraine. The new European Neighbourhood and Partnership In-

---

32 Country Strategy Paper 2002-2006, National Indicative Programme 2002-2003, Summary, http://ec.europa.eu/comm/external_relations/ukraine/csp/index.htm (last accessed February 7, 2010).

33 National Indicative Programme 2004-2006. Available online at: http://ec.europa.eu/comm/external_relations/ukraine/csp/ip03_04_08.pdf (last accessed November 3, 2008).

strument (ENPI) was designed to support cross-border and trans-national cooperation between Ukraine and the EU States, and particularly aimed at developing the infrastructure of the border zones.

But national borders constitute a system, and the western neighbours of Ukraine realize this perfectly. No wonder they required the tightening of control at the border with Russia as a necessary precondition for negotiating a simplified border regime at Ukraine's western frontier. According to Marko Bojcun, "the EU enlargement has concentrated the minds of its decision makers on the need to work more closely with Russia and Ukraine in order to stem the tide of migration pressing on the eastern borders of the EU. What happens to migrants and refugees at the Russian-Ukrainian border is therefore an important concern of the European Union."[34] Understandably, the EU is interested not only in the western border of Ukraine, but in the whole system of border management, including the Ukrainian-Russian border.[35]

The aim of the EU in regard to the eastern border of Ukraine is to monitor illegal migration (transit migration in particular) and to reduce the migration flows by improving the efficiency of border control by training the personal and providing modern technical equipment. The *EU Action Plan on Justice and Home Affairs in Ukraine* (2001) identified as one of the main areas of cooperation the "development of a system of efficient, comprehensive border management (i.e. border control and border surveillance) on all Ukrainian borders and examination of possible participation of the State Border Service in a system of early prevention of illegal migration".[36] Following the EU enlargement in 2004 the *Revised EU-Ukraine Action Plan on Freedom, Security and Justice (2005)* became the main strategic document regulating cooperation between two parties in border management. It lists among the priorities the implementation of an integrated border management strategy, sup-

---

34 Marko Bojcun, "The European Union's perspectives on the Ukrainian-Russian border", http://eurozine.com/pdf/2005-01-12-bojcun-en.pdf (last accessed February 7, 2010).
35 For more on EU politics regarding the Ukrainian-Russian border, see Tatiana Zhurzhenko, "Europeanising the Ukrainian-Russian Border: from EU Enlargement to the Orange Revolution", *Debatte: Review of Eastern and Central European Studies*, no. 13 (2005), p. 137-154.
36 Official Journal of the European Union, March 29, 2003, http://eur-lex.europa.eu/LexUriServ/site/en/oj/2003/c_077/c_07720030329en00010005.pdf (last accessed February 7, 2010).

port for delimitation and demarcation of Ukrainian borders, improvements to border crossing points, basic and specialised training for staff involved in border management, etc.[37]

The EU has been supporting Ukraine's efforts to reform the Ukrainian State Border Guard Service in order to create a law enforcement agency that works as a professional body responsible for border management. For this purpose financial and expert assistance has been provided by the EU, as well as by some of its members (Germany, Austria, now also Poland). The most ambitious EU Programme is EUBAM (European Border Assistance Mission to Moldova and Ukraine, 2005-09) administrated together with the UNDP. More than one hundred customs and border guard experts from 22 EU member states contribute their expertise to enhancing the capacities of the border guard and custom services of both countries.[38] The EU also welcomed the Ukrainian initiative to reduce the number of border guards on the western border in order to strengthen control on the border with Russia. An increasing part of the border management budget is directed to Ukraine's eastern border. For example, in 2002 the EU decided to finance the technical modernization of the Sumy border guard division, which controls one of the longest and busiest sections of the Ukrainian-Russian border, and promised 2.5 million Euros for purchasing the required technical equipment.[39] In 2005-2006, the Border Guard Service was implementing a common project with the European Commission with a total budget of about 31.3 million UAH. In the framework of this project the Chernihiv, Kharkiv, Donetsk and Luhansk units of Border Guard Service received computers, transport vehicles and special equipment for border control. In 2006 another project was conducted with the support of the European Commission (total budget of 26 million UAH) aiming at the improvement of human resources management and personal training.[40]

Another aim of the EU is to encourage Ukraine to harmonize its legislation on migration with the EU requirements and to improve the country's ca-

---

37 Revised EU-Ukraine Action Plan on Freedom, Security and Justice: Challenges and strategic aims (2005), http://ec.europa.eu/world/enp/pdf/action_plans/ukraine_enp_ap_jls-rev_en.pdf (last accessed February 7, 2010).
38 See www.eubam.org (last accessed February 7, 2010).
39 "European Union helps Ukrainian border service and itself", *Den*, October 19, 2002 (in Ukrainian).
40 "State Border Service of Ukraine", http://www.pvu.gov.ua/inf/ums/ums3.htm#bss (last accessed November 3, 2008).

pacities to deal with illegal migrants and asylum seekers after detention. This kind of work has already started within the framework of the TACIS Program. With the support of the EU, refugee centres are now under construction for which the State Budget of Ukraine 2004 has allocated 5.3 million UAH. Such refugee centres are also planned on the eastern border (Kharkiv). In 2002 the State Border Service of Ukraine has also started the introduction of the "Arkan" data exchange system, which is designed for controlling goods, transport and persons crossing the state border. The "Refugee" information system (including a fingerprint database) is in the process of being implemented by the State Committee for Migration and Nationalities. These information systems create a basis for information exchange and cooperation between Ukraine's law enforcement agencies and Europol. In 2001-04 Ukraine adopted basic legislation on migration and asylum according to EU standards. As an instrument for limiting illegal migration, the EU encourages conclusion of readmission agreements between the member states and the third countries. Meanwhile, Ukraine already has longstanding bilateral readmission agreements with Hungary, Poland and Slovakia. In 2005 the EU made the EU-Ukrainian readmission agreement a prerequisite for Ukraine to be granted a simplified visa regime. This agreement was signed and ratified by the Ukrainian parliament in January 2008. For the first two years of the transitional period the agreement required Ukraine to receive back only Ukrainian nationals. But starting in 2010 Ukraine has to receive all of its nationals as well as stateless persons and nationals of other countries who have resided in or passed through its territory and who are expelled from the territory of the EU for reasons of unlawful entry or rejection of claim of asylum. This can create a problem for Ukraine because its readmission agreement with Russia has not been ratified yet by the Russian parliament; moreover, Ukraine has no readmission agreements with Belarus, Moldova and the countries of Caucasus region.[41]

---

41 Viktoriia Poda, "Europe expels all illegal migrants to Ukraine", *Kommentarii*, September 18, 2009 (in Russian).

The United States

The EU is not the only global actor interested in Ukrainian border security. In some respects EU policy coincides with the interests of the US, which after September 11 are especially concerned with the proliferation of weapons of mass destruction (WMD) and possible movements of terrorists across the borders. According to US experts, Ukraine might present a threat for global security because of its geographic location, the length of its state borders, the remnants of the military-industrial complex as well as "a weak economy and corrupt institutions".[42] The famous Kolchuga scandal (the Kolchuga radar system was sold to Saddam Hussein's Iraq in violation of international sanctions) revealed the fact that the Ukrainian government does not control arms exports. There are some US-sponsored programs supporting the professionalization of border control services in Ukraine. For example, with the sponsorship of the US European Command, the State Partnership Program has been supporting an exchange between the California National Guard and the Ukrainian Border Service for the last ten years.[43] In 2002, the US allocated $4 million to upgrade Ukraine's border with Moldova.

In 2005-06 the Ukrainian Border Service together with the US Department of Defence implemented a technical assistance project on the border with Moldova aimed at the detection of WMD and related materials (total budget about 20 million UAH). In 2006, a similar project, called "Prevention of proliferation of nuclear and other radioactive materials", was supported by the US Department of Energy (with a budget of about 10 million UAH). In 2006 the Ukrainian Border Service – with the support of the Pentagon – started a five-year program aimed at raising its capacity in the detection of WMD, nuclear and radioactive materials on the Black Sea and Azov Sea.

International organizations

As a member of the Partnership for Peace Program, Ukraine actively cooperates with NATO. In 2002 the NATO-Ukraine Action Plan was signed by both sides. Some components of this plan concern border security and non-

---

42   Katherina W. Gonzales, "Good Fences Make Good Neighbors. Ukrainian Border Security and Western Assistance", *Problems of Post-Communism*, vol. 51, no.1 (January-February 2004), p. 49.
43   Gonzales, "Good Fences Make Good Neighbors", p. 52.

proliferation of WMD. The Ukrainian Border Service takes an active part in the preparation for NATO membership and is adopting corresponding standards of border security, first of all at the new sections of the state border.[44] Yushchenko's government intensified cooperation with NATO and repeatedly expressed its determination to become a member of this organization. In 2006 the NATO Council announced open door politics towards Ukraine; in 2008 it confirmed the principal decision that Ukraine eventually will become a member of the Alliance. NATO membership is often seen in Ukraine as a counterbalance to Russian's influence; there are hopes that it will help Ukraine finally settle disputed issues of demarcation and delimitation of the eastern frontier and equip it according to international standards. At the same time, the discussion of a possible Ukrainian NATO membership irritates Moscow and certainly complicates Ukrainian-Russian relations. Turning the Ukrainian-Russian border into the frontier of a military bloc will significantly affect Ukraine's relations with the eastern neighbour. Moreover, it can become a serious factor for dividing and destabilizing Ukrainian society.

The International Organization for Migration (IOM) has also launched some projects connected to the Ukrainian-Russian border. As reported in the Ukrainian media, computer registration of all persons crossing the border at the Kharkiv-Belgorod section was implemented in April 2003 with the support of the IOM, which provided technical equipment and expert assistance. In the framework of the UN Development Program "Belarus, Ukraine, Moldova Against Drugs" (BUMAD-2), the Ukrainian Border Service purchased computers and control equipment. In 2005 a joint project with the OSCE studied the possibilities of implementing biometric control at Ukraine's borders.

And finally, with the increasing flow of illegal migrants and asylum seekers, human rights organizations such as Human Rights Watch and No Borders have started to pay attention to Ukraine's borders as well. In November 2005 Human Rights Watch published the report "Ukraine: On the Margins. Rights Violations against Migrants and Asylum Seekers at the New Eastern Border of the European Union" assessing Ukraine's capacity to deal with illegal migrants and asylum seekers and its human rights standards in this field.

---

44 "Euro-Atlantic integration", http://www.pvu.gov.ua/nato.htm (last accessed November 3, 2008).

To summarize, both the EU and the NATO enlargement, the growing pressure of illegal migration, the global threat of terrorism and the changing geopolitical balance in the post-Soviet space have increased the interest of the EU, the USA and international organizations in the Ukrainian-Russian border. Despite the fact that Ukraine is not considered even a potential member of EU, it is de facto involved in the formation of a new comprehensive system of European security. The Ukrainian-Russian border is becoming an important element of this system. While the EU is mainly interested in preventing economic crimes and controlling migration at this border, the interest of the US and NATO is more strategic and military, concentrating on the proliferation of weapons and on the threat of global terrorism.

Conclusion

The Ukrainian-Russian border has emerged as a new geopolitical reality resulting from the disintegration of the Soviet Union and the state building processes in both post-Soviet countries. The visions of the new border have changed during the last two decades from "open" and "transparent" to "normal" and "controlled", as the Commonwealth of Independent States failed to become a framework for re-integration of the post-Soviet space and priority in both countries was given to national sovereignty and territorial integrity. For Ukraine, the current status of the border with Russia is a symbol of unaccomplished nation building and seen as an obstacle to EU and NATO accession. At the same time, the unsolved issues of the delimitation of the Azov Sea and Kerch Strait and the demarcation of the land border were instrumentalized for the power struggle between Moscow and Kyiv, especially after the Orange Revolution. The threat of territorial claims is used as a means of political pressure in the Russian-Ukrainian debates over the gas price, the future of Crimea and the status of Sevastopol. Cross-border cooperation between Ukrainian and Russian regions, which originally was launched as a mechanism for partly compensating broken economic ties and helping overcome the trauma of the Soviet collapse, today faces numerous obstacles, mainly due to the unsettled political framework of the Ukrainian-Russian relations. Moreover, projects of cross-border cooperation today often serve only narrow group interests of the regional business and political elites; they fail to win public attention and to attract serious business investments. In general, as a result of the Orange Revolution and EU enlargement to the East the Ukrainian-Russian relations have been "Europeanized" and internationalized. Despite Ukraine's weak prospects for EU accession, the Ukrainian-Russian border has been integrated into the European security system. As a result, the "Schengen" standards of border management are applied not only to the western, but also to the eastern border of Ukraine.

4 Boundary in Mind: Discourses and Narratives of the Ukrainian-Russian Border

The Ukrainian-Russian boundary, a new political reality since 1991, represents a perfect laboratory for studying processes of border construction. Political parties, state bodies and civil societies in both countries; regional elites and politicians in Moscow and Kyiv; experts, local communities and ordinary citizens have been contributing to these processes in various ways. The geopolitical status of the border, a proper regime of border crossing and forms of border controls have been constantly contested and re-negotiated on international, national and regional levels. In this chapter, I would like to apply a constructivist approach and discursive analysis to the Ukrainian-Russian border as it exists today in the national imaginations of both post-Soviet countries. Constructivist approach does not mean that I consider this border "artificial" or "voluntarily imposed by politicians". The fact that a border is a construct does not mean that it is drawn arbitrarily; it usually has some prehistory, e.g. a former administrative division, a historical or ethno-linguistic boundary which can be used as a basis for delimitation. But neither these "objective" factors (usually disputed between the two sides), nor pure political will are sufficient for creating a border. The border has also to be drawn in the minds of the people. It is shaped by the political rhetoric of "national interests", the dominant discourses of nation and state building, the discussions about national identity and "geopolitical choice". Thus, national borders are constructed not only with border stones and fences, but also with words. In this chapter, I analyse the most representative discourses and narratives about the Ukrainian-Russian border in the two respective countries. I start with elaborating the approach to borders as a symbolic and discursive reality. In the next section I focus on two meta-discourses on the Ukrainian-Russian border – the discourse on security and the discourse on integration – and show how the perceptions and images of the common border reflect geopolitical fears and historical traumas in both countries. As a next step I reconstruct the pro-Russian, Ukrainian nationalist and pro-European discourses in Ukraine as well as the nationalist/imperialist and liberal discourses in Russia on the new border. In conclusion, a brief comparison between the official political discourses in Ukraine and Russia will be offered.

4.1 Soft borders, narrated borders

When talking about national borders, we usually have two dimensions in mind. Borders are a physical reality, which is marked on the territory by fences and crossing points and manifests itself by procedures of passport control. But borders are also a symbolic reality; they separate "us" from "them" and constitute a (territorial) community whose members are supposed to share a common memory, common symbols and historical myths. In the words of Klaus Eder, borders are hard and soft facts at the same time.[1] Hard borders are institutionalized borders, written down in legal texts, drawn on maps and demarcated on the territory. Soft borders are their pre-institutional basis: they are shaped by identities, representations and images of "us" and "them", memories and stories. In other words, soft borders are narrative constructs. However, they are not unimportant and secondary. Rather, "soft borders are part of the 'hardness' of borders in the sense that the symbolic power inherent in soft borders helps to 'naturalize' hard borders, to produce the effect of taking borders for granted."[2] Public debates and discourses on the legitimacy, status and the meaning of a border for a national community contribute to the process of its institutionalization.

The concept of "soft" or symbolic borders comes from social anthropology and draws on a constructivist approach to nation and nationalism. Fredrik Barth, a Norwegian anthropologist, outlined a new approach to the study of ethnic groups, focusing on the on-going negotiations of group boundaries and on the processes of inclusion and exclusion.[3] Emphasizing interaction in shaping the boundaries between groups, Barth refuses to see such groups as culturally isolated or bounded entities. Scholars of nationalism (such as

---

[1] Klaus Eder, "Europe's Borders. The Narrative Construction of the Boundaries of Europe", *European Journal of Social Theory*, vol. 9 (2006), no. 2, pp. 255-271.
[2] Eder, "Europe's Borders", p. 256.
[3] Fredrik Barth (ed.), *Ethnic groups and boundaries*, Boston: Little, Brown & Company 1969.

Deutsch, Gellner, Hobsbawm, Anderson and others) have criticized the primordialist view of the nation and stressed the role of education, communication and print media in nation building as a process led by the elites. Anderson's influential concept of the "imagined community" underlines the role of ideas, images, values and meanings that hold a national community together.[4] As an "imagined community" a modern nation is also inseparably linked to its territory. Political geographer Peter Taylor argued that the modern nation state as a "cultural container" has completely changed the nature of territory, especially the integrity of its borders. "From being parcels of land transferable between states as the outcome of wars, all territory, including borderlands, became inviolate".[5] According to Taylor, starting from the second half of the 19th century the state discovered the efficacy of the "cultural container": "State managers found the idea of nation very conducive to mobilize its citizens behind the state: from sponsoring national 'high culture' to feeding the people their national history in the schools and much more sinister nationalizing programs..., states hitched their destinies to nationalism."[6] A similar approach was developed by another geographer, Davis Harvey, who once called nationalism a "territorial ideology". Anssi Paasi in his influential study on the border between Finland and the Soviet Union / Russia[7] has demonstrated how Finnish national territory and particularly the Finnish-Russian border was constructed throughout the 20th century by a variety of instruments (geography and history textbooks, maps, tourist brochures and images of everyday life). Focusing on the processes of geopolitical, and more specifically, "territorial socialization", Paasi paid special attention to the ideas and representations of national territory, borders and borderlands.

Foucault's analysis of "discourse" and his notion of "formation discursive", along with the discursive analysis approach developed in linguistics, inspired some researchers (e.g. Ruth Wodak) in their studies of nations and

---

4   Benedict Anderson, *Imagined Communities: Reflections on the Origin and Spread of Nationalism*, London: Verso 1991 [1983].
5   Peter J. Taylor, "The State as Container: territoriality in the modern world-system", *Progress in Human Geography*, vol. 18 (1994), no. 2, pp. 151-62, here p. 155.
6   Taylor, "The State as Container, p. 156.
7   Anssi Paasi, *Territories, Boundaries and Consciousness: the changing geographies of the Finnish-Russian border*, London: John Wiley & Sons 1996.

nationalism.[8] This approach to a nation as a discourse, a system of cultural representations, a way of constructing meanings is shared by Stuart Hall and Homi Bhabha who see a nation as being constantly narrated and re-narrated. Various political actors and "discursive communities" produce texts and images of a given territory, region, nation. In addition, borders are narrated and constructed by "discursive communities" of various kinds. State institutions, local self-administration, business groups, NGOs, ethnic communities, political parties and organizations, media, academia, the education system, the all produce narratives and images which "make sense" of a border. Not only national states, but also international organisations (EU, NATO, OSCE, IOM etc.) and transboundary institutions such as the "Euroregions" influence and create border narratives. The discursive approach to national borders has been developed in critical geopolitics, particularly be Gerard Toal, who distinguishes between "high" and "low" geopolitics.[9] High geopolitics is the field of politicians and experts who create concepts they need to justify the foreign policy of a state. Low geopolitics is a set of geopolitical concepts, symbols and images in media, advertising, cinema, cartoons, etc. According to Vladimir Kolossov, the "geopolitical discourse is formed by both politicians and media, and by the system of education and mass culture. The functions and importance of boundaries in the life of state and society are a subject of discussion and compromise, the role of boundaries being differently interpreted by various social groups. Social representations of boundaries constitute an element of ethnic and political identity."[10]

In the context discussed in this chapter, the contribution of media to the construction of "soft" borders is particularly important. The media not only informs the public about what happens on the border, but also creates representations and images that are often highly emotionally loaded. Dangers and threats associated with the border, such as contraband, border criminality and illegal migration are packed into stories, reportages and interviews. Such narratives also reflect positive or negative stereotypes about the neighbours, ap-

---

[8] Ruth Wodak et al., *The Discursive Construction of National Identity*, Edinburgh University Press 1999.
[9] Gerard Toal, *Critical Geopolitics: The Politics of Writing Global Space*, University of Minnesota Press 1996.
[10] Vladimir Kolossov, "Border Studies: Changing Perspectives and Theoretical Approaches", *Geopolitics*, no. 10 (2005), pp. 606-632, here p. 625.

peal for more communication and cooperation across the border, or for more protection and control.

The approach to a border as a discursive construct is particularly applicable to the "young" post-Soviet borders, such as the Ukrainian-Russian one. This border, which gained international status only in 1991, still has to be demarcated on the territory. But the problem with the Ukrainian-Russian border is not just the absence of demarcation or the lack of technical infrastructure; it is also, in the words of Eder, its lack of "narrative plausibility". Indeed, to draw a border across this relatively ethnically and culturally homogenous territory has been a challenge, especially for the new Ukrainian state. Here, people living at the border usually do not see their neighbours on the other side as cultural "others". It is rather economic gradients and different welfare provisions which constitute "us" and "them" across the Ukrainian-Russian border.[11] Ukrainian identity in the borderlands with Russia is not exclusive and dominant, but flexible and situational, easily combined with Russian, "Slavic", regional or post-Soviet identities.[12] According to Klaus Eder, narratives, memories and the production of meaning inherent in "soft" borders are all the more important the more the institutional borders are not finalized and open to political struggles.[13] The recent tensions between Ukraine and Russia around the issue of Ukraine's NATO membership, conflicting official interpretations of Soviet history, and Gazprom's gas wars with Kyiv have sparked fierce discussions and even open conflicts on territorial and border issues which until recently had been considered basically solved.

---

11   This question is discussed in detail in chapter 3.1.
12   For the study of identities in the Kharkiv, Luhansk and Sumy regions cf. Peter W. Rodgers, *Nation, Region and History in Post-Communist Transitions. Identity politics in Ukraine, 1991-2006*, Stuttgart: Ibidem-Verlag 2008.
13   Eder, "Europe's Borders", p. 256.

4.2 Making sense of the Ukrainian-Russian border

There are two meta-narratives on borders: the first and most common presents them as sites of hostility and of potential if not open conflict. This "discourse of danger" describes the neighbour as a source of various threats, and the border itself appears as a dangerous zone generating criminality, permeable for illegal migrants, terrorists and new diseases. Such images and representations constitute the narrative of security. The second, less common and rather new narrative presents borders as sites of contact, cooperation and friendship, sometimes referring to old historical ties and cultural commonality, sometimes stressing mutual interests, common future, or both. This is the narrative of integration. These two narratives have been applied to the internal and external borders of the European Union. In mainstream political discourse, the internal borders between EU member states are usually endowed with positive symbols and connotations. For this purpose, historical narratives of former unity, forgotten regional identities and symbols of a common past are evoked. Dangers and threats (first of all, illegal migration and the export of criminality, but also terrorism, drug trafficking, ecological pollution and transmissible diseases) are associated with the external borders of the EU, for which, as a consequence, better protection and more control are necessary. However, quite often populist politicians and Euro-sceptics in many European countries apply the narrative of security to internal EU borders, calling to re-establish border controls inside the Schengen zone. This particularly concerns the new EU members of Eastern and Southern Europe, which are presented in this case as a source of troubles for their neighbours. Public fears of uncontrolled migration and of a flood of criminals invading from the East are reproduced by some media and exploited by populists of the right.

Both the narrative of security and the narrative of integration shape the Ukrainian-Russian border as a "soft fact". In this case, the two narratives often come into conflict as they reflect two different or even contradictory tendencies which refer to the "construction" and the "deconstruction" of a national border. The first tendency relates to the territorial and cultural consolidation of a new nation, the "nationalization" of the borderlands, the integration of their population and endowing the new borders with real and symbolic power. The second relates to the re-establishing of contacts between the border regions on a new institutional basis of cross-border cooperation, the reinvention of cross-border regions and the rediscovery of common regional identities. Various symbolic resources (historical narratives, memorial sites, calendars of national and regional festivities, etc.) are involved in these processes of (re-)narrating the border. They are often interpreted in different ways within the discourses of security and integration. While some symbols and narratives serve to claim the "national character" of the borderland territories and trace the border back into the past, others refer to a "common history" and shared cultural/linguistic religious identity which has to be preserved despite the new border. The "East Slavic civilization", the memory of the Second Wold War, the Soviet past, Stalinism and the Holodomor in their various political interpretations serve as discursive elements of the "soft" border between Ukraine and Russia.

The narrative of security has been central for the symbolic delimitation between post-Soviet Ukraine and Russia. The political elites of both countries see the nation state as having primordial national interests, which include the protection of borders and proper border management. The security discourse has been dominant in Ukraine since 1991, even under president Leonid Kuchma, who at various moments of his political career supported "Eurasian" integration projects and close cooperation with Russia. Ukrainian diplomats and foreign policy experts particularly lobbied for strengthening control on the border with Russia, emphasising the "dangerous openness" and the "lack of protection" from the East.[14] President Kuchma himself, who preferred to use the language of "friendship" and "close brotherly ties" when meeting with the Russian president, immediately picked up and effectively appropriated the discourse of security during the border dispute with Russia around Tuzla Island.[15] At the same time, the discourse of integration was represented in Ukraine not only by the left and pro-Russian, but also by the centrist part of the political spectrum and became marginalized only after the Orange Revolution. Viktor Yushchenko's presidency clearly marked a decisive shift to "se-

---

14   See for example: *Borders of Ukraine. Effective Policy Implementation*, Center for Peace, Conversion and Foreign Policy of Ukraine, http://cpcfpu.org.ua/en/projects/borders/papers/polls/document_1 (last accessed November 3, 2006).
15   For more details on the border conflict around Tuzla see in chapter 2.1.

curity" in the official political discourse. Dangers and threats associated with the eastern frontier now are not limited to border criminality and illegal migration, but also concern territorial integrity, national sovereignty and the geopolitical choice of Ukraine.

The Russian leadership, though not less concerned with the issue of border security, stuck to the integration narrative during the 1990s. The accent on "transparent borders" between the CIS countries was supposed to legitimize Moscow's ambitions for leadership in the post-Soviet space and reflected the uneasy adaptation of the Russian elites to the loss of imperial status. Even in the difficult 1990s Russian "national interests" were not limited to the protection of borders but also included the ability to exercise political and economic influence beyond them. Thus, "transparent" borders were seen as an instrument of post-Soviet integration. Under Putin, the official discourse has shifted from "integration" to "security", especially during his second presidential term. These new tendencies correspond to the concept of "sovereign democracy" and to Putin's efforts to strengthen the capacities of the Russian state. Controlled and well-protected borders belong to this vision of sovereignty. Thus, the Russian national interests in the "near abroad" remained as ambitious as before, but became more pragmatic and less bound to the idea of "integration".

It is worth noting that both meta-narratives of the Ukrainian-Russian border – the security and the integration narratives – originated to some extent from the European Union, which in the last two decades experienced unprecedented processes of supra-national integration and territorial enlargement. The projects of "post-Soviet integration" were inspired by the European integration and its attributes: cross-border and regional cooperation, transparent borders, a common market, etc. Some of the post-Soviet elites saw no reason why the former Soviet republics should not follow this way: given their common past and the still-existing economic ties and contacts between their populations they were "predestined to cooperate". Borrowing the discourse of EU integration served to legitimize integration projects in the post-Soviet space, which their critics saw as a restoration of the Soviet Empire. Despite the fact that, for various reasons, the European Union failed to become a model for post-Soviet integration, the discourse of integration and cross-border cooperation has been nevertheless used by the national and regional elites of Ukraine and Russia for creating a democratic image and winning political legitimacy.

This European discourse of integration at the Ukrainian-Russian border intertwines with the discourse of East Slavic unity and the common historical destiny of the East Slavic nations, particularly on the Russian side.[16] The affection to a pan-Slavist discourse can be observed in the politics of remembering and naming. In the late 1990s regular meetings of Russian, Ukrainian, and Belarusian politicians and businessmen were organized under the title *Sobor slavianskikh narodov* (Assembly of Slavic Peoples). During the 1990s the regional newspaper *Slavianka* was published in Kursk with the support of the Council of the Border Regions. The *Boian Award* was established by the Belgorod authorities "for the preservation of the spiritual space of the peoples of the Slavic world." In his speech during the parliamentary hearings on Russian-Ukrainian cooperation in 1999 Anatolii Zelikov, the head of the Belgorod Oblast Council, called the cross-border cooperation between the two countries the "healing penicillin for the Belovezh'e wound".[17] According to his words, the common celebration of holidays and historical dates together with the Ukrainian neighbours became a normal practice in his region. Another example is the International Festival of Slavic Culture which takes place in Khotmyzhsk (Belgorod oblast) every autumn; this is the village where, according to a legend confirmed by the local historians, important agreements were reached between the Russian and Ukrainian sides in the time of Bohdan Khmelnytskyi. Another highly symbolic place in the Belgorod region is Prokhorovka, the battlefield of the biggest tank battle of the Second World War.[18] Belgorod authorities proposed to use the museum and the cultural centre built in Prokhorovka as a basis for establishing an ecclesiastic academy to educate the chaplains for the armies of Ukraine and Russia. Accord-

---

16   A detailed analysis of the "East Slavic unity" paradigm is presented in chapter 1.2.
17   "Parliamentary hearings. Russian-Ukrainian cooperation: Dynamics of development after the Treaty on Friendship, Cooperation and Partnership between the Russian Federation and Ukraine" , *Analiticheskii vestnik*, no. 7: 119 (2000), pp. 34-36 (in Russian) http://council.gov.ru/inf_sl/bulletin/item/124/index.html. The metaphor of the "Belovezh'e wound" refers to the act of dissolution of the USSR. The agreement was signed by the leaders of the Russian Federation, Ukraine and Belarus on December 8, 1991, in Belovezhskaia Pushcha.
18   On the Prokhorovka Memorial as a new symbol of East Slavic Unity see chapter 1.2.

ing to Zelikov, the institution of army chaplains "in the absence of political instructors in the army could provide a powerful spiritual ground for Slavic unity."[19]

The discourse on security at the Ukrainian-Russian border also resonates with the EU discourse on the "soft threats" coming from the "new neighbourhood". Ukraine, Belarus, Russia as the new neighbours of the EU are seen as a source of organized crime, illegal migration and environmental threats. In Ukraine, with its ambitions for EU membership, there is a clear tendency to shift these threats further east to the border with Russia. These border-related anxieties[20] correspond with the (imagined and real) threats of authoritarian Russia and its neo-imperial ambitions, impeding Ukraine's democratic pro-European aspirations. The "open border" with Russia becomes a symbol of vulnerability of the Ukrainian state and nation. The EU discourse on security and the global discourse on international terrorism thus resonate with the Ukrainian fears of loosing national sovereignty and falling again under Moscow's control.

The Ukrainian-Russian border, being closely connected to the issue of national identity, is invested with a special symbolic meaning, which can be understood only in the Ukrainian "post-colonial" context. It is the lack of clear boundaries which makes Ukrainian identity problematic: Ukrainian culture, language, historical memory etc. first have to be separated from their Russian counterparts. The continuing coexistence of two cultures and languages in Ukraine, Ukrainian and Russian, is seen as a proof of an "unfinished nation-building", a weakness rather than an asset. Significantly, this "post-colonial condition" is represented not so much by the ethnic Russians, but by the Russian-speaking Ukrainians. Russian speakers, most of them living in the borderlands with Russia, embody the unwanted melange of Russian and Ukrainian cultures (*malorosiiska*, or "Little Russian" identity)[21] and the lack of clear cultural and linguistic boundaries. The symbolic status of the Ukrainian language and culture is reflected in the geopolitical status of the Ukrainian-Russian border. Thus, the non-demarcated and still-porous border with Rus-

---

19 "Parliamentary hearings".
20 In 2005 special disinfection measures were taken at the Ukrainian-Russian border against a supposed threat of chicken flu coming from China.
21 Riabchuk Mykola, *Vid Malorosii do Ukrainy: paradoksy zapiznilogo natsietvorennia*, Kyiv: Krytyka 2000.

sia corresponds to the ambivalence of Ukrainian national identity. No wonder that in Ukrainian political discourse the border with Russia is invested with the strategic meaning of protection from the dangerous openness to the East. From this perspective, the threats coming from the East include cultural influences from Russia and its continuing presence in the Ukrainian media space, the persisting dominance of Russian language undermining Ukrainian linguistic identity, the intervention of Russian business in Ukrainian economy and its massive participation in privatization. The presidential elections of 2004 demonstrated that these factors can be used as an instrument of political pressure on the Ukrainian authorities. Finally, after the Russian-Georgian war in the summer of 2008, the threat of military aggression (particularly in such a vulnerable region as Crimea) was added to this list.[22] Thus, strengthening national identity in post-Soviet Ukraine requires assuming a cultural and political distance from Russia. The new border is not only a symbol of, but also an instrument for the creation of this difference. And the ability to exercise real and symbolic control over the borderlands (through demarcation, development of technical infrastructure and international standards applied to the border regime) supports the legitimacy of the Ukrainian state and its "European" image.

It was the Orange Revolution in 2004 that significantly radicalized the perception of dangers and threats related to the Ukrainian-Russian border. For the part of Ukrainian political elite that supported the Orange coalition, Yushchenko's victory reasserted Ukraine's national sovereignty and independence from Moscow. The Russian political elite saw the Orange Revolution as a dangerous US-inspired plot, aimed at undermining Russia's influence in the post-Soviet space and threatening Russia's political order. The border with Ukraine thus turned for Moscow into a "front line" in the fight against the (highly exaggerated) threat of an "export of the Orange Revolution" into Russia. As the new Ukrainian leadership intensified its political ef-

---

22   Even prior to the Russian-Georgian war, the decision of Russia to suspend its adherence to the Treaty on Conventional Armed Forces in Europe (CFE) in summer 2007 was received negatively in Ukraine. Answering the question on possible threats in connection with Moscow's decision, Arsenii Yatseniuk, at that time foreign minister of Ukraine, said that Russia could in theory move its armed forces closer to the Russian-Ukrainian border, but expressed his hope that this would not be the case. (Radio Free Europe/Radio Liberty, *Newsline* July 16, 2007, http://www.rferl.org/content/article/1143911.html, last accessed February 7, 2010).

forts for the Euro-Atlantic integration of Ukraine, the common border has been increasingly perceived as an embodiment of geopolitical threats not only in Ukraine, but also in Russia.

One of the phobias of the Russian political elites has been to be isolated from the West and cut off from Europe by a *cordon sanitaire* consisting of the hostile "new neighbours". Ukraine's regional initiatives such as GUAM, the projects of the Baltic-Black Sea Association and the Ukrainian-Georgian alliance have been constantly irritating the Russian political elite. Ukraine's planned accession to NATO, which is seen in Moscow as an instrument for the containment and isolation of Russia by the West, is a particularly sensitive subject. For more than the Georgian case, Ukraine's possible NATO membership is seen as a direct threat to Russia's security, and Russian media actively spreads these fears among the Russian public. In this context the Ukrainian-Russian border is acquiring new connotations it has never had before: a "militarized zone", a "line of open confrontation" and a "new Iron Curtain".[23]

As one Russian military expert recently wrote, "the North Atlantic pact was created as a military coalition directed exclusively against the USSR. In the words of the first Secretary General of NATO Lord Ismay, spoken in 1956, the mission of the Alliance is 'to keep the Russians out of Europe'. Today, regardless of all the geopolitical shifts in Europe and the world, NATO remains an anti-Russian alliance. By bringing Ukraine into NATO, the West is in essence replicating the old division of Central Europe, most starkly manifest in the division of Germany and of Berlin. Only now the borders of the 'Western Zone' are being pushed up to Smolensk and Kursk."[24]

---

23   Tatiana Ivzhenko, "Ukraine creates Iron Curtain for Russia", *Nezavisimaia Gazeta*, 28.11.2008 (in Russian).
24   Mikhail Barabanov, "Ukraine, NATO and Russia", *Moscow Defence Brief*, no. 1(15) (2009), http://mdb.cast.ru/mdb/1-2008/item1/article1/ (last accessed November 6, 2009).

4.3 Narratives of the Ukrainian-Russian border

This section offers a reconstruction of the different political and public discourses about the role and the geopolitical status of the Ukrainian-Russian border in both countries. While some of them suggest alternative, even irreconcilable visions of the border, others interweave and complement each other.

Ukraine

In Ukraine, two alternative and mutually exclusive discourses on the border with Russia – the pro-Russian and the Ukrainian nationalist – mark the opposite poles of the political spectrum. While the pro-Russian discourse draws on the concept of "civilisation", pan-Slavism and anti-Western sentiments, the Ukrainian nationalist one operates with the notions of "ethnographic boundary" and "ethnic territory". However, the mainstream political discourse in Ukraine appeals to the pragmatic values of "security" rather than to cultural arguments, and builds on "European integration" as a strategic goal for Ukraine.

The pro-Russian discourse in Ukraine

The easiest task is certainly to reconstruct the discourse created by the pro-Russian political forces in Ukraine, i.e. the political parties and non-governmental organizations supporting a pro-Russian political orientation, economic integration with Russia and Belarus, and the status Russian as a state language. In this discourse the historical, ethnographic, and political legitimacy of the Russian-Ukrainian border is usually denied. The border is seen as an artificial construct, a false decision imposed by "selfish politicians" against the interests of the "ordinary people" who are interested in keeping the border open. In the geopolitical and historical context, the new border is interpreted as a tragic misfortune in the common history of the East Slavic peoples, as an arbitrary and artificial line dividing the single body of "Slavic civilisation". For example, the Christmas issue of the newspaper *Russkii Mir* (Russian World) published in January 2002 came out with the headline "We will live without borders." Another example: in the election program of the "Russian block" formed for the 2002 parliamentary elections the reality of the new border was denied to such an extent that the issues of regional and cross-border cooperation were not mentioned at all. They were absent in the program despite the fact that the document proposed European integration as a model for an inter-state union of Russia, Ukraine, and Belarus. Pro-Russian discourse is organized around the idea of ethnic and cultural similarities between Russians and Ukrainians which make a cultural boundary between the two nations irrelevant. Claiming the right to speak on behalf of all Ukrainians, the "Russian block" program stressed in 2002 that "by Russians we mean not only ethnic Russians and people coming from Russia, but all those who have their origins in ancient Rus".[25] The former member of the Ukrainian parliament, Vladimir Alekseev, who used to be a vice head of the parliamentary committee on information and freedom of speech, argued that most of Ukraine belongs to the "Slav-Orthodox civilization" and has a natural commitment to Russian cultural values. A voluntary incorporation of Ukrainians in Russian society (and vice versa) has been going on for centuries and the violent interruption of this process in 1991 caused the destruction of the common cultural and linguistic space. According to Alekseev, Ukrainian nationalism (and its most radical and traditionally anti-Russian Galician form) serves as an instrument of the West in the "war of civilizations". It seeks to "uproot" Ukrainians as a Slavic nation, to change their "cultural code," and to render them sheer raw material for the alien Western civilization.[26] According to this logic, the "real" cultural border does not separate Ukraine from Russia, but Galicia from the rest of Ukraine together with Russia.

Such versions of the "pro-Russian" discourse, which deny the legitimacy of the Ukrainian-Russian border in principle, have become relatively marginal among the Ukrainian political elite, especially after 2004. Among the parties represented in the parliament or having a chance to get into it, it is only the Party of Progressive Socialists (led by Natalia Vitrenko) that openly uses a pan-Slavist and pro-Russian rhetoric.

---

25 "What is the Russian Block and what does it try to achieve? Ideological questions", *Russkii Blok*, electoral brochure, 2002 (in Russian).
26 Vladimir Alekseev, "Vendée", in Nikolay Shulga et al. (eds.), *Dialog ukrainskoi i russkoi kultur v Ukraine*, Proceedings of the IVth International Conference, December 9-10, 1999, Kyiv: Foundation for the Support of Russian Culture in Ukraine, 2000, p. 66-75. (in Russian).

But in the Ukrainian public space, pro-Russian discourses are still present and particularly visible in Southern and Eastern Ukraine. Usually they are represented by the NGOs and small political parties (to name some of them: *Russkii Blok* / Russian Block, *Russkoe Dvizhenie Ukrainy* / Russian Movement of Ukraine, *Soiuz Sovetskikh Ofitserov* / Association of Soviet Officers, *Russko-Ukrainskii Soiuz* / Russian-Ukrainian Unity, *Soiuz pravoslavnykh grazhdan* / Union of Orthodox Citizens, etc.). Such organizations are often financially supported and instrumentalized by Moscow, which since the Orange Revolution has learnt to make use of civil society initiatives. However, Moscow's active attempts to consolidate the Russian organizations in Ukraine and to turn the "compatriots" into a political factor have led in the last years to increased competition and to contradictions between various organizations which claim to represent Russians in Ukraine.[27]

The main demands, arguments and rhetorical figures have not changed much in recent years. For example, the participants of a meeting organized by the Russian Block in Kharkiv in November 2008 (not by accident symbolically linked to Russia's new national holiday on November 4) asked the Ukrainian leadership to give Russian the status of the second state language, to introduce dual Ukrainian-Russian citizenship, to join the Single Economic Area and to keep the Russian Black Sea Fleet in Sevastopol as a factor "of stability and security of Slavic peoples".[28] Since 2006, when demonstrations against US military manoeuvres took place in Crimea, anti-NATO rhetoric, which dominates the pro-Russian discourse, has evoked narratives of "Ukrainian-Russian historic unity" and of a "war against the Eastern Orthodox Civilization". As the relations between Ukraine and Russia deteriorated, pro-Russian discourse becomes more radical, emphasizing the ideas of Russian nationalism and territorial separatism.

The pro-Russian discourse was used by Viktor Yanukovych and his team during the 2004 election campaign. In his program, Russian-speaking candidate Yanukovych promised to develop the cooperation and economic

---

27   On the internal struggle inside the pro-Russian movement, see for example: Igor Konovalov, "Chernomyrdin splits the Russian movement of Ukraine", *Russkaia obshchina*, http://russian.kiev.ua/archives/2006/0612/061215cp01.shtml (in Russian) (last accessed February 7, 2010).
28   "A meeting for Russian unity took place in Kharkov", *Novyi Region*, 05.11.08, http://www.nr2.ru/kharkov/204664.html (in Russian) (last accessed February 7, 2010).

integration with Russia and Belarus, to protect the rights of the Russian language and to simplify procedures of crossing the border with Russia. This message was addressed first of all to the population of the eastern regions and Crimea.

With the radicalization of the election campaign, as negative PR and dirty political technologies became a common practice used by both sides, the anti-Western, anti-American sentiments characteristic for the pro-Russian discourse were deployed by the Yanukovych team against his opponent, Viktor Yushchenko: on posters the latter was depicted as a cowboy riding Ukraine, or as Uncle Sam. While the pro-Russian discourse was pushed into opposition and even marginalized immediately after the Orange Revolution (as presented for example on the "Anti-Orange" web site),[29] it was partly rehabilitated in eastern Ukraine with the victory of the Party of Regions in the parliamentary elections of 2006.

Operating with the neo-traditionalist concept of "Slavic civilisation" rather than with the idea of modern national identity, the pro-Russian discourse inevitably carries nostalgic and even revanchist overtones. However, its persistence in the Ukrainian public space reflects real problems that Russians and (some) Russian speakers in Ukraine have with the "modernisation" of their identity and the still-open choice between various political options (a national minority, an amorphous linguistic/cultural group, a second titular nation). The pro-Russian discourse also reiterates the enormous difficulties of finding a new model for Ukrainian-Russian relations under the conditions of growing competition between Russia and the West in the post-Soviet space.

The Ukrainian nationalist discourse

On the other pole of the political spectrum, Ukrainian nationalist discourse ascribes a "natural" character to the Ukrainian-Russian border, as an essential line which separates two different ethnic and historical entities.[30]

---

29 http://www.anti-orange-ua.com.ru/; see also: Olga Filipova, "Anti-Orange Discourses in Ukraine's Internet: Before the Orange Split", in: Taras Kuzio (ed.), *Democratic Revolution in Ukraine: from Kuchmagate to Orange Revolution*, London: Routledge 2009.
30 Another element of the nationalist discourse is the representation of the Ukrainian-Russian border as a border between civilizations – between Europe and Asia. This

This narrative operates with the notions of an "ethnographic" or "ethno-linguistic boundary" and of "ethnic lands". One of the main premises of nationalism is that, ideally, "ethnographic boundaries" should coincide with the national/state borders.[31] The concept of "ethno-linguistic boundary" was widely used after World War I in the delimitation of international borders between the new nation states of East-Central Europe. In the Ukrainian context it was introduced by the famous geographer Stefan Rudnytskyi, who was the first to draw a map of the Ukrainian ethnic lands and to give their complete geographic, ethnological and economic description.[32] Other historians (Dmytro Bahalii) and geographers (Volodymyr Kubiiovych) have also dealt with the Ukrainian ethnographic boundaries at various occasions.

According to the Kharkiv historian Bahaliy, the ethnographic boundary of Ukraine in the east and south was formed in the process of colonization of the thin populated lands by the Ukrainian Cossacks and peasants from the 17th to the 19th centuries.[33] Initially rather "wild" and spontaneous, this Ukrainian mass colonization was used by the Muscovite state (and subsequently, from the 18th century, by the Russian empire) for securing its southern and western frontiers, and later became more and more regulated and controlled by the imperial centre. The ethnographic principle was used in the negotiations on the delimitation of the border between the Ukrainian Soviet Republic and the Russian Federation in the 1920s, but sometimes exceptions were made in favour of principles of territorial and economic rationality.[34] If the politics of *korenizatsiia* and the system of national councils (*soviety*) allowed the Ukrainians on the Russian side of the border to exercise territorial rights of self-administration in the 1920s,[35] later Soviet economic and migration politics led to a relative cultural and linguistic homogenization of the Ukrainian-

---

has a long historical tradition starting with the Ukrainian geopolitical writer Yurii Lypa (for more details see chapter 1.1.).
31 Vladimir Kolossov, "Primordialism and contemporary nation and state building", *Polis*, no. 3 (1998), p. 105 (in Russian).
32 See Rudnytskyi's essays "Overview of the national territory of Ukraine" and "The Ukrainian issue from the political geography point of view" (in Ukrainian) in: idem, *Chomu my hochemo samostiinoi Ukrainy?* Lviv: Svit 1994.
33 Dmytro Bahaliy, *Istoriia Slobidskoi Ukrainy*, Kharkiv: Del'ta 1993.
34 Vasyl Boiechko, Oksana Hanzha, Borys Zakharchuk, *Kordony Ukrainy: Istorychna retrospektyva ta suchasnyi stan*, Kyiv: Osnovy 1994.
35 Terry Martin, *The Affirmative Action Empire. Nations and Nationalism in the Soviet Union, 1923-1939*, Ithaca: Cornell University Press 2001.

Russian borderlands. Particularly ethnic Ukrainians in Russia were under pressure to assimilate, while Russians in Ukraine could keep their identity due to the *de facto* dominant status of the Russian language in the USSR.[36]

Although ethnic groups are usually bound to a specific territory, the "ethnographic boundary" is an ideal line projected on an area of mixed settlement. In fact, this concept corresponds to the primordialist vision of a nation, which assumes an ethnographic boundary as a historically unchanging attribute of an ethnic group. For example, according to the contemporary Ukrainian geographer Fedir Zastavnyi, Ukrainian ethnic boundaries "are rather stable and change mainly due to political factors, often with the use of military force and by ethnocide."[37] The ideal of congruence between national and ethnic boundaries can become dangerous when two neighbouring states (or ethnic groups striving for statehood) claim the same territory. Antony Smith introduced the special concept of "ethnoscape" to explain the deep emotional attachment that an ethnic community has with the territory it occupies.[38] This emotional attachment, which is often manipulated by right wing political forces, feeds the nationalist discourse on borders.

In the context of contemporary Ukrainian-Russian relations, the concept of an "ethnographic boundary" as an element of the Ukrainian nationalist discourse has several political implications. First, the fact that the borderlands of Ukraine in the east and south accommodate a significant share of Russians and Russian-speakers is seen as a threat for the unity of the nation and for its territorial integrity. The Russian speaking population is often presented as denationalised and uprooted, as an easy target of the pro-Russian, separatist propaganda. From this point of view, the eastern borderlands should be re-Ukrainized. Second, the Ukrainian ethnographic boundary in the east and south often does not coincide with the national border and runs through Russian territory. This means, that parts of the Ukrainian ethnic lands (in the Belgorod, Kursk, and Voronezh oblasts and in the Krasnodar region) now belong to Russia. Third, the shrinkage of the Ukrainian population on the Russian side of the border is explained by the "ethnocide" committed by the Soviet

---

36 For more on being an ethnic Russian in Ukraine see chapter 3.2. in this book.
37 Fedir Zastavnyi, *Ukrainski etnichni zemli*, Lviv: Svit 1993 (in Ukrainian).
38 Anthony Smith, *Myths and Memories of the Nation*, New York: Oxford University Press 2000, pp. 149-159.

power (political repressions, famine, deportations) and by forced assimilation. The lack of national consciousness among ethnic Ukrainians with Russian passports is considered a result of a forceful Russification imposed by the Soviet authorities. At the same time, the number of Russians on the Ukrainian side of the border has grown due to Soviet migration policy aimed at undermining the ethnic and linguistic homogeneity of Ukraine. Fourth, the existence of the "Ukrainian ethnographic lands" beyond the state borders of Ukraine is an argument in favour of a revival and consolidation of the Ukrainian minority in Russia. This minority has no political voice so far but in the future, it could become a new factor in the Ukrainian-Russian relations, counterbalancing the role of the ethnic Russians in Ukraine.

The argument of the "Ukrainian ethnic lands" is often used in response to the territorial claims to Ukraine voiced by Russian politicians. For example, the contemporary author Yurii Loza wrote: "Regions colonized by Ukrainians were left practically isolated from Ukraine and turned into a testing ground for creating 'a new community – the Soviet people'. There, millions of Ukrainians were deprived of their national character. On a territory which is almost 1/5 of the area of the contemporary Ukrainian state, after the cruel liquidation of the beginnings of Ukrainian schools and media in the early 1930s, Ukrainian life was frozen. Now only Ukrainian family names and the names of the villages recall that there also was a Ukraine. And who knows, maybe our neighbours would not make territorial claims, trying to seize *Kharkivshchyna* or Donbas from Ukraine, if in the adjacent Russian lands of *Belgorodshchyna* or Kuban Ukrainians would be conscious about their [Ukrainian] origins."[39]

Attempts to politicize the issue of the Ukrainian minority in the Russian borderlands regularly appear in the debates on the status of the Russian language in Ukraine. The argument that the cultural rights of Ukrainians are infringed in Russia (noting the absence of Ukrainian schools and lack of Ukrainian language media) is used against those Russian officials and politicians who traditionally express concerns about the future of the Russian language and culture in Ukraine. For example, in August 2000 the Ukrainian World Congress sent a special memorandum to Max van der Stoel, the High Com-

---

39 Yurii Loza, "The Ukrainian-Russian ethnic boundary, contemporary borders and territorial claims", *Pam'iatky Ukrainy,* http://www.heritage.com.ua/PU/istorija/doslidzhenja/index.php?id=21 (in Ukrainian) (last accessed February 7, 2010).

missioner for National Minorities of the Organization for Security and Cooperation in Europe (OSCE), regarding the situation of the Ukrainian national minority in Russia. The memorandum expressed deep concerns about the state of Ukrainian identity, language, and culture in Russia. "The attitude of the Russian authorities towards the Ukrainian minority can be characterized, in one sentence, as benign neglect, at the best, and outright hostility, at the worst. ... The reasons for this lamentable situation stem from the historical relationship between the Russian and Ukrainian peoples, and it is the legacy of the policy of the previous Russian and Soviet state authorities."[40] The number of Ukrainian schools, Ukrainian language and literature courses, and Ukrainian periodicals is too small for the Ukrainian minority in Russia which totals 4,400,000 according to the census of 1989. According to the memorandum, Ukrainians in Russia are also restricted in their confessional rights because the quasi-state Russian Orthodox Church has always been intolerant of any form of independence of the Ukrainian Orthodox or the Ukrainian Catholic Churches. The authors of the memorandum admit that the Ukrainian minority in Russia has not been very active in claiming its cultural rights, but the main reason for this reluctance is the memory of repressions and of the stigma of being labelled a "Ukrainian nationalist."

Ukrainian nationalist discourse presents the borderland territories of Russia as Ukrainian ethnic lands, as territories where ethnic Ukrainians (or their ancestors) who need help to preserve their identity live. This approach can be illustrated by a reportage published by *Ukraina moloda* in January 2003 about a tour through the Russian borderlands organized by the Ukrainian World Coordination Council (UWCC). The aim of the group of Ukrainian journalists, academics, and NGO activists was to learn about the everyday life and problems of ethnic Ukrainians living in the villages and cities of the Belgorod, Kursk, Voronezh, and Kuban regions. The tour participants made two important observations: first, "Russia still continues to live in the ideological-mythical space of the Soviet Union and carefully preserves the myth of a

---

40   UWC Commission on Human and Civil Rights, Memorandum to Max van der Stoel, OSCE High Commissioner on National Minorities regarding the situation of the Ukrainian national minority in Russia, http://ukrainianworldcongress.org/rights/sto00-08.shtml (2000). A subsequent letter was sent in 2009: http://www.ukrainianworldcongress.org/committees/KLHP/Lysty/To-VollebaekOSCE-31.07.09.pdf. (last accessed February 19, 2010).

Ukrainian-Belarusian-Russian united people".[41] And second, Ukrainians living in Russia hardly identify themselves with their ethnic motherland. If they are sympathetic to Ukraine, it is not because of their ethnic origins but rather because of the fact of their neighbourhood and family ties. Most of them do not speak Ukrainian and accept their Ukrainian identity only on the folkloristic level. The UWCC tour participants complained about the lack of a common language: "The notions of 'Ukrainian community', 'Diaspora', 'the rights of Ukrainians' have been replaced by 'cooperation between peoples', 'associations of friendship', joint Russian-Ukrainian sport competitions and exhibitions of achievements."[42] The authors of the reportage in *Ukraina moloda* put the responsibility for the low national consciousness of ethnic Ukrainians in the Russian borderland territories on both Russia and Ukraine. While Russia is accused of cultural assimilation and of neglecting the rights of national minorities, Ukraine is criticized for its lack of support (including financial help) to its compatriots across the border. According to the conclusion of Mykhailo Horyn, head of the UWCC, "organized Ukrainian life in the borderlands is in an embryonic state."

Thus, nationalist discourse usually describes the situation of the Ukrainian culture and identity in the Ukrainian-Russian borderlands as problematic. The unequal status of the Ukrainian language and culture, the underrepresentation of Ukrainians in Russia as a minority group devaluate Ukrainian-Russian cross-border cooperation projects. For example, the newly built Belgorod University attracts Ukrainian academics from Kharkiv through financial and status privileges, while its library does not subscribe to any Ukrainian journals.[43] The asymmetry in the "new" Ukrainian-Russian relations thus remains unchanged. According to this logic, there can be no real Ukrainian-Russian cross-border cooperation unless the rights of the Ukrainian minority in the borderland territories are respected and protected.

---

41 Yaroslava Muzychenko, "We arranged our small Soviet Union here", *Ukraina moloda* , January 21, 2003 (in Ukrainian).
42 Muzychenko.
43 Muzychenko.

The pro-European discourse

The pro-European discourse on the Ukrainian-Russian border relates its geopolitical status and border regime to the strategic goal of Ukraine's integration into the EU. The pro-European politicians and experts call for a "normal" border with Russia and argue that "Ukraine as a European country should have European borders". "European" in this context means first of all borders that are arranged according to European security standards. It is of course not the internal borders between the EU member states, but the external Schengen frontier which is taken as a model for the Ukrainian-Russian border. The discourse of European integration projects the "final choice", which has to be taken between a pro-Russian and a pro-European geopolitical orientation, on the level of "border politics." The central argument is that the "open" border with Russia is a serious obstacle to Ukraine's EU membership. The representatives of the pro-European discourse argue that the negative consequences of the EU and Schengen enlargements on the western border of Ukraine can be softened only at the expense of building a "normal" border with Russia. Ukrainian analyst Anatoliy Baronin wrote already in 2001, three years before the EU enlargement to the East: "It is possible that the model for the future Polish-Ukrainian border can be taken from already existing experiences with the Polish-German and Czech-German borders where the EU accepted 'softer' rules for travel between these countries. However, this type of arrangement would demand changes in the present character of Ukraine's borders with Russia and Belarus. Keeping the status of the presently open and practically unguarded Ukrainian-Russian border would exclude any possibility to successfully negotiate a more liberal regime on the Polish-Ukrainian border. Ukraine cannot have both borders open simultaneously. Ukraine will have to decide between Poland and Russia."[44] After the EU and Schengen enlargements to the East (2004 and 2009), the same argument has appeared in the discussions about the possibility of a visa-free regime between the EU and Ukraine. Despite improvements to the technical

---

44 Anatoli Baronin, "Border Closed?", *Central European Review*, vol. 3 (2001), no. 11, http://www.ce-review.org/01/11/baronin11.html (last accessed February 7, 2010).

infrastructure of the border with Russia, it is still perceived as one of the main obstacle for Ukraine to meet the requirements of the EU.[45]

Another euphemism used for the "European border" is "civilized border". As an attribute of a European nation the "civilized border" is opposed to an uncontrolled, "wild" border abetting criminality, and at the same time to the completely closed, impermeable Soviet frontier. "Civilized borders", as the Ukrainian Ministry of Foreign Affairs explains, are meant to be "transparent for people and business and closed for criminals": "Delimitated and demarcated borders shall become a reliable barrier in the way of illegal migrants and dealers, terrorists and international criminals. At the same time, they shall in no way restrict the right of the law abiding citizens and business circles of Ukraine and all its neighbours to continue visiting their relatives or doing business".[46] In practice, the concept of a "civilized border" has, of course, different consequences for the western and the eastern borders of Ukraine. On the western border, which used to be hardly permeable in Soviet times, it means simplification and standardization of border controls in order to facilitate economic and cultural contacts with Europe. On the eastern border, it rather means further restriction of the still relatively free movement of people for the sake of security and national sovereignty. Here, the unpopular policy of strengthening border controls has been officially presented in recent years as a necessity of having "civilized borders."

Therefore, the pro-European narrative declaring Ukraine's European future as a strategic goal stresses the need to further institutionalize the border with Russia. It does not refer to the concept of "ethnographic boundary" and operates instead with the pragmatic concept of "security". But by assuming explicitly or implicitly that Ukraine belongs to "European civilisation" and that its eastern border should be arranged accordingly to this geopolitical reality, it directly challenges the pro-Russian discourse, which operates with the idea of "East Slavic" or "Orthodox civilisation".

---

45 Vitaliy Martyniuk, "Are Schengen visas to be expected by Ukrainians?", *Ukrainska Pravda*, 25.01.2008, http://www.pravda.com.ua/news/2008/1/25/70432.htm (in Ukrainian) (last accessed February 7, 2010).
46 "Priority Tasks of the Ministry of Foreign Affairs of Ukraine for 2005", http://www.mfa.gov.ua/mfa/en/publication/content/1182.htm (last accessed February 7, 2010).

Russia

In Russia, the issue of the new border with Ukraine is represented in a broad spectrum of discourses, from traditional imperialism to ethnic Russian nationalism. However, both imperialist and nationalist discourses are closely interrelated and easily transformed into one another; sometimes they are even performed by the same institutions and personalities. One of the reasons for this is that the identity of post-Soviet Russia still oscillates between a "nation state" and an "empire" ("civilization"). Olga Malinova, in her study of "empire" in contemporary Russian political discourses, introduced the quite useful distinction between "imperial" and "post-imperial" Russian nationalism.[47] If imperial nationalists indulge in nostalgia and foster projects aimed at restoring the empire, the post-imperial nationalists accept its collapse, but strive for preserving Russia's dominance in the region and consider the imperial heritage an important political resource. The distinction suggested by Malinova roughly corresponds with the differentiation between imperialist and nationalist discourses on the Ukrainian-Russian border which I propose here: while the first assumes a single Slavic civilisation and common cultural and religious space, and considers the border artificial, the second draws on the fact of Ukraine's political independence and sees it as an agent of Western influences and a rival in the region. Liberal discourse that welcomes the pro-European aspirations of Ukraine and sees them in line with Russian national interests is rather marginal.

The imperialist discourse

(Neo-)Imperialists consider Ukraine (with the exception of its western regions) an integral part of the Orthodox / East Slavic / Eurasian civilization. They assume that Ukrainians share cultural and religious roots with Russians and have been united by centuries of "common history". This view was developed in Russian historiography during the 19th century and became an indispensable part of the emerging Russian identity. Indeed, Ukraine was not just a "normal" colonial subject of the Russian empire but a constitutive element for the metropolitan centre. Alexei Miller showed that in the 19th century,

---

[47] Olga Malinova, "Empire as a subject of contemporary Russian political discourses", in: Alexei Miller (ed.), *Nasledie imperii i budushchee Rossii*, Moscow: NLO 2008, pp. 59-102 (in Russian).

among various alternatives there was also the influential project of a "Big Russian nation" which included Ukrainians and Belarusians.[48] Soviet historiography starting from the 1930s re-narrated the unity of Russia, Ukraine and Belarus as the history of three East Slavic peoples having common historical roots in the Kievan Rus.[49] The post-Soviet version of the Russian imperialist discourse emphasizes Orthodox religion as a spiritual basis of the Russian-Ukrainian unity, which provides cultural and historical ground for projects of political and economic (re-)integration. The persistence of this narrative in Russia during the 1990s and its popularity among both the elites and the population made it difficult to think about Ukraine in terms of a separate nation with legitimate borders. While Russia officially recognized the national sovereignty of Ukraine in its present borders, the implicit condition of such recognition was its "geopolitical loyalty" to the former imperial core.[50] Therefore any movement of the Ukrainian leadership in Western direction has been met in Moscow with great suspicion. From the anti-Soviet Solzhenitsyn[51] to the Soviet-nostalgic Prokhanov[52] and the neo-Eurasianist Dugin,[53] the re-emerging Russian empire is hardly imaginable without Ukraine. The historical and cultural unity of Russians and Ukrainians has been constructed in opposition to the West, particularly to the USA as a superpower. Therefore Ukraine with its Euro-Atlantic aspirations is seen as a potential traitor of

---

48   Alexei Miller, *The Ukrainian Question: Russian Nationalism in the 19th Century*, Budapest: CEU Press 2003, p. 26
49   Zenon E. Kohut, "History as a Battleground: Russian-Ukrainian Relations and Historical Consciousness in Contemporary Ukraine", in: Frederick Starr (ed.), *The Legacy of History in Russia and the new states of Eurasia*, Armonk, NY: M.E. Sharpe 1994, pp. 123-145; Serhy Yekelchyk, *Stalin's Empire of Memory. Russian-Ukrainian Relations in the Soviet Historical Imagination*, Toronto: University of Toronto Press 2004, pp. 93-96.
50   Dmitri Trenin, *The End of Eurasia: Russia on the Border between Geopolitics and Globalization*, Moscow: Carnegie Moscow Centre 2001, p. 165.
51   Aleksandr Solzhenitsyn, "How should we rearrange Russia?", *Komsomolskaia Pravda*, September 18, 1990 (in Russian).
52   Aleksandr Prokhanov, *Simfoniia piatoi imperii*, Moscow: EKSMO, 2007; see also: "Russia: The Fiction and Fact of Empire", http://www.rferl.org/content/Article/1072489.html (last accessed February 7, 2010).
53   Aleksandr Dugin, *Osnovy geopolitiki: Geopoliticheskoe budushchee Rossii*, Moscow: Arktogeia-Tsentr 1999.

"Slavic unity" – a pattern which corresponds to the historical clichés of Ukrainians in Russia as "banderists" and "mazepists".[54]

The (neo-)imperial discourse is to a large extent congruent with the pro-Russian discourse in Ukraine (discussed above) and actually induces and legitimizes the latter. The renaissance of imperialist ideologies and projects in Russia during the 2000s is an obvious fact that can be explained by the trauma of the Soviet collapse, the limited success of the liberal reforms and the disappointment of the Russian elites with their Western partners. Post-Soviet Russia is increasingly imagined as an independent centre of power exercising political and cultural dominance in its former imperial space. In this context, Ukraine is perceived as belonging to the "first circle" of this space, as the closest to Moscow geographically, culturally and historically. Therefore the border with Ukraine, in the imperialist imagination, cuts through a single body. Characteristically, open claims to parts of Ukrainian territory could be rarely found in neo-imperial discourse. It is not the Ukrainian-Russian border itself which is at stake there, but its geopolitical status. Will it be an internal boundary running through the single "Slavic civilization" and common economic space, something like an administrative line rather than a political boundary? Or will it cut Russia from Europe and put up a "Huntingtonian wall" – a new Iron Curtain along the very borders of Russia?

The nationalist discourse

If imperialist narratives in Russia put an emphasis on the unity of the two Slavic peoples and see their future perspectives in re-integration and a close political alliance – thus downplaying the issue of the border – nationalist narratives depart from the fact that Russia and Ukraine are divorced for good. Nationalist discourse presents Ukraine mainly as an agent of external influence, as a Trojan horse of the West in the traditional zone of the Russian geopolitical interests. Russian nationalist discourse can be illustrated by the publications and speeches of Konstantin Zatulin, Director of the CIS Institute in Moscow and deputy of the Russian parliament. According to him, "the independence of Ukraine is a hard challenge to Russia, which lost its most

---

54 Andreas Kappeler, "Mazepisten, Kleinrussen, Chochols: Die Ukrainer in der ethnischen Hierarchie des Rußländischen Reiches", in: idem, *Der schwierige Weg zur Nation: Beiträge zur neueren Geschichte der Ukraine*, Vienna: Böhlau 2003.

promising, i.e., European part and dwindled to the size of the Russian Federation. If independent Ukraine is not bound by a special Union with Russia its newly acquainted statehood will unavoidably be placed on an anti-Russian foundation. Ukraine then turns into a second Poland, an alien cultural and historical project that Russia will have to learn to deal with."[55]

In the Russian nationalist narratives the border between Ukraine and Russia is usually presented as artificial, arbitrary and illegitimate. The fact that Moscow accepted Ukraine's political independence in its present borders is seen by nationalists as a tragic failure of Russian diplomacy and a result of its inability to defend national interests. Unlike Ukrainian nationalists, Russian ones rarely use the concept of ethno-linguistic boundary and refer to a historical justification of their territorial claims to Ukraine. The "historical rights" of Moscow to the Ukrainian territories go back to the Russian empire and its territorial possessions or even further, to the Kievan Rus, which is claimed to be the first "Russian state". Crimea is a classical case for territorial claims based on historical arguments. Characteristically, at the occasion of the "Day of Inclusion of Crimea into Russia" Konstantin Zatulin in his address to the Russian community of Crimea praised the colonization policy of Katherine the Great: "The integration of the ancient Crimean peninsula, which in the past was a fragment of the Greek Eukumena and the cradle of Russian Orthodoxy, into a great European state, put an end to centuries of barbarism and robbery on this territory. Crimea ceased to be a horror for the neighbouring peoples, and turned into the Crimea we all love and will never give up in Russia."[56] In this document Crimea is claimed to be "Russian" due to its ancient ties with Byzantium and Eastern Christianity, and also by virtue of the civilizing efforts of the Russian empire in the 18th century.

Finally, the protection of the rights and interests of the "compatriots" (ethnic Russians and the Russian speaking population) is another argument supporting Russian territorial claims to Ukraine and the right of Moscow to interfere in Ukrainian affairs. Indeed the new national borders are constructed

---

55 Konstantin Zatulin, "Fight for Ukraine: What is next?" *Rossiia v globalnoi politike*, no. 1 (2005), http://www.globalaffairs.ru/numbers/12/3638.html (in Russian) (last accessed February 7, 2010).
56 Zatulin, Konstantin, "Address at the Occasion of the 222nd Anniversary of the Inclusion of Crimea into Russia", *Ofitsialnyi sait K.F. Zatulina*,19.04.2005, www.zatulin.ru/index.php?&section=publications&id=135 (last accessed February 7, 2010).

in Russian nationalist discourse to a large extent by raising the issue of the Russians and Russian-speakers in the near abroad (this is the case in relations not only with Ukraine, but also with the Baltic countries and to some extent, with Kazakhstan). Since the majority of the Russian Diaspora in the "near abroad" is of Soviet origin and live in the cities, Russian nationalists, unlike their Ukrainian counterparts, rarely use the concept of ethno-linguistic boundary[57] and instead refer to the great contribution of Russians to Ukrainian economy, science and culture. Russians in Ukraine are presented as victims of forceful Ukrainization who have to be saved and protected; their cultural and political loyalty to Russia as a "homeland" is seen as an important leverage in Moscow's Ukrainian politics.

Thus, territorial claims to Ukraine are typical for Russian nationalists. Such claims are articulated by Yurii Luzhkov, Vladimir Zhirinovskii, Konstantin Zatulin and some other politicians. Zatulin took an especially radical anti-Ukrainian position towards the ratification of the Big Treaty between Ukraine and Russia in 1999. In his official position as director of an academic institution and as a leading Russian expert on Ukraine, he repeatedly questioned the legitimacy of the Russian-Ukrainian border. According to his arguments, Ukraine never existed historically in its contemporary borders: The historical roots of the Ukrainian-Russian border are an illegitimate construct resulting from German occupation of Ukraine in the First World War and thus imposed by foreign armed forces. Being re-established in 1991 this border has forcefully cut millions of ethnic Russians off from their homeland. The agreement on the borders between the Russian Federation and the Ukrainian Soviet Republic was legitimate only within the framework of the USSR, and, according to Zatulin, it was a crime against Russian national interests to accept the existing border under the new conditions.[58]

After the Big Treaty was signed and then ratified by both parliaments, and a compromise on Sevastopol was found by Ukraine and Russia in the early 2000s, the radical discourse of territorial claims was marginalized. In his

---

[57] However, the fact that the Russian authorities do not welcome attempts of Ukrainian self organization in the border regions and regard any cultural activity that goes beyond folkloristic festivals with suspicion shows that they understand the potential force of the "ethno-linguistic" argument.

[58] Konstantin Zatulin and Aleksandr Sevastianov, "Russian-Ukrainian Treaty: Fraud of the Century", *Nezavisimaia Gazeta*, January 26, 1999 (in Russian).

later publications Zatulin argued that his idea was to use the "border issue" as a bargaining chip to force Ukraine to safeguard the interests of Russia in Ukraine, ensuring, first of all, guarantees for the Russian language and the rights of the Russian-speaking population.[59] Already with the Tuzla crisis, however, and especially during and after the Orange Revolution, the radical nationalist discourse of territorial claims reappeared and gained popularity in Russia.

The Russian imperialist discourse of "Slavic unity" and the nationalist discourse of territorial claims to Ukraine can be differentiated only analytically; in reality they are hardly separable and both are based on the assumption of Ukraine as an "artificial" and "unnatural" state formation. If the re-integration scenario and the "East Slavic" alliance does not work, and there is a danger of turning Ukraine into a hostile agent or even a geopolitical rival of Russia, then the option to support federalization, territorial split and separatism would be considered by both imperialist and nationalists as a legitimate alternative.

However, they are also aware that Ukraine's disintegration would threaten Russian security; therefore territorial claims are still more an instrument than a goal in itself (a situation that can change in the future). In one of his recent publications Konstantin Zatulin, speculating about the perspectives of Ukrainian-Russian relations after the change of political leadership in Kyiv resulting from the presidential elections in 2010, formulated the conditions of a "new deal" that would be acceptable for Moscow: the Ukrainian government should guarantee the neutral status of Ukraine and give up its NATO ambitions, introduce a federative system, grant Russian the official status as the second state language and keep the Russian-Ukrainian Orthodox unity in the framework of the Moscow Patriarchy. In exchange Moscow would abstain from territorial claims and the territorial split scenario for Ukraine.[60]

---

59   Konstantin Zatulin and Aleksandr Sevastianov, "Friendship, cooperation, partnership between Russia and Ukraine: Two years after the fraud of the century", *NG - Sodruzhestvo*, January 31, 2001 (in Russian).
60   Konstantin Zatulin, "The Strategy of Russia in Relation to Ukraine", *Ofitsialnyi sait K.F. Zatulina*, 22.05.2009, http://www.zatulin.ru/index.php?&section=publications&id=407 (in Russian) (last accessed February 7, 2010).

The liberal-democratic discourse

In the early 1990s, as the leading part of the Russian political elite saw the future of both Russia and Ukraine in "Europe", the anticommunist, critical attitude towards the "Soviet empire" and the agenda of pro-Western reforms shaped the basis for liberal-democratic discourse on the Ukrainian-Russian relations. Russian liberals and democrats assumed that the heritage of imperial politics was left behind and the newly born nations can build their relations from zero, on the principles of respect and mutual interests. True, Russian liberals occasionally expressed some reservations against Ukrainian independence: for example, "Foreign Minister Andrei Kozyrev spoke out in support of Russian minorities in the New Abroad, and St. Petersburg Mayor Anatolii Sobchak warned against 'forced Ukrainization' of the Russian minority and a potential territorial conflict".[61] However, in the 1990s the loss of Ukraine and its geopolitical consequences were not fully realized by the liberal part of the Russian elites, who were preoccupied with domestic problems.

As Ukraine was reluctant to join Russian integration initiatives, and the traditional dominance of Moscow in the post-Soviet space has been increasingly challenged by Western partners, the liberal-democratic discourse on Ukrainian-Russian relations became marginalized. Even liberal and Western-minded Russian politicians resorted to elements of imperial thinking in their approach to the problems of the post-Soviet space. Characteristically, in 2003 in the wake of parliamentary elections Anatoly Chubais, one of the leaders of the Union of Right Forces and the father of market reforms in Russia, put forward the concept of a "liberal empire". In his interpretation Russia as a liberal empire is not endowed with the cultural and religious attributes of Slavic and / or Orthodox unity and rather represents a regional analogy of the "American Empire". Chubais saw its mission in protecting the interests of Russian business in the "near abroad" and in promoting principles of freedom and democracy in the former Soviet republics. The liberal empire should be based on the "common economic space" of Russia, Ukraine, Belarus and Kazakhstan, while the integrity of national borders and other democratic principles would

---

61 Aurel Braun, "All Quiet on the Russian Front? Russia, Its Neighbours and the Russian Diaspora", in: Michael Mandelbaum (ed.), *The New European Diasporas: National Minorities and Conflict in Eastern Europe*, New York: Council on Foreign Relations Press 2000, pp. 81-159.

be respected.[62] Despite its liberal rhetoric, this project assumed the "natural leadership" of Russia and the legitimacy of its special economic and political interests in the post-Soviet space. While the idea of Russian foreign policy in service of Russian big business reflected the common vision of the new capitalist class in Russia, the critics of Chubais from the liberal camp doubted that the Russian model of democracy would be attractive to its neighbours.[63]

After the Orange Revolution, one could observe a revival of the liberal democratic discourse on the role of Ukraine and Ukrainian-Russian relations. For a rather short period, Ukraine had become a model of democratic transformation for Russia in the eyes of some Russian liberals. Boris Nemtsov, who visited Kyiv in the most dramatic days of the Orange Revolution, solidarized with its leaders and openly supported Viktor Yushchenko. As he explained in an interview, he believed that both Ukraine and Russia should turn towards Europe and become democratic societies.[64]

The liberal democratic discourse avoids the essentialization of ethnic, cultural or religious factors, which allegedly separate/divide Ukraine and Russia, and does not address the issue of the common border. Instead, universal (European) values and principles of democracy, human rights, national sovereignty and the strategic goal of integration into/cooperation with Euro-Atlantic institutions are seen as the basis for Ukrainian-Russian relations. However, the liberal democratic discourse was extremely marginal in Russia against the background of the prevailing negative attitude to the Orange Revolution as a "foreign plot" aimed at undermining Russia's influence. And naturally enough, this discourse could not survive the disappointment caused by the internal conflicts, the persisting corruption and the failure of the political reforms in Ukraine.

---

62 Anatoly Chubais, "The Mission of Russia", official speech at St. Petersburg State Engineering Economic University, *Polit.ru*, 25.09.2003, www.polit.ru//dossie/2003/09/26/625760.html (in Russian). (last accessed February 7, 2010)
63 Malinova, "Empire as a subject", p. 82.
64 "The Orange Revolution is an alarm bell for Russia", interview with Boris Nemtsov, *Boris Nemtsov: Personalnyi sait*, 28.01.2005, www.nemtsov.ru/?id=703960 (in Russian) (last accessed February 7, 2010).

4.4 Official discourses on the Ukrainian-Russian border

The official discourse of Kuchma's presidency combined the "strategic goal" of European integration with a Ukrainian-Russian "special partnership". This ambivalence was reflected in the official rhetoric on the border issue: Kuchma's administration paid lip service to "national security" and the necessity of "civilized borders" while at other occasions promoted cross-border cooperation and integration projects for the "border of friendship" (a metaphor used for the Ukrainian-Russian border in the official discourse). These two discourses – European choice and East Slavic partnership – were successfully combined and instrumentalized by Leonid Kuchma until they got into open conflict before and especially during the Orange Revolution. With the victory of Viktor Yushchenko in the 2004 presidential elections the "security" and "civilized border" discourse became dominant. The new Ukrainian leadership criticized its predecessor for Ukraine's "porous borders" (pointing first of all to the "problematic" borders with Russia and Moldova) and demonstrated compliance with the border policy of the EU. At a press conference in Strasbourg in February 2005 Yushchenko promised that the year 2005 would be devoted to the final settlement of the Ukrainian borders and their modernization according to EU standards in order to stop contraband traffic and illegal migration. The Ukrainian leadership declared its will to cooperate with the EU in settling the Dniester conflict. In April 2005, during his visit to Chisinau, Yushchenko proposed a peace plan, backed by the EU, which featured free elections in the separatist Dniester region under international supervision and an increase of the number of Ukrainian peacekeepers in the conflict zone. Responding to the concerns of both the EU and the US, the Ukrainian government showed its determination to strengthen the relatively open Ukrainian border with Transnistria, a notorious site of smuggling and arms trafficking. Similar concerns and ambitious plans to stop contraband on the border with Russia were expressed by prime minister Yulia Tymoshenko and Petro Poroshenko, in 2005 the head of the Council for Security and Defence.

At the same time, with the political defeat of the "pro-Russian" eastern Ukrainian regional elites in 2004 the discourse of Eurasian integration and cooperation with Russia became marginalized. Although the issue of cross-border cooperation was discussed in March 2005 during the meeting of Viktor

Yushchenko with Vladimir Putin, the agenda of security and national sovereignty dominated, particularly on the Ukrainian side. President Yushchenko called on his Russian colleague "to devote 2005 to solving outstanding border issues – in particular, in the Sea of Azov and the Black Sea, as well as in the Kerch Strait."[65] Later on, with the growing tensions in Ukrainian-Russian relations, this aspect of "border politics" and this type of discourse became predominant in the official Ukrainian rhetoric, represented by the Presidential Administration and the Ministry of Foreign Affairs. In some regions of eastern Ukraine the victory of the Party of Regions in the 2006 local elections partly rehabilitated the traditional discourse of "friendship and cooperation" with Russia. However, the ongoing political crisis in Kyiv and the conflicts among the regional elites made it difficult for them to think and act strategically; the discourse of "integration" became less popular than ever.

The official discourse in Yeltsin's Russia paradoxically combined liberal-democratic and neo-imperial elements. Independent Ukraine was officially recognized in its contemporary borders, but under conditions of close partnership, which included cultural closeness, a geopolitical orientation towards Moscow, economic integration and the transparency of the common border. However, already under Yeltsin the rhetoric of "transparent borders" was combined with a "security" discourse, which supported the reorganization and modernization of the Russian Border Service. With Putin's presidency (especially during his second term) the discourse of "national interests" started to prevail in Ukrainian-Russian relations. At the same time, in contrast to the anti-communist ideology of Yeltsin's regime not only Slavic identity and Orthodox religion but also the partly rehabilitated "common Soviet history" was seen as a uniting factor. The Orange Revolution in Ukraine clearly showed the limits of the Russian neo-imperialist narrative based on the paradigm of "East Slavic unity" and facilitated its transformation into a nationalist one. Thus, since 2005 it has been the discourse on "pragmatism" and "national interests" that dominated in Russian official rhetoric regarding Ukraine. Moreover, in the context of the permanent gas conflict, Yushchenko's plans for NATO accession and Kyiv's refusal to extend the term of Russian naval base

---

65 "Putin, Yushchenko Pledge Partnership, End To Disputes", *Radio Free Europe/Radio Liberty*, 20.03.2005, http://www.rferl.org/content/Article/1058044.html (last accessed February 7, 2010).

in Sevastopol, Ukraine is often presented as an agent of foreign influences at the western border of Russia, an unfriendly neighbour state which tries to "exploit" Russian natural resources and profit from Russia's traditional paternalism.

The lack of progress in post-Soviet integration projects, the inefficiency of CIS institutions and the new accent on "sovereign democracy" as the centre of Russia's national doctrine have rendered the concept of "transparent borders" with the former Soviet republics obsolete. What is now at stake for Moscow is not the "transparency" of the Russian borders with the CIS countries, but their geopolitical status, the ability to exercise political and economic influence in its neighbourhood. While Yushchenko's administration was clearly determined to join NATO, these plans faced the unambiguously negative reaction of Moscow. From the Russian point of view the perspective of Ukraine's accession to NATO destabilizes the very foundation of Ukrainian-Russian relations as Ukraine's territorial integrity was recognized under the implicit condition of its geopolitical neutrality. Therefore, the question of legitimacy of the Ukrainian borders has entered the official discourse in the last years. During a closed meeting of the Russia-NATO Council, Vladimir Putin made some comments which were widely interpreted as a potential claim to Crimea and Eastern Ukraine in case Ukraine joins NATO. According to the Russian newspaper *Kommersant* Putin said: "Ukraine is not even a state! Part of its territory belongs to Eastern Europe, and another part of it they received from us as a gift!"[66] Similar interpretations emerged as in May 2009 while visiting the renovated grave of the White General Denikin, Putin suggested reading "Anton Denikin's diary, specifically the part about Great and Little Russia, i.e. Ukraine. He says nobody should be allowed to interfere between us. This is only Russia's right."[67] These words of Putin, uttered in a non-official situation, but made public by Archimandrite Tikhon who accompanied the Prime Minister, fed numerous speculations in Ukraine. At other occasions, however, Putin convinced German journalists, who asked about possible parallels between South Ossetia and Crimea, that "Crimea is not a disputed territory" and that "Russia has recognized the borders of contempo-

---

66 *Kommersant*, April 7, 2008.
67 "Putin: 'You certainly should read Anton Denikin's diary'", *Kyiv Post*, May 24, 2009, www.kyivpost.com/nation/42032 (last accessed February 7, 2010).

rary Ukraine long ago." He added that any speculations about Russia's claims on Ukrainian territory should be seen as a provocation.[68] However, the very fact that the issue of Ukraine's territorial legitimacy has been raised again in Russian official political discourse although it had been settled in the Big Treaty more than ten years ago indicates serious problems in the relations of two countries.

Conclusion

National borders are not only a physical, but also a symbolic reality; they are drawn on the territory but also in the people's minds. As they are shaped by collective memories, stories, representations, stereotypes and images of "us" and "them", borders are discursive constructs. Not only their location, but their status and regimes of crossing are justified by historical, linguistic and political arguments. Borders as constructs are re-negotiated by the neighbouring states, and also by various political forces and different social groups, not only in international treaties and in the official political discourse, but also in media, school textbooks, through cultural events and commemorative ceremonies.

Since 1991, the Ukrainian-Russian border has been subject to a process of symbolic construction, which reflects problems of post-Soviet nation building, state efforts to nationalise borderlands, to assimilate them as integral part of the national territory and to invest new borders with real and symbolic power. At the same time, establishing contacts between Ukrainian and Russian border regions on the new institutional basis of cross-border cooperation, reinterpreting regional histories and re-inventing new borderland identities invest the new border with alternative meanings of "friendship" and a "common past". Therefore, two competing discourses – the discourse of security and the discourse of integration – shape the perceptions and images of the common border both in Ukraine and Russia. In Ukraine, the pro-European discourse dominates, connecting the issues of national security, sovereignty and European integration perspective with the status of the

---

68 "V. Putin: Crimea is not a disputed territory", *RBK-Ukraina*, August 30, 2008, http://www.rbc.ua/rus/top/2008/08/30/421476.shtml (in Russian) (last accessed February 7, 2010).

Ukrainian-Russian border. While pro-Russian and pan-Slavist discourses have been marginalized (although they are still present on the regional level), the Ukrainian nationalist discourse, which draws on the concepts of ethnic identity and ethnographic boundary, is gaining popularity in Ukrainian society. As for Russia, the visions and narratives of the border with Ukraine belong to neo-imperialist as well as nationalist discourses, fluctuating between the denial of legitimacy of the Ukrainian borders and claims for a common Slavic civilization, on the one hand, and the image of a new "iron curtain" separating Russia from Europe, on the other.

5 "Slobozhanshchyna": Re-inventing a Region in the Ukrainian-Russian Borderlands

The new border between Ukraine and the Russian Federation has been constructed not only from above by the state building policies of Moscow and Kyiv. It has also been shaped from the ground up, by the actual border regions of both countries, which have played an important role in defining the border regime and influencing the mode of cross-border relations. The Ukrainian and Russian regional elites bring their economic interests and political visions into these processes; they interact with each other, use the opportunities of the new border and adapt to its constraints, re-interpret the local history and try to legitimize cross-border cooperation. In this way, the geopolitical reality of the new border becomes one of the crucial factors in "region-making" and in re-inventing the regional identity.

Two neighbouring border regions – the Kharkiv oblast (Ukraine) and the Belgorod oblast (RF) – provide a particularly illuminating example of contradictory tendencies in the Ukrainian-Russian borderlands. First, these two oblasts became initiators of cross-border cooperation between Ukraine and Russia in the early 1990s; they see themselves as pioneers whose experience can be used by others. New institutional forms of cooperation (such as the Euroregion) offer at least a potential opportunity to adopt "European" instruments of cross-border cooperation beyond the EU borders. Second, Kharkiv and Belgorod demonstrate an interesting combination of (remaining) cultural closeness and (growing) social and economic differences between the two neighbouring territories. The differences in the political regimes, in the geopolitical orientations and paths of transformation taken by Ukraine and Russia further complicate the context of cross-border cooperation. Third, the historical and ethno-cultural peculiarities of these territories (as a frontier zone colonized during the 17th century) provide symbolic resources for re-inventing the regional identity. *Slobidska Ukraina* (Sloboda Ukraine), a historical region, which in the 17th century had covered parts of contemporary Kharkiv, Sumy and Poltava oblasts in Ukraine as well as portions of Belgorod, Kursk and Voronezh oblasts in the Russian Federation, has become a popular subject of historical scholarship. Meanwhile, the historical name "Slobozhanshchyna" has been appropriated by the Kharkiv oblast as a cultural brand and used for the new Euroregion established by the Kharkiv and Belgorod oblasts in 2003.

This chapter addresses the cross-border cooperation between the Kharkiv and Belgorod oblasts, particularly in the framework of the Euroregion "Slobozhanshchyna". What are the opportunities and limitations of the Euroregion in the post-Soviet context? Can this institutional form be filled with the contents of real projects? Can a potential cross-border region profit from both European and "Eurasian" integration processes? The chapter also explores mechanisms of discursive construction of the regional identity, the ambiguity of the historical "Slobozhanshchyna" myth and the multiplicity of its political uses. How do Kharkiv elites represent their region's role in Ukrainian history and in Ukrainian-Russian relations? In what way is the history of the region interpreted and instrumentalized in the process of constructing regional identity and creating a new ideology of Ukrainian-Russian cooperation? How does regional history become a symbolic resource in "region making"? This chapter starts with a brief overview of the theoretical debate on regionalization and "region making" in Europe and its relevance for the post-Soviet context. The next two sections address the cross-border cooperation between Kharkiv and Belgorod and the dilemmas of the "Slobozhanshchyna" Euroregion. The following section deals with the history of Slobozhanshchyna (Sloboda Ukraine) and its contemporary political and public uses. In the conclusion I return to the question of the possibility of a Euroregion in the absence of "Europe".

5.1 Constructing the region in the post-Soviet borderlands: the theoretical context

In Ukrainian politics "regionalism" plays a rather ambivalent role. On the one hand, the European discourse of regionalization as an instrument for promoting democratization, good governance and competitiveness is widespread in Ukraine. As a country striving for EU membership, Ukraine needs a comprehensive systemic reform which would delegate a substantial share of political power and cultural autonomy to the regions. According to Ukrainian and foreign experts, cross-border cooperation projects between Ukrainian regions and their western neighbours face serious problems: Ukrainian regions "lack sufficient autonomy from the central power" and "differ substantially from similar institutions in the EU".[1] On the other hand, inter-regional disparities over historical background, political culture and geopolitical orientations are usually seen as a serious challenge for nation and state building. "Regional cleavages" play an important role in Ukrainian politics.[2] During the Orange Revolution, the threat of "regional separatism" in eastern Ukraine was instrumentalized by the political opponents of Viktor Yushchenko. Concerned with the problem of territorial integrity and facing growing regional polarization since 2004, Kyiv has observed the ideas of federalism and of regional autonomy with suspicion. When in 2006 some eastern Ukrainian regional and city councils (including Kharkiv, Luhansk or Donetsk) declared Russian a second official language on the regional level, Kyiv denounced this decision as "language separatism". The tensions with Moscow, which traditionally instrumentalizes the Russian language issue in the "near abroad" and uses the separatist threat as a leverage in its relations with the neighbours, additionally complicate the issue of regionalization in Ukraine. In this light, transnational initiatives and cross-border cooperation projects developed by the Ukrainian border regions together with their Russian neighbours are often seen as ambivalent. Such projects are welcomed on the western border of Ukraine as a common European practice, but in the Ukrainian-Russian borderlands, they are considered a "Trojan horse", smuggling Russian imperial ambitions and the traditional power asymmetry into the bilateral relations.

---

1   "New Neighborhood – New Association. Ukraine and the European Union at the beginning of the 21th century," Policy paper series *On the Future of Europe* (Warsaw: Stefan Batory Foundation, March 2002), Policy Paper no. 6, p. 14.
2   The literature on the regional factor in Ukrainian politics is enormous. Here just some titles: Sarah Birch, "Interpreting the Regional Effect in Ukrainian Politics", *Europe-Asia Studies*, vol. 52, no. 6 (September 2000), pp. 1017-1042; Lowell Barrington and Eric Herron, "One Ukraine or Many? Regionalism in Ukraine and Its Political Consequences", *Nationalities Papers*, vol. 32, no. 1 (March 2004), pp. 53-86; Ivan Katchanovski, *Cleft Countries: Regional Political Divisions and Cultures in Post-Soviet Ukraine and Moldova*, Stuttgart: Ibidem-Verlag 2006; Paul Kubicek, "Regional Polarisation in Ukraine: Public Opinion, Voting and Legislative Behaviour", *Europe-Asia Studies*, vol. 52, no. 2 (March 2000), pp. 273-294; Andrew Wilson and Valeriy Khmelko, "Regionalism, Ethnic and Linguistic Cleavages in Ukraine", in: Taras Kuzio (ed.), *Contemporary Ukraine. Dynamics of Post-Soviet Transformation*, Armonk, NY: M. E. Sharpe 1998, pp. 60-80.

Is regional diversity and regionalization a blessing or a curse for Ukraine? To approach this question we need to look into European debates. The so-called "new regionalism" emerged in Europe in the late 1980s in the context of globalization and the changing role of the nation state. The power of the centralized state was eroded by internationalization and European integration, increased mobility of capital and the rise of transnational corporations. Market liberalization required new forms of competitiveness based on innovation, networking and the quality of human capital. As old industrial regions faced systemic crises and traditional welfare state practices of redistribution became ineffective, the accent was put on "flexible specialization", industrial districts and informal cooperative networks. According to Michael Keating, the new regionalism "pits regions against each other in a competitive mode, rather than providing complementary roles for them in a national division of labour."[3] Opposing new and old regionalism, Keating argues that "the new regionalism is modernizing and forward looking, in contrast to an old provincialism, which represented resistance to change and defence of tradition."[4] However, the old and the new regionalism continue to coexist and typically complement each other.

In the EU countries, regions have not only become decision-making actors, they also represent a new form of territorial solidarity and an important aspect of European citizenship. However, according to Arnoud Lagendijk, "the question is to what extent the roles allocated to the region really require the development of a democratic mandate at the regional level".[5] Lagendijk argues that there is a fundamental contradiction between the roles of the region "as a strategic actor operative in an increasingly competitive battlefield" and "as a form of public policy making which should be democratically legitimized and controlled".[6] Making a cross-European comparison, John Loughlin admits that "there is worrying disaffection from politics in general and from

---

3   Michael Keating, *The New Regionalism in Western Europe. Territorial Restructuring and Political Change*, Cheltenham: Edward Elgar, 1998, pp. 72-73.
4   Keating, *The New Regionalism*.
5   Arnoud Lagendijk, "Regionalisation in Europe. Stories, Institutions and Boundaries", in: Henk van Houtum, Olivier Kramsch and Wolfgang Zierhofer (eds.), *Bordering Space*, Aldershot: Ashgate 2005, pp. 77-92; here p. 80.
6   Lagendijk, "Regionalisation in Europe", p. 81.

local and regional politics in particular on the part of European citizens".[7] Loughlin points to the tendency of national political parties to keep control of local politics. When local and regional elections are seen only as a "stepping stone to national politics", citizens do not take them seriously.

As the state's dominating role in defining and reproducing the national culture has been eroded by globalization, local and minority cultures gain more attention. Regions with a distinctive cultural and historical identity, such as Catalonia or Wales, have in the last two decades succeeded in reaffirming their special status within their respective nation states. However, regional identity is not just a static set of stereotypical cultural features exploited by the tourist industry; it also implies the "search for a 'usable past', a set of historical referents which can guide a regional society on its distinct road to modernization, bridging the past, via the present, with the future".[8] In this sense, Melanie Tatur suggests treating history "as a 'treasury' or 'container' of symbols which may be forgotten, reactivated, or reconstructed and reshaped in communicative interaction. Symbolic resources accumulated in the course of history and activated in discourse refer to meaningful signs, schemes and codes, myth and narratives, concepts, world views and theoretical constructs".[9] Regions, like nations, are "imagined communities" (Anderson); the feelings of solidarity and common destiny among their members are shaped by media, political parties, NGOs and civic initiatives. All of them use the stock of local symbols, narratives and collective memories to mobilize certain social groups, to consolidate political support or to encourage local patriotism. Therefore, "regional identity may be rooted in historical traditions and myths but, in its contemporary form, it is a social construction, forged on a specific context under the influence of social, economic and political pressures".[10]

---

[7] John Loughlin, "Conclusion: The Transformation of Regional and Local Democracy in the European Union", in: idem (ed.), *Subnational Democracy in the European Union: Challenges and Opportunities*, New York: Oxford University Press 2001, pp. 387-400; here p. 397.

[8] Keating, *The New Regionalism*, p. 84.

[9] Melanie Tatur, "Introduction", in: idem (ed.), *The Making of Regions in Post-Socialist Europe – the Impact of Culture, Economic Structure and Institutions. Case Studies from Poland, Hungary, Romania and Ukraine*, vol. 1, Wiesbaden: VS Verlag 2004, pp. 15-47; here p. 33.

[10] Keating, *The New Regionalism*, p. 87.

In the countries of post-socialist Eastern Europe, according to Melanie Tatur, regionalization emerged on the political agenda for a number of reasons: first, "systemic change had abolished the mechanism of central redistribution and thus dismantled the instruments of regional equalization built into the socialist economy"; second, "the processes of opening the national economy to the global markets redefined the competitive advantages" of the regions, disadvantaging former core areas and encouraging former peripheries to rediscover their developmental potential. Third, "political liberalization and democratic procedures created space for regional diversity, regional competition and formulation of 'regional identities'", transformed into political demands. And fourth, the availability of EU funding for local and regional development strengthened these demands.[11] In the last two decades the "region making" process in the countries of Central and Eastern Europe was complicated by the institutional and cultural legacy of state socialism and the dilemmas of a double transformation (simultaneous transition to democracy and market reforms). However, a legal and financial framework for regional policy was created by the late 1990s in most EU accession countries. With EU enlargement and deepening integration, some border regions rediscovered the new geopolitical, economic and cultural advantages of their peripheral (from the national point of view) location. EU funding for economically depressed areas and for cross-border cooperation became an important incentive for their development.

At the same time, regionalization in the post-Soviet context has been further complicated by a number of additional factors. Besides simultaneous market liberalization and democratic reforms, countries like Ukraine faced the challenge of basic state-building and national consolidation. While unitary Ukraine has to deal with deep regional cleavages, Russia struggles with the shortcomings of its under-institutionalized ethnofederalism inherited from the Soviet era.[12] Neopatrimonialism, clientelism, corruption and state capture,

---

11 Tatur, "Introduction", p. 15.
12 While formally Russia is a federation and Ukraine a unitary state, "an authoritarian and pragmatic political culture and specific forms of clientelism dominate both polities and manifest themselves in electoral and budget politics regulating the relationship between the center and the regions". See Kerstin Zimmer, "Not So Different After All? Center-Region Relations: a Ukrainian Comparison", in: Graeme Gill (ed.),

bribery, blackmail and violence are to various degrees characteristic of the post-Soviet states. According to Kerstin Zimmer, the new regional elites in Ukraine emerged due to a fundamental redistribution of property through *nomenklatura* privatization, which preserved the vertical ties among the actors as well as their characteristics.[13] In the Ukrainian neo-patrimonial system "actors at the regional level are not notably differentiated. So far the borders between different organizations and spheres (public, political, economic) are blurred and systemic mechanisms block the emergence of distinct spheres".[14] In the absence of Ukraine's EU accession prospects the external pressure and support for reforms have been quite weak; no funding has been available as an incentive for institutional modernization.

Decentralization efforts in Ukraine have hitherto been inconsistent and insufficient; moreover, the framework for the political system has not been settled yet. As a result, Ukrainian regions suffer from institutional and legal instability[15] and from the lack of a proper financial and economic basis for the local government bodies.[16] Regional and local councils, while formally democratically elected, are lacking in transparency and accountability to the public. Despite the differences in their political systems the regional administrations in Ukraine and in Russia constitute an essential part of the "presidential power vertical".[17] In post-Soviet states the relationship between the centre and the regions is characterized by vertical alliances and weak horizontal integration. Ukrainian "governors depend on the center, but simultaneously they guarantee the administrative and political control of the country".[18]

Politics in the Russian Regions, Basingstoke and New York: Palgrave Macmillan 2007, pp. 108-137, here p. 108.
13 Kerstin Zimmer, "The Captured Region. Actors and Institutions in Ukrainian Donbas", in: Tatur (ed.), *The Making of Regions*, vol. 2, p. 233.
14 Zimmer, "The Captured Region", p. 234.
15 Claudia Sabic and Kerstin Zimmer, "Ukraine: the Genesis of a Captured State", in: Tatur (ed.), *The Making of Regions*, vol. 2, p. 123.
16 Sabic and Zimmer, "Ukraine: the Genesis of a Captured State", p. 121.
17 President Putin undertook some reforms to reinforce the power of the centre and presidential power in particular: In 2000 seven general districts were created, each headed by a presidential envoy appointed by and responsible to the president; in 2004 direct elections for chief executives in the regions were abolished, and the president was given power to appoint them. For more details see Graeme Gill, "Introduction: Power and the Russian Regions", in: idem (ed.), *Politics in the Russian Regions*, pp. 1-15.
18 Zimmer, "The Captured Region", p. 232.

This makes central players dependent on governors and informal leaders – "regional barons" and oligarchs. The exchange of patronage for electoral support is also characteristic of the Russian political system, as "Putin relies on the governors to deliver him electoral support in national level elections. The integration of the governors into United Russia is a reflection of this."[19] In short, regions in both Ukraine and Russia remain strongholds of the clientelist system.

The eastern borderlands of Ukraine (Donetsk, Luhansk, and Kharkiv oblasts) used to be core regions in the Soviet economic system. Being highly urbanized and industrially developed, they kept this core position also in independent Ukraine. During the "wild" 1990s a strong "administrative-economic group" emerged in the Donetsk region.[20] With the creation of the pro-presidential Party of Regions in 2001, and with Donetsk governor Viktor Yanukovych becoming Ukrainian prime-minister in 2002, this so-called "Donetsk clan" turned into an important player in Ukrainian politics. Despite (or rather due to) the Orange Revolution, the Party of Regions continues to hold strong positions in the eastern Ukrainian regions. At the same time, Donetsk, Luhansk and to some extent Kharkiv face serious problems typical of "old industrial regions"; they are also particularly dependent on Russia's energy sources and Russia's markets. And from the nation building perspective, the eastern borderlands of Ukraine are quite problematic due to their significant share of Russians and Russian-speakers, the persistence of a "Soviet" identity and the traditional East Slavic orientations of the local population. However, it would be a mistake to consider the elites of the eastern border regions merely "pro-Russian": it is protectionism and egoistic business interests rather than loyalty to the Ukrainian state which shapes their cautious attitudes to cooperation with Russia and to the post-Soviet integration projects.

The eastern Ukrainian regions share a border with the economically successful and politically stable Central Black Earth Region and South Russia (namely Bryansk, Kursk, Belgorod, Voronezh, Rostov oblasts). Unlike the weakly integrated ethnic territories and rebellious republics of the Russian periphery, these regions are not troublemakers for Moscow. The Ukrainian

---

19   Gill, "Introduction", p. 10.
20   Kerstin Zimmer, "The Donetsk Factor", *Transitions Online*, December 17, 2004. http://www.tol.cz

minority living here is assimilated to the Russian language; it does not claim cultural autonomy or even special cultural rights. Much more than their Ukrainian counterparts, the Russian regional elites cling to pan-Slavism and the vision of Ukrainians and Russians as having been "one people" in the past. These ideological concepts shape the Russian attitude to cross-border cooperation with Ukraine and make it an instrument of re-integration. However in Russia, as in Ukraine, it is the vertical alliances and the relationship with the centre which matter for the regional elites in the first place. In other words, the administrative centralisation and the lack of economic incentives for cross-border cooperation limit the integrationist ambitions of the Russian regional elites despite their pan-Slavist rhetoric.

5.2 Kharkiv-Belgorod as a (potential) cross-border region

Like other neighbouring regions in the Ukrainian-Russian borderlands, Kharkiv and Belgorod oblasts are characterized by a significant degree of cultural similarities, which can be explained by their long history of coexistence in the Russian empire and by their shared Soviet history. The Russians and Ukrainians living on both sides of the border usually belong to the Russian Orthodox Church; cultural and linguistic differences create no problems for migration and mixed marriages. In Kharkiv, the Russian language still dominates in everyday life, and ethnic minorities and migrants are usually assimilated to Russian. Most of Kharkiv oblast and part of Belgorod oblast belong to the same historical region – Sloboda Ukraine – which was colonized by Ukrainian and Russian settlers in the 17th century. The ethnographic differences between Ukrainian and Russian villages, which were still identifiable at the beginning of the 20th century, are hardly visible today. The older generation still shares a common Soviet identity based on the memory of the "Great Patriotic War", Khrushchev's thaw and Brezhnev's "long seventies". In the "post-Soviet discourse" of cross-border cooperation[21] this cultural similarity

---

21 Vendina and Kolossov identify three main discourses of Ukrainian-Russian cross-border cooperation: 1. the post-Soviet integrationist discourse, which denies the necessity of applying international norms to the Ukrainian-Russian border and sees cross-border cooperation as an instrument of reunification or at least re-integration;

and shared cultural memory is usually interpreted as a natural precondition for re-integration. According to this logic, Kharkiv and Belgorod are "predestined to cooperate" because of their common East Slavic roots and centuries-long history in one state.[22] However, from the perspective of Ukrainian nation-building hybrid identities, bilingualism and the historical symbiosis of two cultures in Kharkiv are seen as symptoms of a dangerous weakness and immaturity of the regional identity. Indeed, in the case of Kharkiv and Belgorod their "cultural closeness" plays an ambivalent role: it is an important factor of region building and cross-border cooperation, but at the same time the shared (post-)Soviet political culture and mentality can become an obstacle for modernization.

Another factor fostering cross-border cooperation is the short physical distance between two oblast's centres: Kharkiv and Belgorod are separated by only 70 km, less than one hour by car if one disregards the time for border crossing. Since 2004, a local train, which does not stop at the border, makes this distance in 1 hour and 20 minutes. This short distance allows for intensive personal and business contacts; therefore the border is often perceived by the local residents as an annoying obstacle.

Populations on both sides of the border are connected by family and friendship ties; many visit close relatives on a regular basis and own family property across the border (a house, dacha or piece of land).[23] Less than the border itself, growing transport costs have reduced certain categories of pri-

---

2. the discourse of disintegration, which sees cross-border-cooperation as a rudiment of the past; 3. the pro-European discourse, which promotes "European" forms of cross-border cooperation and the development of partner relations on all levels (including administration, business and civil society). See Olga Vendina and Vladimir Kolossov, "Partnership that Bypasses Barriers", *Rossia v globalnoi politike*, no. 1 (January-February 2007).

22 For example Alexandr Skliarov, vice-speaker of the Belgorod Oblast Duma, at the Second Conference on the Euroregion "Slobozhanshchyna" in Kharkiv, 23 May 2008.

23 According to statistical data cited during the parliamentary hearings on Russian-Ukrainian cooperation in the Russian Duma in 1999, almost 40% of the families in the Belgorod oblast have relatives in Ukraine. Around 45,000 people move from Ukraine to the Belgorod oblast each year, and about 20,000 leave the oblast for Ukraine. Around 30,000 people actually live in Ukraine but are registered in the Belgorod oblast in order not to lose their Russian pensions. See "Parliamentary hearings. Russian-Ukrainian cooperation: Dynamics of development after the enactment of the Treaty of Friendship, Cooperation and Partnership between the RF and Ukraine", *Analiticheskii vestnik*, no. 7 (119) (2000), pp. 34-36 (in Russian).

vate visitors: for the rural population, cross-border trips have become particularly expensive. The number of students who study across the border has also decreased significantly, despite small quotas for the neighbouring regions introduced by the local universities.

At the same time the border has added some new incentives for travelling. The residents of Belgorod come to shop at Barabashovo, the biggest regional market in Kharkiv, attracted by the low prices. Special shopping tours are even organized for this purpose by Belgorod tourist companies. A number of Kharkiv residents look for jobs in Belgorod, with its higher salaries, or sell on the Belgorod markets. This growing intensity of social and economic contacts is likely to persist in the near future and makes Kharkiv-Belgorod a potential cross-border region.

Relations between Kharkiv and Belgorod have been always asymmetrical, but the character of this asymmetry has changed. Both cities were founded at the margins of the Muscovite state and served as military fortresses during the 17th century. Initially Belgorod played a more important strategic and administrative role. From 1727 to 1779 it was the centre of Belgorod guberniia, which included Kharkiv until 1765, when the latter itself became a guberniia centre. The integration of the borderlands into the Russian empire during the 18th century allowed Kharkiv to develop into an important trade centre. In addition, the university established in 1805 made Kharkiv an academic and cultural capital of Left Bank Ukraine. In the second half of the 19th century, Kharkiv went through a capitalist modernization and became an important industrial centre and a transport junction connecting Moscow with Crimea and Caucasus.

During the Soviet decades the role of Kharkiv increased even more. From 1919-1934 Kharkiv was the capital of Soviet Ukraine and in the 1930s became the construction site of the first industrial giants. It was severely damaged in the Second World War, but quickly regained its economic potential.

Before 1991 Kharkiv's industrial sector was deeply involved in the all-Union economic cooperation, and partly subordinated directly to Moscow. Modern aircraft construction and aerospace industry, machine construction, nuclear physics and new materials physics made Kharkiv one of the strong-

Derzhprom / Gosprom building in Kharkiv

Lenin Monument in Kharkiv

V. Karazin Kharkiv National University

holds of the Soviet military-industrial complex. With its University and more than twenty institutes for higher education the city became a students' capital. As an industrial and academic centre Kharkiv attracted students and a labour force not only from eastern Ukraine, but also from the neighbouring regions of Russia, particularly from the Belgorod oblast.

The collapse of the USSR in 1991 has changed the economic role and status of the city. The heavy industry lost its markets, and the research sector was underfunded due to the severe economic crisis of the early 1990s. As a result Kharkiv has been partly marginalized, both economically and politically. In comparison to the more successful Donetsk and Dnepropetrovsk oblasts, it failed to create a significant regional lobby in Kyiv. On the other hand, Kharkiv with its dominant Russian-speaking culture and strong leftist political sympathies struggled to find its proper place in the nation building process and to adapt its hybrid "Little Russian" identity to the new ideology of a "national revival".[24] This task was partly solved under Leonid Kuchma's presidency when Kharkiv mayor Yevhen Kushnar'ov became the head of the presidential administration from 1996-1998 and came back to Kharkiv as a governor from 2000-2004. Since the Orange Revolution Kharkiv's regional elites have been divided: the oblast administration is controlled by "Our Ukraine" while in the city and oblast councils the Party of Regions is dominant. Political conflicts between different segments of the local political elites reveal the competing interests of the administrative-economic groups, but also reflect different visions of regional identity and collective memory.

Unlike Kharkiv, Belgorod during the 19th century remained a small town in the Kursk guberniia. In 1869 the Kursk-Kharkiv railway connected Belgorod with its more dynamic neighbour. Like Kharkiv, Belgorod went through the turbulent times of civil war. In April 1918 it was occupied by the German army and became part of Ukrainian territory according to the Brest Peace Treaty. In December 1918 it returned under the control of the Soviet government and was later included in the Russian Federation. Until the beginning of the Second World War the population of Belgorod was 34,000. The city started to

---

24   Olha Filipova, "Politics of identity and consolidation of Ukrainian society: the situation of a border region", in: *Ukrainsko-rosiiske porubizhzhia: formuvannia sotsialnoho ta kulturnoho prostoru v istorii ta v suchasniy politytsi*, Kyiv: Kennan Institute, 2003, pp. 49-58 (in Ukrainian).

grow from 1954, when the Belgorod oblast was created as a separate administrative unit and Belgorod became an oblast centre. The city grew quickly, but still could not compete with Kharkiv (its population in the end of the 1990s was 340,000 against 1,500,000 of Kharkiv). Until recently it had no university, and few higher education institutions (such as the Pedagogical Institute and the Institute for Agriculture). A lot of students from the Belgorod oblast studied in Kharkiv. Before 1991 many Belgorod oblast residents used to work in the big industrial enterprises of Kharkiv, some of them commuting across the administrative border every day. In the 1990s, according to Vladimir Kolossov and Olga Vendina, the Belgorod oblast recovered from the recession faster than Kharkiv due to its more balanced economic structure and the advantages of its relatively late modernization. The rather profitable extraction and processing of iron ore, as well as the developed construction materials and food industries, helped the Belgorod oblast to become self-sustainable, whereas Kharkiv, with its old and energy-demanding industrial complex, became dependent on the supply of Russian gas.[25] In the early 2000s Belgorod's average wage, pensions and other social benefits had surpassed those of Kharkiv.[26]

Today, the Belgorod oblast exhibits a low poverty rate and relatively high social standards; its authorities succeeded in implementing an effective housing provision program. In the 1990s the region profited from immigration flows from the former Soviet republics. Since most of the newcomers are ethnic Russians or Ukrainians, migration does not create social tensions in the region.

In 1996 the Belgorod Pedagogical Institute was transformed into the Belgorod State University, which became the most important image project of the regional authorities and a stronghold of Russian national identity on the western border.

Belgorod's regional elites are consolidated and political conflicts, if they happen at all, are usually hidden. During the 2005 regional elections, Gover-

---

25   Vladimir Kolossov and Olga Vendina, "The Russian-Ukrainian border: Social gradients, identities and migration flows – The example of Belgorod and Kharkiv oblasts", *Migratsiia i pogranichnyi rezhim: Belarus, Moldova, Rossiia i Ukraina*, Kyiv: NIPMB (National Institute for International Security Issues) 2002, pp. 21-46 (in Russian).
26   Kolossov and Vendina, "The Russian-Ukrainian border".

BORDERLANDS INTO BORDERED LANDS 207

Belgorod oblast administration with Lenin monument

Belgorod State University

nor Evgenii Savchenko managed to block the intervention of outsiders from Moscow (Elena Baturina's business clan[27] and Zhirinovskii's Party, the LDP) and preserved his power. Belgorod has also the reputation of being one of the most conservative regions: it was the first to introduce "Orthodox culture" as an obligatory course into school curricula. The Russian Orthodox Church has a strong influence in Belgorod and is involved in political decision making, and pan-Slavism is almost an official ideology in the region.

The idea of cross-border cooperation between the Kharkiv and Belgorod oblasts emerged as an immediate reaction to the dissolution of the USSR and to the challenges of the new international border. As early as in 1993 Kharkiv and Belgorod regional authorities initiated the creation of the *Council of the Border Regions of Ukraine and Russia* (which was officially established in the following year); in 1995 the first agreement on cooperation between the two regions was signed. The problems to be solved by cross-border cooperation included the development of a legal basis for cooperation between Ukrainian and Russian enterprises, attracting investments for common projects, improvement of tax and custom legislation for cross-border trade, development of regulations for labour migration and providing social guarantees for foreign labour force, cooperation in environmental issues, facilitating academic exchange and scientific cooperation satisfying the needs of near-border residents who work or have families across the border, cooperation of the regional administrations in combating contraband and other forms of border-related crimes and jointly maintaining the border infrastructure.[28]

Some of these projects were launched already in the mid-1990s, though with only relative success; among them was a common program for monitoring and protecting the Siversky Donets water resources, as well as projects for a "free economic zone" and a "special investments regime". But it was the years 2000-2004 that cross-border cooperation began to be seen as one of the priorities in Ukrainian-Russian relations, and both the Kharkiv and the

---

27 Elena Baturina is the wife of Moscow's mayor Yuriy Luzhkov; she owns the INTEKO company and is the richest woman of Russia. According to *Forbes*, her fortune in 2008 was about $ 4.2 billion. http://www.forbes.com/lists/2008/10/billionaires08 _Elena-Baturina_GXNS.html (last accessed February 7, 2010).
28 Vladimir Kolossov and Alexei Kiriukhin, "Cross-border cooperation in Russian-Ukrainian relations", *Politia*, no. 1 (19) (2001), pp. 141-165 (in Russian).

Belgorod elites could consolidate their pioneering roles in this respect. In December 2001 the Fourth Economic Forum of the Russian and Ukrainian business elites took place in Kharkiv. It focused specifically on cooperation and investment projects and defined the main prospects for Ukrainian-Russian cross-border cooperation:

- The formation of a "financial-industrial union of border regions" in the form of a Russian-Ukrainian consortium of banks and industrial enterprises with the aim of encouraging cooperation programs and coordinate export policy;
- Testing a simplified customs and border regime in order to accommodate the social and economic needs of the population of the near-border areas in Kharkiv and Belgorod oblasts with the prospect of a future implementation in other sections of the border;
- Harmonizing the tax systems in both countries in order to eliminate obstacles for trade;
- Inter-regional cooperation in the preservation and rational use of the water resources of the Siversky Donets river basin and the foundation of a Russian-Ukrainian inter-regional ecological fund.

Most initiatives in the ecological, economic and humanitarian spheres were undertaken by the Kharkiv and Belgorod oblasts, which thus became a laboratory for new projects of Ukrainian-Russian cross-border cooperation. This special mission of the two oblasts as pioneers in the development of the new Ukrainian-Russian relations has been actively advertised by local business and political elites.[29]

The cooperation in environmental preservation should be mentioned in greater detail. This entails a large-scale ecological project which touches on the vital interests of several oblasts of Ukraine and Russia belonging to the Siversky Donets river basin (Kharkiv, Luhansk and Donetsk in Ukraine; Belgorod and Rostov in Russia). The upper and the lower parts of the river basin belong to Russia; the middle part belongs to Ukraine. This territory is urbanized, with a high population density, developed industry and intensive agriculture. The water resources are very limited and rather polluted, which causes massive health problems for the local population. Moreover, Siversky Donets

---

29 "The economic mission 'Kharkiv–Belgorod'", *Vestnik torgovo-promyshlennoi palaty*, no. 10 (2001), pp. 12-13 (in Russian).

is one of the main sources of pollution for the Azov Sea, which belongs both to Russia and Ukraine. The problem became extremely urgent after the disaster at the Dykanivka water purification complex near Kharkiv in the summer of 1995, when the Siversky Donets was highly polluted by sewer overflows and the 1.5 million inhabitants of Kharkiv were left without drinking water. This accident, shown worldwide on TV news, demonstrated the unacceptable technical state of the water supply infrastructure, canalization and purification systems. The project, aimed at the ecological restoration of the Siversky Donets River and at improving the quality of drinking water, was supported by the Council of the Border Regions in 1997 but remained mainly on paper. It was during the meeting of the Russian and Ukrainian ministers of foreign affairs in February 2001, that the leaders of the five border regions signed a special memorandum that helped to institutionalize the program.[30] The program priorities include the coordination of the ecological strategies of Russia and Ukraine, the harmonization of ecological legislation, the development of common criteria for the assessment of the water quality, the formation of a joint monitoring system and the identification of the main sources of pollution, and the improvement of the quality of water through the modernization of the infrastructure.

Both Kharkiv and Belgorod oblasts have been interested in using the advantages of their transit location. Therefore they initiated some projects aimed at the improvement of border and customs controls, the modernisation of the border infrastructure and the regulation of transport flows. One of the most urgent problems has been the construction of the new crossing points and the modernization of the existing ones. The new Nekhoteevka international crossing point at the Russian side of the border, arranged according to modern technical standards, was officially opened in June 2002 by the two prime ministers, Anatolii Kinach and Mikhail Kas'ianov. One-fifth of the total goods transported between the two countries now flows through the Nekhoteevka crossing point (and the corresponding Ukrainian crossing point at

---

30 Alexei Kiriukhin, "The cooperation of the territories of Russian-Ukrainian borderlands in environmental issues", *Region: Problemy i perspektivy,* special issue *Ekologia Severskogo Dontsa,* Kharkov 2001, p. 64 (in Russian).

Hoptivka).[31] In order to increase the transit capacities of both oblasts, Ukrainian and Russian experts developed a new scheme of cross-border transport flows and plans for modernization of the transit infrastructure.

Another interesting cross-border cooperation project concerned research and higher education. Once again, the initiative came from Kharkiv and Belgorod universities, which proposed the idea of a consortium, or rather, an association of Ukrainian and Russian universities in the border regions. Such an association, according to the originators, would help to unite available resources, facilitate international cooperation and raise the standards of education in the post-Soviet space. On April 22, 2003 the memorandum creating the Consortium of Near-Border Ukrainian and Russian Universities was signed in Kharkiv.[32]

The aims of the new association, as announced in its official documents, included the exchange of information and sharing of resources; the organization of joint research projects, conferences, seminars; the development of new curricula dealing with the problems of the Ukrainian-Russian borderlands; and the raising of the mobility of students and professors. The founding members of the consortium were three Ukrainian and three Russian universities (Kharkiv, Donetsk, Simferopol; Belgorod, Voronezh, Rostov).

---

31 "The ink has dried – let's start working", *Vechernii Kharkov*, June 22, 2002 (in Russian).
32 For more information see the site of Belgorod University: http://old.bsu.edu.ru/struktura/Consorc/ (last accessed February 7, 2010).

BORDERLANDS INTO BORDERED LANDS 213

Hoptivka-Nekhotkeevka, on the highway Moscow-Crimea, is the main crossing point at the Kharkiv-Belgorod part of the border

5.3 The "Slobozhanshchyna" Euroregion: opportunities and constraints

Both the Kharkiv and the Belgorod regional authorities realized quite soon that all these diverse projects and initiatives would have a better chance if they were institutionalized in the framework of a Euroregion. The idea of the "Slobozhanshchyna" Euroregion, the first one on the Ukrainian-Russian border, was developed by local experts from the Department of Geography at Kharkiv National University. As early as in 1997 the idea of a Euroregion encompassing the territory of the Kharkiv and Belgorod oblasts was discussed by Kharkiv geographers Artur Golikov and Pavel Chernomaz in the regional media.[33] They pointed to the geopolitical, economic, ecological and cultural preconditions for a cross-border region: the traditional economic cooperation between Kharkiv and Belgorod, the emergence of new joint companies operating across the border, the transit location of both oblasts, the ethnic and cultural closeness of the populations, the traditional cooperation between academic institutions and the similarities of the educational systems, and the common media space. The authors referred to the historical and ethnological analysis explicated by the Kharkiv historian Dmytro Bahalii in 1924 to justify the delimitation line between Soviet Ukraine and the Russian Federation. According to contemporary Kharkiv geographers, Bahalii's work proves that both the Ukrainian and the Russian parts of Slobozhanshchyna form a geographic, economic and cultural unity that would provide a solid basis for a cross-border region. This argument was strengthened by an analysis of the intensity of cross border-business contacts between Ukraine and Russia conducted by geographers Alexei Kiriukhin, Pavel Chernomaz and Natalia Korsunova. According to them, Kharkiv and Belgorod demonstrate the highest intensity of such contacts and therefore would be the most suitable candidates for the first Euroregion on the Ukrainian-Russian border.[34]

---

33 Artur Golikov and Pavel Chernomaz, "The Euroregion 'Slobozhanshchyna' as a form of cross-border cooperation between the border regions of Ukraine and Russia", *Region*, no. 4 (1997), pp. 52-54 (in Russian).
34 Alexei Kiriukhin, Pavel Chernomaz and Natalia Korsunova, "The Euroregion 'Slobozhanshchyna' as a model of sustainable development for near border territories", *Biznes-inform*, no. 3-4 (2002), pp. 62-63 (in Russian).

Further discussions about this Euroregion project were inspired by the Russian-Ukrainian political rapprochement of the early 2000s. Projects of regional integration such as the Eurasian Economic Community (EurAsEC) and later the Single Economic Area (SEA), which promised the harmonization of economic legislation, a customs union and the coordination of tax policies, were supposed to provide the geopolitical background and the institutional basis for Euroregions in the post-Soviet space. In February 2002, the Russian and Ukrainian presidents signed the *Program of interregional and cross-border cooperation for 2001-2007*, which encouraged the creation of Euroregions in the Ukrainian-Russian borderlands. The positive experience of the existing Euroregions on the western border of Ukraine gave confidence to the authors of the "Slobozhanshchyna" project; at the same time it raised the ambitions of the Kharkiv regional elite to demonstrate the competitive advantages of eastern Ukraine. Some hopes for financial support from the EU and the possibility to participate in EU programs, such as the "New Neighbourhood", also played a role. In this context the project of the Ukrainian-Russian Euroregion fitted well into Ukraine's "multivector" foreign policy, which combined post-Soviet integration with the "European choice". Being the motor for the project, the pragmatic regional elites of Kharkiv were looking for new forms of cooperation with Russia, but at the same time kept open the option of participating in the EU programs.

The Euroregion was supposed to become an umbrella institution facilitating various projects such as the aforementioned plans for the development of cross-border trade and transport infrastructure, the consortium of near-border universities and the program of environmental protection. In terms of economic development, the Euroregion would help to revitalize the economically depressed border areas, create new jobs drawing on the highly qualified human resources and decentralize the industries in the urbanized zone. This "innovative industrial core" was supposed to give a strong impulse to the economic and social development of the wider area including Kharkiv and Belgorod (the so-called "zone of economic growth").[35] Even more ambitious

---

35 "Kharkov + Belgorod = Evroregion?" (Interview with Alexei Kiriukhin), *Komsomolskaia Pravda in Ukraine*, October 25, 2002, p. 14; Alexei Kiriukhin, "The territorial structure of the Euroregion 'Slobozhanshchyna'", *Biznes-inform*, no. 6 (2000), pp. 48-50 (in Russian).

plans have been developed such as the launch of a "cross-border industrial complex" encompassing the small towns of Shebekino (Russian Federation) and Vovchansk (Ukraine).[36] This territory, endowed with a special investment climate and a high concentration of innovative small and medium-sized enterprises, was supposed to specialize in new technologies. Later on these plans were supplemented by the project of a joint Ukrainian-Russian airport half way between Kharkiv and Belgorod.[37] The new airport would serve citizens of both countries and was supposed to be combined with a business centre, an exposition hall and entertaining facilities, thus providing jobs for the local population and concentrating investments and expertise on one particular territory. There were great hopes that these projects would give a strong impulse for regional development. Inspired by the "new regionalism" in the West, their initiators have nonetheless underestimated the high economic and bureaucratic costs of border crossing and the unfavourable investment climate.

The "Slobozhanshchyna" Euroregion project was eventually made public by the head of the Kharkiv regional administration, Governor Evhen Kushnar'ov, on the occasion of the meeting of the Russian, Ukrainian and Belarusian border regions in Sumy in September 2002. Kushnar'ov made cross-border cooperation (in particular with the Belgorod oblast) one of his priorities and supported the implementation of a Euroregion. In November 2003, an agreement creating the "Slobozhanshchyna" Euroregion was signed by the administrations of the Kharkiv and Belgorod oblasts. Since October 2004 the Euroregion has had an observer status in the Association of European Border Regions (AEBR).[38] In the following years other Euroregions were created in the Ukrainian-Russian borderlands: "Yaroslavna" (Kursk and Sumy oblasts), "Dnepr" (Briansk, Homel and Chernihiv); at present, the "Donbas" Euroregion (Rostov and Luhansk) is on its way.

The initial outcomes of the "Slobozhanshchyna" project are mixed, as most of the declared aims are still far from being achieved. On the one hand, one cannot deny that the Euroregion serves as a communication platform for

---

36 Yurii Klochkov and Alexei Kiriukhin, "Near Border Growth Pole: Perspectives of revitalising trade and cooperation", *Vestnik torgovo-promyshlennoi palaty*, no. 10 (2001), p. 16.
37 For more details see chapter 2.2.
38 See http://www.aebr.net/ (last accessed February 7, 2010).

the regional officials and, to some extent, for the local businesses on both sides of the border. Since 2003 various seminars and round tables for local administration officials and small businesses have been organized within the framework of "Slobozhanshchyna", as well as two international conferences devoted to cross-border cooperation.[39] The Euroregion has also become an instrument of coordination and the solving of common problems related to the regulation of the border regime, the improvement of the technical infrastructure, and the everyday needs of the local population living in the near border zone. As it was reported in the Kharkiv media, in 2007 the Ukrainian state budget and the oblast budget for the first time allocated some funds specifically for cross-border cooperation.[40]

On the other hand, the Euroregion failed in most of its stated goals; it failed to become an instrument of modernization for the regional economies, to bring innovations and foreign investments to the region and to improve its competitive capacities. In other words, the "Slobozhanshchyna" Euroregion failed to keep up with the European pattern of the "new regionalism".

It might be more important, however, that the political context of the Euroregion project has changed with the Orange Revolution: the Ukrainian-Russian cross-border cooperation had to be divorced from the "East Slavic unity" paradigm and from the post-Soviet re-integration projects. With the new governor Arsen Avakov ("Our Ukraine"), the Euroregion ceased to be among the priorities of the Kharkiv regional administration. Before 2005 both Ukrainian and Russian regional elites used the "Slobozhanshchyna" Euroregion as a symbolic resource, associating business projects with the idea of Ukrainian-Russian unity.[41] Since the Orange Revolution the new Kharkiv administration, which is loyal to the pro-Western course of President Yushchenko, has not shown much interest in the Euroregion, while the cooperation with Russia is monopolised by the Party of Regions. Moreover, conflicts and tensions among different segments of the Kharkiv business and political elites in recent years have made long term strategic projects difficult. As a result, in re-

---

39   See the web site of the Kharkiv oblast administration www.kharkivoda.gov.ua/show.php?page=17474
40   "Friendship has to be proved by deeds", *Vechernii Kharkov*, 27 July 2007. www.vecherniy.kharkov.ua/news/14088 (in Russian) (last accessed February 7, 2010).
41   Olga Vendina and Vladimir Kolossov, "Partnership that Bypasses Barriers".

cent years Ukrainian and Russian border regions have tended to focus on pragmatic and technical aspects of cross-border cooperation, such as opening new crossing points and modernizing the old ones.

One of the immanent problems of the Euroregions in the post-Soviet space is their bureaucratic and technocratic nature. Like other Euroregions in this part of Europe, "Slobozhanshchyna" lacks a public dimension: regular contacts and cooperation between civic organisations, academic institutions and cultural associations are the exception rather than the rule. In this respect, the declared cross-border region is far from being an "imagined community"; its (potential) members on both sides of the border are scarcely connected by solidarity or even mutual interest. Information and news from Belgorod almost never appears in Kharkiv television or newspapers; the reverse is true about the Belgorod media. Ordinary citizens hear about the Euroregion mainly in the context of the official visits from the neighbouring country. Problems of Ukrainian-Russian cross-border cooperation are sometimes presented in the regional media, but most of the articles in such newspapers as *Slobidskyi Krai* and *Vechirnii Kharkiv* are official statements or informational announcements from the administration; the attitudes and opinions of the local community rarely find their way into the press. Special publications aimed at a narrow circle of the experts are easier to find. Since 1997 the journal *Region*, devoted to issues of regional development and municipal management, including cross-border cooperation, has been published in Kharkiv. It offers articles on regional economic development, politics and sometimes local history (most of which are in Russian). Among the publications aimed at economists and business circles is the regular newsletter *Business-Inform*. The *Vestnik* of the Kharkiv Chamber of Commerce is also publishing materials about economic and cross-border cooperation with Russia. A special issue of this magazine published jointly with the Belgorod Chamber of Commerce in 2001 was completely devoted to Ukrainian-Russian cross-border cooperation.[42]

Probably most important in this context is the specialized newspaper *Prigranichnoe Sotrudnichestvo* (Cross-Border Cooperation), published in Kharkiv with the support of the Council of the Border Regions since 2002. It

---

42   *Vestnik torgovo-promyshlennoi palaty,* no. 10 (2001).

presents itself as a newsletter addressing a broad audience interested in economic, social and cultural contacts with Russia. This periodical publishes official materials on various aspects of Russian-Ukrainian relations: customs and tax regulations in both countries, texts of interstate agreements, interviews with Ukrainian and Russian officials. It also presents some material on European integration and the experience of cross-border cooperation in Europe. This newspaper addresses not only businesspeople but also the general audience; it publishes practical information for foreigners coming to Russia and Ukraine, recommendations concerning social welfare and citizenship problems, opportunities for tourism and education and even the astrological forecast for those who are going across the border. This can be seen as a positive sign of "democratization" and as a step toward the development of a cross-border public discourse.

To overcome public disinterest and the lack of awareness about the opportunities and prospects for the Ukrainian-Russian Euroregion, some initiatives have recently been launched in Kharkiv and Belgorod. These are intended to draw the attention of the young people from Ukraine and Russia to the problems of cross-border cooperation by bringing them together and involving them in open discussions. For example, in April 2009 a "strategic debate" on the future of the "Slobozhanshchyna" Euroregion was organized in Belgorod for students from Kharkiv and Belgorod Universities. They took part in a role-playing game moderated by specialists from the Institute for State and Municipal Management of Belgorod University.[43] Two competing teams which included both Ukrainians and Russians were supposed to develop projects such as a "green corridor" at the border, a common cross-border cultural space and cross-border tourist routes. In October 2009 the departments of history of Kharkiv National University and Belgorod State University organized a students' school on the cultural heritage of the "Slobozhanshchyna" Euroregion.[44] During one week, students from Kharkiv and Belgorod dis-

---

43 "Debates on the Euroregion are taking place in Belgorod", *Bel.ru*, www.bel.ru/news/slobogan/2009/04/30/37731.html (in Russian) (last accessed February 7, 2010).

44 For information about the Autumn Students' School at Kharkiv National University on "Historical and cultural heritage of the Euroregion "Slobozhanshchyna" see www.kharkivoda.gov.ua/osvita/show.php?page=22209 (in Russian) (last accessed February 7, 2010).

cussed the perspectives of protection and restoration of regional cultural monuments and memorial sites; in the end they presented projects for cross-border tourist routes introducing guests of the region to the rich culture and history of Slobozhanshchyna.

5.4 Reinventing the border region, constructing regional identity

With its origins as an administrative and technocratic project, the "Slobozhanshchyna" Euroregion requires a cultural (historical) legitimization. It was not by accident that the third issue of the periodical *Cross-Border Cooperation* called for contributions about the history of Sloboda Ukraine as a specific borderland territory, about its mixed Ukrainian and Russian cultural roots and its bilingualism as valuable assets of the region.

In this section, I demonstrate how the cultural unity of the historical region *Slobidska Ukraina* or *Slobozhanshchyna*[45] has been (re-)constructed since 1991 as a basis for cross-border cooperation. How do Kharkiv elites see the historical identity of their region and its role in Ukrainian-Russian relations after 1991? How do they adapt the new Ukrainian historical narrative and new national identity to local needs? What elements compose the reinvented regional identity of Slobozhanshchyna? Modern literature on region-

---

45 Although historically, *Slobidska Ukraina* encompassed portions of what are now Belgorod, Kursk and Voronezh oblasts, the name "Slobozhanshchyna" is rarely used for political and cultural branding there today. For the Russian regional elites, this would mean admitting that the Ukrainian Cossacks and Ukrainian culture were part of their own history and, moreover, it would open the door to the dangerous discourse on "Ukrainian ethnic lands". While accepting the name "Slobozhanshchyna" for the cross-border Euroregion project, the Belgorod oblast administration has always preferred to utilize "Slavic" myths and symbols that unify Russians and Ukrainians. It is the Kharkiv intellectual and political elites who have claimed their region to be the successor to the historical Slobozhanshchyna and used this regional history as a resource for shaping the collective identity and branding their cultural and political projects. The Party of Regions, which dominates Kharkiv politics, uses this brand today as a symbol of the close historical ties between Russians and Ukrainians. As a motor of cross-border cooperation between the two countries, Kharkiv oblast has been promoting this interpretation of Slobozhanshchyna to justify its leading role in Ukrainian-Russian economic cooperation. Therefore, in what follows, "Slobozhanshchyna" is used in multiple contexts: as a historical region and as a brand appropriated by the post-Soviet regional elites for the Kharkiv oblast, in addition to its use as a name for the Ukrainian-Russian Euroregion.

alism assumes that regions have a discursive nature: they are not reducible to any single "essence," be it ethnic, historical, economic or administrative; they are social constructs rather than natural entities. According to the Finnish geographer Jouni Hakli, there are as many different kinds of regions as there are "discursive communities" producing texts and images of these regions.[46] In the case of post-Soviet Ukraine the variety of these "discursive communities" and their ability to produce images, concepts and strategies for a region is somewhat limited by the weakness of the local civil society, administrative centralisation and the lack of transparency of the regional administrations. Nevertheless, democratisation and the intensifying contacts with EU institutions on the regional level have been producing a growing demand for a new cultural legitimization of cross-border projects with Russia. Being concerned about their "European image", and not satisfied with the ideologically charged concept of "East Slavic brotherhood", business and political elites of the Kharkiv oblast need more adjustable and "pro-Ukrainian" historical narratives and symbols. The political legitimacy of these elites depends on Ukrainian statehood, but their economic interests are closely connected to Russia. Therefore they have been interested in an ideology of Ukrainian-Russian cooperation which stresses the "Ukrainian character" of the region but at the same time provides a justification for the traditionally close relations with Russia. In opposition to the narrative of shared Soviet history and to the myth of common Slavic origins, which is still widely used by the Russian side to justify the Ukrainian-Russian partnership, the myth of Slobozhanshchyna offers an opportunity to overcome the long-lasting symbolic asymmetry in the relations of the two countries and grants more space for the Ukrainian identity of the region.

The contemporary reconstruction of the identity of Sloboda Ukraine involves various symbolic resources and sometimes contradictory historical narratives: the glorious Cossack past with its democratic traditions, the peaceful character of hardworking Ukrainian peasants, a "multiculturalism" and ethnic tolerance typical for the borderlands, the historical experience of cooperation between Russians and Ukrainians, the settlement mentality with

---

46 Jouni Hakli, "Cross-border identities in the new Europe: Ghost of the past or signpost to the next millennium", http://www.nuim.ie/staff/dpringle/igu_wpm/hakli.pdf (last accessed February 7, 2010).

its liberal and individualistic attitudes, and the merchants' prosperity and capitalist spirit of Kharkiv. All these narrative elements and myths, which are united by the grand narrative of Slobozhanshchyna, meet the ideological needs of the regional ruling elite. As a cultural brand for the region, "Slobozhanshchyna" has much to offer: it is the historical name of a region that was half forgotten during Soviet decades, it refers to a history that is at a safe distance from the current "memory wars" in Ukraine; it is neutral enough not to provoke divisions and exclusions; finally, it is pro-Ukrainian but not anti-Russian. "Slobozhanshchyna" is an ideal myth because it is ambivalent and therefore can be filled with various messages to legitimize different interests.

Slobozhanshchyna or Sloboda Ukraine is a specific historical region which was formed during the 17th century by the colonization efforts of both the Russian state and the Ukrainian settlers – Cossacks and peasants – on the borderlands between Muscovy, the Polish-Lithuanian Commonwealth and the Tatar Khanate. This area, called *Dyke Pole* (Wild Field), was a vast, thinly populated frontier zone. It made Muscovy vulnerable to attacks by nomadic Tatars. The few guard posts were hardly able to prevent such attacks, so once the human and material resources allowed for it, the Muscovy state started the construction of a series of fortresses, which were later united in a single fortification line called the "Belgorod line". In order to complete the garrisons of these new fortresses, and also to enlarge the population of the borderland territories as a guarantee against Tatar invasions, groups of Russian peasants and military servants (called in the documents of this time *sluzhilye liudi* or *boiarskie deti*) were moved there by the Muscovite administration. As such projects relied on ample supply of human resources, the Muscovy state encouraged Ukrainian Cossacks and peasants (called at that time *cherkasy*) from the neighbouring Polish territories to settle there.

Cossacks were given lands to feed their families; they were allowed to keep their customs, military structure and self-organization on condition of providing military service guarding the border against the Tatars. Although the Cossacks had to swear allegiance to the tsar, they retained significant liberties (for example, the freedom of movement: in contrast to the Russians, the Cossacks could leave service) and got some economic privileges (such as tax-free trade and the license to produce and sell alcohol). The name "Sloboda Ukraine" comes from *slobodá* (settlement) and is etymologically connected to the modern Ukrainian word *svobóda* (freedom); *ity na slobodú* means "to go to the free lands".[47] From the middle of the 17th century and almost until the end of the 19th century the territory was populated mainly by Ukrainians, with a Russian population of around 10-15%. From the beginning of colonization the territory of Sloboda Ukraine was organized in five regimental districts (*polki*) of Sloboda Cossacks. Such a regiment had a Cossacks self-administration, which was elected on a democratic basis and was simultaneously under the control of the local Russian administration, which was responsible for general defence policy, criminal justice issues and so on. From the beginning of the 19th century this self-administration was slowly reduced, and the Cossack regiments were transformed into units of the Russian regular army. The territory of Sloboda Ukraine lost its special borderlands status with the expansion of the Russian Empire to the west and south. It was included first in the Azov guberniia and later became part of the Kiev guberniia. The last remnants of the old Cossack self-administration were finally abolished in 1765 and the *Slobidsko-Ukrainska* guberniia (with Kharkiv as a capital) became a regular administrative unit of the Russian Empire. Cossacks of the higher ranks (*starshyna*) were granted officership and *dvorianstvo* (nobility).

During the last two centuries these historical facts have served as a basis for very different interpretations.[48] First, historians of the region, while pointing to the specific history, social structure and traditions of Sloboda Ukraine, represented its history as a successful incorporation into the Russian Empire. For example, Izmail Sreznevskii (1812-1880), a Ukrainophile professor at Kharkiv University, who wrote a short sketch of Sloboda Ukraine history, underlined the role of the region in Russian military history and in the history of Russian colonization. The development of ethnographic and historical studies at Kharkiv University and the foundation of the Kharkiv Historical Philological Society (1877) contributed at the end of the 19th century to the growing awareness of Slobozhanshchyna as a Ukrainian land. The academic

---

47 Cf. Volodymyr Kravchenko's commentary to: Dmytro Bahalii, *Istoriia Slobidskoi Ukrainy*, Kharkiv: Delta 1993 [1918], p. 235 (in Ukrainian).
48 An overview of the historiography on Sloboda Ukraine would exceed the framework of this chapter. For a detailed historiographic account see Volodymyr Masliichuk, *Kozatska starshyna slobidskykh polkiv druhoi polovyny 17th – pershoi tretyny 18th stolittia*, Kharkiv: Rayder 2003, pp. 5-19.

and social activities of Kharkiv professors such as Oleksandr Potebnia (1835-1891), Dmytro Bahalii (1857-1932), Mykola Sumtsov (1854-1922) and others not only stimulated the raising of Ukrainian national consciousness but also prepared the ground for the modernization of regional identity as a necessary element of a nation state and a capitalist economy. As one of the academic and cultural centres of the region, Kharkiv also became an important site of the nationalist movement. With the abolishment of restrictions on the public use of Ukrainian language in the early 20th century one of the leaders of Ukrainian nationalism, Kharkiv lawyer Mykola Mikhnovskyi, founded the newspaper *Slobozhanshchyna* – its title sounding like a challenge to the local Russian-language press, which usually labelled the region as "South Russia".

The works of the Kharkiv historian Dmytro Bahalii (who was also rector of Kharkiv University from 1906-1919 and mayor of the city from 1914-1917) were especially important for the formation of the regional identity of Sloboda Ukraine.[49] They were popularized in Soviet Ukraine in the 1920s, but later denounced as "nationalist". Bahalii was rediscovered and enthusiastically read with new eyes after 1991. In fact it is his interpretation of the regional history which has become widely accepted and thus provided a basis for the post-Soviet identity of Slobozhanshchyna. According to Bahalii, the identity of Slobozhanshchyna is certainly Ukrainian. In addition to the ethnographic and linguistic evidence, he presents historical arguments: the territory was colonized mainly by Ukrainian Cossacks; it had an autonomous status and was under traditional Cossack military administrative order similar to the Hetmanate.[50] The contemporary Ukrainian historian Serhii Plokhy has shown that the myth of the Ukrainian Cossacks was one of the main founding narratives of the Ukrainian nation in the 19th and early 20th centuries. Originally related to a limited territory, the Cossack myth has successfully expanded to other

---

[49] The most important works of Dmytro Bahalii in regard to the history of Sloboda Ukraine are: *Istoriia Kharkova za 250 let ego sushchestvovaniia*, Kharkiv, vol. 1, 1905; *Istoriia Slobidskoi Ukrainy*, Kharkiv 1918.

[50] The Hetmanate (in Ukrainian *Hetmanshchyna*) was the Ukrainian Cossack protostate that between 1649 and 1775 was located in the central and north-eastern regions of today's Ukraine. Its first leader, Bohdan Khmelnytsky, ruled from 1648 to 1657. As a result of the Treaty of Pereyaslav the Hetmanate lost its independence. In 1667 the Treaty of Andrusovo (*Andrusiv*) divided it between Russia and Poland. In 1764 the autonomy of the Cossack state and the position of the hetman were abolished by Catherine II of Russia.

lands (such as Galicia). Later it was used to claim the integrity of Ukrainian territory, united by the same glorious Cossack past.[51] A similar point was also made by Andreas Kappeler: "One could say that the contradiction between the history of elites and the history of the people is reconciled in the Cossack myth. This myth demonstrates the specificity and originality of Ukrainian history in the most articulate way. The socio-political specificities of Cossack tradition and its relation to Orthodoxy and Ukrainian culture are part of the core of Ukrainian history construction, which thus combines elements of "Western" (civic) and "non-Western" (ethnic) models of nation."[52] In his *History of Sloboda Ukraine* Dmytro Bahalii extended the power of the Cossack national myth to Slobozhanshchyna, underlining in this way that it is the core Ukrainian land. He also argued that before colonization during the 17th century *Dyke Pole* did not belong to the Muscovy state (a view contested later by Soviet historiography). For him Sloboda Ukraine was a part of the historical Ukrainian territory because before the Mongol-Tatar invasion it was populated by the Eastern Slavs of the Kievan Rus, which were ancestors of the Ukrainians. At the same time, Bahalii pointed to the peculiarities of Sloboda Ukraine and the Sloboda Cossacks. Without opposing them explicitly to the "original" Cossacks of the Hetmanate, he stressed the peaceful and constructive intentions of the Sloboda settlers, their preoccupation with agriculture rather than with military endeavours and their interest in keeping peace with their neighbours. There are well-known historical facts which have marginalized Sloboda Ukraine in the nationalist historiographic discourse. For example, although Slobozhanshchyna had the same Cossack administrative military order, it had less autonomy than the Hetmanate and was under the direct control of the Russian administration. It was never part of the Hetmanate, despite some attempts to reunite the Ukrainian lands. Slobozhanshchyna stayed loyal to the tsar during the anti-Russian Cossack uprisings and refused to join them. For this loyalty the Cossacks of Slobozhanshchyna were later rewarded by the

---

51   Serhii Plokhy, "Historical Debates and Territorial Claims. Cossack Mythology in the Russian-Ukrainian Border Dispute," in: Frederick Starr (ed.), *Legacy of History in Russia and the New States of Eurasia*, Armonk, NY/London: M. E. Sharpe 1994.

52   Andreas Kappeler, "Die Kosaken-Ära als zentraler Baustein der Konstruktion einer national-ukrainischen Geschichte: Das Beispiel der Zeitschrift *Kievskaja Starina* 1882-1891," in: idem, *Der schwierige Weg zur Nation: Beitrage zur neueren Geschichte der Ukraine*, Vienna: Boehlau 2003, pp. 123-135.

tsar with some trade and tax privileges, which contributed to the prosperity of the region. As the first Ukrainian land incorporated into the Russian Empire, Sloboda Ukraine also underwent a significant loss of Ukrainian traditions and identity. Mykhailo Hrushevskyi (1866-1834), the founder of Ukrainian national historiography, saw the historical role of Sloboda Ukraine rather in negative terms. He believed that in the colonization movement, "extensive energy took over intensive. The issue of Ukraine's independence was destroyed at the price of its territorial expansion".[53] Hrushevsky argued that Sloboda Ukraine was a weaker, paler copy of the Hetmanate and the Sloboda regiments were a touchstone for abolishing Cossack traditions and privileges in the Hetmanate. In Bahalii's interpretation these historical facts did not contradict the true Ukrainian identity of Slobozhanshchyna. He stressed that the proto-Ukrainian elite, with its rich traditions and awareness of the glorious past, never ceased to exist in Slobozhanshchyna. This is illustrated by the founding of Kharkiv University in 1805, which was initiated by the local community. Without denying the contradictions and tensions between Ukrainians and Russians – especially between the Ukrainian settlers and the Russian administration – Bahalii avoided putting national conflicts at the centre of the region's history.

The ambivalence of the historical identity of Slobozhanshchyna persisted in Soviet times. Although Dmytro Bahalii was denounced as a "bourgeois nationalist," Soviet historiography of Slobozhanshchyna was heavily based on his works. It is telling that the name "Slobozhanshchyna" did not acquire negative connotations in the official historical discourse. In Soviet historiography, Sloboda Ukraine became the true embodiment of the "eternal" Russian-Ukrainian friendship. This is demonstrated, for example, by the book by Kharkiv historian Anton Slusarskiy[54], which was published in 1954 on the occasion of the 300th anniversary of the Pereyaslav Treaty. Nevertheless, the historical narrative of Slobozhanshchyna kept its subversive "nationalist" potential even in Soviet times, and by the end of the 1980s a significant part of the Kharkiv intelligentsia was sympathetic to *Narodnyi Ruch* and supported the idea of Ukraine's independence. In this cultural milieu, the historical myth of Slobozhanshchyna was restored in its "nationalist" version, emphasizing

---

53   Cited in Masliichuk, *Kozatska starshyna*, p. 13.
54   Anton Sliusarskyi, *Slobidska Ukraina. Istorychnyi narys 17-18 stolitt*, Kharkiv: Kharkivske knuzhkovo-gazetne vyrobnytstvo 1954.

the "originally Ukrainian" character of the region in opposition to external Russian influences. "Slobozhanshchyna" became associated with the Ukrainian language and culture, which had survived in the rural area if not in the city.

These "nationalist" interpretations challenged both the dominance of the Russian language in Kharkiv and the opportunist attitude of the regional political elites with regard to Ukrainization. In this context the ambivalent Slobozhanshchyna myth once again became politically desirable. The rediscovery of the region's historical identity made Bahalii's works popular in Kharkiv after 1991: they were republished and widely used as textbooks on local history. Kharkiv historian Volodymyr Kravchenko stressed their academic and political relevance in his commentaries to Bahalii's *History of Sloboda Ukraine*, newly edited in 1993: "Bahalii was the first to provide a scholarly understanding of the colonization of Sloboda Ukraine as a meeting and interaction site of the two streams of settlers from Russia and from Ukraine."[55] In Kravchenko's introduction to the new edition, Bahalii is presented as a historian who, contrary to the Hrushevskyi school, studied Ukrainian history in a close connection with Russian history, and who viewed this connection in a positive light.[56] Bahalii's arguments seemed to reinforce the vision of Slobozhanshchyna as a region with a multicultural character (which is in fact a product of Soviet history). According to Kravchenko, the geographical location of Slobozhanshchyna made it a "zone of active contacts and mutual influences of various civilizations and cultures. From approximately the 17th century onwards, the interaction between Ukrainian and Russian cultures in the broad sense became decisive for the historical destiny of this land. Through a kind of joint *reconquista*, Ukrainians and Russians won back the territory of Slobozhanshchyna in a severe fight with the neighbouring states and colonized it. They created a material and spiritual culture which absorbed the various dimensions of the national-cultural elements of both."[57]

The discourses of "traditional multiculturalism" and Ukrainian–Russian bilingualism became very popular after 1991 as one of the ways to construct

---

55 Dmytro Bahalii, *Istoriia Slobidskoi Ukrainy*, p. 236 (in Ukrainian).
56 Volodymyr Kravchenko, "Introduction", Dmytro Bahalii, *Istoriia Slobidskoi Ukrainy*, p. 8.
57 Kravchenko, "Introduction", p. 6.

a specific regional identity around the core issue of Russian-Ukrainian relations. The identity of Slobozhanshchyna was partly reinvented as an alternative to the ethnic concept of the Ukrainian nation and as a counter-narrative to "post-colonial" interpretations of Ukrainian history. In this discourse, the region is represented as bearer of a special historical experience: namely, the voluntary and mutually beneficial interaction of Russians and Ukrainians. Kharkiv historian Serhii Kudelko, who since 2008 has headed the Center for Local History at Kharkiv National University, points to the "uniqueness of Kharkiv among other big cities of Ukraine which lies in the fact that there was not a one case of ethnic, racial or religious conflict here... Kharkiv inhabitants are characterized by traditional hospitality..., negative attitude to xenophobia and religious intolerance... Their native languages are both Ukrainian and Russian".[58] This discourse is also popular in local politics and school education. According to Vladimir Grinev, one of Kharkiv's Russian-speaking politicians of the 1990s, the interconnection of Russian and Ukrainian cultures is crucial for Sloboda Ukraine, as well as the tolerance of ethnic and cultural diversity and traditional bilingualism.[59] The new school textbook on the geography of the Kharkiv region published in 2001 proudly reports about the multinational character of the region (more than 100 nationalities) as an asset. It informs that Ukrainians compose 63% and Russians 33% of the population of the region, and mentions without additional comment that its population speaks both Ukrainian and Russian.[60]

No wonder that the myth of Slobozhanshchyna was also appropriated by those who claim to represent the interests of the Russian speakers in Ukraine. The program *Pervaia Stolitsa* (The First Capital) produced by the young Kharkiv journalist Konstantin Kevorkian has been one such ambivalent attempt to reinvent the local history. His popular version of Kharkiv's history was presented as a documentary series on local television and later published as a collection of historical essays.[61] Although the title of his program

---

58 Serhii Kudelko, "Ethnic and social processes in Sloboda Ukraine", *Mizhnarodna mihratsiia ta mizhetnichni stosunky na Slobozhanshchyni* (seminar proceedings), Kharkiv: Konstanta 2004, pp. 23-26; here p. 26.
59 Vladimir Grinev (Volodymyr Hryniov), "Socio-economic and cultural-historical aspects of regional politics in Ukraine," *Region*, no. 2-3 (1998), p. 13 (in Russian).
60 Viktoria Sadkina, *Heohrafiia ridnoho kraiu*, Kharkiv: Skorpion, 2000, pp. 65-66.
61 Kevorkian, *Pervaia Stolitsa*, Kharkiv: Folio 2002.

Pervaia Stolitsa refers to the years 1919-1934, when Kharkiv was the capital of Soviet Ukraine and a centre of Ukrainization politics, the "golden age" of the city according to Kevorkian was the end of the 19th century, the period of rapid economic growth and cultural flourishing. Thus, his version of Kharkiv history tries to reconcile Soviet and Russian imperial narratives with local Ukrainian narratives and symbols. Kevorkian sees the path to Kharkiv's renewed prosperity and cultural revival in economic regionalization (the idea of a free economic zone) and in turning the city into the "shadow capital of the Russian-speaking culture in Ukraine."[62] Kharkiv emerged as an urban centre connecting Russia and Ukraine and owed its success to this role as a mediator; therefore, it should reacquire this traditional role. The main obstacles in this scenario, according to Kevorkian, are the "Ukrainian nationalists", who are unable to accept the cultural specificity of Kharkiv and are afraid of its potential political influence. According to Kevorkian, Kharkiv's identity as a merchant centre and a mediator between Ukraine and Russia is not related to the Ukrainian rural ethnic environment. Therefore, it could become a capitalist "small tiger" – liberal, multicultural and indifferent to the issue of national identity.

Both the specific history and the cultural ambivalence of Slobozhanshchyna were embraced by the regional ruling elite; for example, shortly after 1991 the main regional newspaper *Sotsialistychna Kharkivshchyna* was renamed in *Slobidsky Kray*. This new narrative gives the region its own identity and provides symbolic resources that go beyond the obsolete Soviet mythology but are still compatible with it. It underlines the originally Ukrainian character of the region, while leaving enough space for the historical justification of the "traditionally close Ukrainian-Russian relations" and a new/old role of Kharkiv as a mediator in the economic cooperation between the two countries. Thus, "Kharkiv is a capital of Ukrainian-Russian cooperation" was the slogan of the pro-presidential political bloc "For a United Ukraine" in the 2002 parliamentary elections.

The specific historical and cultural identity of the region is considered important enough to be reflected in the "Regional Program of Social and Economic Development until 2010". This document stressed that the political

---

62   Kevorkian, *Pervaia Stolitsa*, p. 186.

orientation to Russia and the cultural closeness to Ukraine give the region a specific ambivalence. The text underlines the rich traditions of civil society and academic freedom, but also admits the deficit of national consciousness and the low status of the Ukrainian language. The document states that, in the past, "The specificity of the region expressed itself in the absence of a clear character, avoiding extremities, and in a certain ambivalence. *Kharkivshchyna* very early became a meeting place of various cultures and peoples, therefore tolerance, ability to mutual understanding and dialogue characterized the inhabitants of the Kharkiv oblast from the beginning. Besides, political values and symbols played a less important role in their lives than economic and cultural factors."[63] According to this document, regional values and traditions (pragmatism, civic self-organization, tolerance, openness to innovation, and a mixed Ukrainian-Russian culture) can make a considerable contribution to nation building and provide a "ground for solidarity and social mobilization under conditions of social apathy, cynicism and disorientation".

According to the Regional Program the lack of a clear Ukrainian national character, the political passivity and the indifference to the Ukrainian national idea in the region is compensated by other virtues. The document presents the identity of Slobozhanshchyna as based on the values of market and entrepreneurship. Here, Slobozhanshchyna is a potential bearer of the "capitalist spirit" embodying pragmatic attitudes, openness to innovations and cultural influences, the priority of private interests, orientation to family prosperity, self-confidence and protest against state paternalism, the idea of modest but honest enrichment, and the historical traditions of charity and social responsibility of business.[64] In the early 1990s the idea of a special economic "Slobozhanshchyna" mentality served to legitimize the market transformations and the interests of private business. Being apolitical, but anticommunist at the same time, it played a special role in the self-identification of the region after 1991 in opposition to the "national-democratic" west. This

---

63 Regional Program "Kharkivshchyna – 2010", suspended on February 3, 2009 by decision of the Kharkiv Oblast Council; see http://oblrada.kharkov.ua/dod/1106V38 d07.doc (last accessed February 7, 2010).
64 Regional Program "Kharkivshchyna – 2010".

narrative of "traditional economic pragmatism" has been serving to legitimize Ukrainian-Russian cross-border cooperation to this day.

Conclusion: A Euroregion in the absence of "Europe"?

Is a Euroregion at the Ukrainian-Russian border not a contradiction in itself? Being outside the EU – and not even at the external border of the enlarged EU – how European can this "Euroregion" be at all? Most Ukrainian experts focus on the Euroregions at the western border of Ukraine, which are considered primarily to be important instruments of European integration – in other words, bridges to the EU.[65] The Russian-Ukrainian Euroregions have been given only marginal attention, not only due to their relatively young age, but also because of their ambivalent geopolitical status. Can they contribute to the political and economic modernization of Ukraine and its eventual accession to the EU, or do they instead represent a geopolitical alternative to the "European choice"? If one considers Ukraine's relations with Russia and the EU as a "zero sum game", the Ukrainian-Russian Euroregions are easily associated with post-Soviet re-integration and restoration of Russia's imperial sphere of influence.

However, the very notion of "Euroregion" is as ambiguous as the geopolitical definition of "Europe" itself. Euroregions as a form of cross-border cooperation have no single legal status. The term "suggests simply a feeling of belonging to Europe and a willingness to participate in the process of European integration."[66] For example, the "Carpathian Euroregion" on the western border of Ukraine was created when its neighbours Poland and Slovakia were not yet official EU candidates. Although the "Slobozhanshchyna" project has to be seen in the context of the political rapprochement between Russia and Ukraine in the last years of Leonid Kuchma's presidency, in the broader geopolitical sense the emergence of the new Euroregions at the Ukrainian-Russian border is the result of EU enlargement and European integration. Kharkiv geographers Golikov and Chernomaz suggested a classification of the existing Euroregions according to axes of cross-border coopera-

---

65   Lyubomyr Petrenko, "Euroregion – a bridge to Europe for Ukraine", *JI*, http://www.ji-magazine.lviv.ua/kordon/ostpolitik/2003/dwelle-1204.htm (in Ukrainian) (last accessed February 7, 2010).
66   Cf. the Council of Europe website, http://www.coe.int.

tion: the first axis goes along the borders between Western European countries, the second one along the border of Western Europe and the post-socialist countries of Eastern and Central Europe, and the third one along the western border of the former USSR. Historically, there have been three different types of Euroregions, aimed at solving quite different political problems. Golikov and Chernomaz add to this classification a fourth axis of cross-border regions, which is presently being formed: the zone along the border of the Russian Federation with the western "new independent states," namely Ukraine and Belarus.[67] These Euroregions differ from their predecessors in many respects: they do not have to deal with the burden of historical conflicts and the challenge of ethnic diversity, and they often unite not peripheral but core economic regions while the populations still have intensive family ties and frequent contacts across the border. The Kharkiv and Belgorod oblasts belong to this fourth axis of cross-border cooperation. As the boundaries of Europe are in flux, particularly in the east of the continent, one cannot deny Slobozhanshchyna a Euroregion status.

However, the question still remains: What is behind this "Euro" façade of regional politics? Can the Ukrainian-Russian Euroregions have a modernizing effect on the political systems and economies of both countries or do they just serve to legitimize the particularistic interests of the regional "business-administrative groups"? In fact, the post-Soviet Euroregions are rather ambivalent and fulfil multiple functions. Depending on the political situation, they can be used by the regional elites as a bargaining chip in power negotiations with the centre, as an element of electoral campaigns attracting the voices of the Russian speakers, or as a means to immunize oneself with a "politically correct" pro-European rhetoric against accusations of pro-Russian sympathies. Pragmatic considerations concerning potential EU funding and other benefits of international cooperation also play a role. As Vendina and Kolossov note, creating a Euroregion can be a political manoeuvre that allows a territory to acquire a special economic status or to be granted investment and tax privileges, which are of interest for the regional business groups.[68] A Euroregion is often used as a symbolic resource promoting the "European"

---

67 Golikov and Chernomaz, "The Euroregion 'Slobozhanshchyna'", pp. 52-54 (in Russian).
68 Vendina and Kolossov, "Partnership that Bypasses Barriers", op. cit.

image of the regional authorities and politicians, and helping to attract foreign investments and to get subsidies from the state budget.

Currently the "Slobozhanshchyna" Euroregion serves mostly as an additional communication channel which allows regional authorities from Ukraine and Russia to discuss problems of common interest and even solve some urgent issues, avoiding the mediation of Kyiv and Moscow. To some extent it also works as a learning platform which provides an exchange of information with other Euroregions and the advice of international (European) experts. But apart from its communication and representation functions, it has little modernizing effect on the regional economies of the borderlands. To date, the "Slobozhanshchyna" Euroregion has failed to facilitate economic growth, technical innovation or the creation of new jobs in the border regions; no "breakthrough" has happened in academic and technical cooperation, education and cross-border tourism. The Russian expert Leonid Vardomskiy explains the limitations of post-Soviet cross-border cooperation by the dominance of the traditional "trade" model based on differences in prices on goods and services on both sides of the border.[69] To go beyond the "trade" model, he argues, would require a significant liberalisation of the border regime, including border, migration and custom controls.

Another constraint for the "Slobozhanshchyna" Euroregion is the specificity of post-Soviet regional politics, which serves the economic interests of the "business-administrative groups" and the re-election of local politicians but blocks grassroots initiatives. "Russia and Ukraine remain highly centralized states: in both countries civil societies which force authorities take the interests of local residents into account are rather weak. The main moving forces of 'Euroregion building' have to date been administrations dealing with cross-border problems, some politicians using this topic for self-advertising, and also certain intellectual elites, which support the idea of integration".[70] Without the democratization of the local self-government and a decentralization of power in both Ukraine and Russia the "Euroregion" is just a label. However, as we remember from the first section of this chapter, similar ten-

---

69   Leonid Vardomskiy, "Cross-border cooperation on the 'new' and 'old' borders of Russia", *Evraziiskaia ekonomicheskaia integratsiia*, no. 1 (2008), p. 105 (in Russian).
70   Vendina and Kolossov, "Partnership that Bypasses Barriers".

sions between the economic and administrative roles of a Euroregion and its function of public policy making are not only characteristic of the post-Soviet space.

European enlargement has yet to bring Ukraine into the EU, but it has moved the EU closer to Ukraine's borders. The new European Union has developed a "New Neighbourhood" strategy and (re-)shaped its policies concerning the external EU border. This affects first of all the regime for Ukraine's western border and the status of the respective Euroregions that Ukraine has established together with the new EU members: Poland, Slovakia, Hungary and Romania. However, the Ukrainian-Russian border regions can also profit from the European programs of regional development. In a broader sense, EU enlargement affected the situation on the eastern border of Ukraine no less than on the western side. As the middle-term prospects of EU membership are quite unlikely, Ukraine most probably will develop looser forms of association with the EU and more flexible instruments of integration. The Euroregions can serve as one of them; the question, however, is how to make them more efficient.

At the same time, it is the Ukrainian-Russian Euroregions where two integration projects overlap and come into conflict: the European Union, which becomes more reluctant the further east it expands, and resurrected Russia gathering its former imperial fragments into a new sphere of influence. The political and symbolic role of Europe in Ukrainian politics and society is challenged by Russia, which conceptualizes its integrationist ambitions as a restoration of the common East Slavic / Orthodox space. Since the Orange Revolution, Moscow has changed its political strategy for regaining influence in Ukraine and now works more closely with some segments of Ukrainian civil society and the eastern Ukrainian regional elites, using NGOs and youth movements. One cannot rule out that this new strategy (and the predictable response from the Ukrainian side) will also affect the Ukrainian-Russian Euroregions and turn them into a stage of political conflict.

The prospects of cross-border regionalisation are inevitably limited by the politics of "nationalizing the borderlands" pursued by both Ukraine and Russia. While the common historical "Sloboda" identity did not survive the 20th century and is almost non-existent today, various hybrid and mixed identities combining some elements of Ukrainian and Russian culture, Orthodox belief and Soviet symbols are widespread in the region. Ukrainian nationalist and national democratic discourses try to devaluate these identities as postcolonial and "Little Russian". From this point of view the shared cultural traditions, religious beliefs and linguistic similarities in the Ukrainian and Russian borderlands are interpreted as remnants of an "imperial" past which cannot provide a basis for a "modern" and "European" cross-border regionalization.

But in fact it is not so easy to differentiate between the "new" and the "old" regionalism, even in the contemporary European context where the former imperial provinces reinvent themselves across national borders. As Jouni Hakli asked, "[Is] the emerging regional question merely a logical continuation in the long disintegration process of the great European polyethnic empires, or an altogether new development reflecting the late modern networked form of organization in the areas of communication and technology?"[71] It is legitimate to assume that similar processes are going on today in the post-Soviet – and in particular in the Ukrainian-Russian – borderlands.

---

71   Hakli, "Cross-Border Identities in the New Europe".

III Living (with the) Border

6 Making Sense of a New Border: Social Transformations and Shifting Identities in Five Near-Border Villages

The fact that globalization links national economies and facilitates the flow of ideas, technologies and people does not necessarily make borders irrelevant. Particularly in the post-Soviet space, the effects of globalization and integration into the world economy are often combined with the emergence of new peripheries, with strengthening cultural boundaries and establishing new frontiers. It is especially people living in border regions who experience these transformation processes in their everyday lives. The construction of the new border between Ukraine and Russia brought a lot of changes (such as the introduction of passport and customs controls, reorganization of transport routes, restructuring of local labour markets), which have made the territory of the neighbouring state less accessible[1] and more "distant" for the local inhabitants. People have been adjusting their social contacts, their shopping and leisure habits to the new situation; they take the fact of the border into account in their labour market and education strategies. However, the new situation of becoming a periphery, a borderland territory, is perceived on both sides of the Ukrainian-Russian border in different ways depending on social and economic factors. The emerging economic asymmetry is not only an important factor for the new advantages and disadvantages of living at the border, but also contributes to shaping new national identities – Ukrainian and

---

[1] Visas are not required from Ukrainian and Russian citizens for visiting the neighbouring country. The border can still be crossed with "internal" Ukrainian and Russian passports. Plans to introduce international passports as obligatory for crossing the Ukrainian-Russian border were discussed, but postponed because of the high administrative costs. In the 2004 Ukrainian presidential election campaign, the pro-Russian candidate Viktor Yanukovych promised to make border crossing to Russia easier. In 2007-08 the Russian Ministry of Foreign Affairs repeatedly warned that a visa regime can be introduced for Ukrainian citizens in case the country becomes a member of NATO.

Russian. The spatial reorganization related to the border construction is combined with nation building implemented through education and administrative reforms, thus changing the symbolic links to the territory and causing a disintegration of the former common Soviet space. For example, the respective new national historical narratives have been introduced in local schools on both sides of the border and new national symbols have replaced the old Soviet ones. These changes in the individual and collective mental maps were followed in the 1990s by radical social and economic transformations (land reforms, the dismantling of the kolkhoz[2] system and the emergence of private agricultural companies, a rise of unemployment and social insecurity). In the eyes of the local population these transformations, and first of all their negative effects, are inseparable from the fact of the new border: spatial and temporal boundaries are closely related. The new border represents the irreversibility of the post-1991 political and social changes, thus separating not only Ukraine from Russia, but also the present, real Ukraine from an imagined Soviet Union.

This chapter focuses on social and economic factors that contribute to the different perceptions and images of the border among Ukrainians and Russians and, in this way, to the process of shaping new national identities. By analyzing the results of interviews in villages on both sides of the border the essay seeks to show how the particular experience of "becoming a borderland" has been connected to another experience – of becoming Ukrainians or Russians; how in the narratives of the local inhabitants the new border animates their identity, their political loyalty (or lack of it) and local patriotism. The first section of the chapter provides the necessary information on the fieldwork, the methodology and the site of the research. The second section uses data from group interviews to look at how local inhabitants perceive the reorganization of their habitual space after the establishment of the new border. The third section focuses on local narratives of social change and on

---

2   *Kolkhoz* (Russian) or *kolhosp* (Ukrainian) in the former Soviet Union was a cooperative agricultural enterprise operated on state-owned land by peasants from a number of households who belonged to the collective and who were paid as salaried employees on the basis of quality and quantity of labour contributed. Conceived as a voluntary union of peasants, the *kolkhoz* became the dominant form of agricultural enterprise as the result of a state program of expropriation of private holdings embarked on in 1929. Operational control was maintained by state authorities through the appointment of *kolkhoz* chairmen (nominally elected).

their role in shaping the new national identities. The fourth section addresses the new / old collective "symbolic geography" of the borderlands (the images of "us" and "them", the local discourses of Ukrainian-Russian relations and the role of the national media and the school in the processes of nationalizing the borderlands).

6.1 Methodology and research sites

The research was conducted in the summers of 2003 and 2004 in three villages of the Kharkiv oblast (Ukraine) and in two villages of the Belgorod oblast (Russian Federation). All villages are located in the so-called controlled near-border area.[3] The research was based on focus group interviews and additional individual interviews with local inhabitants. The focus groups consisted of people from various occupations: teachers, village administrators, medical personal, bookkeepers, truck drivers, workers in the agricultural enterprises and small farmers. Pensioners, young people and the unemployed were also represented. The focus group interviews proved to be an effective method for collecting valuable information about people's attitudes and perceptions of the new border: the collective discussion stimulated the participants to recall important details, to talk of interesting examples, and to agree or disagree actively with each other. At the same time, especially in this case, group interviews as a research instrument had their limits: for example, young people were reluctant to talk in the presence of older persons, and questions about illegal cross-border business were sensitive. However, it was possible to collect missing information subsequently in individual interviews or informal talks. In all cases representatives of the village administration took part in the focus groups; in a small village, it is not possible to organize a focus group without their consent and goodwill, which is even truer if one works as a Ukrainian researcher on Russian territory. In some cases the official affirmative discourse on state borders dominated the discussion, but it was still interesting to see how the village administration adapted the official policy to the local needs and the interests of the village community.

---

3   A "controlled near-border area" is a special zone officially established according to the Law on the State Border of Ukraine, where the movement and behaviour of local inhabitants and visitors are regulated according to special rules.

Street in Udy

The focus group interviews were based on three groups of questions. The first group concerned the historical roots of the village, the most important events in its Soviet and post-Soviet history, the ethnic and linguistic identities of the participants, the language issue and attitudes to Ukrainization. The second group of questions dealt with the economic aspects of near-border life: Does the border have an effect on family well-being? Does it create new (legal or illegal) opportunities to earn money, and if so, for whom? Do people cross the border to earn money, to shop or to sell products on the local markets? Does the border itself provide new jobs for the local population? Do people consider living near the border an advantage or a disadvantage? Finally, the third set of questions concerned the sphere of emotional attitudes and perceptions of the border: Does the fact of the border irritate people in their everyday lives, or have they become used to it? Do they feel that the border is an obstacle? Do they feel better protected or rather threatened because of the border? What do they feel while crossing it?

Research was conducted in five near-border villages (Udy, Zemlianky and Hlyboke on the Ukrainian side, and Shchetinovka and Zhuravlevka on the Russian one). They represent different constellations of geographic, social and economic factors and, therefore, various combinations of gains and losses since 1991. Here I briefly present the social and economic background, as well as the particular situation of each village.

The three Ukrainian villages belong to three different administrative districts (raions) of the Kharkiv oblast. Udy (Zolochiv raion) was historically a Russian ethnic village founded in the 17th century by settlers from Russia.[4]

---

[4] In the 17th century the territory where all five villages are situated was a vast, thinly populated frontier zone called *Dyke Pole* (Wild Field) open to the attacks of nomadic Tatars. It was colonized by the common efforts of the Muscovite state and Ukrainian settlers – Cossacks and peasants – coming from the neighbouring Polish territories. Therefore, Russian and Ukrainian ethnic settlements have historically coexisted in this region (more in: Liudmila Chizhikova, *Russko-ukrainskoe pogranich'e. Istoriia i sudby traditsionno-bytovoi kultury (XIX-XX veka)*, Moscow: Nauka 1988). Cultural boundaries between both ethnic groups (clothing, elements of house design and decoration, religious holidays) almost disappeared during the 20th century, especially under the pressure of Soviet rural modernization. In the 1920s the administrative border was negotiated between the Soviet Ukrainian government and the government of the Russian Federation. It was generally drawn according to ethnic and linguistic criteria, but some ethnic enclaves were left on both sides of the border. In the 1920s the Soviet nationalities policy encouraged ethnic differentiation: the administrative division of the territory both in Ukraine and in Rus-

Due to intermarriages and intensive migration in Soviet times it is not predominantly Russian anymore. However, Russian is the common language spoken in the village and most people are aware of its Russian ethnic roots. Women of the older generation can still remember some Russian folk songs, and I was told that traditional religious holidays are still celebrated in the Russian way. Probably more than folklore and half-forgotten traditions, it is the language of instruction at school which is important for reproducing "Russian" identity:[5] the secondary school in Udy is the only Russian-language school in the Zolochiv raion. The village has rather limited public transport connections: the bus to Kharkiv goes only four times a week, the distance to the nearest railway station is 12 km and people usually walk. In Soviet times Udy was part of a flourishing kolkhoz, whose respected head was able to provide investments in the social infrastructure of the village. Today the village is in crisis: buildings from the 1970s and 80s cannot be maintained anymore and lie in ruins.

The second village, Zemlianky, belongs to the Vovchansk raion of the Kharkiv oblast. It is predominantly Ukrainian, but also with a rather mixed population. Teaching in the village school has always been in Ukrainian. Unlike in Udy, where the "Russian identity" of the village was a structuring factor for the discussions, in Zemlianky people were not inclined to emphasize their ethnic identity, perhaps because it is not opposed but rather corresponds to the new national identity. Russian language is taught as an elective subject, but in fact is obligatory, because, as the director told us, "there are many Russians here and the teacher should not lose her job".[6] The fate of Zemlianky is very much determined by its geographic location: 40 km from the raion centre Vovchansk, 130 km from Kharkiv. The bus to Kharkiv goes once a day and takes more than two hours. There is another bus going from

---

sia down to the village councils and *kolkhoz* level was based on ethnic criteria (see Terry Martin, *The Affirmative Action Empire. Nations and Nationalism in the Soviet Union, 1923-1939,* Ithaca: Cornell University Press 2001). From the end of the 1920s ethnic Ukrainians in Russia became a subject of intensive Russification; they did not have access to Ukrainian language education or press. Ethnic Russians in Ukraine usually had access to Russian or bilingual schools. Soviet industrialization and cultural assimilation made ethnic differences between Russians and Ukrainians in this region almost irrelevant.

5   Identity change in Udy is discussed in detail in the next chapter.
6   Interview with the school director, Zemlianky (Vovchansk raion, Kharkiv oblast, Ukraine).

Piatnitskoe (Russia) to Kharkiv via Zemlianky, and it took the village administration and local community a lot of struggle with the regional authorities to defend this route. Because of these poor connections Zemlianky's inhabitants have only limited opportunities to access the Kharkiv market to sell their products. Unemployment is a big problem, as only seasonal work is provided by the local cooperative (a transformed kolkhoz) and by four private farmers. Due to the long distance to Kharkiv and the lack of jobs, the border and the proximity of Russia are important for the economic strategies of the local inhabitants.

The third Ukrainian village, Hlyboke can be called "Soviet" because of its origins: it was founded after World War II and inhabited by newcomers from other regions of Ukraine and Russia. Most houses and the social infrastructure were built in the 1960s and 1970s. Unlike in the other two villages, gas was installed here on a permanent basis. Hlyboke is situated in the Kharkiv raion of the Kharkiv oblast and only 35 km away from the city. People can work and study in Kharkiv while living at Hlyboke. Until recently, the language of school education was Russian, but since 2000 it has been Ukrainian. Most people in the village speak both languages. Hlyboke seems to be in a better economic situation than the other two villages, although unemployment is a problem as the village has no industrial or agricultural enterprises. Most people lease the shares of land they received in the process of privatization to "Kharkivovoshchprom", a large enterprise based in Kharkiv and specialized in intensive vegetable growing. Like in Zemlianky it offers only seasonal jobs. But in the next village, Strilecha, there is a big regional psychiatric hospital with its own small farm. This institution is a very important provider of jobs for the nearby villages; it guarantees relatively high salaries and gives some additional privileges. Last but not least, the proximity of Kharkiv makes it easier to find a job in the city.

Both Udy and Hlyboke have about a thousand inhabitants, Zemlianky about six hundred. For Udy and Zemlianky the population decline is typical. After the kolkhozes were dismantled, peasants got shares of land, but only a small percentage of families managed to launch private farms due to the lack of credit, the unavailability of technical equipment and the opportunism of the local authorities. The remnants of the kolkhozes transformed themselves into cooperatives and limited companies, in some cases they were swallowed up by big agricultural firms. Most peasants lease their shares of land to these new monopolists in the village, which also provide them with seasonal work. Payment is often delayed and "in kind".[7] People earn a living from their household plots (*priusadebnoe hoziaistvo*) which are run on little money and provide food just for the family. In many cases however, part of the produce goes to the market: primarily milk and milk products, but also vegetables and meat. Rural transformation in Russia follows a similar path.[8] But the specificity of the Belgorod oblast is that its economic crisis and agricultural decline was less dramatic than in Ukraine but also, on average, in the rest of Russia. One has to understand that the nostalgia for the kolkhoz has nothing to do with ideology or a "Soviet mentality", but rather with social security and the guaranteed employment usually provided by the kolkhoz.[9] Even more importantly, dissolving kolkhoz farming threatened the household economy as the main source of survival for the rural population: "without resources provided by collectives, household production would not have been sustainable, as rural families depended on collectives to provide agricultural inputs – seed, animal feed, and services such as ploughing".[10]

On the Russian side of the border, focus groups were interviewed in two villages, both in the Belgorod raion of the Belgorod oblast: in Shchetinovka and Zhuravlevka. Shchetinovka is in the close vicinity of Udy, just 5 km away, with a population of about six hundred. The village belonged to the "Frunze" kolkhoz, which, like its Ukrainian counterpart across the border, prospered in the 1970s and 1980s.

---

7   Louise Perrotta, "Coping with the Market in Rural Ukraine", in: Ruth Mandel and Caroline Humphrey (eds.), *Markets and Moralities: Ethnographies of Postsocialism*, Oxford/New York: Berg 2002, pp. 169-190.
8   Jessica Allina-Pisano, "Land Reform and the Social Origins of Private Farmers in Russia and Ukraine", *The Journal of Peasant Studies*, no. 31 (3-4) (2004), pp. 489-514.
9   Jessica Allina-Pisano, "Sub Rosa Resistance and the Politics of Economic Reform. Land Redistribution in Post-Soviet Ukraine", *World Politics*, vol. 56 (2004), pp. 554-581; Maria Amelina, "Why Russian Peasants Remain in Collective Farms: A Household Perspective on Agricultural Restructuring", *Post-Soviet Geography and Economics*, vol. 41, no. 7 (2000), pp. 483-511.
10 Allina-Pisano, "Sub Rosa Resistance", p. 576.

BORDERLANDS INTO BORDERED LANDS 245

Post office in Shchetinovka

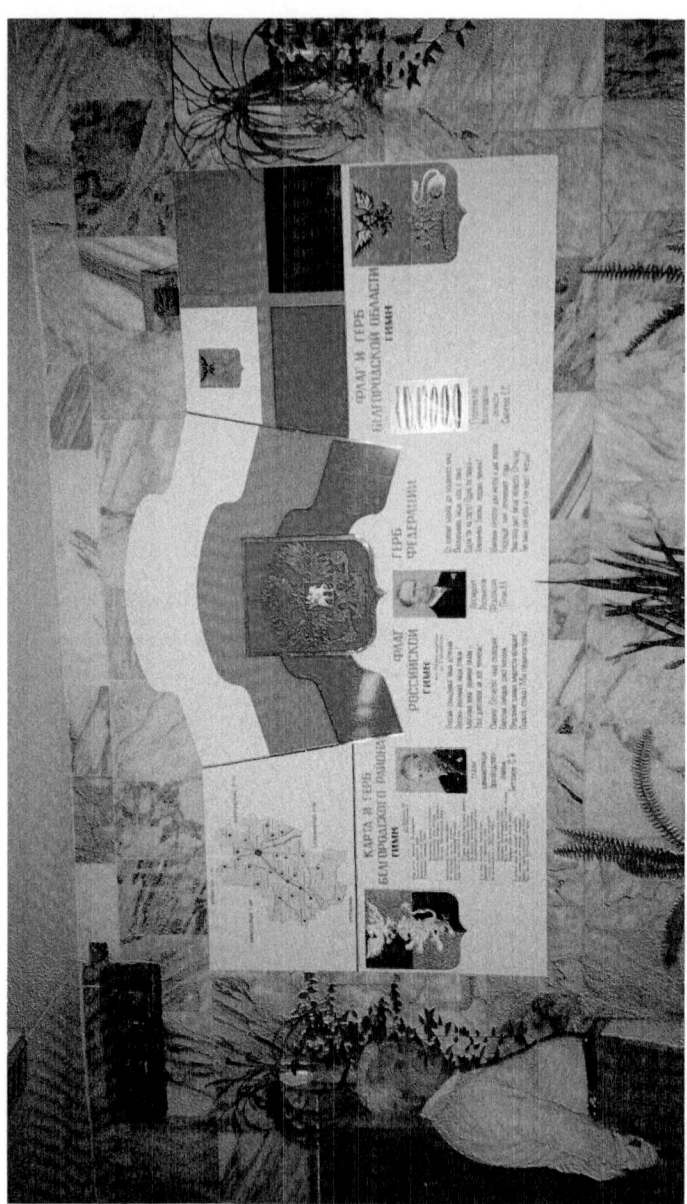

National and regional symbols in Shchetinovka school

But what is unique about the Shchetinovka, is that the "Frunze" kolkhoz is among the few in Russia which were not dismantled in the 1990s. Moreover, it has adapted successfully to the new economic situation under the leadership of the old director, a "Hero of Socialist Labour", who has kept this position for more than thirty years. The kolkhoz invests in the social infrastructure of the village, provides jobs, offers higher salaries to teachers and helps pensioners.

The second village on the Russian side, Zhuravlevka, is a neighbour of the Ukrainian villages of Hlyboke and Strilecha. In Soviet times, some inhabitants of Zhuravlevka worked in the psychiatric hospital in Strilecha and many were employed by Kharkiv industrial enterprises. Zhuravlevka had to adapt to the new border, and the new situation also turned out to be beneficial for the village: the new crossing point and the big Nekhoteevka transport terminal on the Moscow-Crimea highway was built just 5 km away. The terminal provided Zhuravlevka's inhabitants with various jobs at the customs and border control points in auto services, shops and at petrol stations. The proximity to the crossing point also means that the distance to Kharkiv (in physical and symbolic terms) has not changed significantly for the Zhuravlevka inhabitants.

It is important to note that at the time when this field research was conducted, the Belgorod oblast was more prosperous than the Kharkiv oblast. According to a research done by the Russian political geographer Vladimir Kolossov and Olga Vendina, the economic revival after the collapse of the early 1990s started in the Belgorod oblast earlier and was faster than in Kharkiv.[11] They see the reasons for this development in the more balanced structure of Belgorod's economy and in the advantages of a relatively late modernization (after World War II). Although Kharkiv as an industrial city is much bigger than Belgorod, the average salary in the Kharkiv oblast in 2001 was only 80% of that in the Belgorod oblast.

---

11   Vladimir Kolossov and Olga Vendina, "Social gradients, identity and migration flows (by the example of Belgorod and Kharkiv oblasts)", *Migratsiia i pogranichnyi rezhim: Belarus, Moldova, Rossiia i Ukraina*, Kyiv: NIPMB (National Institute for International Security Issues) 2002, pp. 21-46 (in Russian), here pp. 24-26.

Public library in Zhuravlevka

Correspondingly, pensions and other social benefits are higher on the Russian side and a lot of social indicators are better, such as housing provision, medical services and crime rates. A survey conducted in June 2001 among residents of both oblasts who were interviewed when crossing the border shows that the level of social optimism and satisfaction with the social and economic situation in the country is higher among Russian citizens.[12] I am not going to generalize the situation and project it onto other regions, but at the time when my field work was carried out, the economic and social advantages were on the Russian side, and the narratives of the respondents reflected this asymmetry.

In Ukraine the interviews and discussions were conducted in Ukrainian and Russian, depending on the preference of the audience. Here some information on the linguistic situation in the region is needed. In Soviet times some kind of bilingual policy was pursued on the Ukrainian side of the border.[13] Therefore people here usually have competence in both Ukrainian and Russian and understand both languages without difficulty. *Surzhyk*, a Creole of Ukrainian and Russian is widespread. *Surzhyk* is interpreted sometimes as a mixed language or sociolect.[14] In Udy, a formerly ethnic Russian village, the Russian language dominates (some older people still speak the Kursk dialect of Russian); in Hlyboke both languages were present equally and in Zemlianky people speak predominantly Ukrainian. Those with higher education are able to switch from one language to the other, especially school teachers and representatives of the village administration; the same is true for the younger generation. Migrants from other regions (e.g. Western Ukraine) or from Russia do not necessary assimilate to the dominant local language and

---

12   Kolossov and Vendina, "Social gradients", p. 39.
13   Liudmila Chizhikova, *Russko-ukrainskoe pogranich'e. Istoriia i sudby traditsionno-bytovoi kultury (XIX-XX veka)*, Moscow: Nauka 1988, p. 62.
14   On Surzhyk see among other works: Laada Bilaniuk, *Contested Tongues: Language Politics and Cultural Correction in Ukraine*, Ithaca and London: Cornell University Press 2005; Michael Flier, "Surzhyk: The Rules of Engagement", in: Z. Gitelman et al. (eds.), *Cultures and Nations of Central and Eastern Europe: Essays in honor of Roman Szporluk*, Cambridge, MA: HURI 2000, pp. 113-136; Valerii Khmelko, *Lingvoetnichni regionalni osoblyvosti: Tendentsii zmin za roky nezalezhnosti*, Kyiv: KIIS 2004; Nikolai Vachtin, Oksana Zhironkina et al., *Novye iazyki novykh gosudarstv: iavleniia na styke blizkorodstvennykh iazykov na postsovetskom prostranstve*, St. Petersburg: European University 2004 (in Russian), http://eu.spb.ru/ethno/projects/project3/list.htm (February 7, 2010).

keep some linguistic peculiarities for decades. From my experience the choice of the language of communication usually is situational and pragmatic, and rarely loaded with political connotations. On the Russian side of the border my interviews were conducted in Russian. Although a significant part of the population in the villages I visited have ethnic Ukrainian origins, the Ukrainian language is not taught at school and the assimilation pressure is evidently higher than in Ukraine.

As for religion, it does not represent an important factor for constituting different national identities: most residents of the Ukrainian villages, as well as those of the Russian ones consider themselves Orthodox. The role of the church in the political and social life of the villages is not very important, and many people on the Ukrainian side are not even aware which orthodox church they formally belong to: the Kyiv or the Moscow Patriarchy.[15] Indeed, the Ukrainian Orthodox Church of the Moscow Patriarchy keeps a pro-Russian position, but it seems that most people in the villages I visited did not go into such details.

My own ambivalent identity (Ukrainian citizenship but Russian as mother tongue) – which is not unusual for many Ukrainian academics – made it easier for me to understand the situation of my interviewees. On the Ukrainian side, I was considered an outsider not because of my language or ethnicity, but rather due to my urban background. Presenting myself as an "academic from Kharkiv University", I was aware of the common perception of academics as powerless and "harmless" and I used this to gain the trust of my respondents. But in some situations (especially when dealing with the representatives of the village administration) this image proved to be rather disadvantageous. In these cases, my colleague who accompanied me and who is working for the Kharkiv oblast administration would mention her position to give our mission a more "official" status. On the Russian side I was perceived as an outsider because of Ukrainian citizenship. In other words, people were more cautious in discussing with me sensitive issues such as contraband or corruption. In some cases a hidden message was present in the interviews:

---

15 There are four main Christian churches in Ukraine: the Ukrainian Orthodox Church (Moscow Patriarchy), the Ukrainian Orthodox Church (Kyiv Patriarchy), the Ukrainian Autocephalous Orthodox Church, and the Uniate (Greek-Catholic) Church.

"It was you Ukrainians who wanted independence, and you see we live now better without you".

6.2 Becoming a borderland: state, loyalty and social space

Before 1991 the border between Ukraine and Russia hardly existed for those who wanted to cross it. Russians and Ukrainians carried the same Soviet passports, and personal information contained in them (place of birth and current place of registration, as well as "nationality") did not have symbolic links to the territory. "My address in not a house or a street, my address is the Soviet Union" was a popular Soviet song in the 1970s. Limitations on the freedom of movement during the Soviet era mainly resulted from the system of compulsory registration (*propiska*). There were other significant barriers that structured the social spaces and life worlds of the Soviet people: military zones, highly protected areas along the external borders of the USSR and the so-called "closed cities" working for the military-industrial complex were not so easy to enter.[16] But the administrative boundaries between the Soviet republics practically did not matter in the everyday life. People worked, studied, shopped and visited friends across the "virtual" border, but the act of crossing was rarely a subject for discussion.

In eastern Ukraine, and especially in the regions bordering Russia, the collapse of the Soviet Union and the materialization of the new border were seen by many people as a dramatic change, threatening their mobility and social networks. Of course the new border did not emerge overnight and the hopes for some kind of "reunification" or a substitute for the USSR remained very popular in the early 1990s. Russia's position that the borders inside the CIS should stay "transparent" certainly corresponded to the mood of the population, especially in eastern Ukraine.

---

16 Olga Brednikova and Viktor Voronkov, "Border and Social Space Restructuring (the Case of Narva/Ivangorod)", in: idem (eds.), *Kochuiushchie Granitsy*, St. Petersburg: CISR Works (7), 1999, pp. 19-25, here p. 20 (in Russian).

Kozacha Lopan, a railway station at the Ukrainian-Russian border, halfway between Kharkiv and Belgorod. The border guards patrol is on its way to check the local train

But the Ukrainian leadership always saw the national borders and the ability to control them as an important attribute of state independence.[17] In 2003, the Agreement on the State Border between Ukraine and Russia was signed, which finalized four-year-long negotiations on the delimitation of the land part of the Ukrainian–Russian border. Border and customs controls were established at the Ukrainian-Russian border in 1992, first at the main highways and railways with the urgent purpose of preventing massive smuggling caused by the uneven effects of price liberalization and the sudden disruption of the economic ties between Ukrainian and Russian firms. It took a long time before the border control was tightened so that crossing the border from one village to another became an issue and people had to accept that the new border is "serious and for a while".[18]

In social anthropology the border is seen not as a line but as a special zone with its own rules, an area where the power of the state is particularly concentrated, visible and felt by people in their everyday lives. "To the inhabitants of an area adjacent to a state boundary, the degree of compulsion is partially higher than that of residents of the interior of the country".[19] In their study of the Russian-Estonian border, Brednikova and Voronkov highlight "the effects of a border as a political tool of state building on restructuring of the habitual social space, destroying old ties and developing new social networks".[20]

In this part of the chapter I trace similar processes at the Ukrainian-Russian border by showing how state power manifests itself in the borderlands and how people respond to it.

---

17 For more on the issues of border delimitation and border regime in Ukrainian-Russian relations, see chapter 2.1 of this book.

18 The rules for crossing the border have been tightened since the end of the 1990s. In addition to passport and customs controls, in 2003 migration cards were introduced both in Ukraine and Russia, and in 2004 car insurance for the neighbouring country became obligatory on both sides. The summer of 2003 saw the launch of a widely advertised experiment on simplified border crossing (the "green corridor") on the Kharkiv-Belgorod part of the border, but it turned out to be a rather short-lived political campaign.

19 Thomas Lunden and Dennis Zalamans, *Boundary Towns. Studies of Communication and Boundaries in Estonia and Its Neighbours*, Stockholm: Stockholm University Press 2000, p. 2.

20 Brednikova and Voronkov, "Border and Social Space", p. 19.

People waiting for border and customs controls to enter the local train Kharkiv-Belgorod

For the local residents the new border means first of all the necessity of always being prepared to prove their identity. In other words, it means carrying a passport even if one does not intend to cross the border, but just to go, for example, to one's own vegetable garden that adjoins the border. Mobile patrols can stop anybody on the road and search the car; they can temporarily block the road or enforce a diversion. The constant presence of the state authority in the village – border guards who impose new rules of behaviour and control the movement of people – changes the habitual space of everyday life.

To cross the border by private car is not a trivial thing, because any car, even with an empty trunk, has to pass customs control. Customs control points are installed only on the main roads, which often means a significant loss of time and petrol for the local population. For example, residents of Zemlianky, where the nearest control point was closed recently, now have to go to the main crossing point Pletn'ovka, which means some extra 80 km. Together with the unpredictable waiting time at the border it makes people feel the disadvantage of their new situation. From the state perspective, however, the construction of a new border requires special efforts to discipline and educate the local population to bring order to the "chaos" of free movement (in the official rhetoric these unpopular practices are justified as building a "civilized border"):

> *Once me and my husband, we went by car to visit our friends. They* [the border guards] *stopped us... and I had only a student ID, my passport I had left for registration ("dlia propiski") in the administration. So, they forced me to get out of the car... and said: go back and bring your passport. We keep your husband with the car... so I turned and walked back through the fields... then, some minutes later, they reconsidered and said* [to the husband]*... "OK, go drive her home and then come back". Imagine the situation, what they were saying was: "We will seize your car and you go by foot and bring your passport"* (female, 26 years, Hlyboke).

According to the regulations in the near-border controlled zone, the local peasants are obliged to submit information about their fields and cultivated crops to the local border control offices. Some plants, such as maize and sunflowers, are not allowed at the border because smugglers can hide there.[21] The official announcements displayed in the village administration, such as warnings about the danger of illegal migration, of possible crimes and serious diseases connected with illegal migrants, calls to the local inhabitants to report any strange or unknown people they see in the village or its surroundings, or the invitation for voluntary fingerprinting – all this reminds people that their village now belongs to a special zone with extraordinary rules.

How do people cope with these novelties in their narratives? Understandably, they try to "normalize" their situation by means of language: typically, they use phrases such as "this is just an ordinary village," "they (the border guards) have their business, and we do not know much about it," "we got used to them," "nothing has changed." It seems our interviewees try to ignore the imposing power of the state in their everyday lives and pretend that nothing special happens. The attempts to domesticate these new circumstances are reflected in the pejorative term *"pograntsy"* (derivative from Russian *"pogranichniki"*) for the border guards and in the numerous jokes about them. For example, local inhabitants sometimes call the regular patrols of the special anti-contraband commandos, whose members cover their faces, *"Maski-Show"* (the name of a popular TV show). At the same time, some interviewees were eager to tell us extraordinary stories about smugglers' cars racing through the village and border guards chasing them. These stories are usually told from the position of a neutral observer, though our interviewees did not deny they sometimes help smugglers in exchange for money or goods. Typically, to protect themselves, people say they used to do such things in the past, but not anymore. Here is a story told by a 60 year old female pensioner:

> *Once in our village... somebody passed by with a car. I don't know from where... he was chased* [by border guards] *... and the neighbour's gate was open... he sneaked in there...* [people laugh] *and the gate closed... they* [the border guards] *asked me: Did a car pass by? I said: No, I have not seen any* (people laugh). *Four days the car stayed there, hidden... and later they told us it was full of contraband. I said: I thought he was a just a guest* (female, former teacher, 60, Hlyboke).

---

21   Interview with the head of the village administration, Zhuravlevka, Russia.

In most cases we got negative answers to the question as to whether the presence of the border guards made people feel safer (one exception was a fire in Hlyboke, which the border guards were the first to notice and which they helped to extinguish). Often people mentioned the new "dangers" related to the near-border situation: strangers in the village, busy traffic, smugglers' cars speeding along without lights and so on. It seems the border sometimes induces a feeling of a "no-man's land", uncontrollable by both states despite the over-presence of border guards. In Zemlianky, people told us a story which could happen anywhere, but here was immediately connected with the fact of the border:

> There was one case... A girl from our village married and moved to Tishanka [a neighbouring village in Russia]. She came once to visit us and then disappeared. The Russians did not search for her, neither did the Ukrainians [the police]. Just like that! Nobody was searching for her... What had happened to her? She is a Russian citizen... Nobody knows on whose territory she disappeared – Russian or Ukrainian. She went "through the fields". The Russians cannot search here, Ukrainians cannot go there. Only two or three days they searched for her. But she has disappeared... and left two children (male, driver, 43, Zemlianky).

Local administrations usually support the border guards in their attempts to "educate" and discipline the local population. Not surprisingly, an affirmative discourse on the new border is common for village administrators both in Ukraine and in Russia. For them, the border is justified by "state interests" and economic benefits. Deliberately or not, Soviet connotations are often evoked if the authorities call for the "responsibility" and "vigilance" of ordinary citizens:

> Border guards... they make announcements. For example: please tell people who are registered here that they should always carry their passports on them. We understand, this is a border zone ("pogranzona")... in a way, we are proud... we feel responsible, we are a border zone... so we got used to it. If we go somewhere we should have our passports on us (female, administrator, 54, Hlyboke).

> It is a status or something... pride or some kind of responsibility... you know, now the village symbol... it turns out to be a border post ... oth-

> ers have, for example, a chicken – they have a chicken farm... and we have a border post! (female, 40, Zhuravlevka).

In order to mobilize the support of the local population, the border guards willingly cooperate not only with the village administrations, but also with the schools. Special lectures are given to make children aware of possible near-border threats such as illegal migration and contraband and encourage them to cooperate with the border guards. This is maybe the most effective way to anchor the border in the human heads and make its presence natural for the next generation, while for the older people it will always remain rather artificial. The school administration usually finds such cooperation with the border guards useful and adapts it to its own needs:

> We communicate with the border control service. We have a special club at school... the "Young Border Guard". We cooperate very well in terms of "military-patriotic education" [22] (female, school director, Zemlianky).

According to Lunden and Zalamans, border studies usually stress the conflict between the natural tendency of the state to integrate its territory and the interests of the individuals and social groups who profit from the contacts and interaction with the neighbouring state territory.[23] The fact is that the residents of the border areas not only often benefit from the border traffic (legal and illegal), but also sometimes internalize the arguments of the state. In the next fragment the head of the village administration in Zhuravlevka tries to challenge what she thinks is our assumption of the negative role of the border in village life. In her narrative, she avoids the contradiction between the "state interests" and the interests of the village inhabitants:

> All these talks about open borders... you know... in the end... we do not really care. I feel nothing special... in fact this border... it does not limit me... it does not press... it was a moment ... psychological... we overcame it. The thing is... why can't the Russian state give up the borders?... it is not a secret... I think you know... the customs provides the

---

22   Military-patriotic education (*"viiskovo-patriotychna pidhotovka"*) is a school course that was obligatory in the Soviet Union and still exists in Ukraine. It combines basic military skills with patriotic education.
23   Lunden and Zalamans, *Boundary Towns*, p. 1.

(state) budget with money... and this is teachers' and doctors' salaries... who would give this up? Now it is rather comfortable to cross... With the border our people, population found jobs (female, 53, Zhuravlevka).

In no way are the local residents just passive objects of border construction policies. As it was argued by Donnan and Wilson in their anthropological research on state power at the border, "the powerless, among others, have a variety of behavioural options at their disposal, including violence, avoidance, resistance, inclusion and exclusion, many forms of which have been called by James Scott (1985) the 'weapons of the weak'."[24] There are many reasons why people do not always obey the formal rules for crossing the border. First of all because they often just follow routine and do not see illegal crossing as a crime. They do it to save time or to avoid contact with the border officials, especially in the case of small contraband or when they do not have the required documents on them. In most cases local residents do not hesitate to profit from the new situation if the risk is not too high. In their eyes the existence of large-scale organized contraband and corruption justifies their right to slightly adapt the border regime to their own needs. One can better understand such an attitude if we remember how important informal practices were in the Soviet economy: for example, small thefts of kolkhoz property (a pack of seeds or fodder) should have been legally qualified as a crime, but such cases were widely tolerated as a kind of informal economic stimuli in the rigid kolkhoz system. In their narratives people use various euphemisms for illegal crossing: to go "through the fields" (*poliami* or *ogorodami / gorodamy*), by "goats' paths" (*koz'imi tropami*), by "partisans' paths" (*partizanskimi tropami*).

In 2003 special privileges for the inhabitants of the near-border zone were introduced: they got the right to cross the border without filling in a customs declaration if they do not leave the 50 km near-border zone. However, the interviews gave the impression that people were not well informed about the new rules. Besides, because of the low trust in state authorities, they tried to avoid a direct encounter with the border guards:

---

24 Hastings Donnan and Thomas M. Wilson, *Borders: Frontiers of Identity, Nation and State*. Oxford and New York: Berg 1999, p. 63.

There were some talks... we don't know exactly, but... anyway we are afraid to go without a declaration. Somebody will stop me and say: I've never heard about this (male, driver, 53, Zemlianky).

People are convinced, probably not without reason, that the informal (or even illegal) way is simpler and cheaper (*"As everywhere, the legal way is more expensive"* – female, 26, Hlyboke). It is easier to make a deal with a personal representative of the state authorities than to follow the formal rules. This makes sense particularly when the rules are often changing and not clear and therefore leave space for various interpretations and as a result invite for harassment and bribery. One can understand from the interviews that people perceive crossing the border rather a matter of "luck" (it is not by chance that one of the local newspapers used to publish a weekly horoscope for those who were going to cross the border). But at the same time, the everyday informal practices of dealing with the border are based on rational knowledge of a particular kind. It assumes acquaintance with everyday procedures, quite similar to the observations peasant usually make of natural processes: for example, which unit of border police is on duty today, when is the lunchtime etc.

The act of "border crossing" is a structural element of most interviews and discussions with local residents, something that everybody has his or her own stories about. Very often these stories contain an element of challenge and competition ("catch me if you can"). The absence of natural obstacles, such as a big river or mountains, and the peculiarities of the landscape (open space, steppe, cultivated fields) make it difficult for the guards to control the whole border permanently. They have good maps and modern means of communication and observation, while local inhabitants relay on their knowledge of the territory and informal contacts. This local situational knowledge is a valuable resource, which can be offered to the border guards or contrabandists in exchange for material benefits or a good relationship (it seems that deals with smugglers happen more often). Some interviewees tried to convince us that the smugglers now have perfect maps, "made from cosmos" (i.e. based on satellite photographs), and are equipped with advanced military devices to orient themselves on the territory, so that they do not need the help of the locals anymore. These means of surveillance and orientation, used by both smugglers and border guards, create a different perspective on the village and the surrounding fields. While for local residents this is a space of everyday life and regular routes, for a stranger it offers various opportunities to hide and escape.

Illegal crossing, small contraband and sometimes collaboration with the professional smugglers are the typical forms of opportunistic behaviour of the near-border population. As some people admitted, these activities are rooted in a deep distrust in the state institutions, an attitude inherited from Soviet times:

> *The people's mood... the population is inclined to help the smugglers rather than the border guards. People do not trust the police... and this is projected onto the border guards. If they see a guy around the corner with huge bags, full of stuff... everybody will come and tell him: there are "pograntsy"* [a pejorative nickname for border guards] *over there* [people laugh]. *So with us it's the opposite attitude... we have pity for these people: "poor people... they have to earn money". Nobody will go to the border guards and tell them: look, now my neighbour will go... no, this will never happen... despite all these assistance groups. Nobody will inform about the neighbours* [Only in respect to the neighbours? What about strangers? – T.Z.] *... No, it does not matter... to everybody* (female, housewife, 26, Hlyboke).

The restructuring of the social space concerns not only the native village and its surroundings. A new hierarchy of places and destinations has been emerging, reflecting new asymmetries of labour market and education opportunities, changing perceptions of life perspectives and prestige. In Soviet times Kharkiv, as a big industrial city, attracted labour force from Russia; in the early 1990s most of the former workers returned home because of the economic crisis and unemployment. Now labour migration goes rather in the opposite direction because of the higher wages in Russia. However, it is mostly seasonal agricultural work and low skill jobs in the construction industry that are available for Ukrainian citizens. In former times the main incentive for cross-border shopping was a deficit of consumer goods and the regional imbalances in supply. People went across the border to buy particular products (freshwater fish, for example, was more available in Belgorod). Now the main incentive for cross-border shopping is price difference: many Russian residents go in order to shop at the big regional Barabashovo market in Kharkiv, which offers cheaper goods. At the same time, the customs controls and the need for currency exchange on the one hand, and market liberalization on the other push people to shop within their national borders. The same is true about peasants selling agricultural products on the local markets: the costs of carrying them across the border are too high. Again, those who have access to public transport (direct train or bus connection to Kharkiv) have fewer problems, but without a car they still cannot bring much across the border. As already mentioned, Zhuravlevka's location near the main crossing point makes it possible for the local inhabitants to profit from the proximity of the Kharkiv markets. Adjustments to the national borders are also characteristic for choosing one's educational opportunities: in Soviet times young people from the Belgorod oblast often went to study in Kharkiv, which offered a wide range of opportunities, whereas now such cross-border strategy is an exception (for example, if relatives can provide free accommodation for a student). Otherwise, pursuing a national diploma or degree is less complicated. A Kharkiv University diploma or academic degree, which is still prestigious in Ukraine, requires additional formalities for recognition in Russia; the same is true for the Russian academic qualification in Ukraine. Therefore young people from Belgorod oblast usually prefer to study in Belgorod (where an ambitious new University was recently established) or in other Russian cities.

6.3 Narratives of continuity and change

The construction of the new border after 1991 coincided with a decade of radical economic transformations and land reforms both in Ukraine and in Russia. The reforms were aimed at dismantling the kolkhoz system, developing market relations in agriculture and creating a new social class of independent farmers. Not all of these aims were reached, but the economic and social conditions of the peasantry have significantly changed. The transformations of property and economic relations are not irrelevant for the perception of the new border by local residents, their loyalty to the state and new national identities. This section seeks to compare the local narratives of social change in Shchetinovka (Russia) and Udy (Ukraine). Two neighbouring villages at a distance of only 5 km from each other are separated now by the border, but people keep regular personal contacts with their relatives and friends on the other side. As mentioned above, the economic and social dynamics since 1991 were rather different in the Ukrainian and Russian regions on both sides of the border. These differences can be seen also on the local level: the prosperous kolkhoz in Shchetinovka managed by an experienced and influential director has successfully adapted to the new market conditions and was able to preserve a relatively high level of social security, including guaranteed employment and regular payment, and to maintain and even develop the social infrastructure. Despite its peripheral geographic location in the Belgorod raion Shchetinovka is doing well. In the neighbouring Udy, the local kolkhoz was dissolved and the new private agricultural companies did not take on any social obligations, offering only seasonal jobs to peasants. As a result, the unemployment rate is high and the infrastructure of the village is in decay. By answering our question "What has changed in the village since 1991?" people connected the emergence of the new border with the social and economic changes and compared their situation with the neighbouring village. In this way they constructed their collective identities and related them to the bigger national communities – "Russians" and "Ukrainians."

In Shchetinovka, the narrative of stability and continuity dominated the discussion. From a certain point of view, time stopped in this village somewhere in the first part of the 1980s, during the "golden age" of the kolkhoz system. By comparing their situation with the neighbours, people see the advantages of the kolkhoz, mainly as a provider of social security:

> *Our kolkhoz – it is still the same as it was in Soviet times. Our director is twice a "Hero of Socialist Labour"... here people really get paid... it's not like that everywhere else... we are an exception... over there in the Borisov rayon there are also destroyed kolkhozes... I have been working for twenty years here... it has never happened that people were not paid in time... they get wages, additional payments, rewards (premia) – everything as it should be* (male, head of the brigade, 48, Shchetinovka).

TZ: *Are there individual farmers?*

> *No. Everybody works in the kolkhoz. As it was in the seventies, eighties and now...*

TZ: *Do they not want to or is it better to be in the kolkhoz than to be a farmer? Do they not wish to do so or is it not allowed?*

No wish! We see our neighbours, and we lose any wish... Farmer is farmer, kolkhoz is kolkhoz... in the kolkhoz you are paid if you are sick... farmers do not have this... in the kolkhoz you have holidays... a farmer has to work with his family from the morning to the evening... today is for example a holiday... people relax... of course there is always urgent work... now people are sent to mowing... but not by force... they know they will be paid double (from the same interview).

Of course this "socialism in one village" is rather limited. People are aware that their situation is exceptional, and with the death of the eighty years old director and "socialist hero" things might change. Besides, the economic oasis of the "Frunze" kolkhoz exists today in a completely different political and economic environment with new opportunities and risks: one can buy a car without waiting for years, as was the case in Soviet times, but higher education for children has become expensive and sometimes unaffordable for many families. It seems that Shchetinovka residents are well adapted to this new economic situation. They are not at all passive recipients of kolkhoz welfare who just rely on Soviet paternalism. Burawoy and Verdery remind us that "what may appear as 'restorations' of patterns familiar from socialism are sometimes quite different: direct *responses* to the new market initiatives, produced *by* them, rather than remnants of an older mentality".[25] Like in the neighbouring Udy, peasants' households in Shchetinovka are also partly market oriented, and many combine kolkhoz jobs with some kind of private farming or other small businesses. As the research on post-Soviet rural transformations proves, such a flexible combination of a regularly paid secure job with commercial activities is a rather typical family strategy.[26] At the same time, people in Shchetinovka are not really protected from the newly emerged economic and social risks. Besides, during the discussion it also became

---

25 Michael Burawoy and Katherine Verdery, "Introduction", in: idem (eds.), *Uncertain Transition: Ethnographies of Change in the Postsocialist World*, Lanham etc.: Rowman & Littlefield 1999, pp. 1-17. Here pp. 1-2.
26 Olga Fadeyeva, "Rural Families: Ways of Adaptation to the Changing Economic Environment (based on the results of a budget analysis in the Kuban and Volga regions)", in: Theodor Shanin (ed.), *Refleksivnoe krestianovedenie: Desiatiletie issledovanii selskoi Rossii*, Moscow: Moscow School of Economic and Social Sciences 2002, pp. 161-215 (in Russian).

clear that not all are equally prosperous in Shchetinovka: not everybody is happy with the kolkhoz salaries, the teachers and other employees in the public sector have to survive on a third of the average wage in the kolkhoz. Young specialists who come back to the village after graduation also have to accept rather low salaries. What the residents of Shchetinovka seem to appreciate more is not so much the level of income, but the fact that the norms of social life were not totally devaluated in the transition, and some kind of coherence and "order" was preserved. This was possible due to a policy "from above" and not because of the people's own initiative, and this fact is reflected in the interviews ("we were lucky" – this is how the exceptional situation in Shchetinovka is often described).

The narrative of stability and continuity in Shchetinovka is crucial for defining "us" and "them" (the neighbours across the border), the Russians and the Ukrainians, in terms of economic success or failure:

> With Ukraine... with Udy and others... we always had friendly relations. We visited each other, exchanged spare parts, especially during harvesting... Now this all has stopped because... this is ours, this is yours... I tell you... we do not suffer much... at least we have a successful kolkhoz and live better, it is not a secret... But the Ukrainians suffer... they cannot come anymore... although we cannot give much... but some used spare parts (male, agronomist, 47, Shchetinovka).

What was earlier a friendly mutual exchange of help between two collective farms is now an act of charity, paternalism of the rich to the poor neighbour. This new asymmetry was explicitly made clear to us as guests from Ukraine: "The border has not affected our situation, but yours!" The new border therefore is constructed through this collective narrative of economic stability and continuity with Soviet times, as opposed to the radical (and negative) changes across the border. In the interviews with Shchetinovka residents the border as a symbol corresponds to the collapse of the Soviet Union as being induced by non-Russian republics: it was Ukraine which "separated" (moved away) from Russia (which stayed where and as it was). Therefore there is some kind of justice in the fact that now the Ukrainians have to deal with the consequences of their recklessness and egoism. That the border "does not matter" in Shchetinovka (as it was claimed in the interview above) only underlines the relative prosperity of the village. The "poor Ukrainians" on the other side of the border who would be happy to get help are not cultural "others" yet; they are rather perceived as economic losers. Shchetinovka inhabitants apply this new hierarchy not only to their village vs. neighbouring Udy, but also to Belgorod / Kharkiv and sometimes to Russia / Ukraine in general. The reason for this is that Ukrainians in this Russian region have a specific image: they are perceived either as seasonal workers or small traders, forced to cross the border out of economic necessity:

> *Kharkiv residents come every day to our markets to sell. In Belgorod... if you go from the stadium to the central market... it is only Kharkiv there... they stand in a row... I personally always thought that Ukraine will flourish... But I forgot it has no oil and gas* (male, agronomist, 47, Shchetinovka).

During the interviews in Udy, on the Ukrainian side of the border, the theme of crisis and decay dominated the narrative of village life, and unlike in Shchetinovka, past and present were radically opposed. As in Shchetinovka, in the 1970s and early 1980s people in Udy enjoyed the advantage of working in a rather successful kolkhoz. During the focus group interview, people enthusiastically indulged in memories about that time: "What a village it was!" People recalled that the kolkhoz provided excellent employment opportunities and could afford to make investments in the social infrastructure, including a big trade centre, a "palace of culture" with a public library, a hospital and a kindergarten. The director enjoyed respect in Kharkiv, and Udy was more than an ordinary village.

In Udy, the discussion of the present situation was structured around the comparison with the neighbouring Russian Shchetinovka on the one hand, and with the Soviet past on the other. Here are some extracts from the focus group discussion:

> *In terms of the economy, of course... the whole Ukraine, not only our village... I go to Russia regularly, and literary after 10 km you can see... their fields... those reforms that are implemented on the Russian territory... and our fields, you cannot even compare. The roads are good. And even if it comes to clothes... if I have to go there for a wedding, it is always a problem – what to wear? Because I have fifty-six adult rela-*

tives there, and every year somebody gets married (female, medical assistant, 44).

I have relatives in Russia... we visited them recently. They live much better than us, better "obespecheni" [well being] ... They consider us... just as poor. An ordinary worker there earns more than me... And I am a kind of boss in the village council! What then do our peasants earn? They [the Russians] are just wondering how we can live with our money (female, administrator, 46).

It seems that residents of Udy reproduce the same "us" and "them" opposition as in Shchetinovka, but the other way round ("the neighbours" are prosperous, and "we" are poor). But in Udy "border matters", and the neighbouring Russian village is an important point of reference. The situation in Udy, described in the interview of its residents, is partly seen through the neighbours" eyes: "What do they think of us", "we are ashamed", "I have nothing to wear when I go there". This external perspective, "the neighbours' gaze", and the reference to Russia in general seems to be important for the self-image of Udy. Interestingly, some interviewees said that "reforms are going faster in Russia", while others were convinced that "everything is still working orderly there as it was under Soviet rule". For the middle aged people, the Belgorod oblast (and Russia in general) represents a more dynamic development, more successful not only in terms of economic growth, but also in terms of social security. For the elder generation, however, Russia still represents the Soviet Union, and the border with Russia is also a symbolic boundary separating the idealized past (guaranteed employment, working social infrastructure, salaries paid on time) from the problematic present. The border separates Udy's inhabitants from their past Soviet life, but also from the better life in Russia which they imagine they also could share if the Soviet Union had not collapsed. The border therefore turns out to be spatial as well as temporal. In this sense the village cultivates a kind of collective myth, or rather, more than one: one of the "golden times" of kolkhoz, and another one of the "better life" across the border.

A similar pattern of constructing an "us" and "them" opposition was characteristic for the discussion in Zemlianky, also lying on the Ukrainian side. As in Udy, people in Zemlianky admitted that the Russian neighbouring village is developing more dynamically and successfully:

> The neighbour village is much bigger. 1,200 residents. They are building a new big school... they live better than us. Gas supply is installed... A lot of construction sites (female, pensioner, 63). You know, we were on the same level (female, head of council). But now they have developed (male, driver, 43). Maybe the administration has changed, I don't know... but the last five years they have lived much better... (head of council). They started to build houses... one can see it while passing the village... they earn good money, they are employed the whole year... As it was in Soviet times, they still have jobs... they kept their collective farm, everything (male, driver, 43).

Both in Udy and Zemlianky the problem of gas supply was addressed in the discussion. Because of the peripheral location of Udy, to install a gas pipeline from Kharkiv is not easy. In the eighties Udy had hoped for cheap gas supply from the Belgorod oblast where full gas supply was already provided to all villages. But the breakup of the Soviet Union made these plans obsolete and now it is virtually impossible because of the border. At the same time, the village has no money to install gas supply from Kharkiv, which is a much longer distance. In this way, the lacking gas infrastructure becomes a visible marker of the border. Zemlianky has the same problem: gas cannot be supplied from the Russian side of the border, but the village has even less chance than Udy to get it from Kharkiv because it is even more distant. The problem of gas supply illustrates the mechanism of negative identification through the feeling of isolation and of lost chances:

> Across the border, in Russia, they have gas supply installed. If only the border would have happened three years later... this would have been just enough to extend the gas supply here... just 2 kilometres. Only three years and we would have gas" (group discussion, Zemlianky).

Another problem concerns transport connections. Local connections were reduced after 1991 because they were not profitable enough; most local train and bus connections to Russia were discontinued, ticket prices were raised. The consequence is that, in addition to the border controls, in many cases also the limited availability of local public transport creates obstacles for cross-border contacts. But what makes the near-border villages feel isolated is not only the restricted contacts with the Russian neighbours; it is also a fact that they were not compensated by a better integration into the Ukrainian territory, first of all by better connections to Kharkiv. Only in Hlyboke did people admit that transport connections with Kharkiv have improved in the last years.

Although economic indicators in the Belgorod oblast seem to be better than in Kharkiv, the situation in each village is influenced by a complex combination of geographic, political and social factors. The village of Hlyboke, also on the Ukrainian side, experienced the same difficult transition from the kolkhoz to private farming. Like in Udy, unemployment is a problem here. But the advantageous geographic location makes a big difference: Hlyboke is situated close to Kharkiv (35 km) and to the crossing point of the Moscow-Crimea highway. It is connected with Kharkiv by a regular bus route five times a day, and there is a regular bus across the border to Zhuravlevka. Hlyboke's inhabitants can work in Kharkiv, have better access to its markets and enjoy the other opportunities of the big city. Unlike in Udy, the gas supply had already been installed here in Soviet times. Its location offers better chances to get attention for local needs. Moreover, at the time of our research the village was under the patronage of an influential Kharkiv politician, the Rector of the Institute for Internal Affairs, Oleksandr Bandurko (who was nominated as a candidate to the Ukrainian parliament from the electoral district which includes Hlyboke). He helped to improve medical services and to provide a regular mini bus connection to Kharkiv. Although it is a near-border village, Hlyboke is not a periphery. Interviews and discussions showed that unlike in Udy the "collective identity" of Hlyboke is constructed around positive symbols, and not so much determined by comparison with the Russian neighbours and by the myth of the Soviet kolkhoz prosperity.

Social and economic factors which determine the situation on both sides of the border but also in every particular village turn out to be very important for shaping the new national identities in the Ukrainian-Russian borderlands. Among these factors are: the pace and format of economic reforms, the success of rural transformations in Ukraine and Russia, tendencies of regional development in both countries, the geographic location of the village (proximity to the border, main highways and crossing points, big cities), access to the distribution of economic resources and clientelist ties to oblast politicians, economic infrastructure (gas, electricity, roads), transport connections, the demographic situation and so on. The priority of economic and social factors for national self-identification is illustrated by the following answer given by one of the interviewees to the question: Does it happen that sometimes you ask yourselves if you are Ukrainian or Russian?

> *No, not today, I don't ask myself anymore... but before... when the currency was changing... I felt humiliated... but not now. Now it's OK. My salary has been raised. Before I was not paid in time... I had to ask for help* [from Russian relatives], *now I am more or less independent. It is better now* (female, bookkeeper, 37, Hlyboke).

6.4 The new borderlands: Ukrainian, Russian or (post-)Soviet?

The social and cultural integration of the borderlands into the national territory is one of the important tasks of a nation state, often crucial for preventing political instability and limiting the territorial claims of the neighbours.[27] The last century witnessed various strategies for such integration: from cultural and language politics to forced resettlements and even ethnic cleansing. At first glance, nothing like that has been happening in the Ukrainian-Russian borderlands since 1991. Until 2005 Ukrainian leadership did not pursue any special "nationalizing" policy towards its eastern borderlands. The lack of political determination and limited economic resources combined with Ukraine's regional diversity, the high proportion of Russian-speakers and the pressure of Russia claiming support for Ukrainian Russophones – all these factors prevented the central government from forced Ukrainization in the east and south. It was the Orange Revolution of 2004 that revealed potential risks of separatism in the east and of territorial disintegration. National consolidation and the promotion of national identity based on ethno-cultural and linguistic characteristics have become the declared goals of President Yushchenko's politics. This has increased the pressure of Ukrainization in the eastern regions and in Crimea and provoked conflicts be-

---

27 John P Augelli, "Nationalization of Dominican Borderlands", *Geographical Review*, vol. 70, no. 1 (1980), pp. 19-35.

tween the regional political elites and Kyiv. However, the politicisation of the language issue is limited to the big cities; the rural population, which in the east often speaks *surzhyk,* a mixture of Ukrainian and Russian, usually stays indifferent to the cultural wars of the elites. The Kharkiv oblast has since 1991 experienced a half-hearted Ukrainization of education and the administrative system, which left enough space for compromises and flexibility for the local actors, especially in the countryside.

As for the Russian regions bordering Ukraine (and the Belgorod oblast in particular), they are less problematic for Moscow, which is more concerned with the southern and eastern frontiers of the country. As a result, on both sides of the Ukrainian-Russian border there was no particular need for "nationalizing the borderlands". Nevertheless, unlike in the core territories, in the border regions the social experience of "becoming Ukrainians" or "becoming Russians" is inseparable from the experience of "becoming a borderland". How have these transformations of collective identity – of turning Soviets into Ukrainian or Russian citizens – been experienced in the Ukrainian-Russian borderlands? How do the emerging local "border" identities correspond to the processes of shaping the new national identities and state loyalties?

Analyzing post-Soviet identities in relation to territory and ethnicity, the Russian political geographer Vladimir Kolossov came to the conclusion that "hierarchical" multiple identities are common in many parts of the post-Soviet space.[28] He refers to the concept of "matreshka" nationalism[29] which takes into account the complexity of the eastern Ukrainian situation: Soviet, national, ethnic, regional and local identities fit into each other like Russian nested dolls. Paul Pirie argued, particularly in relation to eastern Ukraine, that a strong ethnic identification is not typical here. A marginal identification (i.e., a weak or unstable identification with two or more ethnic groups), or even

---

[28] Vladimir Kolossov, "After Empire", in: John Agnew, Katharyne Mitchell and Gerard Toal (eds.), *A Companion to Political Geography,* Oxford: Blackwell 2003, pp. 251-270, here p. 253.
[29] Ray Taras, "Making sense of matrioshka nationalism", in: Ian Bremmer and Ray Taras (eds.), *Nations and Politics in the Soviet Successor States,* New York: Cambridge University Press 1993, pp. 513-38.

"ethnic nihilism" (rejection of ethnic identity) and "pan-ethnic" identification are more characteristics for this situation.[30]

This approach can help to explain transformations of collective identities in the Ukrainian-Russian borderlands. Although people had to indicate their nationality in Soviet passports, the choice was often pragmatic; self-identification depended on such factors as ethnic environment, percentage of intermarriage, or the language of school instruction.[31] After 1991 both Ukrainian and Russian passports no longer have the "nationality" column. Mixed marriages between ethnic Ukrainians and Russians are common, and most people have relatives both in Ukraine and in Russia. According to sociological studies conducted during the late 1990s, ethnic Ukrainians in Kharkiv and in the Belgorod oblasts "feel closer" to Russians than to Ukrainians from the western regions.[32] The villages on both sides of the border have a high proportion of newcomers from the central regions of Russia or from the rest of Ukraine, but also from other Soviet republics. Migration to this region, which is famous for its fertile soil but had been devastated during the Second World War, was encouraged by the Soviet authorities. After the collapse of the USSR, migrants from the new "conflict zones" in the Caucasus and Central Asia (ethnic Ukrainians, Russians as well as other nationalities) often found a new home here. The Belgorod oblast is today one of the biggest recipients of migrants and is rather successful in terms of their social integration. In the Kharkiv oblast former residents of the Chernobyl zone were resettled, as well as refugees from the "conflict zones".

Due to all these factors, "ethnic nihilism" or keeping a "supra-ethnic" Soviet identity were common attitudes among those who lived near the "virtual" administrative boundary between the two republics. Almost fifteen years after 1991, people still often referred to their native village as "multinational", as a "small Soviet Union":

> *People were coming here from all Republics of the former Soviet Union... When we had statistics in the village council... by nationality...*

---

30   Paul Pirie, "National Identity and Politics in Southern and Eastern Ukraine", *Europe Asia Studies*, vol. 48, no. 7 (1996), pp. 1079-1104.
31   Chizhikova, *Russko-ukrainskoe pogranich'e*, p. 54.
32   Olga Fillipova, "Specificities of Border Region and their Influence on Ethnonational Identity", *Region: Problemy i and Perspektyvy*, no. 3 (1997) (in Russian).

there were about sixteen nationalities here... All are newcomers; we do not have native people, because it is a new village... Only children who were born here... they are native (interview with the secretary of the village council, Hlyboke).

References to the Soviet past are very common and almost always positive, but today most of our interviewees would hardly call him or herself "Soviet". As research on another Ukrainian border region, the Donbas, demonstrates, the role of "Soviet" identity is constantly diminishing.[33] In fact, "Soviet" no longer refers to a particular political system, ideology, or way of life; rather, it signifies the absence of other terms for this disappearing common social and cultural space.

This border... we did not feel it at all... we felt ourselves as one people... we did not feel we are a separate republic... later of course, when the border was built... it has changed... the border mood: here is Russia and we are Ukraine... it was a bit painful that we do not belong to Russia... we would like to... we would so much like to stay together [ostatsia obshchimi – to belong to both Ukraine and Russia at the same time] (female, teacher, 40, Udy).

Look, Vladimir Vladimirovich [Putin] *was recently in Ukraine... they were sitting with him... your leaders... and nobody supported Vladimir Vladimirovich... OK, we have separated... but he said... brotherly peoples... it is possible to re-unite again... what do your leaders think about it?* (group discussion, Zhuravlevka).

In many respects the new Ukrainian-Russian borderlands in 2003-04 still appeared a non-differentiated "Soviet" space. On both sides of the border people were keeping traditions of celebrating old Soviet holidays, which in some cases have lost their original meaning: Women's Day, the Day of the Soviet Army, Victory Day. Russian and Ukrainian schools continue old traditions of jointly organized art festivals and sport competitions (one devoted to the memory of an Afghanistan war hero, coming from a near-border village, was mentioned by several respondents). The new Ukrainian and Russian state symbols coexist with the old Soviet ones, especially those related to the

---

33   Yaroslav Hrytsak, "Ukrainian Nationalism, 1991-2001: Myths and Misconceptions", in: J. Miller and I. Gyoerge Toth (eds.), *CEU history Department Annual* 2001-2002, Budapest: CEU Press 2002, pp. 233-250.

commemoration of the Second World War. For the war veterans, cross-border excursions to the memorial sites are organized by the local administrations. Not surprisingly, Ukrainian-Russian relations are usually formulated in the old discursive forms referring to "brotherly peoples" who are historically destined to stay together.

In some sense this common (post-)Soviet space is preserved due to the dominance of Russian media, and particularly Russian television. At the border with Russia people do not need expensive satellite antennas to watch Russian TV; they have access to more or less the same channels as the residents of the Belgorod oblast. Taking this opportunity, most people indeed prefer to watch Russian TV: because of the language or because they are accustomed to it, or find it more interesting. This results partly from the fact that some people virtually live in Russia rather than in Ukraine. The dominance of Russian TV and press over the Ukrainian media market can be observed in the big cities as well, but it is more visible in small near-border villages. The following story (which had happened some years earlier, when the border was not so strictly controlled) is particularly illustrative:

> *Once we took part in an election campaign as agitators. So we went to Kazachok, a small village not far from here. It was the first time we went there. We went through the fields. We entered ... looks like a small village. So we go, with the newspapers... Elena puts posters with Moroz [the leader of the Ukrainian Socialist Party] on the walls. And we meet an old woman... we tell her: Babushka, you should vote for Moroz! – And she answers: And what about Putin? First we did not realize we are on the Russian side! We said: Babushka, do you watch only Russian channels?* (female, teacher, 34, Udy).

What is interesting in this example is a double confusion: the agitators are sure the old woman is confused, because she does not follow Ukrainian political events and watches only Russian TV. But in reality they are the ones who are confused because they entered Russian territory by mistake. This local anecdote demonstrates very well the still non-differentiated symbolic space of the Ukrainian-Russian borderlands.

At the same time, on both sides of the border, in Ukraine and Russia, new political /civic identities are taking shape. Reference to territory and citizenship is the most widespread (and at the same time formal and superficial) way of self-identification: *We live here... and the passports are Ukrainian... so we are Ukrainians* (female, pensioner, 60, Hlyboke). In many cases (particularly on the Ukrainian side) one has a feeling that this new "national identity" imposed from above just needs time (and positive social changes associated with the new state) to be internalised by the population.

> *We do not regret, I guess,* [that we live on the Ukrainian side], *we are conscious* (soznatelnye) *people. Before... there was something... when the passports were changed... a little bit... now not* (female, administrator, 54, Hlyboke).

Deeper layers of identity most often refer to the mother tongue and place of origin. People often pointed to the semi-voluntary assimilation to Russian, due to its higher status as an "urban" language, better perspectives for children's education and so on. Many of them would call themselves "Russian-speaking Ukrainians", a highly disputable (and politically charged) ethnic category in Ukraine.[34] Here again, the example of Hlyboke is very illustrative:

> *You know, talking about the language, if we take only the language... we are Russians. We studied... and our children... in Russian. But when it comes to the nationality... we have many Ukrainians... about 50%. And also migrants... they were coming from other oblasts, from western parts, also from Donetsk... I guess, some were real Ukrainians, but it's easier here in Russian... maybe because Kharkiv is near* (female, 54, Hlyboke).

In Soviet times the Ukrainian speaking population in the Russian Federation had no alternative to the assimilation to Russian because Ukrainian was not taught at school (this situation has not changed much since then). In the following extract from an interview, the respondent is aware of his ethnic Ukrainian roots though he is comes originally from Russia.

---

34   Andrew Wilson, "Redefining ethnic and linguistic boundaries in Ukraine: indigenes, settlers and Russophone Ukrainians", in: G. Smith et al. (eds.), *Nation-building in the Post-Soviet Borderlands. The Politics of National Identities*, New York: Cambridge University Press 1998, pp. 119-38.

> *I am also from Russia... We were neighbours with the Savchenko family, who is today a governor of the Belgorod oblast. Then we moved here with my parents [to Udy, Ukraine], I went to the fifth school grade. The interesting thing is that in Russia... our village, they were Ukrainians there, a Ukrainian speaking population... a kind of Zolochiv dialect. But school was in Russian... So many years passed, almost thirty-five, and now I realize, it was discrimination by the teachers, they always accused us of speaking Ukrainian outside the school. When we moved here, I was surprised... some children speak Ukrainian at home, but they don't have to learn it* [in Soviet times, parents in Ukraine could apply to the school administration to exempt their child from studying Ukrainian] (male, administrator, 49, Udy).

If we look into the future, will Russians in Ukraine and Ukrainians in Russia constitute new diasporas, will they assimilate or is there a third option? Our research does not provide enough material to answer this question. The example of Udy shows that the language of schooling is sometimes crucial for preserving or transforming national identity. Here the language of school teaching (which is Russian) attracted newcomers who for some reason were looking for a Russian-speaking village or a school with Russian as a language of instruction. This became one of the main factors for the reproduction of the "Russian" identity of the village even after 1991.[35]

Hlyboke is a more typical case. The village was founded after the Second World War. In Soviet times it was Russian speaking and had a Russian language school. Russian still dominates everyday communication, but the language of schooling was switched to Ukrainian at the end of the 1990s. The administration of the village has switched to Ukrainian as well. Hlyboke's habitants successfully combine their new political loyalty and the official use of Ukrainian with their private usage of Russian. Interestingly, here the narrative of adaptability and flexibility dominated the group discussion:

> *I worked in the kindergarten as a nursery teacher... and sometimes brought children to school. So we go and speak Russian... As soon as we reach the school, they see the fence and immediately switch to Ukrainian ... They adapt so quickly... good children!* (female, 60, Hlyboke).

---

35 This aspect is analyzed in more detail in the next chapter.

Ethnic Russians and Russian-speakers in Ukraine still profit from the former superior status of the Russian language in the Soviet Union and its still important role in post-Soviet Ukraine. Due to this factor (and the proximity of Russia), the option of combining a Ukrainian political identity with a "private" Russian or Russian-speaking identity might stay attractive for a long time.

The situation of the ethnic Ukrainians on the Russian side of the border is not the same. For example, the school in Zhuravlevka hosts the "Club of Ukrainian-Russian friendship" (traditional Soviet discourse), but offers no Ukrainian language courses, even though around thirty percent of its inhabitants come from Ukraine and the school director is ethnic Ukrainian. The absence of such an opportunity is explained by the passivity of the local Ukrainians:

> *Our Ukrainians... they do not want Ukrainian to be taught... if they would want it... something could be done... but they do not require it... why? They forgot their language. They came here at seventeen years old* (Zhuravlevka, group discussion).

It is not only Russian education policy that determines this situation, but first of all the existing hierarchy of Russian and Ukrainian languages, with its long history. The de facto still high status of Russian language in the Ukrainian-Russian borderlands explains the pragmatic choice people often make in favour of assimilation to Russian.

To summarize briefly, Russia and Ukraine today face quite different challenges in the processes of cultural and social integration of their borderlands as they pursue different nation-building projects. Soviet Ukraine was a republic of the titular "Ukrainian nation" and thus Soviet Ukrainian identity assumed already a symbolic link between the Ukrainian language/culture and the national territory. However, this link was only a potential one; "Ukrainians" in terms of cultural identity still had to be created. Udy, Hlyboke and other villages at the border with Russia demonstrate the challenge of cultural integration which Ukraine faces as a nation-state in progress.

The territorial definition of Ukrainian identity still has to be filled with a cultural substratum – Ukrainian language, history and symbols – in order to consolidate the nation around its ethnic core. Ukrainian, formally the official state language, still has to conquer cultural space from Russian, especially in the eastern border regions. The Ukrainian historical narrative is based on a break with the old Soviet one; Soviet politics and their outcomes are considered as anti-Ukrainian (e.g. the Holodomor, collectivization, repressions against the Ukrainian elite). The challenge for building a Ukrainian national identity is that in order to "make Ukrainians" one has to "unmake Soviets", which is still a long-term project.

In case of Russia, the new national identity is merged with the supranational (post-imperial) Soviet identity. Unlike in Ukraine, there is no explicit policy to make the cultural (*russkiye*) and political (*rossiyane*) definitions of the nation congruent. In Russia, the ethno-cultural component of the national identity is less important: the latter refers rather to the continuity of Russian statehood and its history. At the same time, the status of the Russian language is unchallengeable, so that the problem of cultural integration is not as urgent as it is in the Ukrainian borderlands. Hence the making of Russians does not require the unmaking of "Soviets". The new historical narrative integrates not only symbols of the imperial Russian past but also, selectively, Soviet myths and symbols.

This means first of all that the inertia of the common Soviet cultural and political space in the borderlands poses more challenges to Ukraine than to Russia. It is Ukraine as a new state which has to pursue an affirmative "nationalization" policy, particularly in its eastern borderlands, but has limited political opportunities and economic resources for doing so. On the opposite, in the Russian regions bordering Ukraine the share of national minorities is insignificant and no special "nationalization" efforts are required from the state. The heritage of Soviet nationalities politics, which assumed voluntary assimilation to Russian as the dominant language, poses challenges first of all to Ukraine.

At the same time, its better economic situation and the relative consolidation of political elites allow the Russian state to pursue an active cultural politics (for example, the new Belgorod University founded in 1996 presents itself as an outpost of Russian science and Russian identity in the borderlands). The same applies to the new World War II Prokhorovka memorial in the Belgorod oblast, which represents the new Russian identity and can be seen as a symbol of the Russian military glory at the country's new western frontier.

Conclusion

The narratives of the villages' residents concerning their everyday lives near the new border connect the particular social experience of "becoming a borderland" with the national identity formation in both Ukraine and Russia. However, it is not only school education, language policy and media, but also economic development and social provision that contribute to the different perceptions and images of the new border among local Ukrainians and Russians. As the border becomes a "natural" fact of social life, people try to "domesticate" the new reality and present their special circumstances as a part of their everyday routine. Despite similar themes in their narratives the images of the new border and attitudes to it are quite different in the two neighbouring countries.

For the Ukrainians, the closeness of Kharkiv as a big city with its employment, education and shopping opportunities compensates to some extent for the reduction of contacts with Russia. But the growing economic differences in favour of the Belgorod oblast (Russia) sometimes make Ukrainian residents feel nostalgic about the common Soviet past, which represents stability and social security in collective memory. This nostalgia and the persisting common (post-)Soviet cultural space poses challenges to the process of "making Ukrainians". In the eyes of the Russian citizens, the new border is also artificial, but is seen as more legitimate and acceptable because of the better economic situation on their side. And unlike on the Ukrainian side, on the Russian side there is no need for a nationalization policy. Neither by Russian nor by Ukrainian citizens is the new border perceived as a cultural boundary. Instead, different social provisions related to citizenship as well as economic asymmetry make the border "real" for local populations.

But the attitudes to the new situation differ not only across the border. The situation of every single village depends on the constellation of various social and economic factors. The ability of people to adapt to the new border location (and even profit from it) depends on such factors as the efficiency of the local administration, availability of financial resources, support from oblast authorities, closeness to the big cities and to the border infrastructure, transport connections and employment opportunities. As a consequence, the attitude to the border and the perception of the new near-border situation is not so much a question of political loyalty, but rather a function of economic well-being and social mood.

The spatial reorganization of social life resulting from the border construction has coincided with the radical social and economic transformations (such as land reform, dismantling of the kolkhoz system, emergence of unemployment and decay of the social infrastructure). Understandably, in the narratives of the residents of near-border villages these social changes are inseparable from the emergence of the new border. The spatial boundary (the new international border) and the temporal boundary (the end of the communist system and the collapse of the Soviet Union in 1991) are closely related. The new border represents the irreversibility of the post-1991 political and social changes, thus separating not only Ukraine from Russia, but also the present, real Ukraine from an imagined Soviet Union. In the Russian case this effect is less visible. But one can suppose that with the passing of time and with the generational change the border will become a "natural" feature of the social landscape; it will be integrated in the routine practices of everyday life and lose its negative association with the Soviet myth.

7 Becoming Ukrainians in a "Russian" Village: Local Identity, Language and National Belonging

In the process of post-socialist transition and nation building citizenship, language, ethnicity and regional/local identity interact in a complex way. New border regions are particularly interesting sites of such interaction,[1] because this is where the nationalizing efforts and the imposing authority of a state are often confronted with the everyday practices of cross-border movement and with passive resistance and the persisting feeling of "otherness". The social and cultural effects of the border on small rural communities deserve special research. As Elena Nikiforova wrote, "one of the implications of the Soviet type of modernization was the tremendous gap between urban and rural settlements and the formation of two different cultures. The countryside has not been the subject of consideration and discussion. Very little sociological research of the countryside has been done ... In the sphere of 'border studies' this gap is particularly evident. There are numerous studies of divided cities... However, very little is known about the transformation of the rural social space due to the establishment of a political border."[2] What meaning do ethnic, national and linguistic identities have for rural inhabitants? How has the

---

[1] Among numerous publications on post-Soviet borderlands see, for example: Olga Brednikova, "Historical text *ad marginem* or: a divided memory of divided towns", *Ab Imperio*, no. 4 (2004), pp. 289-312 (in Russian); Elena Nikiforova, "The Disruption of Social and Geographic Space in Narva", in: Risto Alapuro, Ilkka Liikanen and Markku Lonkila (eds.), *Beyond Post-Soviet Transition. Micro Perspectives on Challenge and Survival in Russia and Estonia*, Saarijärvi: Kikimora Publications 2003, pp. 148-164; Laura Assmuth, "Nation building and everyday life in the borderlands between Estonia, Latvia and Russia", *Focaal – European Journal of Anthropology*, no. 41 (2003), p. 59-69. On the Ukrainian-Russian borderlands in particular see: Peter Rodgers, "Regionalism and the Politics of Identity: A View from Ukraine's Eastern Borderlands", in: Madeleine Hurd (ed.), *Borderland Identities: Territory and Belonging in Central, North and East Europe*, Eslöv: Förlags ab Gondolin 2006, pp. 163-194; Margrethe Sovik, "Language, Identity and Boundaries in a Ukrainian-Russian Borderland: Talking about History and Identity", in: Hurd (ed.), *Borderland Identities*, pp. 195-224.

[2] Elena Nikiforova, "Is a Border a Factor of Ethnic Community Formation? Case study: the Setus, Petchory district, Pskov region, Russia", in: Olga Brednikova and Viktor Voronkov (eds.), *Kochuiushchie Granitsy*, Proceedings of the seminar held in Narva, 12-16 November 1998, St. Petersburg: CISR 1999 (Working Paper no 7), pp. 133-138, here p. 133.

hierarchy of social identities in the village been changing with the emergence and institutionalisation of a new border?

This chapter is based on a case study on Udy, a near-border village in the Zolochiv raion, Kharkiv oblast (Ukraine). This village is located at the border between Ukraine and the Russian Federation, a fact that since 1991 has affected the lives of local inhabitants probably more than any other transformation or reform. While adapting slowly to the new realties, most families still keep close contacts to their relatives and friends in neighbouring Russia. Thus, for them the experience of "becoming Ukrainians" has been definitely connected to the experience of "becoming a borderland". Udy residents traditionally consider their village "Russian"; it is indeed predominantly Russian-speaking and the language of instruction in the local school has always been Russian. Despite the de facto mixed population and the progressive assimilation to the Ukrainian language, this ethnic "otherness" is an important marker of the village in the eyes of the local residents as well as their neighbours. Combined with the proximity of the Ukrainian-Russian border this creates a particular discrepancy between the new citizenship and ethno-cultural identity and makes the integration of the village into the Ukrainian cultural and political space more complicated. Since the beginning of the 1990s Udy has been experiencing an economic crisis and a decay of its social infrastructure, which is especially visible in comparison with the relatively prosperous neighbouring village of Shchetinovka on the Russian side. Unemployment, depopulation and the negative side effects of the land reform make people think about the new border not only in spatial but also in temporal terms: it symbolizes the irreversible break with the Soviet era, nostalgically related to social security and relative prosperity in a common state.[3] Economic and social factors shape the popular attitudes to the new border and contribute to political loyalty (or lack of it), local patriotism and the feeling of national belonging. In many respects Udy is an ordinary village struggling with the problems typical of rural Ukraine. At the same time, due to its specific location and exceptional "language minority" status, this case demonstrates the challenges of political and cultural integration in the borderlands in a very tangible way.

---

3   On the spatial and temporal dimensions of the Ukrainian-Russian border see previous chapter.

I first visited Udy in 2003, when I was conducting individual and group interviews for my research project on the Ukrainian-Russian border. Udy was one of three near-border villages on the Ukrainian side I had chosen for my research.[4] The aim of the project was to analyze the perceptions and attitudes of the local population in relation to the new border and the role this border plays in restructuring social relations and shaping national identity in the borderlands.

All three villages on the Ukrainian side of the border represented particular cases interesting in their own way. But it was Udy where the contrasts between "here" and "there", "now" and "then" seemed to be most dramatic at that time. In 2003 it looked like Udy, more than any other village I had visited, was "lost in transition". The nostalgic myth of the "golden kolkhoz age" underlined the sharp contrast with the problematic present. People were typically looking across the border with envy. They preferred Russian TV channels to the Ukrainian ones and were better informed about the political life on the other side than at home. The specific ethno-linguistic identity and the official status of a "Russian" village left the future of Udy rather open. The question I asked myself at that time was: Will Udy "catch up" and culturally assimilate to the Ukrainian language or will it, while preserving its Russian school and reproducing its ethno-cultural "otherness", instead contribute to reshaping the amorphous "Russian-speaking population" into a new national minority group?

During the dramatic 2004 presidential elections in Ukraine I often thought about Udy and promised myself to go back there. I did so in summer 2005 when the political passions of the Orange Revolution had calmed down a bit, but the first crisis in the new coalition had not yet emerged. During this visit I found out that although most Udy residents quite expectedly had supported Viktor Yanukovych, the village was becoming in a way "more Ukrainian" then it had been in 2003. Nobody stayed indifferent to the recent political events in Kyiv, and the Ukrainian TV channels had definitely become more popular. At the same time, important changes had occurred in the local

---

4   Some results of this project are presented in the previous chapter. See also: "The New Post-Soviet Borderlands: Nostalgia, Resistance to Changes, Adaptation. A case study of three near border villages in Kharkiv Oblast', Ukraine", in: Hurd (ed.), *Borderland Identities*, pp. 57-88.

school changing the balance of Russian and Ukrainian languages in favour of the latter. In this light I had to reformulate my initial approach: what I had believed were two alternatives for Udy as a Russian speaking village (assimilation or turning into a national minority) looked now as two tendencies which are developing simultaneously and interact in a complex way. The aim of my second research trip to Udy in summer 2005 was therefore to analyze the national identity as a process by observing changes in people's attitudes and perceptions during the previous two years. I assumed that the more critical view of Putin's Russia and the emotional engagement in Ukrainian politics could affect political loyalties and sympathies of the near border residents and change the hierarchy of their identities. I was interested in how the presidential elections were perceived and experienced in a small Russian-speaking village at the border with Russia, and what kind of local tensions and conflicts they made visible.

This chapter is based on two focus group interviews in Udy (one in summer 2003, the other in summer 2005) and 18 individual interviews with present (and former) residents of Udy (conducted also in 2003 and 2005). More than half of the participants of the second focus group had already taken part in the first one. As for the individual interviews, I talked with indigenous Udy residents as well as with newcomers. The interviews with the teachers were particularly important for me.

The first section of this chapter provides basic information about the history and contemporary economic and social situation of Udy. The second section offers different, often contradictory narratives of the local residents about their native village and shows how local identity is constructed through "us" vs. "them" oppositions and comparisons with the "others". The third section is devoted to the issue of language in relation to ethnic/national identities and focuses particularly on the role of the Russian language school in the ongoing reproduction of Udy's "Russianness" . The fourth section seeks to explain the "Ukrainization by de fault" and the non-politicization of the language issue in Udy. And finally the fifth section focuses on the experiences of the 2004 presidential elections and the effects of the Orange Revolution on the village community.

7.1 Udy as a site of research

Udy is a village in the Zolochiv raion in the north of the Kharkiv oblast, with a population of around 1,300. It is the centre of a *silrada/selsovet*, i.e. an administrative subunit of the raion that includes four other smaller villages, most of them in decay and inhabited mainly by pensioners. Udy is situated 16 km from the town Zolochiv (the raion centre) and 12 km from Kozacha Lopan, the closest station of the Kharkiv-Belgorod-Moscow railway. The bus to Kharkiv goes only four times a week and is relatively expensive for the local residents, who are rarely paid in cash. Quite often those who have no private transport walk to Kozacha Lopan and then take the local train to Kharkiv.[5] Recently a couple of young people in Udy organized some kind of private taxi service. With three to four passengers in the car the price of a ride to Kharkiv's central market is comparable with a bus ticket. This is of course an informal business, nobody is registering it and paying taxes. The neighbouring Russian village *Shchetinovka*, situated 5 km from Udy across the border, belongs to the successfully reformed "Frunze" kolkhoz, a rather prosperous agricultural enterprise well-adapted to the new economic situation.[6]

Compared to other settlements in this region Udy is an old village.[7] Its name presumably stems from the old Russian word *"Ud"* ("body part"), which is also the name of the local river.[8] According to archive materials Udy was founded in 1685 by Russian settlers from Volkhov. Later, Ukrainians also settled here (the Ukrainian part of the village was called "*Maiaki*", named after the watch towers used by Ukrainian Cossacks for observing the surroundings and preventing attacks of nomadic Tatars). The residents of the village had the status of "state peasants" and were not serfs. In former times Udy hosted a community of Old Believers (*starovery*), with their own church and ceme-

---

5 A bus ticket was 6 UAH in 2003, a local train ticket 2 UAH (exchange course in 2003-05 was about 1USD = 5.5 UAH).

6 The director of the "Frunze" kolkhoz, eighty-six-year-old Vasilii Gorin, was awarded twice "Hero of Socialist Labour" and is famous not only in Belgorod, but in all of Russia for his successful management. See, for example: "Important is human life, not the economic indicators", http://www.bel.ru/news/officially/2007/01/09/22172.html (in Russian) ((last accessed February 7, 2010).

7 On the history and ethnic composition of Sloboda Ukraine see endnote 5 in the previous chapter.

8 The historical data on Udy are based on: Pavel Kuznetsov, "Istoriia sela Udy", unpublished manuscript, 1984 (in Russian).

tery.[9] Today only a few old people remain from this community. The Old Believers church was dismantled after the Second World War, because the village desperately needed material for reconstruction. Under the Russian Empire Udy was a flourishing village; it had a population of around 4,000, a two-storey school, a hospital and a bank office, and the main streets were covered by cobblestones. In the 1920s the population rose to 7,000, but then declined significantly due to the famine of 1933 and the Second World War.

In the 1970s and 1980s, a modern social and economic infrastructure was created in Udy. However, this could not prevent young people from leaving for the big cities, first of all to Kharkiv. In the last two decades of Soviet rule, Udy residents enjoyed the advantage of working in a rather successful and developing ("*perspektivnyi*") kolkhoz. It could afford to build a trade centre, a "palace of culture" with a hall seating 200 and a big public library, and to maintain a hospital and a kindergarten with a swimming pool. Other employment opportunities included the so-called ATS (the kolkhoz garage), a fishery, a small clothing factory, and six state-run shops. As one woman illustratively told, in 1985 there were over hundred phone numbers of enterprises and organizations in the Udy telephone book, and now only twelve.

After 1991, as everywhere else in Ukraine, the Udy kolkhoz was dissolved.[10] Everybody received a share in the form of a plot of land (usually one hectare), but only a few families were able to cultivate it on their own. Most people had no choice but to lease their shares to the new agricultural enterprises, which are monopolists in the village and dictate their conditions.

In case of Udy this is first of all the big private farm "Sevelir" and three Ltds. They hire local people for agricultural work, but only on a seasonal basis. The rent that people get from these enterprises is often paid in kind (i.e., wheat, sugar, etc.); "real" money is rare.

In their households, people produce vegetables, meat and milk for their own needs. Some families grow vegetables for sale, others sell milk to middle

---

9   The Old Believers (Starovery) became separated from the hierarchy of the Russian Orthodox Church after 1666-67 as a protest against church reforms introduced by Patriarch Nikon. Old Believers continue liturgical practices which the Russian Orthodox Church maintained before the implementation of these reforms.
10 On land reform in Eastern Ukraine after 1991 see: Jessica Allina-Pisano, *The Post-Soviet Potemkin Village: Politics and Property Rights in the Black Earth*, New York: Cambridge University Press 2008.

BORDERLANDS INTO BORDERED LANDS 287

The monument for the liberation of Udy from German fascist occupation dominates the central square of the village. 506 inhabitants of the village died in the Second World War

men and bitterly complain about the low prices. As people reported in 2005, many got rid of their cows because milk production has become unprofitable.

Cross-border shopping is a common practice in the village, but only a few families are involved in "professional" smuggling activities. Typical goods smuggled across the border in recent years have included petrol, liquid gas, vodka, cigarettes and sugar. Due to the lack of contacts, information and initial capital, peasants have very few opportunities to profit from cross-border trade; instead, they are consumers of smuggled products (for example, liquid gas smuggled from Russia is very popular in Udy).

Employment opportunities across the border include first of all seasonal agricultural work, which pays better then on the Ukrainian side. Occasional construction work is also an option. Long-term employment in Russia seems more problematic because of the border and bureaucratic restrictions.

Compared to the 1980s, the social sphere in Udy is in decay and people are leaving the village. The "palace of culture" and the trade centre are abandoned and falling apart. The hospital is closed, and only a medical assistant is left. In 2003, only 10 children attended the kindergarten. The number of children at school is also decreasing, threatening teachers' jobs. Paid jobs in the village are rare.

A gas supply infrastructure has not been installed, and together with the high unemployment this is one of the main reasons why people leave the village. As a consequence, houses are rather cheap. The project to install a gas supply infrastructure for Udy has been in preparation for many years; the first phase was scheduled for spring 2004. Yanukovych's election campaigners had promised Udy residents that the gasification of the village will be on top of the agenda, but in 2005 the project was postponed again.

Due to mixed marriages and intensive migration in Soviet times, Udy has now a rather mixed population (the majority consists of Ukrainians and Russians, but there are also representatives of many other former Soviet nationalities).[11] Indigenous residents are, however, still aware of the historical roots of Udy as a "Russian village". There are a couple of families in Udy who

---

11   Unlike in Soviet times, the local administration today keeps no statistics showing the ethnic composition of the village, and the "nationality" is not inscribed in Ukrainian passports. So it is difficult to estimate changes in the ethnic makeup.

BORDERLANDS INTO BORDERED LANDS   289

The remnants of the trade centre in Udy, built in the 1970s

are considered a kind of "local aristocracy" and trace their origins back almost to the founding of the village. People of the older generation speak a kind of Russian dialect similar to the one spoken in the Kursk oblast. Some women can still remember Russian folk songs, and I was told that traditional religious holidays still are celebrated in the Russian way. However, the role of religion in village life should not be overestimated: Udy's church was destroyed in the 1930s with the support of the new local communist elite and Komsomol activists, and to this day, most village inhabitants have been paying their rare church visits in Zolochiv, mainly to baptise children.

In 2005 a small group of local enthusiasts initiated the re-opening of a church in the former kolkhoz cafeteria (a fact that became a subject of numerous jokes in the village). The newcomers from the western regions of Ukraine stress the absence of a communal church life in Udy as a striking difference to their home villages.

Probably more than folklore and half-forgotten traditions it is the language of instruction at the local school which is important for preserving the "Russian" identity. Udy has a Russian language school, practically the only one in the Zolochiv raion (Ukrainian language and literature are also taught as obligatory subjects).

There is an almost mythical story about another Russian school in the same raion, which was destined to be closed because of the low number of children. But then, almost magically, a former resident of this village appeared who had made a fortune in the oil business in the Russian North. He invested some money and saved the school, at least temporarily.

Memorial cross erected after 1991 at the place of the old Orthodox church destroyed in the 1930s

New Orthodox church recently opened in the former Udy cafeteria

7.2 Conflicting narratives of local identity

How do people living in Udy talk about their village, and how is it represented in the local narratives? What does it mean for them to live in Udy? Are people proud of their native village or rather ashamed of it? Not surprisingly, there are varying narratives about Udy among its residents. Those who were born in Udy, the newcomers and those who had left to Kharkiv speak about their village in a different way. Some just deny that there is something specific about "being from Udy"; others refuse to answer question about "Udy's identity" because "too many new people came here". In the interviews several layers of local identity, from language and culture to labour ethics and drinking habits, could be found; interestingly, some characteristics (such as "Soviet" and "multinational") appear as positive or negative depending on the context. In this section I would like to show the self-representations of Udy in the semi-official discourse and in the informal narratives of the locals. I will trace the local identity as being constructed through various oppositions of "us and them" and comparisons with the "others".

One common narrative presents Udy as an old village, a village with three and a half centuries of history, "Russian" by its origins. In most cases it is the local school teachers who tell about the history of Udy, or sometimes also the village administration workers and other inhabitants. In fact, those who were born here and went to the local school are more or less aware of the history of Udy. They owe this feeling of a distinctive historical identity first of all to the former teacher and school director, Pavel Konstantinovich Kuznetsov, who is now over 80.

As a local history enthusiast, Kuznetsov has collected rich materials about the history of Udy. He set up a small school museum with an ethnographic and historical collection, which is located now on the premises of the former primary school. Unfortunately, the village council has difficulties in maintaining the museum due to a lack of money. The roof is damaged and the old one-storey building is falling apart. Some of the museum's stock is certainly valuable and drew the attention of the Kharkiv Historical Museum.

Pavel Kusnetzov, the former Udy school director and local history enthusiast, with one of the teachers

Kuznetsov wrote also a history of Udy (unpublished manuscript finished in 1984), based on archival materials. He has often been interviewed by Kharkiv ethnographers and journalists. Even today he remains highly respected in the village, and almost everybody recommended that I talk to him. Kuznetsov was not a member of the Communist party, but certainly identified himself with Soviet ideology and politics. He started his teaching career in Udy in the 1930s; in 1941 he was mobilized for the Red Army and sent to the front. After the War he came back to Udy and from the 1950s through the 70s was highly appreciated in the Zolochiv raion as a school director and a teacher. Not surprisingly, his manuscript, while extensively presenting Udy's pre-revolutionary past, folklore and traditions, focuses mainly on the Soviet period of Udy's history. It describes in detail the successful collectivisation and does not mention the Famine of 1933; it glorifies Udy's contribution to the victory over Nazi Germany and hardly mentions Stalin's terror. In Kuznetsov's manuscript Udy is presented in fact as a Soviet village with ethnic Russian roots. His interest to the pre-revolutionary history of his village, rather unusual for a Soviet school director, was certainly limited by the ideological constraints of that time.[12]

As in post-Soviet society in general, the rediscovery of Udy's local history was encouraged by the *perestroika* and the collapse of communism – for example, a cross was erected in the 1990s on the central square, where the Orthodox church had been destroyed in the 1930s. As the value of the "historical roots", of local traditions and national culture was increasingly appreciated, Kuznetsov's amateur studies were rediscovered in Udy as some kind of fundament for the newly constructed "Russian identity". Today Kuznetsov believes that ethnic Russians still form a majority of Udy's population and that the Ukrainian newcomers usually assimilate to the Russian language. In his interview given in 2005 he opposed to what he calls the "Ukrainization" of the local school pursued by the new director (see below) and insisted that Udy's Russian identity should be protected.

---

12 After World War II, Kuznetsov, who later would become an enthusiastic historian and ethnographer of Udy, initiated the dismantling of the Old Believers church because bricks were needed for the reparation of the local school. However in his manuscript he does not regret this fact, but focuses on the successful post-war reconstruction of the village.

This "Russian identity", which is to some extent an intellectual construction, clashes with everyday stereotypes about Russians and Ukrainians (pej. *Katsapy/Khokhly*). Although a cultural boundary between local Ukrainians and Russians hardly exists in this region, in some situations ethnicity becomes an important reference for (self-)identification. In the Zolochiv raion, which is predominantly Ukrainian, being a "Russian village" means being distinct from the other villages:

> You know, when I first came to Udy... I am from the Zolochiv raion...in this raion there was always such an attitude... Udy is a Russian village... even in those times. I also shared it... it is a different village, not like others... and people are strange... In the Zolochiv raion there was always ... and even now... such an attitude...condescending... because this is a Russian village. Katsapy... they are called katsapy. I also had such an impression, before I moved here... but now I say "here in our village, in Udy" (female, mathematics teacher, 34).

The locals sometimes perceive this distinctiveness as an asset, but more often as a burden, something that makes them a "black sheep" (this attitude will be illustrated below by the example of the Udy Russian language school). In any case, in this context "Russian village – Ukrainian environment" is one of the main dichotomies shaping the local identity.

The second common narrative focuses on the Soviet past and the "golden age" of the kolkhoz in Udy. Most Udy inhabitants remember the late Soviet era as a period of growing economic stability and relative well being. With Khrushchev's liberalization policy, agricultural work in the kolkhoz became better paid, housing construction was supported and the social infrastructure in the village was improved. Several small collective farms were merged in two bigger ones and later into one single kolkhoz. This enabled large-scale mechanization and the improvement of labour conditions. As one can conclude from the interviews, the 1970s and early 1980s were the "golden age" of Udy. The renowned and respected head of the kolkhoz belonged to the oblast's Party elite and could provide investments and credits for the village. He is remembered as a good manager ("strict but just") who successfully combined administrative control with a lot of (often informal) economic incentives. This was the time when, among other things, the "palace of culture" and the big supermarket were constructed in the village. In their interviews people enthusiastically indulged in memories of that time: *What a village it was!* As the retired teacher told us: *When the three-hundred-year anniversary of Udy was celebrated, there was a performance with horse races and a tank parade!*

Not surprisingly, the present situation in Udy, which is determined by economic and social problems, is often described in terms of discontinuity: as a radical break with relative stability and prosperity of the kolkhoz and with the Soviet system in general. Particularly for the older generation memories are coloured by nostalgia. It seems sometimes that there are actually two different villages: the one which lives in the memory and imagination of the people, where nobody had to be afraid for his or her future and the kolkhoz administration took care of their workers, and the real Udy ruined by chaotic reforms and dishonest management. This idealization of the kolkhoz is rather strong despite the low payments and hard work that most our interviewees readily admitted. In their eyes it is first of all "order" and "a real master" (*khoziain*) that the village lacks today. In this context people often compared Udy with the flourishing neighbouring village of Shchetinovka on the Russian side of the border.[13] Here are some extracts from the interviews:

> *If somebody goes through our fields and theirs, the difference is not to our favour. Sometimes I feel ashamed... for Ukraine, for myself... in front of those people who can compare* (male, head of the village council, 49).

> *In Shchetinovka the living standards have been always high... because of Gorin* [a famous kolkhoz director]. *The whole village has permanent gas supply... they earn well... Why I know this? I used to work in Bezsonovka* [another village in the Belgorod oblast] *in school... I was fired here and I used to go there for two years... and often passed Shchetinovka. A simple example: if someone gives me a ride here, I have to pay. And there if you ask someone for a ride... he is offended if I offer money. He just says: I don't need your change... I earn enough, I am not interested in your ridiculous money. In Shchetinovka they have a kolkhoz bus... it goes every morning from Shchetinovka, it picks up the farm workers and brings them to the farm... the same at lunch time and in the evening. Here we don't have something like that. And labour*

---

13 See the comparison between Udy and Shchetinovka in the previous chapter.

> *conditions you cannot compare... When our women from the pig farm go home – you don't even have to ask where they work. But in Shchetinovka I was surprised when I once caught a bus... I saw women wearing leather jackets and fur caps and I asked my acquaintance: Are they going for excursion? No, she said, they work at the pig farm! How is that? She said, they have a shower, changing rooms there... everything. Imagine, they come, change clothes... they have a dining room, a relaxation room... after work they take shower... they change clothes again... this is just normal* (female, teacher, 47).

Thus, the idealised past of Udy is often projected across the border, to the neighbouring Shchetinovka. Of course the "Frunze" kolkhoz, one of the very few left in Russia, functions today according to market rules, as a big capitalist enterprise, and most people in Udy understand this. They are also aware that Shchetinovka and Russia are not the same, and there are enough villages in the neighbourhood that are not so lucky: "speculators buy land and nobody cares about people". But still "kolkhoz Gorina" is associated with Russia as a more successful model of transition and remains an important reference point in the discussions about Udy's difficult situation. The border separates Udy's inhabitants from their past Soviet life, but also, as they sometimes feel, from the better life in Russia, which they also could share if the Soviet Union had not collapsed. In this context it is not ethnicity and language, but economic gradients and (new) social contrasts that constitute the opposition of "us" and "them", depressing Udy and flourishing Shchetinovka. "Here" and "there", Ukraine and Russia as spatial categories turn into temporal ones associated with the problematic present and the nostalgic past.

Some other informal narratives about Udy contradict its representation as a "village with deep historical roots". Motifs characteristic for these counter-narratives include the lack of original culture, the high number of migrants and forced "multiculturalism", alcoholism, theft and the decay of the labour moral. In this view it is the Soviet system and the kolkhoz that bear the responsibility for the negative features of the local society. This alternative narrative is characteristic for the younger generation, and also some newcomers put the myth of the "kolkhoz golden age" into doubt. A local taxi driver who asked me about the purpose of my visit to Udy was very eager to share his opinion:

> *People in our village – it is a wild mixture... Here there is no specific culture... because people are from everywhere... they came from Western Ukraine, from Caucasus. Mentality is very bad. Udy is a particular place. Here the soil is very good... black earth. This soil Germans brought home by trucks... After the rain...you will not get out from here. There is a climate anomaly in Udy... and the same with people: one lived happily...moved to Udy... and got crazy... got lost (because they start to drink* – commented a taxi passenger, an elderly women).

Udy folklore offers numerous stories on drinking habits in the village; here are some examples (told by the same taxi driver):

> *Once a man went by car to sell cabbage and stopped in Udy by accident... I don't know how, but he came across some of our guys... they invited him to share a bottle... the next morning he needed a drink because of his hangover... so they started anew... he was drinking for five days and could not leave Udy... his cabbage got rotten... he told us later, never in his life he had drunk like in Udy...*

> *Once I was driving fishers to Udy and told them this story* [see above]... *and on the way back they said... there is something to it... they told me, they came to Udy and got lost... one of them got drunk and lost his way... he had a bag with vodka and beer on him...after some time he came to the Russian customs control point... and they sent him in the wrong direction... he was away for two days...they* [his friends] *went to the policy and wanted to report him as missing...*

Good soil and climate conditions combined with the rather successful kolkhoz management on the one hand, and a mass exodus of young people to industrial Kharkiv on the other created in Udy a labour shortage in the 1960s and 70s and attracted newcomers from other regions. They came for various reasons: for example, families from "*neperspektivnye*" (futureless) villages[14] in the Kursk oblast were invited to resettle in Udy; seasonal workers from Western Ukraine often stayed in Udy and married locals; a bit later, in the 1990s, Russians and other nationals from Caucasus moved to Udy because of the political instability at home. As a result, Udy has become rather a multinational village than a Russian one. Even now in the semi-official dis-

---

14 Cf. Stefan Hedlund, *Private Agriculture in the Soviet Union*, London: Routledge 1989, p. 55.

course Udy is often presented in terms of "internationalism" ("a small Soviet Union"), whereas in informal discussions this multinationalism is often made to be responsible for the decay of the village morals. The newcomers (although some of them have been living in the village for ten or more years) are blamed by older people for the widespread alcoholism and theft. As some people believe, thefts committed by newcomers were often tolerated by the kolkhoz administration, because it was interested in keeping a labour force in the village at any price, and "it is from them that locals learned to steal". In this context, the symbolic boundary is often drawn between "us", native Udy residents, and "them", the newcomers:

> *Before the newcomers came no one drank as much as they do now, and there was more order...Yes, and there was less theft...no one ever stole anything...everyone knew each other...But now you see people...you don't know who they are...because there are many newcomers, many strangers...And they've taught our people how to steal...While we worked in the collective farm, we didn't steal...we might have taken some fodder but that was all. But when 'they' came...ours learned...and stole by the truck load* (from an interview with an Old Believers couple, Saveliy and his wife, both in their 80s).

As mentioned above, drawing parallels with the neighbouring Russian village across the border (Shchetinovka) is an important element of the narratives on Udy's identity. In a similar way, a comparison is often made between Udy and a generalized "Western Ukraine" as its cultural antipode. A lot of Udy residents come from the western regions of Ukraine; many natives are married to western Ukrainians and have relatives there. But while in the case of Shchetinovka well-being, social security and working conditions are usually compared, in case of Western Ukraine comparisons are made on the way of life, labour ethics and mentality. Western Ukrainians are characterized as hardworking, open and friendly – in opposition to Udy's inhabitants (who in this case are not differentiated into Ukrainians and Russians). Here is an extract from an interview with a couple in their forties, with two children of school age (Ivan is a Ukrainian from Transkarpathia, Vera is a native Russian from Udy):

Ivan: [In Transkarpathia] *they work...they're hard working... They left for a season – they made money. They left for a month or two...in the spring they planted potatoes – and they went. There is a one month interval...the wife stays by herself somehow and takes care of the household. In two months they are back to harvest hay. Harvesting hay takes about two or three weeks...they cut the hay – and they then have three months to work. Again they come home with money...and therefore they live much better...*

Vera: *Who from Udy would go to earn money? We don't have workers like that, who would go somewhere else to earn money. Who would go to support their families...here they think only about what to steal...the whole village has been taken apart...they take things apart and sell them... that's how it's done around here...here, in Udy...*

An important distinction which is often mentioned concerns community life, leisure time and celebrating holidays. An old women, who just visited her relatives in the Rivno oblast, shared her impressions:

On Trinity day [a religious holiday in May] *– what a feast they had! The whole village came. There was a band from America! They decorated a scene with rushnyky* [traditional stitched towels], *pottery... And here in Udy on Trinity day: I saw my neighbour, she went to her vegetable garden to work! There are no jobs over there either, but everybody has a hothouse, some kind of business. They do not drink as much as here in Udy.*

Here is another extract from an interview with Ivan and Vera:

Ivan: *They prepare everything for Easter one week before. Before Friday they have to cook... on Friday, Saturday there is almost no work. And they go to the church... these three days... and then three Easter holidays... everybody goes to the church. There you feel it is really a holiday... it is such a holiday, that...*

Vera: *They do not have fences like here... Here every house is fenced... One builds a Berlin wall, that's it...*

Ivan: *There they only have low fences... so that chicken do not run on the road. And the neighbours, when they go to the church...they always pass by. If it is a holiday – they always pass by. There nobody invites officially... people just pay visits... in every house.*

7.3 What makes Udy "Russian"?

As it was already mentioned, in the narratives of the local residents Udy is usually presented as a "Russian" village. But what exactly makes it "Russian"? Is it the language spoken in the village, the remnants of ethnic tradition (folklore, religious holidays, etc.), or is it the historical narrative promoted by Kuznetsov and represented by the school museum? How has this "Russianness" been preserved/reproduced/reinvented, particularly in the independent Ukrainian state? The case of Udy can help us to understand how Russian "ethnic identity" is constructed today (if at all) in a small rural community at the border with Russia.

On the one hand the "Russian identity" of Udy is based on collective memory, it is still performed through some traditional customs and religious holidays. On the other hand, Udy as a "Russian village" is a relatively new construction. Before 1991 Russian language was not a marker of ethnicity as was the case with other languages in the Soviet Union; it was not a "property" of a particular ethnic group but rather a supranational and de facto dominant *lingua franca.* Unlike other Soviet nationalities the Russians had not been subject to affirmative action policies: their ethnic traditions and folklore were not promoted systematically and Russian identity was in a way dissolved in the Soviet one.[15] The collapse of Soviet Union turned Russians in the new post-Soviet states into national minorities, a potential diaspora[16] with a new collective identity still in the making. The consolidation of a new national minority is a function of many factors, such as the politics of the "ethnic homeland" (in this case the Russian state), the activities of the local cultural activ-

---

15 One could assume that Udy as a Russian village had advantages in the 1970s and 80s, conventionally seen as a period of Russification policy in Ukraine. However, the reality was more complicated. At that time it might have been indeed easier for young people from Udy to enter Kharkiv institutions of higher education where Russian was the predominant language of teaching. But even though Russian was in fact the dominant language in public life, Russian "ethnicity" was not privileged on the regional level, sometimes just the opposite. According to the former village club director, the folklore ensemble in Udy was "encouraged" by the Zolochiv raion authorities to perform Ukrainian songs and dances rather than Russian ones.
16 Pal Kolsto, "Russian Diasporas in the 'Near Abroad': Implications for International Peace", *Diaspora*, no. 2, vol. 10 (Fall 2001), pp. 297-305; Pal Kolsto, "Territorialising Diasporas: The Case of Russians in the Former Soviet Republics", *Millennium. Journal of International Studies*, vol. 28, no. 3 (1999), pp. 607-631.

ists, the existence of ethnic conflicts, the level of politicization of language issues etc.[17] In the case of Udy two factors became important for the partial reinvention of Russian identity on the local level: the proximity to the Russian border and the Russian language school.

Those who live at the border have more intensive contacts with relatives and friends in Russia, they travel there more often and have more opportunities to compare changes in both countries. For example, milk prices and the profitability of milk production on both sides of the border was one of the central motifs during the focus group discussion in Udy in 2003. Pensions, salaries, social provision, electricity and gas supply were also compared, usually not in Ukraine's favour. *When the electricity supply is interrupted here, we look across the border – there are a lot of lights there – and we think: Why doesn't Putin take us back?* This remark made by a women from Udy during an informal conversation demonstrates that the economic effects of the border can have some influence on the feeling of national belonging and on state loyalty. The proximity of the border alone does not make Udy inhabitants Russian, but allows them to imagine other scenarios and leaves some options open. Elena Nikiforova, who studied the effects of the new Estonian-Russian border on the local rural population, also noticed that national identity is usually seen by peasants rather pragmatically as an access to certain economic and social benefits.[18]

Another aspect of border proximity is the dominance of the Russian media, particularly Russian TV. This situation is of course not unique for

---

[17] From the recent literature on ethnic Russians in the NIS and in Ukraine, see in particular: David D. Laitin, *Identity in Formation. The Russian-Speaking Populations in the Near Abroad*, Ithaca and London: Cornell University Press 1998; Anna Fournier, "Mapping Identities: Russian Resistance to Linguistic Ukrainisation in Central and Eastern Ukraine", *Europe-Asia Studies*, vol. 54, no. 3 (May 2002), pp. 415-33; Edwin Poppe and Louk Hagendoorn, "Types of Identification Among Russians in the 'Near Abroad'", *Europe-Asia Studies*, vol. 53, no. 1 (January 2001), pp. 57-71; Lowell Barrington, "Russian-speakers in Ukraine and Kazakhstan: 'Nationality,' 'Population,' or Neither?", *Post-Soviet Affairs*, vol. 17, no. 2 (April-June 2001), pp. 129-158; Marion Recktenwald, "The 'Russian Minority' in Ukraine", in: Ted Gurr (ed.), *Peoples Versus States: Minorities at Risk in the New Century*, Washington, DC: U.S. Institute of Peace 2000, pp. 57-64; Roman Solchanyk, "Russians in Ukraine: Problems and Prospects", in: Zvi Gitelman et al. (eds.), *Cultures and Nations of Central and Eastern Europe. Essays in Honor of Roman Szporluk*, Cambridge, MA: Harvard University Press 2000, pp. 539-554.

[18] Nikiforova, "Is a Border a Factor of Ethnic Community Formation?"

Udy.[19] But at the border with Russia this influence is particularly visible – here people do not need expensive satellite antennas to watch Russian TV, they have access to the same channels as the residents of the Belgorod oblast. Therefore most people prefer Russian TV channels because they find Russian entertaining programs more interesting than Ukrainian ones, or because they prefer Russian language, or just due to some kind of inertia. As a result they are well informed about what is going on in Russia and often disinterested in Ukrainian political life. In summer 2003 our interviewees told us about embarrassing situations, which have become local jokes.

> *We watch mainly Russian TV. Children come to school and tell me: Valentine Ivanovna, do you know today is Putin's birthday? ... The ORT channel* [Russian TV] *showed it... Larissa Viktorovna asks: Children, do you know who is our president? – Yes! Putin! – And what is the flag of Ukraine? Red!* (people laugh). *And the day before I had just told them: blue and yellow!* (female, mathematics teacher, 34).

But the decisive factor for Udy's persisting Russian identity still is the language of instruction in the local school.

As it was mentioned above, Udy's school is practically the only one teaching in Russian in the Zolochiv raion (the second one in Gur'ev Kazachok is on the verge of being closed because of the small number of pupils). Already before 1991, but especially in the 1990s, when other schools in the neighbourhood switched to Ukrainian, Udy attracted newcomers who for some reason were looking for a Russian-speaking village or a school with Russian as teaching language. In some cases these were families from Russia or other post-Soviet republics with school-age children who had not spoken Ukrainian before. But more importantly, this concerned school teachers for whom language competence is decisive in performing their job. Here are a couple of typical stories:

> *I came to this village in 1995, after finishing Kharkiv Pedagogical College. The first thing I was interested in when I came to the Ukrainian re-*

---

19 The dominance of the Russian media in Ukraine is often seen as a serious problem threatening the "informational security" of the country. Since 2005 the Ukrainian government has been undertaking various steps to limit the audience of Russian TV channels.

gion – *if there is a Russian village here, with Russian school. Because I am Russian, I almost did not know Ukrainian. Just I had no chance to learn it in school... Two years in the college, but I knew very little... And thanks God I was sent to this Russian village* (female, primary school teacher, 40).

I am native ["korennaia"]. *In which sense "native"? I am coming from the Zolochiv raion, I am Ukrainian, "real" Ukrainian* [laughs]. *It happened that after graduation from the Pedagogical Institute I was appointed here* ["po raspredeleniu"]. *Why in Udy? Because my husband is Russian. For me it was no difference. And now... to tell the truth, here in Udy I mainly speak Russian. In the family, with my parents I speak only Ukrainian. Although now of course... to teach mathematics in Ukrainian I would not be able to...because five years in the Institute and 13 years here... to switch to Ukrainian is very difficult* (female, mathematics teacher, 34).

The Udy school reinforces "Russian identity" not only because it still teaches in Russian, but also because it attracts the Russian-speaking newcomers, among them teachers. In some cases they have very low competence in Ukrainian and see Udy as a some kind of linguistic asylum. The case of the Udy school is interesting to compare with a similar case studied by the Finnish anthropologist Laura Assmuth: this is the Estonian language school in Pechory, a small town in Russia at the Russian-Estonian border.[20] This school existed until 2005 and was attended not only by local Estonians (Setu),[21] but also by children from mixed families and by some ethnic Russians. Assmuth sees the reason for the school's relative success in the "new positioning of Estonian in Russia: from an odd and disregarded minority language it is developing into a prestigious foreign language worthy of intensive study. This is because studying and mastering Estonian has become an asset, at least in this region bordering Estonia."[22] While most Estonian-speakers resettled to Estonia in recent years, the status of the Estonian language is growing in this region of Russia as it helps to obtain Estonian citizenship and opens access to the EU labour market.

---

20 Laura Assmuth, "Politicizing language at a post-Soviet border: an Estonian school in Russia", *Journal of Finnish Anthropological Society*, no. 1 (2007), p. 36-46.
21 The Setu is an ethnic group living at the border between Estonia and Russian Federation. The Setus speak an Estonian dialect, but are of Orthodox denomination.
22 Assmuth, "Politicizing language", p. 42.

Udy's school (built in 1910) is the only one in the Zolochiv rayon to teach in Russian

Compared to the Pechory school, the Russian school in Udy brings its pupils (and teachers) no particular advantages. Mastering Russian is not seen as a special asset, because most families are oriented to the higher education opportunities offered by Kharkiv as the nearest big city, where the knowledge of Ukrainian has become a crucial factor in recent years. In this region everybody has some language competence in Russian regardless which school, Ukrainian or Russian, he or she attended. This usually allows local people to work across the border. Attending a Russian school in Ukraine can even pose problems, as the informal discussions with teachers showed. They claimed that in local school competitions Udy pupils are sometimes disadvantaged (or even discriminated) because everybody can identify their anonymous tests by their use of Russian language, and in case of a choice between two potential winners the preference is normally given to the test answered in Ukrainian. During our meeting in 2003 the Udy teachers complained about the lack of school textbooks in Russian; the few that were available on the market were translated from Ukrainian, therefore published only with a delay, and were more expensive. Parents have to look for schoolbooks in Russian themselves, often without success. Two years later the problem was still there, and the teachers told me that they often use textbooks in Ukrainian, especially for the older children.

Despite the politicization of the language issue in Estonia and strained relations between Estonia and the Russian Federation (or maybe because of that), the Estonian school in Pechory received significant support from Tallinn. The textbooks were provided from Estonia and even the teachers' salaries were paid by the neighbouring state. In contrast to this case, the Udy school got no attention, not to mention real support neither from Russia, nor from pro-Russian organizations or politicians active in Kharkiv. "We even wanted to write to Putin about the problem with the textbooks!" said one of the teachers in 2003. But evidently a small school in a stagnating village was not worth a political investment, not to mention that it has only very limited autonomy to shape teaching on its own.

As we can see both factors reinforcing the "Russian identity" of Udy – the language of instruction in the local school and the proximity of border – work only to a limited extent. Although most teachers in 2003 were determined to preserve Russian as a language of teaching, they did not openly oppose Ukrainization and stressed their readiness for compromise. In the absence of external support and of visible benefits, Russian as a language of instruction offers no advantages for both pupils and teachers. Since the curricula is the same as in the Ukrainian language schools (it includes Ukrainian history and culture, geography of Ukraine etc.), it produces Russian speaking Ukrainians rather than "ethnic Russians". And as we have seen above, Udy residents are well-informed about the political developments and cultural life in Russia due to the proximity of the border and the popularity of Russian TV. However, with the passage of time Russia becomes for them increasingly a foreign country, with its own rules, sometimes rather unfriendly to Ukrainian citizens (such as obligatory registration in a police office for Ukrainian visitors staying in Russia longer than three days). It is not so much contemporary Russia that Udy residents feel attached to, but rather the common past and common Soviet space not divided yet between the two countries:

> We felt ourselves as one people...it was a bit painful that we do not belong to Russia... we would so much like to stay together [*ostatsia obshchimi* – to belong to both Ukraine and Russia at the same time] (female, teacher, 40, Udy).

As Andrew Wilson once noticed "ethnic Russians in Ukraine... have an ambiguous notion of 'homeland', located partly in Ukraine, partly in the Russian Federation and partly in both at the same time. Russians in Ukraine do not yet define themselves as 'diaspora', in terms of irredenta of a broader homeland... The logic of the Russian position therefore drives them towards support for the restoration of the some kind of overarching political unity between Ukraine and Russia, rather than towards local separatism".[23] Even the admiration for Vladimir Putin, which one could feel in the interviews with Udy residents in 2003, has little to do with their political loyalties. Rather, Putin is a symbolic figure who represents the lost (or imagined) stability and security and cannot be blamed for the difficulties of the Ukrainian transition. Udy as a "Russian village" does not identify with the new Russia of Putin. It is instead

---

23 Andrew Wilson, "Redefining ethnic and linguistic boundaries in Ukraine: indigenes, settlers and Russophone Ukrainians", in: Graham Smith et al. (eds.), *Nation-Building in the Post-Soviet Borderlands: The Politics of National Identities*, New York: Cambridge University Press, 1998, pp .119-138, here p. 131.

the fading nostalgia for the Soviet past and the feeling of being "others" in the Ukrainian linguistic environment which keeps the "Russian identity" of Udy residents alive.

7.4 Becoming Ukrainians

Due to mixed marriages and labour migration from the 1960s through the 1980s, Udy received a lot of Ukrainian newcomers. However, most of them assimilated to Russian – not only because of the Russian-speaking environment in Udy, but also due to working and studying in Russian-speaking Kharkiv, military service, etc. Children who are born from mixed marriages in Udy are usually Russian-speaking. The demographics alone could not make Udy Ukrainian, but it helps to understand why attitudes to the language issue have been rather flexible and pragmatic in the village since 1991.

Since the use of Russian in the local school and in the village administration is guaranteed by law, the village has not experienced an abrupt and forceful Ukrainization. But Udy inhabitants do not live on an island and the Ukrainian language slowly permeates their lives. Informal incentives often encourage people to use Ukrainian, first of all in the professional sphere and in communication with local authorities. Although the local administration is officially allowed to use Russian internally, the language for communication with the raion authorities is Ukrainian. Therefore, in order to avoid doing double work, the village administration often issues its internal documents in Ukrainian. The same is true for the Udy school: it has to submit all reports to the raion department of public education in Ukrainian, so the teachers are required to have a certain level of language competence. In many cases professional communication encourages people to use Ukrainian: when taking part in raion meetings or training courses they prefer Ukrainian to avoid looking like a black sheep. The school in Udy teaches in Russian, but its curriculum has changed in favour of Ukrainian language, literature and cultural studies. In fact it is the village school that is responsible for building the new Ukrainian identity, and it does it as everywhere in Ukraine: on the basis of national history and culture. Paradoxically, it is the Russian-speaking teachers who have to carry the main work of "making Ukrainians" in Udy. No wonder that this situation affects their personal identities:

> *At our lessons we try of course to educate children as Ukrainians...* [T.Z.: Do you also introduce children to Ukrainian traditions?] *We try to keep neutrality... there is a course of Ukrainian studies* ["narodoznavstvo"]*... we teach the history of the Ukrainian people. Maybe it has become less distant also for us...* (female, teacher, 40, 2003).

Between 2003 and 2005 things have changed significantly in Udy's school. The new school director, who was appointed in the end of 2002, is Ukrainian and lives in Zolochiv. She is an advocate of Ukrainization, and tries to introduce the Ukrainian language in the curricula and school administration. Six new teachers now come from Zolochiv, almost half of the school team, and most of them are Ukrainian speakers. Newsletters, announcements and posters are often issued in Ukrainian; Ukrainian is widely used in extracurricular activities such as school celebrations, folklore concerts, etc. And when addressing children the school director uses Ukrainian. The Ukrainian-language classroom is decorated not only with a portrait of Taras Shevchenko and other national symbols, but also with objects of Ukrainian folklore and everyday culture. Characteristically, a self-made poster on the wall reminds the children about their duty to "love and cultivate their mother tongue" (*ridna mova* – Ukr.). No doubt, the language implied by this poster is Ukrainian, not Russian.

Not everybody welcomes these changes, but during my visit in summer 2005 the teachers supported in principle this turn. As I had found out that most of them supported Yanukovych in the 2004 presidential elections I asked them if their choice was affected by the fear of a systematic Ukrainization in case of Yushchenko's victory. The answers were definitely negative:

> *"No, not at all... Moreover, I think – the school should be Ukrainian. In Ukraine school should be Ukrainian"; "It is difficult for children to study further after our Russian school"; "I am also for it. Children do not know Ukrainian terms; if they want to continue their study, they have problems. They should learn both Ukrainian and Russian"; "If we are Ukraine, if we are a country, we should be Ukrainians".*

BORDERLANDS INTO BORDERED LANDS 311

The class room for Ukrainian studies in Udy's school. Objects of Ukrainian folklore are presented to promote Ukrainian national identity among pupils

Even taking into account the evident compliance with the director's new policy, the teachers' attitude to the Ukrainian language has become more affirmative and the reasons for this are mainly pragmatic. To some extent the teachers of the Udy school are tired of being an exception: they long for normality and do not want to be treated as a special case. Textbooks and pedagogical materials are better available in Ukrainian, and the training courses they have to attend from time to time are also in Ukrainian. Teachers also see the disadvantages if their pupils are taught only in Russian. The lack of resources, limited autonomy and dependence on the raion administration makes teachers' motivation pragmatic, and they eagerly demonstrated this pragmatism and flexibility in the interviews. Most teachers stressed their neutral position in relation to the language issue and underlined the absence of conflicts in the local community and in school on this matter: "We never put Ukrainian and Russian in opposition"; "we do not emphasize language differences". On the one hand, it seems to be true that social and political conflicts in the village are not framed in linguistic and ethnic terms (as, for example, the election campaign of 2004 showed). On the other hand, the discourse of neutrality and flexibility is probably the only way for an ordinary teacher, who is in a powerless position, to protect her- or himself and affirm her or his cultural and professional identity in a Russian school led by a Ukrainian-speaking director. This accent on adaptability and flexibility can be found not only in the teachers' interviews but in the narratives of other Udy residents:

> Children from Svetlychna [a neighbouring village] *came to us to study... their school was closed – only preliminary classes are left. For them it is easier in Ukrainian. They answer in Ukrainian – and we understand them perfectly. We do not make this a problem for the children: "Here is a Russian school, you must speak Russian!" No, we do how it is easier for children* (female, geography teacher, 34).

> *My son is in the sixth class – just finished... For example, he is at home and does his homework in history. He has a textbook in Ukrainian, but at school he is taught in Russian. I ask him: "How do you answer in school?" He says: "Just as it comes... sometimes in Russian... sometimes in Ukrainian. If I do not understand the term – I use Ukrainian." He does not even reflect* (female, 43).

The extracts from the interviews above give an impression that the Udy school is already de facto bilingual. On the one hand, Ukrainian is actively promoted by the new director as an important state and national symbol. On the other hand, the active use of Ukrainian in class results from the lack of resources and of the teachers' pragmatic attitude. It is difficult to foresee what kind of future is waiting for the school and the village. As a "national minority" Russian residents of Udy have a formal right for a Russian language school. But unlike other national minority languages, Russian is seen in Ukraine as a de facto still-dominant language that does not need state support.[24] While no one is pushing for complete Ukrainization, some symbolic concessions in favour of the Ukrainian language are evidently welcomed by the raion authorities. It might happen one day that Udy inhabitants themselves will find it easier to give up their particular status of a "Russian village" for pragmatic reasons. They might keep using their Russian in the family, but further Ukrainization of higher education and public administration will encourage them to opt for a Ukrainian school. With the passing of time, the inhabitants of Udy seem to have accepted Ukrainian political identity and do not see it as opposing their local Russianness:

> We have become a Ukrainian village already... it seems. There is no communication with Russia... as there used to be. I think we feel more like a Ukrainian village...despite the fact people here speak Russian. We have become a part of Ukraine (female, mathematics teacher, 36).

Most likely, this process would be accelerated by the positive social and economic changes that people will associate with an independent Ukraine. Unfortunately, in the case of Udy, the economic situation instead supports a nostalgic mood. Political developments in the country are another important factor in national identity formation. The majority of Russian-speaking Udy residents voted for Yanukovych and in summer 2005 were not too sympathetic for the new "Orange" leadership. Did the presidential elections of 2004, which had instrumentalized linguistic and cultural stereotypes more than ever

---

24   On the ambivalent status of the Russian language in Ukraine see: Tatiana Zhurzhenko, "Sprache und Nationsbildung. Dilemmata der Sprachenpolitik in der Ukraine", *Transit - Europäische Revue*, no. 21 (2001), pp. 144-170; English version: http://www.iwm.at/index.php?option=com_content&task=view&id=322&Itemid=486 (last accessed November 8, 2008).

before, contribute to the consolidation of Udy's specific "Russian identity", or did they accelerate the process of becoming Ukrainians? This is the question I will try to answer in the last section of this chapter.

7.5 The 2004 presidential election campaign in Udy

Not surprisingly, the overwhelming majority of Udy residents voted for Viktor Yanukovych in the 2004 presidential elections, strongly encouraged by the village administration and the raion authorities.[25] But there was also a small minority of "dissidents" in the village who actively supported Viktor Yushchenko. As almost everywhere in Ukraine, the Udy community was split into two camps and the degree of political passions in the last months of 2004 was rather high. In summer 2005, most people were still ready to defend the choice they had made half a year before and did not change their political sympathies. During the focus group and in the individual interviews in June 2005 the presidential election campaign in Udy was discussed in detail. Understandably, people avoided thematizing conflicts inside the village community in the presence of an outsider. They tried to belittle the political split and to present a more peaceful picture of the dramatic political events. The Yanukovych advocates (and among them were most of the local school teachers)[26] typically stressed that the "aggression" and the attempts to divide people were coming from outside and positioned themselves on the side of civic peace and harmony. One of the teachers presented the political mood of local pupils in this way:

> There was no sharp division in the village. As far as I talked to children... they of course discussed this subject ... they were interested and asked the teachers' opinions. But to say for example "I am only for Yanukovych" or "only for Yushchenko" – thanks God, our children did

---

25   Yevhen Kushnar'ov, governor of the Kharkiv oblast at that time, was one of the leaders of the Party of Regions and a fierce opponent of the Orange Revolution. As in other regions of Eastern and South Ukraine the "administrative resource" was widely used in the Kharkiv oblast to guarantee the victory of Yanukovych, the "candidate of power".

26   School teachers were actively involved in the election campaign as agitators and constituted an important part of the "administrative resource".

not put such barriers. Sometimes they were making jokes... there was no hostility (female, teacher, 34).

The election campaign in Udy was not very different from campaigns in other villages and small towns in Eastern Ukraine: the local authorities mobilized all available resources to guarantee Yanukovych's victory. Yushchenko's election campaigners practically did not show up in Udy and most people got rather distorted information about him and his program from the Ukrainian (and Russian) TV. In their interviews people often tried to justify their choice by referring to the lack of information on Yushchenko's program. However when more information became available later, after the second round of elections, it did little to change the choices people had already made.

> We had no information... to read what he proposes. A car passed through the village with the slogan: "Vote for Yushchenko!" and that was it. And another car was parked on the marketplace (female, administrator, 48).

Pensioners, who compose more than half of Udy's population, voted for Yanukovych because of his promise to increase pensions; others believed Yanukovych's election campaigners that in case of his victory the most urgent problems in the village would be solved. Among the typical promises were the installation of a permanent gas supply infrastructure in Udy and, no less important for the near-border village, the liberalization of cross-border traffic regulations:

> Pensioners... you talk to a babushka and she immediately says: "I am for Viktor Fedorovich!" She even does not call him Yanukovych, but Viktor Fedorovich! She has his portrait... The election campaigners did a good job... everybody had photos of Yanukovych. He promised to install gas... and that life will be better... and the border with Russia will be opened a little bit. Open border... it would be easier to communicate... this is very important! (female, teacher, 36).

Massive agitation for Yanukovych combined generous promises with hidden threats and even blackmail. In most cases it was enough to convince people that they have no alternative. Gas supply in Udy offers a good example how such mechanisms of manipulation work. Gas supply had been promised to Udy already in the late 1980s. The technical planning was already prepared, but because of the collapse of the Soviet Union and the economic crisis the project of gasification was postponed (there was even a pipeline built to Udy, but, as people told, the pipes got rotten after several years). The next attempt to gasify Udy was undertaken in 2002. Once again money was allocated and the technical documentation updated. Gas was scheduled to be installed in spring 2004. But like the first time, nothing happened. With the beginning of the election campaign in summer 2004, the gasification of the village was again promised as a reward for the "right" choice and used as a means of persuading people. (One might even assume that this was the reason why gas had not been installed according to the initial schedule).

> *You know why many of us voted for Yanukovych? His election campaigners approached people and asked: What do you need most? – Of course this is gas. – You will get gas for sure, hundred percent! – And now we are told: Yanukovych was not elected – how can you expect gas?* (female, unemployed, 40).

However, it would be wrong to explain the support for Yanukovych in Udy only through populism and the political manipulations of his local representatives. Some positions in his widely advertised program corresponded to the hopes of Udy residents; the most important among them seem to be a "union with Russia", the cooperation in the framework of the Single Economic Area, cross-border cooperation and "opening borders". While explaining their preference for Yanukovych, people sometimes referred to the "common Slavic culture", but more often they argued that, economically, Ukraine will experience hard times without Russia. In the case of Udy as a near-border village, this combination of an economic and a cultural orientation to Russia resulting in the popularity of Yanukovych as a presidential candidate is easy to understand.

At the same time, it seems that another item in Yanukovych's program – the support he promised for the Russian language – impressed Udy inhabitants less than one would expect, given that it is a Russian-speaking village. The people I interviewed usually denied that their choice in favour of Yanukovych was determined by the language issue. As I already described above, they stressed the flexibility and absence of conflicts concerning the language issue. Indeed, as in Udy most people are busy with agricultural or other physical work, they do not care much if Russian has an official status and agree that their children need to learn Ukrainian. The only professional group in Udy that could be concerned about the language issue is the school teachers, but as we have seen they take a rather pragmatic attitude. Most of them denied that the language issue was the reason why they supported Yanukovych, and underlined their sufficient competence in Ukrainian and their loyalty to Ukrainian as a state language. Thus, contrary to what one would have expected, language and ethnicity were not instrumentalized and did not become a mobilizing factor in the 2004 election campaign in Udy.

Did the Orange-Blue divide in Udy correspond to ethno-linguistic criteria? I do not have enough information to speculate about that. It seems that Russians indeed usually preferred Yanukovych, whereas among Ukrainians there were advocates of both political camps. Referring to the stereotypical opposition of the east and west of Ukraine, commonplace in the political discourse, some interviewees particularly stressed that "our Western Ukrainians (*zapadentsi*) also were for Yanukovych". Several examples were mentioned when political conflicts emerged inside the family, between generations. In general, it seems that ethnicity and mother tongue did not correspond directly with personal political preferences, and such correlation was usually denied by people. Rather, it was the occupation and social position in the village which in the interviews was sometimes related to a political choice. A teacher from the Udy school, who actively supported Yanukovych because of both personal conviction and of her official position, tried to define her opponents in a following way:

> Those people who campaigned for Yushchenko here – they are not respected in this village... You understand? If he would be represented by people who have authority here, the attitude to his candidature could be different. But it happened that these were people who are not respected... it played a role. If someone is unemployed and does not look for a job, does not want to work – and he supports Yushchenko – what kind of reaction could one expect? (female, teacher, 36).

Who were these Yushchenko advocates who, according to this teacher, do not enjoy respect in the village? In some cases they belong indeed to the outsiders of the village community, such as the private farmer Vasyl who moved to Udy from Kharkiv and in former times was a member of *Narodnyi Ruch*. He spent years in endless bureaucratic wars with the local administration trying to get a plot of land for private framing. Vasyl has a reputation of an exotic person and a Yushchenko freak. In the days of the Orange Revolution he even went to Kyiv and spent some days on Maidan. Photos of him on Maidan together with symbols of the Orange Revolution are proudly presented on the wall of his modest house.

The other example is the officially unemployed former tractor driver Ivan, who in fact earns much better than his former colleagues by doing all kind of woodworking and producing *samogon* (homemade alcohol) together with his wife. It was he who in his interview criticized the labour moral and heavy drinking in Udy (see section two of this chapter). In both cases these are people who do not fit to the post-kolkhoz political economy of Udy based on a mixture of traditional solidarity and paternalism. They are indeed marginal in the village because they are not dependent economically on the local authorities (or even in conflict with them) and not afraid for their jobs.

In summer 2005, half a year after the elections of 2004, this event was not such a hot subject anymore, but it seemed to me that people still stuck to the choice they made at that time. Those who had voted for Yanukovych, still distanced themselves from the symbols of the Orange Revolution and Maidan and were rather sceptical about the new government. Old anecdotes from the time of *perestroika* were popular again; their message is that the "wind of changes" which blows "above" will never reach the small village Udy. At the same time Yushchenko's advocates are also sceptical:

> *They are there, above... they now need time to recover. Before something comes here – one needs decades. I tell you – we live here in Brezhnev times ... we have wage-rates here as in Brezhnev times – one rouble seventy per hour... can you imagine? And you expect something changes immediately, in one year* (male, unemployed, 42).

BORDERLANDS INTO BORDERED LANDS   319

Vasyl, private farmer and Yushchenko supporter

Most of Udy had bet on the loser, and the mood in the village in 2005 was not very bright. The head of the village council told us that the only consequence of the Orange Revolution he expects for Udy is that the gasification project will be postponed again. But paradoxically enough, despite the hostility to the "Orange" rhetoric and symbols, despite the sceptical attitude to the first steps of the new government and the disappointment with the economic situation, in summer 2005 Udy seemed to be more integrated in the Ukrainian political and cultural life as it was two years ago. Putin's popularity has decreased[27] and the political developments in Kyiv attracted people's attention and emotions. Although people still watch Russian TV channels for entertainment programs, Ukrainian TV news and information programs have become popular in the village. People now follow the political developments in the country more closely, and though they do not identify themselves with the victory of the Orange political camp, they seem to feel more "Ukrainian" than before.

Conclusion

The case of Udy illustrates well the complex interaction of language, ethnicity and national belonging in a rural near-border area. Most people speak Russian in Udy, but this "Russian identity" based on collective memory and the language of everyday communication is a subject of constant contestation and renegotiation. Multiple meanings, positive as well as negative, are associated with this specific identity, from local cuisine and drinking habits to work ethics and the level of communal solidarity. While the neighbouring Russian village of Shchetinovka, across the border, serves as a point of reference for economic success and well-being, western Ukrainian villages, where many local residents have relatives, are often compared with Udy in terms of culture and religious life.

More than folklore or religion, it is the Russian language school that reproduces the specific ethnic identity of Udy by attracting teachers and pupils lacking the proper competence in Ukrainian. At the same time, the same

---

[27] The direct interference of the Russian leadership in Ukrainian affairs and the failure of Moscow to guarantee the victory of its favourite Yanukovych damaged the image of Putin and decreased his popularity even among the pro-Russian part of Ukrainian population.

school as an instrument of state cultural policy promotes Ukrainian national identity not only among children but also among their parents. Seeing their linguistic "otherness" as a disadvantage in everyday life, many Russian speakers opt for Ukrainian for pragmatic reasons. Like other villages at the border, Udy is particularly exposed to Russian informational influences as people here can watch the same TV channels as in Russia. However, it seems that the choice in favour of Russian or Ukrainian TV is not a question of language preferences. It was rather the fact that political life in Ukraine all of the sudden became interesting and its coverage more professional and controversial, which attracted viewers to domestic TV. As Jessica Allina-Pisano noted in regard to the historically Hungarian village of Kisszelmenc on the Ukrainian-Slovak border, "identity is not a category of being but of practice";[28] it results from the pragmatic choices people make in their everyday lives.

The presidential elections in 2004 and the Orange Revolution made visible hidden conflicts and dividing lines inside the Udy community. The majority voted for Viktor Yanukovych, attracted first of all by his promises to install gas supply infrastructure and liberalize the border regime with Russia. At the same time some "dissidents", who were in conflict with the local authorities on the issue of land property and/or critical about the village administration, openly supported the opposition and even went to Kyiv to demonstrate on the "Orange" Maidan. In any case, the growing awareness about Ukrainian political life and the emotional engagement in Ukrainian politics have strengthened national identity and accelerated the break-up with the Soviet past.

---

28 Jessica Allina-Pisano, "From Iron Curtain to Golden Curtain: Remaking Identity in the European Union Borderlands", *East European Politics and Societies*, vol. 23, no. 2 (2009), pp. 266-290, here p. 281.

SOVIET AND POST-SOVIET POLITICS AND SOCIETY

Edited by Dr. Andreas Umland

ISSN 1614-3515

1 *Андреас Умланд (ред.)*
Воплощение Европейской
конвенции по правам человека в
России
Философские, юридические и
эмпирические исследования
ISBN 3-89821-387-0

2 *Christian Wipperfürth*
Russland – ein vertrauenswürdiger
Partner?
Grundlagen, Hintergründe und Praxis
gegenwärtiger russischer Außenpolitik
Mit einem Vorwort von Heinz Timmermann
ISBN 3-89821-401-X

3 *Manja Hussner*
Die Übernahme internationalen Rechts
in die russische und deutsche
Rechtsordnung
Eine vergleichende Analyse zur
Völkerrechtsfreundlichkeit der Verfassungen
der Russländischen Föderation und der
Bundesrepublik Deutschland
Mit einem Vorwort von Rainer Arnold
ISBN 3-89821-438-9

4 *Matthew Tejada*
Bulgaria's Democratic Consolidation
and the Kozloduy Nuclear Power Plant
(KNPP)
The Unattainability of Closure
With a foreword by Richard J. Crampton
ISBN 3-89821-439-7

5 *Марк Григорьевич Меерович*
Квадратные метры, определяющие
сознание
Государственная жилищная политика в
СССР. 1921 – 1941 гг
ISBN 3-89821-474-5

6 *Andrei P. Tsygankov, Pavel
A.Tsygankov (Eds.)*
New Directions in Russian
International Studies
ISBN 3-89821-422-2

7 *Марк Григорьевич Меерович*
Как власть народ к труду приучала
Жилище в СССР – средство управления
людьми. 1917 – 1941 гг.
С предисловием Елены Осокиной
ISBN 3-89821-495-8

8 *David J. Galbreath*
Nation-Building and Minority Politics
in Post-Socialist States
Interests, Influence and Identities in Estonia
and Latvia
With a foreword by David J. Smith
ISBN 3-89821-467-2

9 *Алексей Юрьевич Безугольный*
Народы Кавказа в Вооруженных
силах СССР в годы Великой
Отечественной войны 1941-1945 гг.
С предисловием Николая Бугая
ISBN 3-89821-475-3

10 *Вячеслав Лихачев и Владимир
Прибыловский (ред.)*
Русское Национальное Единство,
1990-2000. В 2-х томах
ISBN 3-89821-523-7

11 *Николай Бугай (ред.)*
Народы стран Балтии в условиях
сталинизма (1940-е – 1950-е годы)
Документированная история
ISBN 3-89821-525-3

12 *Ingmar Bredies (Hrsg.)*
Zur Anatomie der Orange Revolution
in der Ukraine
Wechsel des Elitenregimes oder Triumph des
Parlamentarismus?
ISBN 3-89821-524-5

13 *Anastasia V. Mitrofanova*
The Politicization of Russian
Orthodoxy
Actors and Ideas
With a foreword by William C. Gay
ISBN 3-89821-481-8

14 Nathan D. Larson
    Alexander Solzhenitsyn and the
    Russo-Jewish Question
    ISBN 3-89821-483-4

15 Guido Houben
    Kulturpolitik und Ethnizität
    Staatliche Kunstförderung im Russland der
    neunziger Jahre
    Mit einem Vorwort von Gert Weisskirchen
    ISBN 3-89821-542-3

16 Leonid Luks
    Der russische „Sonderweg"?
    Aufsätze zur neuesten Geschichte Russlands
    im europäischen Kontext
    ISBN 3-89821-496-6

17 Евгений Мороз
    История «Мёртвой воды» – от
    страшной сказки к большой
    политике
    Политическое неоязычество в
    постсоветской России
    ISBN 3-89821-551-2

18 Александр Верховский и Галина
    Кожевникова (ред.)
    Этническая и религиозная
    интолерантность в российских СМИ
    Результаты мониторинга 2001-2004 гг.
    ISBN 3-89821-569-5

19 Christian Ganzer
    Sowjetisches Erbe und ukrainische
    Nation
    Das Museum der Geschichte des Zaporoger
    Kosakentums auf der Insel Chortycja
    Mit einem Vorwort von Frank Golczewski
    ISBN 3-89821-504-0

20 Эльза-Баир Гучинова
    Помнить нельзя забыть
    Антропология депортационной травмы
    калмыков
    С предисловием Кэролайн Хамфри
    ISBN 3-89821-506-7

21 Юлия Лидерман
    Мотивы «проверки» и «испытания»
    в постсоветской культуре
    Советское прошлое в российском
    кинематографе 1990-х годов
    С предисловием Евгения Марголита
    ISBN 3-89821-511-3

22 Tanya Lokshina, Ray Thomas, Mary
    Mayer (Eds.)
    The Imposition of a Fake Political
    Settlement in the Northern Caucasus
    The 2003 Chechen Presidential Election
    ISBN 3-89821-436-2

23 Timothy McCajor Hall, Rosie Read
    (Eds.)
    Changes in the Heart of Europe
    Recent Ethnographies of Czechs, Slovaks,
    Roma, and Sorbs
    With an afterword by Zdeněk Salzmann
    ISBN 3-89821-606-3

24 Christian Autengruber
    Die politischen Parteien in Bulgarien
    und Rumänien
    Eine vergleichende Analyse seit Beginn der
    90er Jahre
    Mit einem Vorwort von Dorothée de Nève
    ISBN 3-89821-476-1

25 Annette Freyberg-Inan with Radu
    Cristescu
    The Ghosts in Our Classrooms, or:
    John Dewey Meets Ceauşescu
    The Promise and the Failures of Civic
    Education in Romania
    ISBN 3-89821-416-8

26 John B. Dunlop
    The 2002 Dubrovka and 2004 Beslan
    Hostage Crises
    A Critique of Russian Counter-Terrorism
    With a foreword by Donald N. Jensen
    ISBN 3-89821-608-X

27 Peter Koller
    Das touristische Potenzial von
    Kam"janec'–Podil's'kyj
    Eine fremdenverkehrsgeographische
    Untersuchung der Zukunftsperspektiven und
    Maßnahmenplanung zur
    Destinationsentwicklung des „ukrainischen
    Rothenburg"
    Mit einem Vorwort von Kristiane Klemm
    ISBN 3-89821-640-3

28 Françoise Daucé, Elisabeth Sieca-
    Kozlowski (Eds.)
    Dedovshchina in the Post-Soviet
    Military
    Hazing of Russian Army Conscripts in a
    Comparative Perspective
    With a foreword by Dale Herspring
    ISBN 3-89821-616-0

29 *Florian Strasser*
Zivilgesellschaftliche Einflüsse auf die Orange Revolution
Die gewaltlose Massenbewegung und die ukrainische Wahlkrise 2004
Mit einem Vorwort von Egbert Jahn
ISBN 3-89821-648-9

30 *Rebecca S. Katz*
The Georgian Regime Crisis of 2003-2004
A Case Study in Post-Soviet Media Representation of Politics, Crime and Corruption
ISBN 3-89821-413-3

31 *Vladimir Kantor*
Willkür oder Freiheit
Beiträge zur russischen Geschichtsphilosophie
Ediert von Dagmar Herrmann sowie mit einem Vorwort versehen von Leonid Luks
ISBN 3-89821-589-X

32 *Laura A. Victoir*
The Russian Land Estate Today
A Case Study of Cultural Politics in Post-Soviet Russia
With a foreword by Priscilla Roosevelt
ISBN 3-89821-426-5

33 *Ivan Katchanovski*
Cleft Countries
Regional Political Divisions and Cultures in Post-Soviet Ukraine and Moldova
With a foreword by Francis Fukuyama
ISBN 3-89821-558-X

34 *Florian Mühlfried*
Postsowjetische Feiern
Das Georgische Bankett im Wandel
Mit einem Vorwort von Kevin Tuite
ISBN 3-89821-601-2

35 *Roger Griffin, Werner Loh, Andreas Umland (Eds.)*
Fascism Past and Present, West and East
An International Debate on Concepts and Cases in the Comparative Study of the Extreme Right
With an afterword by Walter Laqueur
ISBN 3-89821-674-8

36 *Sebastian Schlegel*
Der „Weiße Archipel"
Sowjetische Atomstädte 1945-1991
Mit einem Geleitwort von Thomas Bohn
ISBN 3-89821-679-9

37 *Vyacheslav Likhachev*
Political Anti-Semitism in Post-Soviet Russia
Actors and Ideas in 1991-2003
Edited and translated from Russian by Eugene Veklerov
ISBN 3-89821-529-6

38 *Josette Baer (Ed.)*
Preparing Liberty in Central Europe
Political Texts from the Spring of Nations 1848 to the Spring of Prague 1968
With a foreword by Zdeněk V. David
ISBN 3-89821-546-6

39 *Михаил Лукьянов*
Российский консерватизм и реформа, 1907-1914
С предисловием Марка Д. Стейнберга
ISBN 3-89821-503-2

40 *Nicola Melloni*
Market Without Economy
The 1998 Russian Financial Crisis
With a foreword by Eiji Furukawa
ISBN 3-89821-407-9

41 *Dmitrij Chmelnizki*
Die Architektur Stalins
Bd. 1: Studien zu Ideologie und Stil
Bd. 2: Bilddokumentation
Mit einem Vorwort von Bruno Flierl
ISBN 3-89821-515-6

42 *Katja Yafimava*
Post-Soviet Russian-Belarussian Relationships
The Role of Gas Transit Pipelines
With a foreword by Jonathan P. Stern
ISBN 3-89821-655-1

43 *Boris Chavkin*
Verflechtungen der deutschen und russischen Zeitgeschichte
Aufsätze und Archivfunde zu den Beziehungen Deutschlands und der Sowjetunion von 1917 bis 1991
Ediert von Markus Edlinger sowie mit einem Vorwort versehen von Leonid Luks
ISBN 3-89821-756-6

44 *Anastasija Grynenko in Zusammenarbeit mit Claudia Dathe*
   Die Terminologie des Gerichtswesens der Ukraine und Deutschlands im Vergleich
   Eine übersetzungswissenschaftliche Analyse juristischer Fachbegriffe im Deutschen, Ukrainischen und Russischen
   Mit einem Vorwort von Ulrich Hartmann
   ISBN 3-89821-691-8

45 *Anton Burkov*
   The Impact of the European Convention on Human Rights on Russian Law
   Legislation and Application in 1996-2006
   With a foreword by Françoise Hampson
   ISBN 978-3-89821-639-5

46 *Stina Torjesen, Indra Overland (Eds.)*
   International Election Observers in Post-Soviet Azerbaijan
   Geopolitical Pawns or Agents of Change?
   ISBN 978-3-89821-743-9

47 *Taras Kuzio*
   Ukraine – Crimea – Russia
   Triangle of Conflict
   ISBN 978-3-89821-761-3

48 *Claudia Šabić*
   "Ich erinnere mich nicht, aber L'viv!"
   Zur Funktion kultureller Faktoren für die Institutionalisierung und Entwicklung einer ukrainischen Region
   Mit einem Vorwort von Melanie Tatur
   ISBN 978-3-89821-752-1

49 *Marlies Bilz*
   Tatarstan in der Transformation
   Nationaler Diskurs und Politische Praxis 1988-1994
   Mit einem Vorwort von Frank Golczewski
   ISBN 978-3-89821-722-4

50 *Марлен Ларюэль (ред.)*
   Современные интерпретации русского национализма
   ISBN 978-3-89821-795-8

51 *Sonja Schüler*
   Die ethnische Dimension der Armut
   Roma im postsozialistischen Rumänien
   Mit einem Vorwort von Anton Sterbling
   ISBN 978-3-89821-776-7

52 *Галина Кожевникова*
   Радикальный национализм в России и противодействие ему
   Сборник докладов Центра «Сова» за 2004-2007 гг.
   С предисловием Александра Верховского
   ISBN 978-3-89821-721-7

53 *Галина Кожевникова и Владимир Прибыловский*
   Российская власть в биографиях I
   Высшие должностные лица РФ в 2004 г.
   ISBN 978-3-89821-796-5

54 *Галина Кожевникова и Владимир Прибыловский*
   Российская власть в биографиях II
   Члены Правительства РФ в 2004 г.
   ISBN 978-3-89821-797-2

55 *Галина Кожевникова и Владимир Прибыловский*
   Российская власть в биографиях III
   Руководители федеральных служб и агентств РФ в 2004 г.
   ISBN 978-3-89821-798-9

56 *Ileana Petroniu*
   Privatisierung in Transformationsökonomien
   Determinanten der Restrukturierungs-Bereitschaft am Beispiel Polens, Rumäniens und der Ukraine
   Mit einem Vorwort von Rainer W. Schäfer
   ISBN 978-3-89821-790-3

57 *Christian Wipperfürth*
   Russland und seine GUS-Nachbarn
   Hintergründe, aktuelle Entwicklungen und Konflikte in einer ressourcenreichen Region
   ISBN 978-3-89821-801-6

58 *Togzhan Kassenova*
   From Antagonism to Partnership
   The Uneasy Path of the U.S.-Russian Cooperative Threat Reduction
   With a foreword by Christoph Bluth
   ISBN 978-3-89821-707-1

59 *Alexander Höllwerth*
   Das sakrale eurasische Imperium des Aleksandr Dugin
   Eine Diskursanalyse zum postsowjetischen russischen Rechtsextremismus
   Mit einem Vorwort von Dirk Uffelmann
   ISBN 978-3-89821-813-9

60 Олег Рябов
    «Россия-Матушка»
    Национализм, гендер и война в России XX
    века
    С предисловием Елены Гощило
    ISBN 978-3-89821-487-2

61 Ivan Maistrenko
    Borot'bism
    A Chapter in the History of the Ukrainian
    Revolution
    With a new introduction by Chris Ford
    Translated by George S. N. Luckyj with the
    assistance of Ivan L. Rudnytsky
    ISBN 978-3-89821-697-5

62 Maryna Romanets
    Anamorphosic Texts and
    Reconfigured Visions
    Improvised Traditions in Contemporary
    Ukrainian and Irish Literature
    ISBN 978-3-89821-576-3

63 Paul D'Anieri and Taras Kuzio (Eds.)
    Aspects of the Orange Revolution I
    Democratization and Elections in Post-
    Communist Ukraine
    ISBN 978-3-89821-698-2

64 Bohdan Harasymiw in collaboration
    with Oleh S. Ilnytzkyj (Eds.)
    Aspects of the Orange Revolution II
    Information and Manipulation Strategies in
    the 2004 Ukrainian Presidential Elections
    ISBN 978-3-89821-699-9

65 Ingmar Bredies, Andreas Umland and
    Valentin Yakushik (Eds.)
    Aspects of the Orange Revolution III
    The Context and Dynamics of the 2004
    Ukrainian Presidential Elections
    ISBN 978-3-89821-803-0

66 Ingmar Bredies, Andreas Umland and
    Valentin Yakushik (Eds.)
    Aspects of the Orange Revolution IV
    Foreign Assistance and Civic Action in the
    2004 Ukrainian Presidential Elections
    ISBN 978-3-89821-808-5

67 Ingmar Bredies, Andreas Umland and
    Valentin Yakushik (Eds.)
    Aspects of the Orange Revolution V
    Institutional Observation Reports on the 2004
    Ukrainian Presidential Elections
    ISBN 978-3-89821-809-2

68 Taras Kuzio (Ed.)
    Aspects of the Orange Revolution VI
    Post-Communist Democratic Revolutions in
    Comparative Perspective
    ISBN 978-3-89821-820-7

69 Tim Bohse
    Autoritarismus statt Selbstverwaltung
    Die Transformation der kommunalen Politik
    in der Stadt Kaliningrad 1990-2005
    Mit einem Geleitwort von Stefan Troebst
    ISBN 978-3-89821-782-8

70 David Rupp
    Die Rußländische Föderation und die
    russischsprachige Minderheit in
    Lettland
    Eine Fallstudie zur Anwaltspolitik Moskaus
    gegenüber den russophonen Minderheiten im
    „Nahen Ausland" von 1991 bis 2002
    Mit einem Vorwort von Helmut Wagner
    ISBN 978-3-89821-778-1

71 Taras Kuzio
    Theoretical and Comparative
    Perspectives on Nationalism
    New Directions in Cross-Cultural and Post-
    Communist Studies
    With a foreword by Paul Robert Magocsi
    ISBN 978-3-89821-815-3

72 Christine Teichmann
    Die Hochschultransformation im
    heutigen Osteuropa
    Kontinuität und Wandel bei der Entwicklung
    des postkommunistischen Universitätswesens
    Mit einem Vorwort von Oskar Anweiler
    ISBN 978-3-89821-842-9

73 Julia Kusznir
    Der politische Einfluss von
    Wirtschaftseliten in russischen
    Regionen
    Eine Analyse am Beispiel der Erdöl- und
    Erdgasindustrie, 1992-2005
    Mit einem Vorwort von Wolfgang Eichwede
    ISBN 978-3-89821-821-4

74 Alena Vysotskaya
    Russland, Belarus und die EU-
    Osterweiterung
    Zur Minderheitenfrage und zum Problem der
    Freizügigkeit des Personenverkehrs
    Mit einem Vorwort von Katlijn Malfliet
    ISBN 978-3-89821-822-1

75 *Heiko Pleines (Hrsg.)*
Corporate Governance in postsozialistischen Volkswirtschaften
ISBN 978-3-89821-766-8

76 *Stefan Ihrig*
Wer sind die Moldawier?
Rumänismus versus Moldowanismus in Historiographie und Schulbüchern der Republik Moldova, 1991-2006
Mit einem Vorwort von Holm Sundhaussen
ISBN 978-3-89821-466-7

77 *Galina Kozhevnikova in collaboration with Alexander Verkhovsky and Eugene Veklerov*
Ultra-Nationalism and Hate Crimes in Contemporary Russia
The 2004-2006 Annual Reports of Moscow's SOVA Center
With a foreword by Stephen D. Shenfield
ISBN 978-3-89821-868-9

78 *Florian Küchler*
The Role of the European Union in Moldova's Transnistria Conflict
With a foreword by Christopher Hill
ISBN 978-3-89821-850-4

79 *Bernd Rechel*
The Long Way Back to Europe
Minority Protection in Bulgaria
With a foreword by Richard Crampton
ISBN 978-3-89821-863-4

80 *Peter W. Rodgers*
Nation, Region and History in Post-Communist Transitions
Identity Politics in Ukraine, 1991-2006
With a foreword by Vera Tolz
ISBN 978-3-89821-903-7

81 *Stephanie Solywoda*
The Life and Work of Semen L. Frank
A Study of Russian Religious Philosophy
With a foreword by Philip Walters
ISBN 978-3-89821-457-5

82 *Vera Sokolova*
Cultural Politics of Ethnicity
Discourses on Roma in Communist Czechoslovakia
ISBN 978-3-89821-864-1

83 *Natalya Shevchik Ketenci*
Kazakhstani Enterprises in Transition
The Role of Historical Regional Development in Kazakhstan's Post-Soviet Economic Transformation
ISBN 978-3-89821-831-3

84 *Martin Malek, Anna Schor-Tschudnowskaja (Hrsg.)*
Europa im Tschetschenienkrieg
Zwischen politischer Ohnmacht und Gleichgültigkeit
Mit einem Vorwort von Lipchan Basajewa
ISBN 978-3-89821-676-0

85 *Stefan Meister*
Das postsowjetische Universitätswesen zwischen nationalem und internationalem Wandel
Die Entwicklung der regionalen Hochschule in Russland als Gradmesser der Systemtransformation
Mit einem Vorwort von Joan DeBardeleben
ISBN 978-3-89821-891-7

86 *Konstantin Sheiko in collaboration with Stephen Brown*
Nationalist Imaginings of the Russian Past
Anatolii Fomenko and the Rise of Alternative History in Post-Communist Russia
With a foreword by Donald Ostrowski
ISBN 978-3-89821-915-0

87 *Sabine Jenni*
Wie stark ist das „Einige Russland"?
Zur Parteibindung der Eliten und zum Wahlerfolg der Machtpartei im Dezember 2007
Mit einem Vorwort von Klaus Armingeon
ISBN 978-3-89821-961-7

88 *Thomas Borén*
Meeting-Places of Transformation
Urban Identity, Spatial Representations and Local Politics in Post-Soviet St Petersburg
ISBN 978-3-89821-739-2

89 *Aygul Ashirova*
Stalinismus und Stalin-Kult in Zentralasien
Turkmenistan 1924-1953
Mit einem Vorwort von Leonid Luks
ISBN 978-3-89821-987-7

90 Leonid Luks
    Freiheit oder imperiale Größe?
    Essays zu einem russischen Dilemma
    ISBN 978-3-8382-0011-8

91 Christopher Gilley
    The 'Change of Signposts' in the
    Ukrainian Emigration
    A Contribution to the History of
    Sovietophilism in the 1920s
    With a foreword by Frank Golczewski
    ISBN 978-3-89821-965-5

92 Philipp Casula, Jeronim Perovic
    (Eds.)
    Identities and Politics
    During the Putin Presidency
    The Discursive Foundations of Russia's
    Stability
    With a foreword by Heiko Haumann
    ISBN 978-3-8382-0015-6

93 Marcel Viëtor
    Europa und die Frage
    nach seinen Grenzen im Osten
    Zur Konstruktion ‚europäischer Identität' in
    Geschichte und Gegenwart
    Mit einem Vorwort von Albrecht Lehmann
    ISBN 978-3-8382-0045-3

94 Ben Hellman, Andrei Rogachevskii
    Filming the Unfilmable
    Casper Wrede's 'One Day in the Life
    of Ivan Denisovich'
    ISBN 978-3-8382-0044-6

95 Eva Fuchslocher
    Vaterland, Sprache, Glaube
    Orthodoxie und Nationenbildung
    am Beispiel Georgiens
    Mit einem Vorwort von Christina von Braun
    ISBN 978-3-89821-884-9

96 Vladimir Kantor
    Das Westlertum und der Weg
    Russlands
    Zur Entwicklung der russischen Literatur und
    Philosophie
    Ediert von Dagmar Herrmann
    Mit einem Beitrag von Nikolaus Lobkowicz
    ISBN 978-3-8382-0102-3

97 Kamran Musayev
    Die postsowjetische Transformation
    im Baltikum und Südkaukasus
    Eine vergleichende Untersuchung der
    politischen Entwicklung Lettlands und
    Aserbaidschans 1985-2009
    Mit einem Vorwort von Leonid Luks
    Ediert von Sandro Henschel
    ISBN 978-3-8382-0103-0

98 Tatiana Zhurzhenko
    Borderlands into Bordered Lands
    Geopolitics of Identity in Post-Soviet Ukraine
    With a foreword by Dieter Segert
    ISBN 978-3-8382-0042-2

Quotes from reviews of SPPS volumes:

On vol. 1 – *The Implementation of the ECHR in Russia*: "Full of examples, experiences and valuable observations which could provide the basis for new strategies."

Diana Schmidt, *Neprikosnovennyi zapas*

On vol. 2 – *Putins Russland*: "Wipperfürth draws attention to little known facts. For instance, the Russians have still more positive feelings towards Germany than to any other non-Slavic country."

Oldag Kaspar, *Süddeutsche Zeitung*

On vol. 3 – *Die Übernahme internationalen Rechts in die russische Rechtsordnung*: "Hussner provides a detailed, focused study dealing with all relevant aspects and containing insights into Russian legal thought."

Herbert Küpper, *Jahrbuch für Ostrecht*

On vol. 5 – *Квадратные метры, определяющие сознание*: "Meerovich provides a study that will be of considerable value to housing specialists and policy analysts."

Christina Varga-Harris, *Slavic Review*

On vol. 6 – *New Directions in Russian International Studies*: "A helpful step in the direction of an overdue dialogue between Western and Russian IR scholarly communities."

Diana Schmidt, *Europe-Asia Studies*

On vol. 8 – *Nation-Building and Minority Politics in Post-Socialist States*: "Galbreath's book is an admirable and craftsmanlike piece of work, and should be read by all specialists interested in the Baltic area."

Andrejs Plakans, *Slavic Review*

On vol. 9 – *Народы Кавказа в Вооружённых силах СССР*: "In this superb book, Bezugolnyi skillfully fashions a candid record of how the Soviet Union employed ethnic groups in its World War II effort."

David J. Glantz, *Journal of Slavic Military Studies*

On vol. 10 – *Русское Национальное Единство*: "A work that is likely to remain the definitive study of the Russian National Unity for a very long time."

Mischa Gabowitsch, *e-Extreme*

On vol. 14 – *Aleksandr Solzhenitsyn and the Modern Russo-Jewish Question*: "Larson has written a well-balanced survey of Solzhenitsyn's writings on Russian-Jewish relations."

Nikolai Butkevich, *e-Extreme*

On vol. 16 – *Der russische "Sonderweg"?:* "Luks's remarkable knowledge of Russian history gives his observations a particular sharpness and his judgements exceptional weight."

Peter Krupnikow, *Mitteilungen aus dem baltischen Leben*

On vol. 17 – *История «Мёртвой воды»*: "Moroz provides one of the best available surveys of Russian neo-paganism."

Mischa Gabowitsch, *e-Extreme*

On vol. 18 – *Этническая и религиозная интолерантность в российских СМИ*: "A constructive contribution to a crucial debate about media-endorsed intolerance which has once again flared up in Russia."

Mischa Gabowitsch, *e-Extreme*

On vol. 25 – *The Ghosts in Our Classroom*: "Inan-Freyberg's well-researched and incisive monograph should be required reading for those Eurocrats who have shaped Romanian spending priorities since 2000."

Tom Gallagher, *Slavic Review*

On vol. 26 – *The 2002 Dubrovka and 2004 Beslan Hostage Crises*: "Dunlop's analysis will help to draw Western attention to the plight of those who have suffered by these terrorist acts, and the importance, for all Russians, of uncovering the truth of about what happened."

Amy Knight, *Times Literary Supplement*

On vol. 29 – *Zivilgesellschaftliche Einflüsse auf die Orange Revolution*: "Strasser's study constitutes an outstanding empirical analysis and well-grounded location of the subject within theory."

Heiko Pleines, *Osteuropa*

On vol. 33 – *Cleft Countries*: "Katchanovski succeeds in crafting a convincing, well-supported set of arguments. His research constitutes a step forward in dealing with the notoriously thorny concept of political culture."

Thomas E. Rotnem, *Political Studies Review*

On vol. 34 – *Postsowjetische Feiern*: "Mühlfried's book contains not only a solid ethnographic study, but also points at some problems emerging from Georgia's prevalent understanding of culture."

Godula Kosack, *Anthropos*

On vol. 35 – *Fascism Past and Present, West and East*: "Committed students will find much of interest in these sometimes barbed exchanges."

Robert Paxton, *Journal of Global History*

On vol. 37 – *Political Anti-Semitism in Post-Soviet Russia*: "Likhachev's book serves as a reliable compendium and a good starting point for future research on post-Soviet xenophobia and ultra-nationalist politics."

Kathleen Mikkelson, *Demokratizatsiya*

On vol. 39 – *Российский консерватизм и реформа 1907-1914*: "Luk'ianov's work is a well-researched, informative and valuable addition, and enhances our understanding of politics in late imperial Russia."

Matthew Rendle, *Revolutionary Russia*

On vol. 43 – *Verflechtungen der deutschen und russischen Zeitgeschichte:* "Khavkin's book should be of interest to everybody studying German-Soviet relations and highlights new aspects in that field."

Wiebke Bachmann, *Osteuropa*

On vol. 50 – *Современные интерпретации русского национализма*: "This thought-provoking and enlightening set of works offers valuable insights for anyone interested in understanding Russian nationalism."

Andrew Konitzer, *The Russian Review*

On vol. 57 – *Russland und seine GUS-Nachbarn*: "Wipperfürth's enlightening and objective analysis documents detailed background knowledge and understanding of complex relationships. "

Julia Schatte, *Eurasisches Magazin*

On vol. 59 – *Das sakrale eurasische Imperium des Aleksandr Dugin*: "Höllwerth's outstanding 700-page dissertation is certainly the, so far, most ambitious attempt to decipher Dugin's body of thought."

Tanja Fichtner, *Osteuropa*

On vols 63-68 – *Aspects of the Orange Revolution I-VI:* "These 45 papers and supplemental election reports provide an excellent overview of the Ukrainian 2004 events, as well as their historical and political context."

Uwe Dathe, *Osteuropa*

On vol. 80 – *Nation, Region and History in Post-Communist Transition*: "Rodgers provides with his analysis an important contribution to a specific view on Ukraine."

Marinke Gindullis, *Zeitschrift für Politikwissenschaft*

Series Subscription

Please enter my subscription to the series *Soviet and Post-Soviet Politics and Society*, ISSN 1614-3515, as follows:

❏ complete series   OR   ❏ English-language titles
                                                               ❏ German-language titles
                                                               ❏ Russian-language titles

starting with
❏ volume # 1
❏ volume # ___
    ❏ please also include the following volumes: #___, ___, ___, ___, ___, ___, ___
❏ the next volume being published
    ❏ please also include the following volumes: #___, ___, ___, ___, ___, ___, ___

❏ 1 copy per volume   OR   ❏ ___ copies per volume

Subscription within Germany:
You will receive every volume at 1st publication at the regular bookseller's price – incl. s & h and VAT.
Payment:
❏ Please bill me for every volume.
❏ Lastschriftverfahren: Ich/wir ermächtige(n) Sie hiermit widerruflich, den Rechnungsbetrag je Band von meinem/unserem folgendem Konto einzuziehen.

Kontoinhaber: _____ Kreditinstitut: _____
Kontonummer: _____ Bankleitzahl: _____

International Subscription:
Payment (incl. s & h and VAT) in advance for
❏ 10 volumes/copies (€ 319.80)   ❏ 20 volumes/copies (€ 599.80)
❏ 40 volumes/copies (€ 1,099.80)
Please send my books to:

NAME_____ DEPARTMENT_____
ADDRESS _____
POST/ZIP CODE_____ COUNTRY_____
TELEPHONE _____ EMAIL_____

date/signature_____

A hint for librarians in the former Soviet Union: Your academic library might be eligible to receive free-of-cost scholarly literature from Germany via the German Research Foundation. For Russian-language information on this program, see
         http://www.dfg.de/forschungsfoerderung/formulare/download/12_54.pdf.

Please fax to: **0511 / 262 2201 (+49 511 262 2201)**
or mail to: *ibidem*-Verlag, Julius-Leber-Weg 11, D-30457 Hannover, Germany
or send an e-mail: ibidem@ibidem-verlag.de

***ibidem*-Verlag**
Melchiorstr. 15
D-70439 Stuttgart
info@ibidem-verlag.de

www.ibidem-verlag.de
www.ibidem.eu
www.edition-noema.de
www.autorenbetreuung.de